Social Change
in Rural Societies

Social Change in Rural Societies

An Introduction to Rural Sociology

Third Edition

EVERETT M. ROGERS
University of Southern California

RABEL J. BURDGE
University of Illinois

PETER F. KORSCHING
Iowa State University

JOSEPH F. DONNERMEYER
Ohio State University

PRENTICE HALL, Englewood Cliffs, NJ 07632

Library of Congress Cataloging-in-Publication Data

ROGERS, EVERETT M.
  Social change in rural societies.

  Includes index.
  1. Sociology, Rural.   2. Social institutions.
3. Social change.   I. Title.
HT421.R6   1988   307.7'2   87-38191
ISBN   0-13-815481-3

Editorial/production supervision and
  interior design: Rob DeGeorge
Cover design: Wanda Lubelska Design
Manufacturing Buyer: Ray Keating

Printed in the United States of America

10   9   8   7   6   5   4   3   2   1

ISBN 0-13-815481-3

PRENTICE-HALL INTERNATIONAL (UK) LIMITED, *London*
PRENTICE-HALL OF AUSTRALIA PTY. LIMITED, *Sydney*
PRENTICE-HALL CANADA INC., *Toronto*
PRENTICE-HALL HISPANOAMERICANA, S.A., *Mexico*
PRENTICE-HALL OF INDIA PRIVATE LIMITED, *New Delhi*
PRENTICE-HALL OF JAPAN, INC., *Tokyo*
SIMON & SCHUSTER ASIA PTE. LTD., *Singapore*
EDITORA PRENTICE-HALL DO BRASIL, LTDA., *Rio de Janeiro*

Dedicated to our colleague,
the late A. Eugene Havens.
He made rural sociology a revolutionary force
for the poor farmer and the poor peasant.

Honoring the Fiftieth Anniversary
of the Founding of the Rural Sociological Society
1937–1987

11191l

No nation has ever achieved permanent greatness unless this greatness was based on the well-being of the great farmer class, the men who live on the soils for it is upon their welfare, material and moral, that the welfare of the rest of the nation ultimately rests.

—President Theodore
(Teddy) Roosevelt, writing
to Professor Liberty Hyde
Bailey, Country Life
Commission, 1910

So long as freedom from hunger is only half achieved, so long as two-thirds of the nations have food deficiencies, no citizen, no nation, can afford to be satisfied. We have the ability, as members of the human race, we have the means, we have the capacity to eliminate hunger from the face of the earth in our lifetime. We need only the will.

—President John F.
Kennedy, on the occasion
of his inaugural address,
January 1960

Contents

PART III

11 FARMER ORGANIZATIONS AND MOVEMENTS   *232*

12 AGRICULTURAL INDUSTRIES   *260*

PART IV

13 AGRICULTURE AND ENVIRONMENTAL QUALITY   *275*

Preface

Since the second edition of *Social Change in Rural Societies* was published in 1972, this textbook has added two authors but keeps the same title. We continue to emphasize the entire corpus of sociology toward cross-cultural comparison. Our textbook reflects this wide perspective, as rural sociology is the subfield of sociology with the earliest and most complete interest in the study of social change in Third World countries. The third edition of our book profits from our personal experience in this internationalization of the field.

One of the authors has taught and conducted research on university faculties in Latin America, Asia, and Europe. He directed a large research project on the diffusion of innovations in Brazil, Nigeria, and India. The other authors have conducted research or taught in Africa, Sri Lanka, Canada, New Zealand, Australia, and Western Europe. One of the authors has traveled in the People's Republic of China to study rural health systems. Examples and insights derived from these cross-cultural experiences are scattered throughout the present book.

Our book seeks to represent all major rural regions of the United States and other parts of the world. The authors' teaching, research, and program experience includes The Ohio State University, Michigan State University, The Pennsylvania State University, the University of Florida, the University of Michigan, the U.S. Air Force Academy, Iowa State University, the University of Kentucky, Purdue University, Stanford University, the University of Illinois, and the University of Southern California, as well as teaching appointments in Australia, the Agricultural University of the Netherlands, and in several other non-United States settings.

This third edition deemphasizes mere sociological description of rural institutions, and stresses sociological analysis, with examples from rural life. This analytical approach yields generalizations and propositions which are italicized throughout the text. Part I provides explanations of the most relevant sociological concepts drawn from cultural anthropology, from social psychology, and from social organization. In Part II, we show the relationships among these concepts in the four chapters on the major institutions of rural community life. Next we detail the changes in the occupation of farming and in the organization of agriculture. We conclude with a four-chapter unit on the process and consequences of directed social change.

In spite of major improvements like the international and analytical emphases, as well as the focus on rural development and environmental issues, much of the content of this textbook is similar to editions one and two. We sought to stress findings from sociological research of the past decade or two, to make liberal use of visual presentation, and to retain a level of writing aimed at the undergraduate reader. The product, we hope, is a "turned-on" textbook with relevance for students who wish to understand contemporary rural society in an international context.

We follow a functionalist approach to understanding social change, rather than a Marxist conflict approach. Functionalism is the main approach in U.S. sociology, and it has been since this social science was launched in North America around the turn of the century. Functionalism fits with the intellectual tradition in which we four coauthors were trained, and it fits best with the thinking of most rural sociology teachers and students. Marxist-conflict theory can uniquely provide understandings of certain types of rural social changes; but that is left for another rural sociology textbook, to be written by someone else in the future. Here, we stick mainly with functionalism.

However, over the 27 years since the first edition of the present book was published, rural sociology has become a more critical science. U.S. rural sociologists no longer tend to assume that the powerful institutions in society (like the Farm Bureau, the agricultural chemical industry, rich farmers, and land-grant universities) make decisions for the benefit of everyone else in rural society. A questioning stance toward agricultural technology is now often thought to be appropriate, given the unanticipated, negative consequences that have accompanied certain farm innovations in the recent past. The farm crisis of the 1980s shows that very severe social problems characterize U.S. rural society. Understandably, we come down hard here on those organizations and institutions that have helped cause these social problems or that are not combating them effectively. Thus in this volume we point to needed social changes in U.S. societal institutions. But we are not issuing a call to revolution.

Professors often detail to their graduate students some of the tedious aspects of writing, such as preparing a book's index. In 1970, Donnermeyer and Korsching prepared the index for the second edition. Now they are equal authors. A special advantage of multiple authors of a textbook is that each author can write in his or her area of professional expertise. Thus Rogers drafted our chapter on the diffusion of innovations, Burdge wrote on agriculture and environmental quality, Korsching on rural development, and Donnermeyer on rural community. We feel that a textbook gains when each chapter is written by an individual with in-depth knowledge of that subject. The four authors represent 70 years of accumulated professional experience in this field. Here, we attempted to write for a reader who is meeting rural sociology for the first time. We hope you get along well.

We wish to take this opportunity to thank the following individuals for their superb job in reviewing the manuscript for this book: James H. Copp, Texas A & M University; David J. O'Brien, University of Akron; and Larry M. Perkins, Oklahoma State University.

Everett M. Rogers	Los Angeles, CA
Rabel J. Burdge	Urbana, IL
Peter F. Korsching	Ames, IA
Joseph F. Donnermeyer	Columbus, OH

Social Change
in Rural Societies

Chapter 1

Introduction: Social Change and Rural Sociology

Everything nailed down is coming loose.

—The angel Gabriel in
Green Pastures

The efficient U.S. farmer is in fact becoming a highly capitalized specialist, anxious and able to become still more efficient. Most U.S. city dwellers know in a general way that the hayseed stereotype of the farmer is a bit out of date; how heavily educated, mechanized, capitalized, and specialized U.S. farming has become, just how swiftly the technology of the farm is moving, is something very few Americans have grasped.

—Gilbert Burck (1955)*

The theme that runs like a red thread through the fabric of rural society today is social change. In this book, we shall deal with those social changes in the United States and abroad that have made rural life today markedly different from that of several decades ago. These changes are permanently transform-

*Courtesy of *Fortune* magazine, Vol. 51: pp. 99–101.

ing the way food and fiber are produced and have altered the very nature of rural society.

Consider a few of these social changes. One major trend is a move toward more complex groupings of all kinds. Businesses, schools, churches, farms, and even communities are consolidating. Other social changes include farming as a second business or permanent part-time job, rural industrialization and tourism, and the advent of computer-based farm management. A separation of farmers (at least in First World countries) into two categories is occurring: Both have a primary occupational interest in farming, but the smaller farmers must rely upon off-farm income. Farmers are increasingly efficient and urban-oriented with access to improved transportation, allowing people to move easily from one place to another. The farmer with a microcomputer has replaced the farmer of previous generations with a business suit, who long ago displaced the country hick. Rural and urban values are mixing and merging. Changes affecting farmers are similarly jolting their small-town and suburban cousins. These domestic social changes in the United States are matched by alterations abroad, as millions of peasants in the Third World countries of Latin America, Africa, and Asia are caught up in a worldwide agricultural revolution.

Only if one is fully aware of the changes taking place is it possible to plan to meet these changes and adjust to them. A major reason for this book is to help the reader understand the social changes taking place in the family, the community, schools and churches, and other organizations. By studying rural sociology, the reader can understand more fully the social changes affecting rural societies.

PURPOSES OF THIS BOOK

In order to understand the nature of this textbook, try to answer the following questions:

1. In Chapter 2, you will learn that approximately 100,000 Old Order Amish reside in Pennsylvania, Ohio, Indiana, Iowa, and other states. They live without automobiles, electricity, lipstick, or public education. The Amish deliberately try to follow a lifestyle like that of their ancestors in Switzerland, Germany, and Holland, where the sect originated some 300 years ago. *How can such a nonchanging culture continue to exist in the midst of dynamic American society?*

2. The urban poverty classes in Latin American cities average about six children per family, while the typical middle class family has one or two children. *Why do those Latin Americans who can least afford them, have the largest families?*

3. India's current population of about 760 million is growing at such an

alarming rate that it will double in the next century. Farm production cannot feed these hungry mouths unless farmers adopt such innovations as improved crop varieties, irrigation, and chemical fertilizers. Yet there is much resistance to these new ideas by traditional peasants. Fertilizer could almost double crop yields, but peasants perceive it as an artificial substance. They prefer the more "natural" fertilizer of cow manure, which is unfortunately in short supply. *How would you successfully introduce fertilizers to India's 600 million peasants living in 560,000 villages?*

4.   The amount of herbicides and pesticides that American farmers put on their crops increases every year and has almost quadrupled since 1969. These agricultural chemicals not only destroy the insects and weeds, as intended, but also eliminate native grasses, animal life, and the natural microbial processes in the soil. *Why do U.S. farmers continue to use such large amounts of agricultural chemicals when the long-range consequences may be soil depletion, chemically resistant pests, and infertile soil?*

5.   The U.S. Department of Agriculture is made up of many different government agencies (as you will see in Chapter 15). Some agencies pay farmers not to grow certain farm products, while other agencies encourage farmers to adopt agricultural innovations that cause higher farm production. One agency pays farmers to adopt soil conservation practices, while another agency has yet to recommend conservation tillage. *Why do many government agricultural agencies work at cross-purposes?*

6.   In the past 20 years, divorce, crime, and mental illness have been increasing in rural communities. *Do these increased rates mean that rural areas are no longer desirable places to live?*

One of the objectives of this book is to enable you to understand questions like these, and their answers, in order to better comprehend the social changes presently underway in rural societies. The main purposes of this textbook are:

1.   To acquaint you with the effect of social change on rural institutions in the United States and in other countries.
2.   To convey an understanding of sociology which will help you in your family, your job, your community, and in other group situations.
3.   To acquaint you with the concepts and points-of-view held by sociologists. Concepts such as social class, bureaucracy, and culture will be introduced to you in the following chapters.

SOCIAL CHANGES IN U.S. RURAL SOCIETY

The magnitude of social changes in rural society is illustrated by the following descriptions of a North American farmer; the first was written in 1928 and the second, in the contemporary era:

In rural America . . . the farmer goes along as he always has and his father had before him and still keeps going. . . . The farmer holds tenaciously to old and outgrown ways long after new and better ones are known to him. He fears experiment. . . . His record is generally one of opposition to reform in economic policies. He habitually votes down schemes of tax reform, steadfastly upholds the protective tariff, defeats programs . . . unless he can see some direct benefit to himself. . . . Further evidence of dogged adherence to custom is seen in moral and religious behavior. (Sims, 1928, pp. 229–231)

At 5:30 one Indiana morning last week, Farmer Warren North rolled out of bed to get at his chores. After a light breakfast of juice and toast, he left the kitchen and walked briskly to his office overlooking the barnyard. In the early morning mist the low lying white barn surrounded by five giant, blue-black silos rode the prairie like an ocean liner. Like the rumble of surf came the hungry bellowing of 400 white-faced Herefords and the grunting of 500 Hampshire hogs, waiting at row on row of troughs to be fed. Once inside the office, Farmer North activated his personal computer and typed in the appropriate instructions. All around, the barn came to vibrant life. From one side dropped ground corn, from another silage, from a third shelled corn.

By modifying his feeding program, Farmer North shot in supplementary vitamins, minerals, and hormone nutrients. In a channel in front of the silos a snakelike auger began to turn. As it writhed, it propelled the feed up a steep incline and sent it tumbling out through a conduit that passed directly over 330 feet of feed troughs. At regular intervals trap doors automatically distributed the individual animal's feed.

Ten minutes later, Farmer North was through with supervising a job that would have taken five men half a day working with buckets and pitchforks. He was ready to indulge in his hobby. He returned to his farmhouse and poured himself another cup of coffee. While it cooled, he read a story on the farm problem in the *Wall Street Journal*. Carrying his cup, he walked into his living room, 40 feet long and carpeted wall-to-wall. It was dominated at the far end by a two-story pipe organ flanked by two electronic organs and a grand piano. Farmer North sat down at the console, and after running through a few warm-up chords and arpeggios, began to play Johann Sebastian Bach's chorale, "Jesu, Joy of Man's Desiring" ("Agriculture: The Pushbutton Cornucopia," 1959).

Farmer North is a symbol and a prime example of the profound changes that have been wrought in U.S. agriculture by the personal computer, mechanization, and automation (Figure 1-1). Warren North is very different from the typical U.S. farmer. He is more affluent, more cosmopolite, and more innovative in adopting new ideas than most farmers. Nevertheless, he provides one scenario of just how much the farmer's lifestyle has changed during the twentieth century. Just as this farmer's living patterns are useful to our understanding and projection of the nature of rural society in the future, so the trends underway in U.S. rural society are helpful in depicting possible directions for Third World countries. We distinguish seven major alterations in U.S. rural society that have specific impact upon the rural social institutions in Chapters 6 through 12.

Figure 1-1.   **An efficient grain-handling operation on an Iowa farm.**

A few decades ago, the typical Iowa farmstead included a corncrib and a small grain storage building. Today, its much larger counterpart consists of the expensive grain-handling equipment shown above, which represents a substantial investment. This operation includes the capacity to dry grain, grind it, mix it, and move it automatically from one bin to another. The Iowa farmer who owns this setup is likely to buy and sell grain futures on the Chicago Board of Trade, and to follow closely weather news and crop yields in the Ukraine and in China. The expensive equipment shown in this photo symbolizes the changing nature of the farming business in the United States, as it becomes larger, more highly mechanized, and more dependent on off-farm buyers and suppliers.

Source: Peter Main, staff photographer, *Christian Science Monitor*, May 2, 1986. Used by permission.

1. An increase in productivity per farmer has been accompanied by a continuing decline in the number of farm people in the United States and in the other First World countries of Canada, Australia, New Zealand, and Western Europe.
2. An agricultural transition has occurred in the past 50 years that will permanently alter the business and the occupation of farming.
3. U.S. agriculture is becoming increasingly interdependent on and competitive with agriculture around the world.
4. Rural-urban differences in social values have diminished, primarily due to the influences of mass media communication.
5. Rural people are increasingly linked to the larger society through advances in telecommunications. The result is a cosmopolite rural person closely linked to the larger society through the realignment of locality groups.

6. A continuing long-term trend toward the regionalization and merger of rural services and institutions is occurring.

7. Changes in rural social organizations include farming as a permanent part-time occupation (with an off-farm job), and an increase in the importance of secondary relationships (such as with government agencies, business firms, and agricultural pressure groups). However, certain traditional aspects of rural family life are being maintained in urban settings.*

Now we shall discuss each of these seven social changes.

1. Increased Farm Productivity and Fewer Farmers

An increase in productivity per farmer is accompanied by a continuing decrease in the number of farm people in the United States and in other First World countries. Agricultural mechanization and other technological innovations have allowed each farmer to increase both per-unit productivity and the size of farm operations in acres. One consequence of increased technological innovation is a major decrease in the farm population. Most analysts of U.S. rural society see new technology at the heart of most social changes, although there are other causes of rural social trends. For example, the nonfarm sector of U.S. society has bid up the price of labor to a level where machines must be widely substituted to replace costly agricultural labor.

The value placed on competition among farmers may indirectly be a factor in rural social changes by causing a more rapid adoption of agricultural technology (Chapter 14). The innovator has a relative advantage over the laggard. The innovator adopts new ideas relatively sooner and thus increases productive efficiency. The laggard must struggle to catch up. This competitive value placed on the adoption of technological innovations speeds up rural social changes.

Increased productivity   A tremendous increase in U.S. farm productivity has occurred in recent decades. In 1960, one U.S. farm worker supplied the food, fiber, and tobacco for 26 persons at home and abroad. In 1985, this figure was about 78. In 1940, seven farmers were required to feed those 78 persons (Figure 1-2).

Fewer farmers   The average number of farm workers declined by about one-half from 1930 to 1980. The number of farmers decreased by one million during the decade of the 1950s, and again in the 1960s. Since 1970, the number of farmers has continued to decline, but not as dramatically. There are actually more individuals employed full-time in U.S. universities than in farming.

U.S. farms are fewer, but larger (Figure 1-3). The average acreage per

---

*Larson and Rogers, 1964, pp. 39–67; trends presently underway were foreseen by McCormick, 1931; Dillman and Hobbs, 1982, have a recent update.

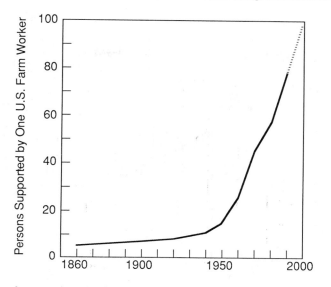

Figure 1-2   Increased productivity of U.S. farmers.

The number of persons supported by one U.S. farmer is a handy index of farm productivity. This indicator required 80 years to double from 1860 to 1940 but then doubled again in 20 years (1940 to 1960) and yet again from 1960 to 1980. This agricultural revolution caused a massive rural-to-urban migration in the United States, as much less labor was needed in farming. Another important social change (not shown above) is that an increasing proportion of the people supported by U.S. farmers are not Americans; in the mid-1980s, about 40 percent of the 78 persons supported per farmer lived overseas.

farm has tripled in the past 40 years. Since the total amount of land in U.S. farms has remained relatively unchanged, the decrease in the number of farms and the increase in average acreage was achieved by the demise of smaller farms and incorporation of their land into the remaining units. The decrease in number of farmers has been especially rapid among blacks, especially sharecroppers and tenant farmers in the South.

Specialization   Farm production is becoming more specialized. An example of such specialization is the change in the number of farms that have animals (either milk cows, beef cattle, or hogs and sheep). Each year about 4 or 5 percent of the U.S. farmers stop keeping animals, yet the total number of animals on U.S. farms has actually increased. In 1950 the average cattle herd per farm was about 20; in 1982 the average was about 170. So, larger numbers are raised on fewer farms. One reason for specialization is technological innovation. For example, smaller dairymen cannot afford to purchase expensive dairy equipment. Other farm enterprises are becoming specialized. For

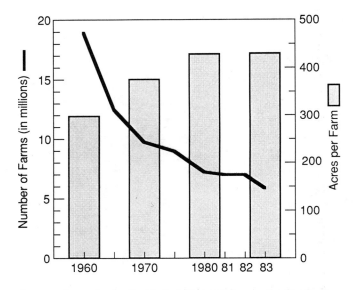

Figure 1-3   **Average farm size in the United States is increasing, while the number of farms is decreasing.**

The agricultural revolution in farm efficiency (shown in Figure 1-2) makes it possible for the average U.S. farmer to operate a much larger-sized farm. As the total acreage of U.S. farmland has remained fairly constant, the number of farms has dropped rapidly.

instance, only 3 percent of U.S. farms in 1984 raised chickens, compared with 59 percent in 1966.

As farmers become increasingly specialized, the locales in which specialized farm products are concentrated are also changing. Cotton has moved from the old Cotton Belt, east of the Mississippi, to the southwestern and western states of Texas, New Mexico, Arizona, and California. Irrigation in the high plains of Nebraska, Colorado, Wyoming, and Kansas has allowed the production of row crops like corn. Soybeans have been added to the Corn Belt, as that region moved outward. The Cotton Belt of the southeast has now diversified to include livestock production. As one observer of U.S. rural society has remarked, "Cotton is moving West, cattle are moving East, corn is moving North, and industry is moving South."

Concentration   Agricultural commodities are also becoming more *concentrated*. As an example, corn and soybean production increasingly are located in the central portions of the United States. In 1987, Iowa, Indiana, and Illinois produced 48 percent of the corn and 40 percent of the soybeans. These areas have fertile soils, adequate rainfall and long growing seasons. In Champaign County, Illinois, the percentage of grain-only farms increased from 65 percent in 1966 to 89 percent in 1986. The environmental and production consequences of concentration in agriculture are discussed in Chapter 13.

2. The Agricultural Transition

The social changes in U.S. agriculture outlined above have led to a permanent change in U.S. farming and other agriculture-related industries. The main transition is from farming as a way of life, to agriculture as a business (Figure 1-4). This pattern is similar to that for other large-scale natural-resource-based rural industries in First World countries. (By *First World countries* we mean the industrialized democracies of the West, e.g., Japan, Australia, New Zealand, Western Europe and North America.)

The *agricultural transition* refers to the change in the nature of farming and other rural industries in response to technology and the changing world economy. During the 1970s and 1980s, a decline in prices for agricultural commodities, combined with a rapid fall in land prices produced a very high debt level for many farmers. Farm foreclosures were common and reminiscent of the depression era of the twenties and thirties. Most First World countries have followed this up and down cycle since the beginning of commercial agriculture in the late 1800s. Chapter 10 on the Nature of Farming provides the details of the agricultural transition.

Rural sociologists describe farm size as a bimodal distribution, with many very big farms, a modest, and diminishing number of medium-sized farms, and very large number of small farms. The large farms often are a combination of owned and rented land. For example, the largest (Class I)

Figure 1-4   U.S. agriculture has changed dramatically since the horse and buggy days of the 1900s. We continually demonstrate that farming now is much like any other business. However, the Amish buggy shown in this photograph represents a way of life that has changed very little in the last four hundred years.

Source: Pennsylvania Dutch Visitors Bureau®

farms produce 70 percent of all the agricultural products sold in the United States.

3.   The Internationalization of Agriculture

When the first edition of this book was published in 1960, only Canada and Argentina competed effectively with the U.S. for world grain markets. Today, Western Europe, Brazil, and Australia, as well as many Southeast Asian countries export grain crops. This internationalization of agriculture is demonstrated by:

1.   The number of nations in the past decade or two that have switched from being net importers to net exporters of agricultural products. Technological innovations like agricultural chemicals and improved crop varieties (especially the high-yielding wheat and rice varieties that set off the "Green Revolution" in many Third World countries in the 1960s) were mainly responsible. By *Third World countries* we mean all those not privileged to become industrialized and wealthy during the past several centuries.

2.   New crop varieties that have allowed wheat, corn, and soybeans to be raised under a wide range of different soil, water, and temperature conditions.

3.   Loosening of government restrictions on individual agricultural production in Second World countries like Poland, Yugoslavia, and Russia has boosted production and thus reduced the need for agricultural imports.

4.   Improved transportation and reduced tariff restrictions now allow many more farmers to access the food markets of the world. Not only is the typical farmer linked more closely to urban society, but agricultural commodities are now linked to worldwide markets and trends. The price received by a U.S. farmer for wheat may be highly dependent upon weather conditions or radioactive fallout in the Ukraine.

From importer to exporter   The model of the efficient U.S. farmer is now being followed around the world. At the end of World War II, the Marshall Plan was inaugurated by the United States to put Europe back on its feet. Industrialization was the major emphasis, but agriculture also received priority. Europeans then provided a ready market for North American agricultural products, but by 1986 most European countries (all members of the Common Market) were producing more than they could consume. There are no price restrictions or tariffs within the European Common Market. However, each country subsidizes individual farmers for what they produce, even though the market price is often much lower. Wine production in European nations is an interesting example of no restrictions on production, coupled with a government subsidy. Wine production has expanded in recent years to the point where very good wines are now available at table wine prices. This glut in Europe has produced export pressures and lowered prices worldwide. Australia, New Zealand, the United States, and the Eastern European countries, also are producing wine in greater quantities for what may be a diminishing market. Many religions in the world do not permit consumption of alcohol, and some people in countries with expanding populations do not have a cultural history of alcohol use. So much more wine is now available for about the same number of drinkers.

New crop varieties   The production of major grain crops like corn, wheat, and rice traditionally has been restricted by temperature, soil, and weather conditions. Improved varieties (many developed by U.S. agricultural experiment stations and international agricultural research centers) are now available for the major grains. Many marginal agricultural areas, particularly in Third World countries, are now being planted in the new grain varieties. However, the world food crisis has not been solved, nor has famine been eliminated. But the present problem is one of matching surpluses in some nations with needs in other countries.

Second World agricultural production   Second World countries in Eastern Europe and other nations whose economies are centrally planned are replacing controls on agricultural production with individual marketing initiatives. These free market forces usually have the effect of increasing farm production. A recent example of higher production due to introducing capitalistic incentives occurred in the People's Republic of China.

International transportation   Advances in both air and surface transportation allow food commodities to move more quickly and easily across international boundaries. For example, each morning Dutch farmers bring truckloads of flowers to Skipol Airport near Amsterdam. These flowers are grown nearby in "glass houses" (as the Dutch call greenhouses). In central Holland, many polders (land reclaimed from the sea) are covered with glass houses. Inside, a variety of vegetables and flowers are grown. Fresh-cut flowers are found in every Dutch home. Now, that Dutch custom is being exported to the United States. Each day wide-bodied jets leave Skipol, loaded not with people, but with fresh flowers bound for Philadelphia, New York, and Boston. Because these west-bound jets follow the sun, the Dutch flowers arrive in time for same-day morning markets in the United States. The Dutch flower industry is booming, but U.S. florists are not happy with the Dutch competition.

So we see how the agricultural markets of the world are becoming increasingly international.

4.   Rural-Urban Value Differences

Rural-urban differences in social values are decreasing as the United States moves toward becoming a more homogeneous society. The many linkages of people and ideas between the farm and nonfarm sectors of U.S.

society result in an interchange of values between rural and urban people. The breakdown of isolation, once characteristic of rural life, aids the trend toward a mass society. Mass media communication transmits essentially the same ideas to everyone in a society at about the same time. One result has been an increase in delinquency rates among rural youth.

Despite the trend toward a mass society, important rural-urban value differences still exist. They stem from historical, occupational, and ecological differences. Rural-urban value contrasts are such that "the modern American farm population resembles the urban population more than it does the farm population of 1950."

Cosmopoliteness   Rural people are increasingly cosmopolite in their outlook and social relationships due to improved mass communication and transportation and the realignment of locality groups. *Cosmopoliteness* is the degree to which an individual's orientation is external to the community of residence. At one time, a rural person's social relationships were almost entirely limited to the people within the boundaries of the local community. The increasing separation of place of residence and place of work, exemplified by farming as a part-time occupation and the rural-nonfarm commuter, has led to more cosmopolite relationships outside of the community of residence.

The Sears catalogue now offers assorted travel packages, ranging from "Two glamorous weeks in Las Vegas," to an "Exciting four-month trip around the world." Road-building efforts in the 1930s and 1940s to get farmers "out of the mud" have had the unanticipated consequence of getting the husband and wife and their children out of agriculture. Cable television of the 1980s brought the TV catalog. The farmhouse with a satellite dish can do mail-order shopping at home. Soon the electronic catalog will be substituted for the printed catalog. All this is breaking down the traditional isolation of rural communities.

Centralization   The trend is toward centralization of decision making in rural institutions. Policy decisions once made within the rural community are now reached in complex governmental or business organizations external to the local community. The growing centralization of farm marketing is indicated by fewer but larger-scale buyers, regional and national marketing operations, and a shift away from local markets. The number of farmers' marketing cooperatives declines as pressures for larger-scale operations bring consolidation and mergers.

Food processing is being centralized in fewer plants located in larger centers. For example, in dairy regions, the conversion to bulk tank pickup at the farm increased the dairy producer's dependence on centralized authority.

The trend throughout rural society is toward centralization of both economic and political power. Prior to the U.S. Supreme Court decision of 1962 on equal apportionment, rural areas were rather heavily overrepresented in state legislatures in relation to their share of the total population. Reapportionment decisions in the 1960s and 1970s led to decreased rural political power. One result has been a still greater centralization of authority and power.

5. Linkage of Rural People to the Larger Society

Linkage of farm and rural areas with nonfarm sectors of U.S. society is increasing. Evidence of this linkage is manifested in several ways:

1. "Telecommuting"
2. Nonfarm work by farmers
3. The trend to agribusiness
4. Contract farming and vertical integration
5. The integration of rural communities into centralized organizations
6. Increased rural-urban interaction

"Telecommuting" In Don Dillman's 1984 presidential address to the Rural Sociological Society, he stated: "The advent of the information age has potentially enormous implications for rural people in rural places, providing potential for being left further behind." In this book we provide many examples of the potential of the new information technologies for overcoming the barrier of distance for rural people (for example, by means of communication satellites).

The most unique application of the new communication technologies is telecommuting. You need only a personal computer, an electrical outlet, and a telephone connection (a modem) to communicate with any other computer in the world. Such easy computer communication means that an individual is free to work from any location. Thus he or she can become a "telecommuter," living perhaps in a pastoral setting, but linked to a central workplace by computer. Work is done from a home office through computer hook-ups with fellow workers at a distance. Physical commuting to the central workplace occurs only when necessary, perhaps once or twice a week for a few hours. Among the advantages of "teleworking" is the saving of commuting time, energy conservation, and reduced costs for buildings and parking lots. Optimistic predictions for the United States are for 5 percent of the workplace to be "telecommuters" by 1990 (Rogers, 1986). In Chapter 5 we talk more about the impact of "telecommuting" on the workplace.

Nonfarm work by farmers The disparity between farm and nonfarm income has widened in recent years, and this gap is still increasing. The average income of farm people is about half the average income for nonfarm people. Not only is the income differential becoming more pronounced, but in recent years it has also become more visible to rural people.

One result of this income differential is that a growing proportion of farmers engage in off-farm work part-time and are dependent on nonfarm sources for the major part of their income. The occupational role of farmers has been changing as their connections with the nonfarm economy and non–farm-oriented systems increase.

Agribusiness   Another link between farm and nonfarm systems is the increasing dependence of farmers on agribusiness representatives to supply input resources for the farm firm. For example, U.S. agriculture today includes the $7 billion seed and feed industry, the $5 billion farm equipment industry, and the $2 billion fertilizer and lime industry. The increasing dependence of farmers on agribusiness representatives is one index of the trend from subsistence farming to modern agriculture. The trend toward agribusiness illustrates the increasingly complex division of labor that occurs as the social change from a traditional to a modern society takes place. The U.S. nonfarm agricultural labor force has grown, while the farm labor force has decreased.

Increased rural-urban interaction   Increased interaction of rural and urban people results from the growing proportion of the U.S. population living in or near large urban centers. Nonfarm people, who make up over 80 percent of the total rural population, link farm people with metropolitan centers (Figure 1-5).

Suburban commuting is a type of rural-urban linkage, as is the trend to farming as a part-time occupation.

6. Reorganization and Merger of Rural Institutions

In the first edition of this book, we described the consolidation of schools in Hamilton County, Iowa. In 1946 there was one high school for each township of 36 square miles and an elementary school for each 4 square miles. By 1966, all of the one-room elementary schools in Hamilton County had been closed, and only four high schools were open. In 1932 there were 127,500 school districts in the United States. Today there are fewer than 16,000. Reorganization, merger, and consolidation continue in rural social institutions. For example:

1. Schools now consolidate across county boundaries.
2. Health care facilities are organized on a regional basis.
3. Government services have become centralized.

Consolidation of schools   Major reasons for continuing school consolidation include a declining tax base, and the general unwillingness of local communities (particularly their older persons) to vote needed tax increases.

Figure 1-5   **Improvements in transportation have lessened rural-urban value differences in the United States.**

Superhighways are symbolic of the greater access rural people now have to the same goods and services as urban persons.

Also, higher educational standards and stricter requirements for graduation and college entrance often require school consolidation, since small school districts may not have the certified faculty to offer specialized math, language, and science courses.

Regionalization of health-care facilities A recent state-wide needs assessment survey in Illinois showed that a major need of rural people was more doctors, hospital facilities, emergency ambulance services, and dental care. However, it is often impossible to locate a full-time doctor for a small rural community. One answer to this problem is the regionalization of health care facilities and location of health clinics in small communities that are staffed only once or twice a week.

Centralization of government services Many centralized government organizations locate their professionals in the rural community. The Agricultural Stabilization and Conservation Services (ASCS), the Extension

Services, Soil Conservation Service (SCS), Farmers Home Administration (FHA), the Bureau of Land Management (BLM), and other agencies are linked to the rural community through their professional staffs. Many decisions once reached solely within the community are now being made in the state capital or in Washington, DC.

7. Changes in Rural Social Organization

Changes in rural social organization include a decline in the relative importance of primary relationships (such as locality and kinship groups), and an increase in the importance of secondary relationships (such as special-interest formal organizations, government agencies, and business firms). The social relationships of rural people are becoming more formal, impersonal, and bureaucratized.

Farming as a part-time occupation has affected the behavior of household heads who must hold an off-farm job. The primary relationships of the small community are partially replaced by the bureaucratized nature of factory or business life. As the economic firms with which rural people deal become larger and more complex, a depersonalization of social relationships occurs.

The traditional rural neighborhood is generally declining. Group relationships once based upon territoriality and proximity shift to relationships based upon such common interests as kinship, flying airplanes, or feeding cattle. Locality groupings are important in the daily lives of rural people, but the ties that bind are more voluntary and psychological than in the past.

So a major change in rural social organization is from primary to secondary group relationships.

When rural people move to the city, they often maintain their cultural values and behavior patterns. Vietnamese immigrants to the United States have encountered hostility from Louisiana shrimpers because they work long hours, rely on family labor, and use their profits to improve their fishing equipment and to help other family members. The work ethic of the native-born American shrimp boater is quite different. Only males work on the boats and such male bonding activities as drinking go along with shrimp fishing. So the clash of the two cultures leads to conflict.

WHAT IS SOCIAL CHANGE?

Social change is the process by which alterations occur in the structure and function of society. We define *society* as a collection of individuals and social groups that perform different functions and that work together in joint problem solving toward common goals. The *structure* of a society is the pattern of relationships between individuals and social groups. *Function* refers to the consequences of these relationships. *Desirable consequences* are the functional effects that help individuals and social groups achieve common goals and solve problems. Undesirable consequences are the dysfunctional effects that block achievement.

Examples of social change are adaptations to international terrorism, the use of a new plant variety, the founding of a village improvement council, the adoption of contraceptive methods by a peasant family and the emergence of a farmers movement. Alteration in both the structure and function of society occurs as a result of such actions.

In this textbook, we emphasize the social changes occurring in such rural social institutions as the family, church, and community. We are mainly concerned with consequences as they affect rural people and social groups and the way in which technological innovations are diffused (especially in Chapter 14).

Planned Social Change and Development Programs

Directed change (or planned change) is caused by outsiders who, on their own or as representatives of change agencies, seek to introduce new ideas in order to achieve goals they have defined. The innovation, as well as the recognition of the need for the change, originates outside the community. Government-sponsored development programs in Third World countries designed to introduce technological innovations in agriculture, education, health, and industry are examples of directed change. These development programs (described in Chapter 16) usually rely on change agents to diffuse innovations. A *change agent* is a professional who influences innovation decisions in a direction deemed desirable by a change agency (see Chapters 14, 15, and 16).

Many development programs in the Third World and in the United States have not been successful. The desire for rapid change has outrun the application of social scientific knowledge about how to introduce innovations. Rural sociologists conduct research directed toward improvements in development programs. Our main concern in this book is with programs of directed change because this is the most frequently occurring type.

WHAT IS RURAL SOCIOLOGY?

In the language of the sociologist, *sociology* is the scientific study of people in group relationships. Sociologists utilize the scientific method in their research studies to develop a body of accurate and reliable knowledge about human relationships. Our definition implies that sociology is scientific, and is concerned with people who are studied not as individuals but rather as members of groups. Sociologists study people organized in families, friendship networks, churches, schools, manufacturing plants, and other organizations. The term "sociology" was coined by Auguste Comte, a French scholar, in the nineteenth century, but sociology did not evolve to a position of importance until World War II. Now sociology courses are offered in every U.S. college and in most universities throughout the world.

Rural sociology is one of several subfields of sociology; there are many others, including family sociology, industrial sociology, criminology, and educational sociology. *Rural sociology* is the scientific study of rural people in group relationships. In comparison to its companion fields, rural sociology is more often applied to the solution of social problems. Because of its focus on social change and problems, rather than only on the intellectual discipline, rural sociology often includes aspects of other social sciences, such as social psychology, political science, economics, and anthropology. Social problems, of course, do not stop at academic boundaries.

History of Rural Sociology

About 1900, the first sociology department was founded at the University of Chicago. Many early sociologists were ministers and wanted to utilize sociology to improve society by solving social problems. In this period of the early 1900s, many problems resulting from industrialism and urbanization were coming to public attention. The University of Chicago was funded by contributions from John D. Rockefeller, the Standard Oil mogul. Within a few years, the Chicago Department of Sociology was founded, and the social problems it studied were mainly urban ills: prostitution, poverty, and crime.

The Country Life Commission, created by U.S. President Theodore Roosevelt in 1910 and chaired by Liberty Hyde Bailey (at the time, Dean of the College of Agriculture at Cornell University), identified the main social problems of rural America, and was a forerunner of many other groups that performed rural social surveys. These investigations fostered the emergence of rural sociology as a problem-oriented and applied discipline. Rural sociology (and agricultural economics) was formalized as a teaching, research, and extension activity within state colleges of agriculture with passage of the Purnell Act in 1925. Today, rural sociology is a formal curriculum in 46 of the 50 states, most Canadian provinces, and in many agricultural colleges around the world (Hooks and Flinn, 1981; Nolan et al., 1975, p. 442; and Sewell, 1965).

The Rural Sociology section of the then American Sociological Society voted to establish a separate society in 1937. The first issue of the journal *Rural Sociology* had been published a year earlier.

The applied problem-solving orientation of rural sociologists is reflected in the present book. The last four chapters of this book, Part IV, deal with the key issues that have emerged in the past 50 years concerning the impacts on the environment of herbicides, pesticides, and fertilizers used to create the agricultural surplus referred to previously, and attempts to deal with the problems of rural communities as they adjust to a decline in the numbers of farmers. The diffusion of agricultural and other innovations as they affect the economic well-being and the environmental quality of rural life are discussed in Chapters 13 and 14. Rural sociologists increasingly attend to the consequences of the agricultural transition that are taking place in U.S. rural society, as outlined in Chapter 15, and international development issues, as described in Chapter 16.

Why Study Rural Sociology?

Some observers point to the decreasing number of farm people as a sign that the study of rural sociology is obsolete. But rural sociologists are not only concerned with the study of the farmer. They have long focused on the small town resident, the urban commuter who lives in the rural-urban fringe, and the city worker who lives in a farm home. Of course, rural sociologists still study farm people in group relationships, but they study much more than that, and this book is concerned with much more than just farm sociology.

The world's population is much more heavily rural than that of the United States. About four out of five people in the world live in rural areas. Many of these people are in the Third World countries of Latin America, Africa, and Asia. This book provides the reader with an understanding of rural life in these nations, as well as of that in the United States.

What does the term *rural* mean? The U.S. Census Bureau divides the nation's population into rural and urban people on the basis of where they reside, rather than on the basis of their occupations, personal values, or other characteristics. Persons who live in the country or in towns of less than 2,500 population are said to be *rural*. All others are *urban*. According to the definition adopted by the Census Bureau in 1950, *urban areas* also include the densely settled fringe around large cities and the unincorporated places (as well as incorporated places) of over 2,500. Most other First World countries utilize definitions of rural and urban that are somewhat similar to those of the United States.

The rural United States population consists of both farm and nonfarm people. Rural farm people live in the open country on farms, and make up less than one-tenth of the U.S. rural population. People living in villages or in the open country, but not on farms *per se,* are considered *rural-nonfarm.* The 1980 Census defined the *farm population* as persons living in rural territory on places of ten or more acres from which annual sales of farm products amount to $250 or more, or on places of less than ten acres from which annual sales of farm products amount to $1,000 or more.

In 1987, about 76 percent of the U.S. population was urban and 24 percent was rural. Since World War I the number of rural people has been increasing or holding steady with each census, but urban numbers have been increasing at a faster rate. So the percentage of rural people in the total population has been decreasing.

However, in the 1970s the rural population increased at a faster rate than the urban population. This rural renaissance took place primarily in rural counties near metropolitan areas, but most rural counties in the United States experienced some increase. In the 1980s the pattern of faster increase of the urban population resumed.

Although U.S. cities are increasing in size, the suburbs are really booming. The 1980 census showed that more people live in suburbs than in either cities or rural areas. Migration out from urban centers to surrounding rural areas stems from a desire to combine certain advantages of rural life, such as "the grass and trees" and "a place for the kids to play," with the economic security of an urban job.

The major changes in the U.S. work force are shown in Figure 1-6. Today, the United States is an *information society*, a nation in which a major-

Figure 1-6   **The agricultural society in the United States gave way in 1900 to the industrial society, which in turn changed to the information society in 1950.**

The agricultural society was the dominant form for about 10,000 years, and most Third World countries are still agricultural societies today. The Industrial Revolution, caused in part by the application of the steam engine to industrial manufacturing and to transportation, began in England about 1750. In the United States, the agricultural society gave way to the industrial society much later, around 1900. The revolution in communication centering around applications of the computer, led to replacement of industrial workers by information workers, until, by 1950, information workers became more numerous than either industrial workers, farmers, or service workers.

Source: Beniger (1986). Used by permission of Harvard University Press.

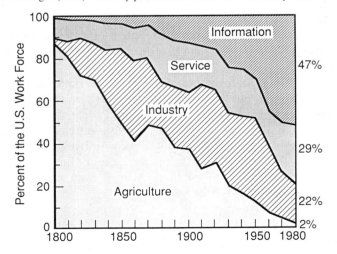

ity of the labor force is composed of workers whose main activity is producing, processing, or distributing information, or producing information technology. Typical information workers are teachers, scientists, newspaper reporters, computer programmers, consultants, secretaries, and managers. These individuals teach, write, sell advice, give orders, and otherwise deal in information. Their main work is not to raise food, put nuts and bolts together, or deal with physical objects.

While U.S. farmers are not mainly information workers, an important and increasing part of their daily activities entails information work: reading reports and magazines, obtaining weather and market news, and dealing with farm suppliers and buyers. A symbol of this information role of the farmer is the office now found in most farm homes, which is often equipped with a microcomputer. Most agribusinesspeople are information workers. U.S. agriculture exists in the context of the information society, which is one reason for the close linkage of rural and urban people.

Back in 1800, farmers constituted about 87 percent of the U.S. work force; the percentage fell to one-third by 1900. Today it is only 2 percent. The number of farm people in the total population continues to decrease as farmers become more productive. There were about 14 million U.S. farms in 1910–1920; this number had declined to about 3 million by 1970, and a further decrease to about 2.5 million is predicted by the year 2000.

Even though the number of farm people is decreasing, the amount of farmland remains approximately constant. Numbers of livestock and amount of fertilizer, machinery, and other resources per farm are increasing. This trend indicates that even though the number of U.S. farmers is declining, the need for veterinarians, extension service workers, agricultural salespersons, and other agribusiness representatives will continue. In 1985, about 35 million workers of the 104-million-person U.S. labor force were engaged in agriculture-related occupations, although only a few million were farmers. Agribusiness (including farming) in the United States accounts for 20 percent of the gross national product (GNP).

Uses of Rural Sociology

In order to demonstrate the usefulness of rural sociology, we shall discuss five specific situations in which the work of rural sociologists has led (or could have led) to an important improvement in rural societies.

1. *Extension Service Use of Diffusion Research:* One illustration is the use by agricultural extension services of research studies by rural sociologists on the diffusion of innovations. The efficiency of U.S. agriculture has increased dramatically in the past 50 years, due to such farming innovations as hybrid seeds, fertilizers, weed sprays, and new machines. These innovations stem from tax-supported agricultural research. The cost of such research is an

unrealized public investment until these innovations are adopted by farmers. Extension services have been set up in every nation in the world to diffuse agricultural innovations from scientists to farmers.

At first, extension workers assumed that every farmer would be eager to adopt technological innovations, most of which are profitable to use. But it soon became apparent that most farmers were not eager. For example, the average Iowa farmer waited seven years before adopting hybrid corn seed. So extension service administrators asked rural sociologists to study how agricultural innovations diffused to farmers, and how the diffusion process could be speeded up. To date, 800 diffusion studies have been completed by rural sociologists, leading to useful recommendations for extension workers. In fact, diffusion research has provided a theoretical basis for carrying out extension work. It is impossible to find an extension worker any place in the world who is not knowledgeable about the diffusion research of rural sociologists (Rogers, 1983).

One finding from the sociological research on diffusion is that the innovative farmers in every community are always the first to adopt new ideas. Laggards are the last to adopt an innovation. Extension workers are not perceived as credible by the laggards, so extension agents must use an indirect approach to reach them, such as by demonstrating an innovation on the farm of an opinion leader in the community. Extension agents have been trained by rural sociologists to identify opinion leaders. The efforts of 14,000 professional extension agents in the United States are multiplied many times by a corps of hundreds of thousands unpaid opinion leaders.

It makes a great deal of difference whom the extension agent selects as a leader. Diffusion research shows that innovators, the first people to adopt new ideas, are not regarded as credible sources of farming advice by their neighbors. So extension workers should ignore the eager innovators and conduct their demonstrations on the farms of somewhat less progressive farmers, who function more effectively as role models for the total community. Sociological research on the diffusion of innovations has provided strategies useful to extension agents in diffusing new ideas to farmers.

2. *The Gezira Scheme in the Sudan:* The Gezira scheme was a huge irrigated plantation for cotton growing in the Sudan. A description of this development program is instructive not because rural sociological research was utilized, but because it was not. Had it been, the managers of the Gezira scheme could have avoided mistakes that caused the eventual collapse of the program.

Sudanese farmers were recruited for the Gezira plantation project and taught to grow cotton on the irrigated land. The project planners arranged for adequate technical training of the farmers, who became good cotton growers. Yields and market prices of cotton were adequate, and the farmers had more money than ever before. But the British-owned Gezira company ignored the need for social development of the farmers. Housing, hygiene, education, and recreation remained at a low level. The company taught the farmers how to make money by growing cotton, but not how to spend this money wisely, so as to improve their level of living.

Worse, the Gezira planners were quite out of touch with the 20,000 farmers. One of the goals of the tenants was to become rich enough to hire laborers to operate their cotton land, so they could cease working. But the project planners assumed that the sole goal of each farmer would be higher family income. Had the company executives utilized social research to understand the needs of the farmers, they could have operated the plantation so as to avoid conflict with the farmers' values and beliefs. Perhaps if this had been done, the disagreements between the company and the tenants could have been minimized (Constandse, 1964, pp. 39–44).

As one analyst of the Gezira scheme concluded: "One of our difficulties was to know the true facts. No one living outside the villages could really tell the extent of all these or other needs and their comparative importance. There seemed a real need for an intelligent social investigation" (Gaitskell, 1959, p. 44). But it was not done. So the officials of the Gezira scheme managed an image that did not correspond with reality.

3. *Polder Development in the Netherlands:* A contrasting illustration of the usefulness of sociological research comes from a massive program in the Netherlands to reclaim farm land from the North Sea by the construction of dikes. The polders, or reclaimed lands, are a responsibility of the government of the Netherlands. Extensive use is made of rural sociological studies as a basis for governmental policy decisions concerning the polders.

In 1930, when the first big polder was drained, villages were established on the newly drained land at a distance of two miles. It was assumed that farmers would live in the villages and travel daily on foot or by horse to their farms. It soon became apparent that many of the villages were too close.

So in the 1940s, when the second polder was drained, rural sociologists were asked to conduct research on ideal settlement patterns. These studies indicated the need for one market town, which was located in the center of the polder. Around this regional center, ten villages were built in a circle. These villages were spaced so that the maximum distance from home to farm was about three and one-half miles, considered appropriate for an era of bicycles and motor cars.

When the third polder was constructed, a sample of 500 farm families were interviewed by rural sociologists. They found that 70 percent of the polder farmers owned a car. Sixty percent of the farm laborers, who lived in the villages, did not even possess a motorized bicycle and almost none had a car. These data dispelled the idea held by the government officials that "all the workers have motorized bicycles nowadays and distances no longer matter."

On the basis of the survey data, Dutch planners were able to decide on an ideal settlement pattern for the third polder. They avoided a costly mistake which would have been difficult to rectify (Constandse, 1964, pp. 45–54).

4. *Needs Assessment:* In the 1970s and 1980s rural sociologists in several states carried out mail questionnaire surveys of large samples of a state's population to assess what citizens saw as the major problems facing their community and the state. The research results were used by county extension advisory councils, as well as other citizen committees to establish priorities for extension program efforts.

Legislators in several states used the data to tap public opinion on certain issues, for background information about needed legislation, and to provide documentation about existing bills. One Illinois legislator best captured the importance of the needs assessment survey when he said: "I had a hunch about what people in my state thought, but I never had any empirical evidence to support my intuition. Now for the first time I have real numbers to back up what I have always suspected" (Burdge, Kelly, and Schweitzer, 1978).

5. *Social Impact Assessment:* Social impact studies attempt to predict the consequences of a development prior to its taking place. Examples include reservoir construction, highway development, the siting of hazardous waste sites, and the location of industrial plants and large recreation facilities in rural areas. Rural sociologists have contributed to social impact assessment research. For example, the town of St. Johns, Michigan, needed to widen Highway 127 through the community due to increased recreational traffic. Instead of arbitrarily imposing a solution, the Michigan Department of Highways hired social assessors to explore alternatives to solve the traffic congestion problem in St. Johns.

A social impact assessment (SIA) identified five alternatives ranging from a bypassed four-lane expressway (very costly) to changing the sequence of traffic lights along the main travel route.

Personal interviews were conducted with local people, the final result being that the community approached the Michigan Department of Highways with a plan to rebuild an existing county road around the town. Thus the daily routine of the local community was preserved, and traffic moved more quickly. More importantly, the local population felt they had an input into the decision and were willing to support its consequences.

We see that rural sociological studies can provide development programs with information about their clients' needs, so that a program can be designed to scratch where the clients itch. Social research can provide feedback to the change agency as to how its program is functioning, so it can be modified to become more efficient and/or more appropriate. We have not been able to illustrate many other common types of rural sociological research. For instance, social research is often a channel through which the poor, the disadvantaged, and the powerless can speak to the power elites of a society. Surveys of Third World peasants, migratory workers, Southern blacks, and Appalachian farmers helped bring their plight to public attention, and led to the initiation of programs to help them. The reader will gain a more adequate picture of these studies in future chapters.

SUMMARY

We distinguish seven major changes in U.S. rural society: (1) increased farm productivity and fewer farmers, (2) the permanency of the agricultural transition, (3) the internationalization of agriculture, (4) decreasing rural-urban differences in social values, (5) closer linkage of rural people to the larger society, (6) regionalization and merger of rural institutions, and (7) changes in rural social organization.

Social change is the process by which alteration occurs in the structure and function of society. *Society* is a collection of individuals and social groups that perform different functions and that work together in joint problem solving toward common goals. *Directed change* (or planned change) is caused by outsiders who, on their own or as representatives of change agencies seek to introduce new ideas in order to acheive goals they have defined. A *change agent* is a professional who influences innovation decisions in a direction deemed desirable by a change agency.

In the past 70 years, the rural population of the United States has been fairly constant because the increase in rural-nonfarm households has balanced the decrease in the number of farm people. However, the urban population has increased sharply, which means that rural people now make up a smaller fraction of the total U.S. population. In the past decade the rural population as a proportion of the total U.S. population has been stabilizing.

Rural sociology is the scientific study of rural people in group relationships. Rural people (in the United States) live in the country or in towns of less than 2,500 population. This category includes (1) rural farm people and (2) rural-nonfarm people. U.S. rural population remains stable at about 26 percent of the total population. About 80 percent of the world's population, however, lives in rural areas.

REFERENCES

"Agriculture: The Pushbutton Cornucopia." (1959). *Time.*

BENIGER, JAMES R. (1986). *The Control Revolution: Technological and Economic Origins of the Information Society.* Cambridge, MA: Harvard University Press.

BURCK, GILBERT. (1955). "The Magnificent Decline of U.S. Farming." *Fortune, 51,* 99–101.

BURDGE, RABEL J., RUTH M. KELLY, and HARVEY J. SCHWEITZER. (1978). *Illinois: Today and Tomorrow,* Urbana, IL: Cooperative Extension Service. University of Illinois, Special Series 1.

CONSTANDSE, A. K. (1964). *Rural Sociology in Action.* Rome: FAO Agricultural Development Paper 79.

DILLMAN, DON A. (1984). "The Information Society: Implication for U.S. Agriculture." *Rural Sociology, 47* (2), pp. 410–423.

DILLMAN, DON A., and DARYL J. HOBBS, eds. (1982). *Rural Society in the U.S.: Issues for the 1980s.* Boulder, CO: Westview Press.

GAITSKELL, ARTHUR. (1959). *Gezira: Story of Development in the Sudan;* London: Faber.

HOOKS, GREGORY M. and WILLIAM L. FLINN, "The Country Life Commission and Early Rural Sociology," *The Rural Sociologist,* 1 (March, 1981) 95:100.

LARSON, OLAF F., and EVERETT M. ROGERS (1964). "Rural Society in Transition: The American Setting." In JAMES H. COPP, ed. *Our Changing Rural Society: Prospectives and Trends*. Ames: Iowa State University Press.

McCORMICK, THOMAS C. (1931). "Major Trends in Rural Life in the United States." *American Journal of Sociology, 36*, 721–734.

MILLSAP, WILLIAM (ed.). (1984). *Applied Social Science for Environmental Analysis*. Boulder, CO: Westview Press.

NOLAN, MICHAEL F., ROBERT A. HAGAN, and MARY S. HOEKSTRA, "Rural Sociological Research, 1966–1974: Implications for Social Policy," *Rural Sociology* 40 (Winter, 1975): 435–454.

ROGERS, EVERETT M. (1983). *Diffusion of Innovations*. New York: Free Press.

ROGERS, EVERETT M. (1986). *Communication Techology: The New Media in Society*. New York: Free Press.

ROSS, EDWARD ALSWORTH. (1933). *The Outline of Sociology*. New York: Century.

SEWELL, WILLIAM H., "Rural Sociological Research, 1936–1965," *Rural Sociology,* 30 (December, 1965) 428:451.

SIMS, NEWELL LEROY. (1928). *Elements of Rural Sociology*. New York: Crowell.

SLOCUM, WALTER L. (1962). *Agricultural Sociology: A Study of Sociological Aspects of American Farm Life*. New York: Harper.

Chapter 2

Culture

Human beings the world over have very different ideas about what is pleasant and unpleasant, polite and rude, true and false, right and wrong. All these differences, found within a single biological species, are expressions of human culture.

—John J. Macionis (1987)

As stated in Chapter 1, sociology is the study of people in group relationships, and as a science, it seeks to determine patterns of human interaction within different societies. Even the untrained observer would agree that throughout different societies of the world, there are an unlimited number of such patterns.

Many patterns seem quite bewildering. For example, the Yanomano tribesmen of eastern Venezuela endeavor to prove their manhood by engaging in chest-pounding contests. A representative or "champion" from one village is designated to compete with the champion of another village. The competition begins by one of the contestants slamming his fist into the chest of the other contestant with as much force as he can muster. The latter must stoically withstand the blow, for if he flinches, he brings shame on all males of his village. Then it is his turn to inflict a similar blow on his competitor, with the same expectations for unflinching behavior. The contest continues until there is a winner and a loser. Barring a clearly identifiable victor, the contest escalates into head-clubbing with wooden sticks. Yanomano men wear their scars with pride (Stewart, 1976, p. 149).

How "strange" is this pattern of human interaction? It depends on one's perspective. Other societies have other ways of proving bravery and superiority, especially among their male members. In Pamplona, Spain, it is the annual "running of the bulls." In the United States, these ideals are embodied in playing gridiron football and in boxing.

Each example illustrates a different pattern of behavior. These patterns become the blueprints by which each individual learns to function within society. Through childhood as well as adulthood, each of us learns and relearns expectations for how we should or should not behave. Altogether, these expectations represent what is called "culture."

The purpose of this chapter is to acquaint the reader with the concept of culture, the reasons for cultural variability, ethnocentrism and stereotyping, and the practical implications of understanding why cultures differ so widely from society to society.

THE CONCEPT OF CULTURE

Before we define the concept of culture, let us indicate what it is not. Unfortunately, the common or everyday usage of the word "culture" does not correspond to its sociological meaning. In the nonsociological sense, culture means serious music, literature, and art. The person who enjoys these activities is considered "cultured." In the United States, a cultured person is associated with the upper social class.

The sociological definition of culture is very different. To be human is to have culture. All persons have some form of culture, that is, a design or blueprint for living. With humans, this blueprint is expressed through symbols. *Symbols* are representations of ideas so their meaning can be communicated among individuals within the same society. There are three types of symbols. Symbols can be objects, such as a national flag, a corporate trademark, or the color of a sports team's uniform. Symbols also take the form of gestures. For example, in different societies, a smile, a frown, or the shrug of a shoulder can have different meanings. In many societies, certain gestures with the hand represent symbols of defiance and derision. The same hand gesture in another society may have a sexual connotation.

Finally, the most important type of symbol for humans is language. The word which represents a small, shallow, oval-shaped bowl with a handle used as an eating utensil is called a "chamuch" in the Bengali language of Bangladesh, a "kumpga" among the Limba tribes of Sierra Leone, and a "spoon" in the English language. Even the word "symbol" is a symbol to designate gestures and words that we use to represent the meaning of different aspects of our culture.

Defining Culture

Culture consists of material and nonmaterial aspects of a way of life, which are shared and transmitted among the members of a society. Several important points must be made about this definition.

1. Culture includes the material products of a society. In U.S. society, eating out at restaurants is a highly popular activity. Restaurants include tables and chairs, utensils and napkins, lighting and wall decorations, uniforms for the waiters and waitresses, and thousands of other physical objects. However, the price we expect to pay for a restaurant meal is determined by the meaning we give these objects. A high-priced restaurant includes objects that in our culture we define as expensive, such as crystal chandeliers for lighting. We do not expect to find crystal chandeliers in a low-priced, fast-food eatery (if we bothered to look, we would find fluorescent lighting).

2. Culture includes the beliefs, values, norms, attitudes and behavior of its members. These are called the nonmaterial aspects of culture. Humans assign meaning and have emotional attachments to objects, such as to a national flag. We express ideas and abstract concepts with words and language. We believe in one god, two gods, three gods or more, depending upon the religious beliefs expressed through the culture in which we were raised. We expect others, and they in turn expect us, to behave in particular ways based on who we are within a society. For example, a married woman with children in U.S. society has several different sets of responsibilities, including mother, wife, breadwinner, homemaker, daughter-in-law, and so forth. In the Yanomano culture, a woman's responsibilities are much different. During important feasts the men do the cooking because they consider women "too clumsy" to handle the pottery. A mother may kill a firstborn girl baby in order to please her husband, in accordance with a culture that places high value on maleness and bravery (Stewart, 1976, p. 148).

3. Culture is shared. Most of the members of a society have similar patterns of behavior, but this common behavior does not mean that every member of a particular society will have a complete sharing of the total culture. Specific groups within a society may have unique beliefs, values, and norms that make them distinctive in some ways. For example, the Amish represent a religion-based rural subculture that is different in both its material aspects (the Amish drive buggies, not motor vehicles) and nonmaterial aspects (the Amish follow a simple, agriculture-based lifestyle) (Hostetler, 1968).

A *subculture* may be defined as a group that shares many elements of the broader culture of which it is a part, yet can be characterized by particulars that set it apart. We often speak of differences in rural-urban lifestyles as if there were two different cultures. It must be understood that in the United States rural society represents a variation from the national culture. Rural society is a subculture, and one that is the specific focus of this textbook.

4.   Culture is transmitted. It is passed on to new members entering a society (such as infants or immigrants) by the process of socialization. *Socialization* is the process by which culture is transmitted to and learned by society's members. Formal education in the classroom is only one of many ways in which culture is transmitted to the members of a society. The family, peer groups, religious institutions, and television are also important mechanisms for the learning of culture. Each member of society is continually learning and relearning culture. Socialization is not a process which stops with the transition from childhood to adulthood. We show in Chapter 3 that adult socialization and resocialization goes on throughout an individual's lifetime.

The whole of a culture is not completely transmitted. Obsolete aspects of a culture are continually left behind as new cultural patterns replace them. For example, notice how rapidly popular music changes.

5.   Culture is possessed by the members of society. When we browse through a museum, we may develop the erroneous perception that the material remains of ancient cultures represent a total portrait of their way of life. However, pottery and ceremonial masks cannot give a very complete picture. Often lost forever are the beliefs, values, expectations, and feelings of these peoples who shared an ancient culture.

As members of our society, we learn a culture and our behavior is guided by it. In other words, we internalize our culture. *Internalization* is the process by which we learn the rewards and punishments of conforming to a culture and hence constrain our own behavior.

6.   Finally, culture is *normative.* Culture provides the blueprint about how we ought to behave and what we ought to believe. Each member of a society may choose to follow this blueprint. Some individual members choose not to. These individuals may be society's innovators, who pioneer and develop new ideas and things; or these individuals may be society's deviants and criminals, those who violate the basic beliefs, values, and norms of a society (Horton and Hunt, 1984, pp. 57–59).

As members of a society, we often feel the pressure to conform to its expectations. For example, even riding on an elevator involves pressure toward conformity. It is expected that everyone face the elevator door or the lighted floor indicators. There is little conversation outside a request to press the button for the third floor, or an occasional "excuse me" from someone standing in the back who wishes to exit at a certain floor. Generally, only small children squeezed between a forest of taller adults are allowed to behave beyond these expectations. If you wish to test the cultural norms of elevator behavior, try singing in a loud voice on an elevator. Are the other passengers annoyed? Do they look nervous because of your actions? Do they try to ignore you and avoid your eye contact? Do they verbally express their dislike of your unexpected behavior? Guaranteed: They will react because you are violating the general expectations of proper behavior for riding on an elevator.

The conservative religious group known as the Old Order Amish provides a sharp contrast to modern U.S. society because there has been little change in their way of life for over two and one half centuries. "The Amish are like an archeological find . . . except that the Amish are in our midst [and] are still part of the present American scene" (Nimkoff, 1947, p. 254). Several examples of cultural differences between the larger society and the Old Order Amish are provided by the following case study.

BOX 2-1   *A PEOPLE WHO SAID NO TO CHANGE: THE OLD ORDER AMISH*

If you were an Old Order Amish person living in the United States today, you would not believe in using buttons (instead you would fasten your clothing with hooks and eyes), tractors, automobiles (which you would consider too "worldly"), birth control, wallpaper, cigarettes, wristwatches, or neckties; you would not engage in dating, military service, or voting; and you would have no education above the eighth grade. On the other hand, you would believe that large families are good (the average Amish family has seven to nine children), that the only proper occupation is farming, and in marrying only an Amish mate. And you would feel genuinely sorry for anyone who is not a member of the Old Order Amish, for you would know that they will not get to heaven.

The Amish are a religious sect who began in Switzerland during the 1690s when the followers of Jakob Ammann (hence the name "Amish") split off from the Mennonites, which had earlier split off from the Lutheran Church. Because they believed in adult rather than infant baptism and in the strictest separation of church and state, the Amish were subjected to extreme persecution by the Lutherans. The Amish began migrating to Pennsylvania prior to the Revolutionary War of 1775 (Smith, 1961, pp. 43–45). About 500 Amish came during this initial wave. This pre–Revolutionary War movement was supplemented by a later wave of migration just after the War of 1812, when about 3,000 more Amish formed communities in Ohio, Indiana, Illinois, Iowa, New York, Maryland, and Ontario (Hostetler, 1968, p. 38).

Today, about 100,000 Old Order Amish live in U.S. rural communities. Ohio has the largest Amish population, followed by Pennsylvania and Indiana. Over the years, Amish settlements have expanded into twenty states, several Canadian provinces, and even countries of Latin America (Crowley, 1978, pp. 249–255).

The Amish have increased in population more than fivefold in the past sixty years, while the U.S. population as a whole has only doubled. Because it is impossible to remain Amish without marriage to an Amish mate, inbreeding has been a problem. For example, only eight family names account for nearly 80 percent of all Amish in Ohio, Pennsylvania, and Indiana. Virtually all of the several thousand Amish people in Lancaster County, Pennsylvania, are descendants of Christian Fisher, who was born in 1757, 230 years ago. The selection of

Figure 2-1   The Old Order Amish are a rural U.S. subculture.

The Amish have a distinct way of life yet share many elements of U.S. culture. They are therefore an example of a subculture. This picture shows an Amish crowd at a farm sale in Pennsylvania. Amish culture forbids bright clothes, buttons (note the hooks and eyes), and store-bought haircuts, and requires that married men wear beards.

Source: Mel Horst and Exposition Press.

marriage partners among the Amish is narrowly limited by their horse-and-buggy means of transportation; they seldom marry an individual living outside of their community.

The Amish offer a fascinating example of cultural differences because they are surrounded by modern U.S. society, but still continue their own unique way of life. The Amish view of the world is one of strict obedience to the will of God. The major goal of each member of the Old Order Amish is to get to heaven by obeying God's word. Maintenance of the proper cultural norms of the Old Order Amish is therefore essential at all times.

The Old Order Amish believe that they are God's chosen people who have been called upon to be separate from the world. They believe in maintaining a self-sufficient community with as little reliance on the outside world (government, insurance companies, public education and so forth) as possible (Hostetler, 1968, pp. 48–51). The desire for distancing themselves from modern American society is due to the historical fact that they are a dissenting religious splinter group from a reform movement of a reform movement. Perhaps the cultural standoffishness of the Amish traces from their early persecution in Europe.

Within this self-sufficient community, there is little room for deviance from the norms, or *Ordnung* (Hostetler, 1968, p. 58). The *Ordnung* is a set of unwritten normative standards for dress, use of machinery, and all other cultural aspects of behavior. Each church (which consists of about 30 families) has its own *Ordnung*. There is no church hierarchy, hence, from community to community, there is considerable variation in the cultural standards set by the Old Order Amish. For example, in some Pennsylvania Amish communities, the men are permitted to drive automobiles, but only if they are very old models. In another Pennsylvania community, the Amish may own a car with the condition that all the chrome is stripped off or painted black; they are sometimes referred to as the "Black Bumper Amish" (Heickes, 1985, p. 54). In one Amish congregation in Ohio, the men are not permitted to cut their hair; they are appropriately referred to as the "long-hair Amish."

The Old Order Amish place great value on leading a "simple life" as the way

Figure 2-2 The Amish have difficulty in maintaining a separate subculture amidst the dominant U.S. culture. The photo shows the wreckage of an Amish buggy that was struck by a truck. Amish depend on horse-drawn buggies for transportation, but are forced to use roads and busy highways.

Source: Michael A. Schenk, *The Wooster Daily Record.*

to maintain separation from American society, and they consider pride to be the most serious sin of all. Not to follow the strict teachings of the *Ordnung,* such as by wearing a colorful shirt, would be committing the sin of pride and thus risking punishment.

When an Amish person deviates from church teachings, he or she is punished by a form of excommunication known as shunning or *Meidung.* The practice of *meidung* exerts considerable social control over an individual's behavior. When a person is shunned, no other Amish individual may speak to him or her. As a member of the Old Order Amish only knows others of the same faith, shunning means that the individual hasn't a friend in the world. Even the member's children, brothers, sisters, and spouse must refuse to speak to the individual, or even to eat at the same table. Marital relations are forbidden (Hostetler, 1968, p. 34). Only upon public repentance of the sinner is the excommunication lifted. For example, a young Amishman in Ohio was shunned for driving a car. After a week of such punishment, he came before the local congregation and repented symbolically by tearing up his driver's license (Hostetler, 1968, pp. 86–88).

The Amish have no church buildings, but they meet every other Sunday for religious services at a member's home. These meetings usually rotate from one home to the next. The services last from two to four hours. At the service, men sit in front and women in the rear. Sermons are conducted in a German dialect. The service itself is presided over by a "bishop" (or leader of the local church), who enforces the *Ordnung* and mediates disputes among members. The bishop also presides at weddings, funerals, baptisms, and communion services. The bishop receives no remuneration for his services. Like his fellow members, he is a farmer (Heickes, 1985, p. 67).

Courtship patterns among the young Amish have changed in recent years. The practice of bundling, whereby a young Amish man visits his girlfriend in her bedroom at night is seldom practiced today. The major opportunity for courting occurs when young men drive their girlfriends to and from the Sunday "sings" in their horse-drawn buggies (Heickes, 1986).

Mutual assistance is important in Amish communities. Everyone is expected to help in a barn-raising. Amish communities maintain contact with each other through a weekly newspaper called *The Budget.* Published in Sugar Creek, Ohio, it contains announcements of weddings, visits to out-of-town relatives, weather, crop and livestock reports, accidents, illnesses, births, deaths, and other community events. Most Amish communities designate a scribe whose responsibility it is to submit announcements for publication in *The Budget.* The newspaper is circulated to every Amish community, including those in Canada and Latin America.

If a young Amishman retains his religious faith, he is established in farming by his parents after his marriage. Most Amish boys are encouraged by their parents to "sow a few wild oats" before settling down to married life; but at the same time, Amish girls are rather closely supervised. Even this is beginning to change. In one Amish community in Ohio, a group of young Amish girls may get a ride into town. They carry with them oversized purses in which modern clothes are stashed. They change clothes in the public restroom of the Greyhound bus station, and then proceed to enjoy themselves at the local night spots. At the

Figure 2-3
Amish, who depend on horse-drawn buggies for transportation. This photo shows the dashboard of an Amish teenager's buggy, the decorations of which suggest that he is oriented toward the general U.S. society. About 20 percent of Amish youth leave the subculture.

conclusion of the evening, they return to the bus station, change into their Amish clothes, and exit the "English-speaking" world for their parents' farms.

Amishwomen often influence the young men to live by the *Ordnung* of the congregation. The result is that if an Amish boy intends to marry and enter farming, he must become a good Amishman; otherwise his bride and his parents will refuse to cooperate. Among the Old Order Amish, only Amishmen who are married are allowed to grow a beard. Facial hair is symbolic evidence that an Amishman has passed into adulthood.

Despite the social pressure exerted by Amish parents on their youth, not all of them remain in the religion. An estimated 20 percent defect (Erickson et al., 1980, p. 56). The high birth rates of the Amish, however, more than make up for the attrition. Although some who leave the Amish faith also leave the local community, many relocate to a nearby town and most maintain contact with close family members. Many who leave the Amish faith join the Mennonite church, which is closely related in its lifestyle, but less strict (Ericksen et al., 1980, pp. 61–64).

Amish subculture continues to flourish within the broader U.S. culture. Childhood training and the punitive measure of shunning allow the Old Order Amish to perpetuate their cultural differences. Reliance on animal power rather than machine power to run the farm has allowed many Amish farmers to avoid bankruptcy (Olshan, 1981, p. 302). However, it will become increasingly difficult for the Amish to continue their isolation in the face of increasing dependence upon the rest of U.S. society. As their population continues to grow, they must find new farmland and establish new Amish communities, which is extremely difficult to do. Thus many young Amishmen today are forced to enter such occupations as carpentry, blacksmithing, and cheese-making. However, these occupations bring the Amish into increasing contact with the non-Amish and increase the rate of defection from the simple life.

THE ELEMENTS OF CULTURE

Earlier in this chapter, we stated that culture includes the beliefs, values, norms, and attitude and behavior of its members. Here we define and illustrate these concepts.

Beliefs

A *belief* is a symbolic statement about reality. It states what is real and what is not real, or what is true or false. Sometimes specific beliefs may be subjected to the test of hard evidence, but often are accepted without recourse to empirical fact. For example, have you ever debated with your friends about whether ghosts exist?

There are belief statements about every aspect of reality, from the nature of the physical universe, to the characteristics of people who live in other societies, to religious beliefs about god and morality. The Talmud (Jewish), the Veda (Hindu), the Bible (Christian), and the Koran (Islamic) are books containing the essential beliefs that embody their major religious doctrines and prescriptions for leading a "holy" life.

BOX 2-2   *CARGO CULTS IN NEW GUINEA*

A most interesting set of religious beliefs developed in the post–World War II years in New Guinea. In New Guinea, people believed in a god named "Old Mansren," who created them and their island. They also believed that "Old Mansren" could restore himself to youth.

During the war, Allied armies occupied the island and built airstrips in order to move men and supplies to the battlefront. The New Guinea natives saw the airstrips being built, and subsequently witnessed large cargo planes (which they had never seen before) land and unload many tons of cargo. From their point of view, the way to obtain food was to grow it, and tools and other objects had to be made by hand. Through the eyes of the islanders, these "red men" (which is what they called the American and Australian soldiers, for red men referred to "ghosts" and the Allied soldiers were white like ghosts) did not have to work for their food and supplies, and they did not have to make their own tools. These "red men" had all the cargo they needed, supplied by large planes that came out of the sky.

Meanwhile, the local residents found the biblical account of the "second coming of Jesus," which they learned from Christian missionaries, similar to their own belief in "Old Mansren" and his powers of restoration. Once the war was over and the troops had left, the local people took over the airstrips (or built airstrips of their own), burning fires along the runway in an imitation of landing lights. The New Guineans believed that "Old Mansren" would have the planes land to give them cargo. These Cargo Cults, believe that if one's people is favored by god, he will send them cargo from the sky.

Source: Stuart, *Evolving Lifestyles,* 1973, pp. 157, 388.

The cargo cults of New Guinea illustrate the importance of beliefs in culture. Beliefs provide explanations for why events happen as they do. For those who embrace particular beliefs, they provide order and understanding about the world.

Do not confuse personal beliefs with cultural beliefs. A cultural belief is a symbolic statement that is shared by the members of society, and hence has the force of authority. You may believe that the earth is being bombarded by sigma rays from the fourth planet in the Alpha Centauri star system, but unless this belief is shared by others, it is no more than a personal, idiosyncratic belief without a basis in your culture (Babbie, 1982, p. 54; Stewart, 1976, p. 157).

Values

Values are symbolic statements of what is right and important. Social values vary from culture to culture (Young and Mack, 1959, p. 70). In some societies, for instance, premarital chastity is highly valued; in others, the bride is required to be pregnant.

Values and beliefs are often closely related. For example, Yanomano tribesmen believe that in the far past a god whom they call Periboriwa (spirit of the moon) came to earth to devour the souls of their children. Their ancestors became angry at this situation, and shot arrows at Periboriwa as he descended to earth. Periboriwa was wounded in the stomach, and it is believed that wherever his blood dropped, a Yanomano man was created. This belief in their origin is compatible with the value they place on fierceness among males (Stewart, 1976, p. 148).

Norms

A *norm* is a symbolic statement of expected behavior. Unlike beliefs and values, which are symbolic statements of ideas and preferences, norms represent the actual rules of the game as defined by a culture. The norms of society provide standards for behavior that are generally consistent with its values and beliefs, specifying which is appropriate or inappropriate, and the limits of what is allowable. Many norms are designed for specific roles within large organizations: In a large university, there are norms to indicate the proper behavior and responsibilities of the president, dean of students, department chairs, professors, students, and so forth.

Norms can be of two types: prescriptive and proscriptive. *Prescriptive* norms specify what should be done, that is, the dos. *Proscriptive* norms specify what should not be done, that is, the don'ts. Often the same behavior may be prescribed in one culture, and proscribed in another culture. For example, belching during dinner is approved in some cultures as a sign of satisfaction with the meal, while in other cultures belching is viewed as extremely rude.

Norms are enforced within a culture by sanctions. *Sanctions* are society's motivations to ensure conformity to norms by specifying the consequences of an individual's behavior. There are two types of sanctions: rewards and punishments. *Rewards* are culturally defined benefits derived by conformity to norms. Rewards are positive sanctions and in many societies include wealth, prestige, and approval or recognition from others. For example, Christmas bonuses depend upon job performance. A long-term, hard-working volunteer in a civic organization is elected president by its members. If a student scores well on an exam, the teachers note approval by assigning a high grade.

Punishments are culturally defined penalties for nonconforming behavior. Punishments are negative sanctions, and include for most societies such actions as infliction of physical pain, restriction of movement, fines, loss of prestige, and disapproval. In most societies, children are painfully taught life's lessons with a firm swat on the backside by their parents. In some Middle Eastern countries, stealing is punished by having the right hand cut off.

Another form of punishment used in most societies is the restriction of movement for those who violate its more important norms. In the United States, violations of the criminal law may result in a jail sentence. During a typical year, over 400,000 persons are serving in federal and state correctional institutions (U.S. Department of Justice, 1985, p. 614).

A third type of punishment is a fine. In U.S. society, traffic laws are enforced through means of citations, which specify how much money is to be assessed against the violator, usually corresponding to the severity of the violation. Which of us has not felt the impact of this sanction? In other societies, the fine for violations of normative standards may be heads of livestock or a specified amount of grain.

Another way to distinguish norms is on the basis of their seriousness, that is, the degree to which they are enforced within a culture. *Folkways* are norms that are only weakly punished if they are violated. In the earlier example of proper elevator behavior, disapproval of improper behavior would not be serious.

Two special types of folkways are fashions and fads. *Fashions* are temporary statements of expected behavior. For example, during the 1960s men were expected to wear their hair long. To do otherwise, was considered old-fashioned. *Fads* are even shorter in duration than fashions, and are usually adopted by only a segment of society. For example, a recent fad among eight to ten year olds is Garbage Pail Kids cards, which depict children who resemble Cabbage Patch Kids (a previous fad) in various deviant roles and situations.

Both fashions and fads are referred to as *popular culture* (in contrast to high culture). Popular culture represents the latest trends in clothes, music, art, toys, food, and other items that are available to us as consumers.

Mores (pronounced *morays*) are more important norms, whose violation is severely punished. Examples of the most serious mores are those prohibiting murder or the molestation of children. A culture's mores are often expressed in terms of a set of laws. *Laws* are formal sanctions in the sense that they are in written form and specify situations under which a violation occurs and the severity of the punishment.

Many norms that indicate what is correct and approved in a society are accompanied by *norms of evasion* which provide the means to circumvent the norms. For example, orthodox Hindus are forbidden by religious norms to touch tobacco with their lips. So they smoke through clenched fists, with the mouth at one end of the fist and the cigarette at the other. The Amish have proscriptive norms against driving automobiles (but not riding in them), and their primary means of transportation is the horse and buggy. However, several Amish may approach a non-Amish neighbor with the proposition that they will buy him a car in return for the equivalent of a taxi service.

In every culture, norms are always changing. In rural North America, there once was a folkway that the homemaker should do the washing every Monday. Clothes seen hung on the washline on a Tuesday were likely to be the subject of gossip by neighbors. This folkway has broken down in recent decades, in part due to employment of both spouses outside the home and to the advent of clothes dryers, which makes violation of the Monday washing folkway less visible to neighbors.

Attitude and Behavior

We often find it useful to know how other people feel about certain issues and things. We read newspaper reports or watch television news programs in which the results of the latest Gallup opinion poll are presented. Another word for opinion is attitude. *Attitude* is a relatively enduring set of beliefs possessed by an individual about an object. The objects about which we have opinions or attitudes include people, actions, and ideas.

Attitudes represent our evaluation or feelings about the world around us. Attitudes are possessed by each of us, and as such, individuals within the same society may display widely divergent opinions about the same thing. However, one's culture (beliefs, values, and norms) is important in determining our attitudes. For example, members of the Yanomano tribe feel differently about female infanticide than do members of modern Western societies.

Attitudes are generally indicative of how people will behave. They are predispositions to act. The practical utility of knowing an individual's attitudes is that they provide us with a partial basis for predicting behavior. If we learn that an individual feels the same way about certain political issues as does a candidate running for office, then we can expect that the individual will vote for the candidate on election day.

Many other factors intervene, so attitudes do not always correspond to, and may even be contradictory with, actual behavior. For example, studies of juvenile delinquents indicate that most adolescents have strong attitudes about not breaking the law. However, under certain circumstances, such as when with a group of friends (see our discussion of peer groups in Chapter 5), these same individuals may go along with the crowd and participate in the commission of vandalism, shoplifting, and other crimes (Sagarin et al., 1984, pp. 9–10).

Another example is the high value placed on honesty in U.S. society, and our preference to avoid cheating on exams, evaluations, and in most other circumstances. However, we also abide by norms of evasion to avoid "snitching" on our less honest fellow students and coworkers.

We may even elevate to folk-hero status those who cheat or "rip off the system." Dan Cooper became a hero in 1974 when he hijacked a Northwest Airlines plane in flight, received a ransom of $200,000, and parachuted into the forest of the Pacific Northwest, never to be seen again.

CULTURAL VARIABILITY

There are differences between cultures, and cultures change over time. Yet there are common elements found in all cultures and throughout history. These *cultural universals* include religion, family, economic institutions, and government.

Although every culture yet studied has had some type of family, the specific forms of family life vary widely. These differences among cultures are called *cultural variability*. For example, when most North American couples marry, they prefer to set up housekeeping in a residence separate from that of either of their parents. However, among the Hopi Indian culture of northeastern Arizona, the new couple lives in the home of the bride's parents.

Both the North American and the Hopi cultures make provisions for breaking marriage bonds through divorce. There is variability, however, as to the specific methods by which divorce takes place. The only possessions of a Hopi husband are his clothes. When he climbs the steep path up the cliff from his wife's fields, where he has been working all day, and finds his shoes placed outside the door of his wife's adobe house, he has been divorced. There is no court action and no alimony. The Hopi man knows it's time to go home to mother.

Cultures vary for a number of reasons. The physical environment, climate, amount of rainfall, topography, and other factors determine how and what type of food is hunted, grown, or gathered. In turn, how food is obtained determines many aspects of a society's culture. Among the Masai and Barabaig tribes of East Africa, rainfall is irregular. When rain comes, the crops grow and livestock have adequate forage. If the rains fail, hardship and starvation follow. Ritualistic magic for rainmaking is very important, and families whose members are considered effective rainmakers are held in high regard. In India, the annual monsoon season is essential to successful agriculture. In the Hindu religion, the sacred book of writings is called the Veda, and the primary god in Vedic writings is Indra, the god of rain.

Cultures may also change due to technology. For example, farming in First World countries is highly mechanized, reflecting the industrial character of the societies. These societies over the past 200 years have been revolutionized by such inventions as the steel plow, the cotton gin, the tractor, and by new seed varieties. Changes in these material aspects of farming culture have been followed by changes in the nonmaterial aspects such as norms that stress farming as a business.

A third way in which cultures vary is through isolation. The Yanomano tribes of Venezuela illustrate societies that have evolved over long periods of time, immune from contact with other cultures.

The fourth way in which cultures change is through contact with other cultures. A specific cultural element from one society may diffuse to another society, thereby causing its culture to change (Chapter 14). The cargo cults of New Guinea developed due to the introduction of American and Australian soldiers, cargo planes, Christian missionaries, and a reinterpretation of their traditional religious beliefs.

Subcultures

Every society can be viewed as having a set of dominant cultural themes which are characteristic of that society and which set it apart from other societies. The Yanamano culture is characterized by the high value placed on fierceness among its male members. Yet within most societies, despite a common core of cultural traits, there exists a great deal of variety. Certain human groups within society exhibit variations from the dominant culture.

They differ from the dominant culture of the society in which they reside by the uniqueness of their beliefs, values, norms, attitudes, and behavior. These differences can be due to many factors, such as age. Consider the following remark by an obviously overwrought teacher:

> The young people of today love luxury. They have bad manners, they scoff at authority, and lack respect for their elders. Children nowadays are real tyrants; they no longer stand up when their elders come into the room where they are sitting, they contradict their parents . . . eat gluttonously and tyrannize their teachers.

The origin of this quotation? Socrates, who said it nearly 2,500 years ago. His words will ring true for many teachers and other adults in contemporary U.S. society. These remarks represent one way in which subcultures are formed: on the basis of age, that is, differences in the way of life of different generations within the same society and culture.

Subculture was defined earlier as the distinctive way of life shared by a specific category of individuals within a larger culture. Members of a subculture may share much of the way of life of the dominant culture, while still maintaining some distinctiveness. Other foundations on which subcultures evolve include religious beliefs, ethnic background, race, geography, and occupation.

A special type of subculture is the counterculture. A *counterculture* is a group having unique beliefs, values, norms, and attitudes that are in direct opposition to or conflict with those of the dominant culture. Examples of countercultures include motorcycle gangs, survivalists, and some religious cults and communes. Countercultures often develop among groups who feel that their access to achieving the goals of the dominant culture have been blocked. For example, countercultures often evolve among youth from working- and lower-class backgrounds who see that they have little chance to be successful in Western society.

Rural Subculture

Many sociologists point out that there remain unique and distinctive features of contemporary rural life in U.S. society that qualify it as a subculture. Two hundred years ago, over 90 percent of the population lived on farms, and an agrarian lifestyle represented the dominant cultural framework. Today, less than 25 percent of the population lives in small towns and rural areas, and a scant 2.2 percent of the population actually lives on farms. As the United States evolved from an agrarian to an industrialized nation, the dominant culture became urban in character. Today, both geography (open country and small towns) and occupation (employment in farming and related agribusinesses) form the basis on which the distinctive way of life of rural people may be seen as a subculture, despite the "homogenizing" influences of television, and the spillover of urban development into the countryside.

One rural-urban difference which has maintained itself over time is views toward morality. For example, Gallup polls find consistent rural-urban differences of opinion on such matters as divorce (rural people are more disapproving) and premarital sex (more disapproving) (Larson, 1978, pp. 96–97).

Likewise, there remain some differences in behavior. Surveys consistently find that rural people attend church more often, read the Bible more often, and are more willing to volunteer for service on committees dealing with local community problems and issues (Larson, 1978, p. 102).

A recent fashion in U.S. society has been the revival of rural culture. For much of this century, rural life was associated with backwardness. However, crime, traffic, pollution, the expense of big-city living, the impersonality and anonymity of metropolitan life, and other perceived urban ills began to reverse this image. Today, rural living is viewed as simpler, cleaner, healthier, safer. Opinion polls indicate that most members of U.S. society judge rural environments to have a higher quality of living, and if they had a choice would prefer to live in a rural area (Williams, 1981, p. 198; Zuiches, 1982, p. 248).

A *Rural Sociology* study of the back-to-the-land movement found that the migrants were ideologically committed to pursuing a rural lifestyle (Jacob and Brinkerhoff, 1986, pp. 43–59).

Evidence for the recent popularity of rural lifestyles is plentiful: the growth of new journals and books about rural folklore, "mountain crafts," and gardening and landscaping, as illustrated by the *Foxfire* books, *Organic Farming and Gardening,* and the popularity of log cabin catalogs. Farmers' markets have been resurrected in response to dietary concerns about the quality and freshness of supermarket food. One of the highest-rated radio shows in the 1980s was the Minnesota-based weekly broadcast of homespun wit and wisdom from Garrison Keillor's "Lake Wobegon Days."

Within the rural sector of U.S. society there also exists considerable cultural variation that grew out of the unique historical circumstances under which different regions of the country were settled. In the South, the sharecropping/tenancy system of farming developed in response to abolition of slavery and post–Civil War reconstruction policies. In the Midwest and Great Plains, the family farm system arose based on the Jeffersonian values of the farmer as the backbone of society, and the utilization of family members as labor in the absence of surplus wage workers. In California, corporate farming predominates based on a history of large landed estates founded by Spanish settlers, and later, on a ready supply of farm laborers in the form of migrants from the far East and Chicanos from Mexico (Pfeffer, 1983).

ETHNOCENTRISM AND STEREOTYPING

Suppose that you just met a foreign student from India at the airport in your city. She has not previously had direct contact with the U.S. culture. She asks you, "What is the American way of life?"

You would probably respond in terms of democracy, a high standard of living, science and technology, and Christian ethics. After having resided in your country for several years, the Indian student might actually have noticed the following aspects of North American life: discrimination against people with dark skin, dirty politics, overemphasis on materialism, and easy but shallow friendships.

Sometimes American tourists overseas return home complaining about the smell of the people in the country they visited. "Don't those people believe in taking baths!" they exclaim. What is the opinion of "those people" from the host country? "Do all Americans smell of soap? How awful!"

Why do these differences of opinion occur? The answer is *ethnocentrism,* the tendency to perceive and value other cultures in terms unconsciously based upon one's own, and hence to regard one's own culture as superior. Every society tends to think that its culture is best.

Ethnocentrism even pervades our sense of body language. In U.S. cultures we distribute ourselves more distantly than members of most other cultures. One study showed that we stand about 20 inches or more away when talking face-to-face. In contrast, Latin Americans stand as close as 8 inches. In U.S. culture, two people talking that closely often has a sexual connotation (Babbie, 1982, p. 56).

The upshot of this cultural difference is that when someone from U.S. society is talking face-to-face with someone from Latin America, both have vague feelings of discomfort or anxiety and gradually begin to adjust. The Latin American tries to get closer, and the U.S. citizen attempts to back away. The person from the United States views Latin Americans as pushy, and the Latin American believes that U.S. citizens are cold, distant, aloof.

One indication of ethnocentrism is provided by the words used in many languages for the category of people who speak that language. For instance, among the Hopi the term *Hopi* means *moral behavior,* while *Kahopi* (literally, non-Hopi) means *bad behavior.*

One reason that ethnocentrism exists is because we tend to compare our *ideal* patterns with other cultures' *real patterns.* The Indian student mentioned previously compared the ideal aspects of her own culture with the real aspects of U.S. culture (which she views as foreign), and judges the former to be inferior. Likewise, North Americans compare their own ideal culture with the real aspects of a foreign culture, and come to the same conclusion.

Ideal patterns are those which members of a society believe they ought to follow, while real patterns are those which they actually follow. The ideal aspects of a culture are more often taught in school and in religious training, while the real are taught informally by peers, or are learned in real situations (the "school of hard knocks").

Earlier in this chapter we discussed norms of evasion. While norms were defined as "rules of the game" (the ideal pattern), norms of evasion refer to "working the system" (the real pattern). This difference also explains why we often behave in ways that contradict how we feel. For example, Americans view virginity as desirable, but few Americans are virgins at the time of their first marriage.

A frequent ethnocentric error is to pick out one element from a different culture and label it as exotic or undesirable without viewing it in relation to the complete cultural context. Certain East African tribes regard the liquid excrement which gathers at the bottom of anthills as a great delicacy. While individuals from other cultures might not regard ant excrement as a very desirable food, nutritionists have found that the ant liquid is rich in certain minerals and vitamins.

The intellectual position that judgments about cultural elements should be relative and must be based upon an understanding of the total culture is *cultural relativism.* The concept of cultural relativism indicates that the worth of any part of a culture should be evaluated in terms of its contribution to the total culture of which it is part. There is no universal standard by which cultural elements can be judged as good or bad.

One danger of ethnocentric attitudes is our tendency to think in terms of *stereotypes,* an exaggerated and preconceived image of a category of people, which affects the way in which we actually see these people. Because of stereotypes, we tend to see all members of that category (regardless of their individual differences) in terms of the preconceived image.

For example, Germans are seen as scientific-minded and industrious, Jews as shrewd and good at making money, and so forth (Katz and Braly, 1952, pp. 67–73). Often our stereotypes of other cultures are formed by what we see on evening television news or in other mass media. The frenzied, angry faces of demonstrators massed around the gates of a U.S. embassy form a lasting stereotype of those people. Likewise, they view U.S. society through the narrow sieve of information they receive about America.

If any culture should have little reason to be ethnocentric, it is the United States, because it borrowed so much from other cultures, as is illustrated by the following.

BOX 2-3   *ONE HUNDERED PERCENT AMERICAN*

There can be no question about the average American's Americanism or desire to preserve our precious heritage at all costs. Nevertheless, some insidious foreign ideas have already wormed their way into our civilization without our realizing it. Morning finds a typical unsuspecting male patriot garbed in pajamas, a garment of East Indian origin, and lying in a bed built on a pattern that originated either in Persia or Asia Minor.

Breakfast over, he places upon his head a molded piece of felt, invented by the nomads of Eastern Asia, and if it looks like rain, puts on outer shoes of rubber, discovered by the ancient Mexicans, and takes an umbrella, invented in India. He then sprints for the train—the train, not the sprinting, being an English invention. At the station he pauses for a moment to buy a newspaper, paying for it with coins invented in ancient Lydia. Once on, he settles back to inhale the fumes of a cigarette invented in Mexico, or a cigar invented in Brazil. Meanwhile, he reads the news of the day, imprinted in characters invented by the ancient Semites by a process invented in Germany upon a material invented in China. As he scans the latest editorial, pointing out the dire effects of accepting foreign ideas, he will not fail to thank a Hebrew God in his Indo-European language that he is one hundred percent (decimal system invented by the Greeks) American (from Amerigo Vespucci, Italian geographer).

THE IMPORTANCE OF CULTURE

In every culture, some parts change and others never do. In the realm of fashion and fad, changes are rapid, and sometimes come full circle (such as hair styles). However, in the realm of more basic beliefs and values (such as parents' beliefs about what is good or bad for their children), changes come more slowly.

As members of society, we live our lives constantly learning and relearning culture. Both the material and nonmaterial aspects of our culture are changing, and the pace of change often varies from one aspect to another. For example, medical technology relative to birth control has placed many new devices for avoiding pregnancy on the consumer market for purchase. However, our beliefs, values, and attitudes about premarital affairs have not changed as rapidly. From the pulpit, the political stump, and TV talk shows, debates about our society's sexual mores abound. Public concern about the rise of AIDS has further intensified the debate over sexual mores.

Cultural change may seem confusing to us at a personal level. However, if we take the viewpoint of cultural relativism discussed above, we can see that, if anything, culture creates order and stability in society. Culture is *integrative* because all members of society learn expectations about how to think and behave, and what their role is within society (Babbie, 1982, p. 62).

Without culture to help us define expectations about how we ourselves and others will act, there would be complete chaos. For example, every day we drive a motor vehicle weighing several tons down a narrow concrete or asphalt ribbon at varying rates of speed. No more than several feet to our right are similar vehicles of equal weight and speed that are coming at us from the opposite direction. What keeps us from sheer panic? Our trust in our belief that the persons controlling the vehicles coming from the opposite direction have been taught (socialized) to stay on their side of the road, just as we have been taught to stay on ours. They in turn have the same expectations of us. Somehow, with the exception of accidents, the system works. When deviations from the system occur (a vehicle swerves across the center line of the road), we have developed laws in the form of fines, revocation of drivers' licenses, and jail terms that punish the transgressor.

Culture is also *problem solving*. Culture helps us develop ways of adapting to our natural environment, and regulates our interpersonal environment. Nearly every society develops a culture that provides for a system of leadership (government), exchange of goods and services (economy), reproduction of its members (family), and socialization of its members (family and schools).

By being sensitive to how culture solves problems and integrates society, we become more appreciative of the way of life of other societies. Hence, we reduce our own natural ethnocentric tendencies.

This can have very practical benefits for the businessperson on an overseas trip or the government employee assigned to work in a foreign country. Many agribusinesses trade and sell internationally. Your value as an employee is greatly enhanced if your skills include an ability to negotiate with people from different backgrounds. State Department employees, Peace Corps volunteers, and many others are required to work in cultures in which they were not raised. To be effective in their jobs, they must possess the ability to rapidly internalize the language and customs of these societies.

Even within our own society, there is great diversity and change in our culture. Sensitivity to the role culture plays will give us greater understanding of the issues and events that affect our lives and the communities in which we live. As the famous anthropologist Ralph Linton once stated: "The last individual to understand water is someone living on the ocean floor."

SUMMARY

The purpose of this chapter has been to acquaint the reader with the concept of culture and to illustrate the great diversity of cultures throughout the world. Culture is transmitted through *symbols* or representations of ideas and objects. *Culture* is the material and nonmaterial aspects of a way of life that are shared and transmitted among the members of a society. *Subculture* is a group that shares many elements of the broader culture of which it is a part, yet can be characterized by particulars that set it apart. The Old Order Amish represent a religious subculture.

The elements of culture include <u>belief, value, norm,</u> and <u>attitude</u> and <u>behavior.</u> A belief is a symbolic statement about reality. A value is a symbolic statement of what is right and important. A norm is a symbolic statement of expected behavior. An attitude is an enduring set of beliefs which predispose toward behavior.

Cultural universals are elements found in all cultures, such as religion, family, economic institutions, and government. *Cultural variability* refers to differences between cultures. Cultures vary due to differences in the physical environment, technology, isolation, and contact with other cultures.

Despite the urbanization of the United States, rural-urban cultural differences remain. Rural culture also varies based on differences in farming systems, religion, and ethnicity.

Ethnocentrism is a tendency to perceive and value other cultures in terms unconsciously based upon one's own and to regard one's own culture as superior. *Cultural relativism* is the intellectual position that judgments about the elements of other cultures should be based upon an understanding of the total culture. *Stereotyping* is an ethnocentric attitude that exaggerates elements of other cultures in a negative way. Culture is *integrative* because all members of society learn expectations about how to think and behave and what their roles are within society. Culture is also *problem solving* because it helps individuals and groups adjust to change.

REFERENCES

BABBIE, EARL. (1982). *Understanding Sociology: A Context for Action.* Belmont, CA: Wadsworth.

CROWLEY, WILLIAM K. (1978). "Old Order Amish Settlement: Diffusion and Growth." *Annals of the Association of American Geographers, 68,* 249–264.

ERICKSEN, EUGENE P., JULIA A. ERICKSEN, and JOHN A. HOSTETLER. (1980). "The Cultivation of the Soil as a Moral Directive: Population Growth, Family Ties, and the Maintenance of Community Among the Old Order Amish." *Rural Sociology, 45,* 49–68.

HEICKES, JAN. (1985). Use of Public Health Services Among the Amish of Wayne County, Ohio. Columbus, OH: Department of Agricultural Economics and Rural Sociology, Ohio State University. M.S. thesis.

HEICKES, JAN. (1986). Telephone interview, February 21.

HORTON, PAUL B., and CHESTER L. HUNT. (1984). *Sociology* (6th edition). New York: McGraw-Hill.

HOSTETLER, JOHN A. (1968). *Amish Society* (revised edition). Baltimore: Johns Hopkins University Press.

JACOB, JEFFREY C., and MERLIN B. BRINKERHOFF. (1986) "Alternative Technology and Part-Time, Semi-Subsistence Agriculture: A Survey for the Back-to-the-Land Movement." *Rural Sociology, 51* (1), 43–59.

KATZ, DANIEL, and KENNETH W. BRALY. (1952) "Verbal Stereotypes and Racial Prejudice." In Guy E. Swanson et al., eds. *Reading in Social Psychology,* pp. 67–73. New York: Holt.

LARSON, OLAF F. (1978). "Value, Belief, and Normative Systems." In Thomas R. Ford, ed., *Rural USA: Persistence and Change,* pp. 91–112. Ames: Iowa State University Press.

MACIONIS, JOHN J. (1987). *Sociology.* Englewood Cliffs, NJ: Prentice-Hall.

NIMKOFF, MEYER F. (1947). *Marriage and the Family.* Boston: Houghton Mifflin.

OLSHAM, MARC A. (1981). "Modernity, the Folk Society, and the Old Order Amish: An Alternative Interpretation." *Rural Sociology, 46,* 297–309.

PFEFFER, MAX J. (1983). "Social Origins of Three Systems of Farm Production in the United States." *Rural Sociology, 48,* 540–562.

SAGARIN, EDWARD, JOSEPH F. DONNERMEYER, and TIMOTHY J. CARTER. (1984). "Crime in the Countryside: A Prologue." In Timothy J. Carter, G. Howard Phillips, Joseph F. Donnermeyer, and Todd N. Wurschmidt, eds. *Rural Crime: Integrating Research and Prevention,* pp. 10–19. Totowa, NJ: Allenheld, Osmun Publishers.

SMITH, ELMER LEWIS. (1961). *The Amish Today: An Analysis of Their Beliefs, Behavior and Contemporary Problems.* Allentown, PA: Pennsylvania Folklore Society.

STEWART, ELBERT W. 1976. *Evolving Life Styles: An Introduction to Cultural Anthropology.* New York: McGraw-Hill.

U.S. DEPARTMENT OF JUSTICE, BUREAU OF JUSTICE STATISTICS. (1985). *Sourcebook of Criminal Justice Statistics.* Albany, NY: The Hindelang Criminal Justice Research Center.

WILLIAMS, JAMES D. (1981). "The Nonchanging Determinants of Nonmetropolitan Migration." *Rural Sociology 46,* 183–202.

YOUNG, KIMBALL, and RAYMOND W. MACK. (1959). *Sociology and Social Life.* New York: American Book Company.

ZUICHES, JAMES J. (1982). "Residential Preferences." In Don A. Dilman and Daryl J. Hobbs, eds. *Rural Society in the U.S.: Issues for the 1980s,* pp. 247–255. Boulder, CO: Westview Press.

Chapter 3

Socialization

The purpose of this chapter is to explain how personality is developed in the individual. The socialization of personality is a process that occurs through a child's communication with family, friends, and others.

PERSONALITY SOCIALIZATION

Personality is the sum total of the attitudes, values, and habits of an individual, including both observable and unobservable traits, both physical and mental. Personality is the individual's unique share of culture. Each society has a culture, and each individual has a personality. We are born with the physical equipment for the potential development of personality, and it emerges as we gradually learn the culture in which we are reared. *Socialization* is the process by which an individual's personality is shaped through the transmission of culture to the individual. Socialization makes us what we are. The process continues throughout a lifetime, but much of an individual's personality is determined in childhood, especially in the period after about two years of age, when the child learns to talk, until about five.

Isolates show that personality is learned, not inherited. *Isolates* are children who have been raised in complete seclusion since birth. One such case is

Isabelle, who was discovered at six years of age after being kept in seclusion in the attic of a farm home by her deaf-mute mother (Davis, 1947). Isabelle essentially did not have a personality, for she could neither talk nor understand spoken language. After two years of special treatment, however, she learned to talk as well as other children her own age. Eventually Isabelle made a complete recovery, graduated from high school, married, and raised a family. Once she began to interact regularly with other humans, Isabelle belatedly was socialized into a human personality.

Socialization of Culture

Culture has an important influence on the personality of an individual in a society, as pointed out in Chapter 2. Culture defines what is considered normal or abnormal for an individual's behavior. For example, homosexuals are not regarded as normal by many people in the United States. However, homosexuals in one South Pacific tribe are highly respected religious leaders, and are regarded as perfectly normal. In fact, every young boy must engage in homosexuality before becoming an adult and engaging in heterosexual relations. So culture defines the normal range of behavior.

The violation of norms leads to sanctions, which vary from a disapproving look, to ostracism from the group, to death. Chapter 2 described the three kinds of norms: folkways, mores, and laws. Examples of folkways include the way we greet others, the way we eat, the way we smell, and other behaviors that are widely accepted. Examples of mores include commandments derived from religious doctrine, incest taboos, and rules about what is acceptable to eat (for example, eating the meat of dogs and cats is unacceptable in the United States). *Laws* are norms codified by a national, state, or city government, and enforced with penalties if a law is broken. So mores are stronger than folkways, and either may be enacted as a law.

The sanctions imposed for violating a folkway are mainly through an individual's interpersonal relationships with others. For example, if you were to "slurp" your soup in a restaurant in the United States, you would receive disapproving glances from other people (who might also comment to their friends about your impolite behavior). If you did not slurp your soup in some other cultures, you would receive disapproving glances. If you were to wear jeans to a black-tie dinner in the United States, people would look at you disapprovingly, but they would not use more severe sanctions. So violating a folkway is not as serious as breaking a norm.

An infant is not born knowing the folkways, norms, and other aspects of a culture. They must be learned through the process of socialization.

BOX 3-1   *SOCIALIZATION AMONG THE AMISH*

The Amish methods of maintaining their separate subculture in modern American society offer some interesting examples of social control and personality socialization. Amish children are trained in Amish ways from birth, just as non-Amish children are socialized according to their culture. Two rural homes may be located across a road from each other; in one, Amish children are learning that their way of life is right, while non-Amish children are learning the same thing for their own culture.

Amish children have almost no contact with the non-Amish world around them. TV, radio, magazines, and non-Amish schooling are forbidden. Friendships with non-Amish children are also banned (Figure 3-1). Amish teenagers are forbidden to attend public high schools where their parents fear they will be lost to popular music, fast cars, and the practice of going steady. A distinctive language also is important in maintaining control over the young: The Old Order Amish speak a special German dialect. Outsiders are referred to by the Amish as the "English."

The religious persecution of the Amish during their European beginnings several centuries ago led to a strong value on independence from the society within which they live. The Amish stress this history of persecution in socializing their children; each schoolchild must read about the Amish martyrs who were tortured, raped, and killed by their Christian countrymen in Europe. Certain of these injustices were at the hands of soldiers, which may explain why the Amish are avowed pacifists today. Professional soldiers in Europe generally wore mustaches, which is why adult Amish men all shave their upper lip and grow a full beard. The high value the Amish give to independence may also explain why they do not use electricity, motor vehicles, or other expensive products that must be purchased. Instead, the Amish prefer to invest their money in buying more land.

The Old Order Amish began as a religious sect in Europe about 290 years ago. The oldest continuous Amish settlement in America is Lancaster County, Pennsylvania, where the Amish have lived for over 230 years. The Amish today have spread to 17 states in America, and number about 100,000 people (see Chapter 2). The Amish in Europe became extinct in 1937 (Crowley, 1978).

Why did the Old Order Amish subculture survive in the United States but become extinct in Europe? The answer is socialization in a community context. The European Amish never developed their own communities. In the United States, their system of land acquisition permitted the Amish families to settle together in local communities.

The Amish in Europe have disappeared, assimilated into the Mennonite, Protestant, or Catholic religions. The Amish were never able to live in compact settlements in Europe. Scarcity of farmland prevented them from forming tight-knit Amish communities. Instead, they rented or purchased land wherever they were given protection from religious persecution. Thus, each Amish family became a separate social unit.

Geographic distance made communication between Amish families extremely difficult. Many could attend religious services only once or twice annually. Under such conditions, the scattered Amish families associated more with local non-Amish persons than with other Amish. Although marriages outside the religions were forbidden, they began to occur.

The importance of the community for socialization into a subculture is illustrated by the Amish costume. In Europe, where the Amish did not live in close-

Figure 3-1   **Amish children walking home from their one-room country school in Lancaster County, Pennsylvania.**

Old Order Amish children are socialized into a very different culture than are other young Americans. The Amish culture prohibits using cars or tractors, wearing colorful clothes, or displaying pride in one's possessions or accomplishments. The Plain People continue to flourish and increase in numbers in the United States (see Chapter 2). Lancaster County is the heartland of Amish culture in America; over 14,000 Amish people (about one-seventh of all the Amish in the United States) live here on the fertile soils of central Pennsylvania. Large-size families are functional for the labor-intensive farming of the Amish.

Source: R. Norman Matheny, staff photographer, *Christian Science Monitor*, May 9, 1986. Used by permission.

knit rural communities with other Amish, they wore the same clothing styles as their non-Amish neighbors. A distinctive Amish costume never developed in Europe. In North America, however, the Amish dress was quite different from that of their frontier neighbors. This difference gave them a definite and symbolic way of recognizing their own kind. The resulting social isolation served to insulate them psychologically against social changes taking place in U.S. society that might otherwise have swept away their cultural distinctiveness.

Today, most Amish people in the United States are concentrated in Ohio, Pennsylvania, Indiana, and Iowa, with other Amish settlements in 13 other states from New York to Virginia to Oklahoma to Minnesota (Figure 3-2). At various times in the past, the Amish have also migrated to North Dakota, Oregon, South Carolina, Alabama, Tennessee, Nebraska, Colorado, and New Mexico. All these Amish settlements are today extinct, providing evidence of the cultural vulnerability of a single community that is geographically isolated from other Amish people. U.S. Amish families have also migrated to Canada, Mexico, Belize, and Paraguay. What explains the success or failure of an Amish community?

Figure 3-2   Location of Amish church districts in the United States.

The approximately 100,000 Old Order Amish living in the United States today are found in 17 states, with the core in Ohio, Pennsylvania, Indiana, and Iowa. In the mid-1970s, the approximately 450 church districts, each with from 150 to 200 members, were located as shown in this map.

Source: Crowley (1978). Used by permission.

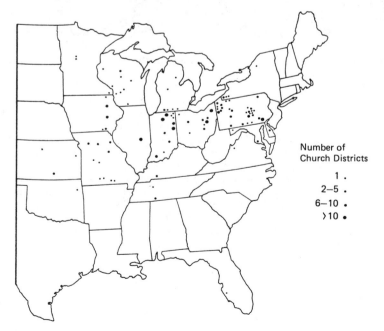

Number of
Church Districts

    1 .
  2–5 .
 6–10 .
  >10 •

One key ingredient is rich soil, which the Amish farm in a labor-intensive manner, growing tobacco, vegetables, fruit, and specialty crops; they also carry on such livestock enterprises as dairying and raising chickens. The Amish average seven children per completed family, and families seek to set up each of their offspring in farming. Tractors are rejected in order to maintain labor opportunities for Amish children (Stoltzfus, 1973). Hard work and high fertility go hand-in-hand for the Amish, as they seek to balance their rapidly increasing population with their environment. In recent years, escalating land prices threaten the Amish way of life. Today about half of the adult Amishmen in Lancaster County work in such nonfarm employment as carpentry, blacksmithing, crafts, and cheese-making. There is even an Amish business that converts tractor-drawn farm implements to horse-drawn equipment, replacing pneumatic tires with metal rims. Nevertheless, nonfarm work brings the Amish into increasing contact with the non-Amish. Today from 10 to 30 percent of young Amish people leave the religious sect (Ericksen et al., 1980). If a young Amish couple live more than a buggy-ride of about ten miles from their parents, visiting is less frequent, and the isolated family is likely to drop out (Ericksen et al., 1980). Spatial isolation lessens the social pressures for conformity to Amish norms.

So despite the threat of shunning if the subcultural norms are violated, and despite the effectiveness of personality socialization into the Amish way of life, the long-range future of the Old Order Amish in America is problematic. Nevertheless, over the several hundred years of Amish experience in the United States, as the subculture has become more and more different from the dominant American culture, its membership has become larger and larger (Crowley, 1978). In fact, over the past 80 years, the number of Amish in America has increased 700 percent (see Chapter 2).

CHILDHOOD SOCIALIZATION

A newborn human infant is one of the most helpless creatures on earth. Other animals are able to stand up and move about within a few hours of birth, but it takes us about 12 months to be able to stand up and several more months to learn to walk. It takes humans 14 years or more to attain sexual maturity (compared with about six years for chimpanzees). All human infants are born much more dependent on adults than are any other animal. Most of our development as humans takes place outside of the womb.

From the moment we are touched by a doctor in the hospital delivery room, we are interacting with other people. A gradual product of interaction with other humans is a child's awareness of *self*—his or her sense of identity, a feeling of "who I am" as a separate and unique person. When children recognize that other individuals are different, they begin to acquire a sense of themselves as distinct. An eminent early sociologist, Charles Horton Cooley (1902), called the changing image that people have of themselves the *looking-*

glass self. We use the people around us as a mirror to define who we are. So it is through the social process of human communication with other people that we gradually develop our personality.

George Herbert Mead (1934) of the famous Chicago School of Sociology showed how the process of developing a social self takes place. First, small children begin role-playing. They play at being Momma, Daddy, a fireman, and so on. By pretending to be other people, children gain firsthand experience about different perspectives. Then children begin acting out relationships through role-taking. They may play themselves hitting the baby, then mother being angry with them for hitting the baby. The child takes the role of the other by putting himself or herself in the other person's shoes. In this way children learn to see themselves through others' eyes. By about age seven they can take the role of the other in their imagination, without acting out the part. They can think about how others would see them.

This ability to look upon themselves as others look upon them is a turning point in personality development, Mead argued. To see themselves and their behavior from other people's points of view is fundamental for children to gain a sense of "me." Until this point in a child's development, the child only has an "I," a conception of his or her individual identity. The "I" is based upon a child's direct experiences through the senses. But then the child gains a point of view of their own behavior; this perspective is the "me." Without the ability to exchange information through the use of language, the "me" cannot develop. Isabelle, the isolate described previously, did not have a "me" until after several years of interaction with other people. The "me" is an individual's perspective of how others see him or her.

The stages of personality development are illustrated by how children at different ages play games. When infants play together in the same room (as in a nursery school), they pay little attention to each other. Each is rather completely occupied with his or her own toy or game. They may quarrel with each other over a toy, but they do not engage in cooperative play. Infants do not possess language, and without word-symbols and ideas, they cannot have expectations of others. They have not yet learned to take the role of the others.

Next, children begin to participate with others in reciprocal relationships such as organized games. Thus children learn to see themselves as part of a larger society, as more than just individuals. George Herbert Mead used a baseball game to illustrate this idea. To play baseball, a child must be able to see the game not only from his or her own point of view (as a pitcher, say) but from other players' viewpoints as well. The child must anticipate what the batter, baserunner, and fielders will do, and what they expect of him or her. One must also understand the rules of baseball. The child moves from understanding personal expectations ("Momma wants me to drink from a cup") to general expectations ("People must drink without spilling"). Mead called this broad image of social expectations the *generalized other*. Instead of anticipating how a particular individual such as father or older sister will react, children learn to plan their behavior according to the expectations of others in general.

At the age of six or seven, children can be trained to be more, or less, collaborative in their relationships with others. In nations like Russia and the People's Republic of China, the behavior of children is structured so as to stress interdependence on peers. For example, in nurseries in Russia and China, the children's play clothes may button up the back, so they must depend on others for help in dressing and undressing themselves. Further, the children's wooden blocks are large-sized (a foot or so on each side), so that two children are required to lift a block and a third is needed to push it into position.

Each individual gradually develops a concept of himself or herself through the process of personality socialization. *Self-concept* is developed mainly through interaction with others. The individual comes to view himself or herself, at least partly, as others see him.

The family is the primary agent of socialization for the child's first years and remains a strong influence for many years thereafter (Figure 3-3). Other important agents of socialization are one's peers (people one's own age) and

Figure 3-3
Parents are the most important socialization agents of their children's personalities.

Parents are particularly important in a child's language development and in socializing the child in role-taking (the ability to put oneself in the shoes of another person). Gradually the child learns to perceive himself or herself the way that others do; thus socialization occurs through the individual's interaction with others.

Source: University of Illinois, College of Agriculture, Office of Agricultural Communication. Used by permission.

teachers. Charles Horton Cooley (1902) called these main agents of socialization "primary groups" because (1) their influence comes first in a child's life, and (2) they are so crucial in personality development.

Interaction and Language

Interaction is the process of exchanging messages with other persons and lies at the heart of all human behavior. Through interaction we become socialized: We learn the motives, values, prejudices, norms, and attitudes of our culture. The example of the isolate Isabelle discussed earlier in this chapter shows the crucial importance of interaction in the socialization process. One's self-concept cannot develop unless one has other persons with whom to interact. The norms and values of society must be communicated to an individual or a self-concept cannot develop. Isabelle had no self-concept because she had no opportunity to see herself through the eyes of other persons.

Benjamin Lee Whorf, an influential linguist, maintained that language is not only a method of voicing ideas but is a very important force in shaping them. For example, the Hopi Indians call "insect," "airplane," and "aviator" by the same word, a notion as surprising to us as our practice of combining all 12 types of "snow" into one category is to the Eskimo—we even have difficulty in perceiving the 12 types of snow that are so clear to the Eskimo. So language has a determining influence on thought and behavior. Individuals think with, and through, language. When an individual learns a language, he or she not only acquires a way of talking, but also a way of perceiving, of organizing experiences, and of relating to other persons. Built into the grammar and vocabulary of a language is a structure of perceptions. Individuals discriminate among objects and events in terms of the vocabulary that is provided by their language.

If the particular culture from which a language is derived has not experienced a certain idea, it will not have a word for it, and will have to coin one, or borrow one from another language. For example, most Spanish words for the game of baseball are taken from our English terms. Likewise, English uses many words from other languages; examples are *tycoon* (from Chinese), *orangutang* (from Indonesian), and *khaki* (from Hindi). Many English words with the letter *z* were originally borrowed from Arabic (for example, *zebra* and *azimuth*), as were many words beginning with *al*, like *algebra*.

Consider the following language and note its use of words as symbols.

BOX 3-2   *EVRI SAMTING YU WANTEM FAENEM AOT ABOUT VANUATU PIDGIN*

Was part of the above title difficult to read? How would you like to learn a new language? This title can be translated as: "Everything you want to find out about Vanuatu pidgin."

These words are part of the official language of the Republic of Vanuatu (formerly New Hebrides), which is a chain of 80 islands located several hundred miles east of Australia and north of New Zealand. Vanuatu became an independent nation in 1980.

Pidgin represents a hybrid language formed from the words of two or more different languages. Historically, various forms of pidgin English were used as the language of trade between colonizers and the local population in Vanuatu.

The difficulties of communication in the country of Vanuatu are particularly acute. As an island chain, its various tribes have been isolated for centuries, resulting in the evolution of over 104 distinct languages among a population of only 130,000 people. To complicate matters further, for years the islands were jointly administered by the English and the French, who used their respective languages as weapons in their struggle for influence with the local population.

The solution to this mishmash of linguistic confusion developed out of the major export commodity of the islands: the sea slug. In China, sea slugs from the waters of Vanuatu were considered a culinary delicacy. A form of pidgin developed as a means of communication between the English-speaking sailors (who transported the sea slugs to China) and the Vanuatu population. As the established language of commerce in the New Hebrides islands, it was later adopted sa the official language of this new nation.

The Vanuatu language is quite inventive. Can you translate the passages below? How long would it take before you could communicate through their language to the citizens of Vanuatu? The word *blong* is an all-purpose word that means to do, to make, or to be.

1. Let's start with some words for objects familiar to you.

   mixmaster blong Jesus
   small box blong musik
   aesbokis
   aeskrim

2. An advertisement for a fast-food outlet reads like this:

   "Namba wan takeaway long Port Vila. I gat fresh fish mo chicken wetem chips."

3. An advertisement in a newspaper for the Vanuatu Motor Repair Shop:

   "Yufala we I wantem riperem trak, motobaek, aotbotmoto, lon mowa, no enikaen narafala enjin. Plis kontaktem mifala long telefon namba 3570."

4. A man found guilty and sentenced for stealing would exclaim:

   "Gavman jaj hem se I kalabus blong tri manis."

5. A special day for Vanuatu is:

   Long 30 Julai 1980 yumi kam wan niufala indipenden nesen.

6. A song written for this special day would be the:

    nasional sing sing blong Vanuatu

Answers:

1. Helicopter, tape recorder, refrigerator (or icebox), and ice cream
2. "Number one carryout along Port Vila (a street). I got fresh fish, plus chicken with chips."
3. "You out there. I want to repair trucks, motorbikes, outboard motors, lawn mowers, and any kind pf other engine. Please contact me at telephone number 3570."
4. "The government judge sentenced me to three months in jail."
5. On July 30, 1980, we became an independent nation.
6. National anthem of Vanuatu

This particular form of pidgin works in Vanuatu because it provides a common set of expectations (in word form) so that its members are able to communicate. Hence, language is an essential part of culture because it serves as the means by which its members share the common meanings of symbols. Without language, personality socialization could not occur.

Source: James P. Sterba, *The Wall Street Journal,* January 15, 1986, pp. 1, 6.

Rural-Urban Differences in Personality Socialization

In the United States today, the main agents of socialization (parents, peers, teachers, and the mass media) are similar for both rural and urban children. Nevertheless, certain important differences in personality socialization exist.

A special aspect of the socialization of farm children is their direct exposure to their parents' occupation (Figure 3-4). This day-by-day observation of the farming role gives this occupation a kind of immediate reality that most urban occupations do not have for the children of parents holding these jobs. Indeed a great deal of useful information is learned by farm children's observation of and participation in farming. As a result, urban boys with a college degree in agriculture may still not know how to farm. For this reason, many colleges of agriculture suggest that urban students work in farm internships if they intend to enter farming.

Not only are the special skills and types of knowledge needed for farming learned by a young person growing up on a farm, but favorable attitudes toward the occupation are also acquired. Unfortunately, too many farm youth want to enter their parents' occupation, at least in light of the limited number of farming opportunities that are available to the next generation.

Figure 3-4   The occupational socialization of farm children is different than for urban children because of direct observation of the farming role.

This young boy is being socialized into the farming occupation through participation and observation of adult work roles. One distinctive aspect of the personality socialization of farm children is their much greater knowledge and understanding of their parents' occupations.

Source: University of Illinois, College of Agriculture, Office of Agricultural Communication. Used by permission.

There are also many types of information that farm youth do *not* learn, as a result of their socialization in a rural setting. For example, farm youth are less likely to understand the importance of formal education as a means of achieving upward social mobility. Nor are farm youth exposed to the full range of urban occupations available to them. Nevertheless, most Americans today, whether rural or urban, consider the farm an ideal place in which to raise children.

GENDER ROLE SOCIALIZATION

Children at an early age begin to see themselves as being either male or female, and they behave accordingly. Even at two or three, boys and girls tend to choose different toys and play different games (little cars versus dolls), and these differences increase with age. Most four year olds are convinced that

Figure 3-5   Gender role socialization begins at a very early age.

A *gender role* is the pattern of behavior expected of a male or female in a society. The different toys that children play with at home and at school suggest the early age at which gender role differences begin to emerge among boys and girls in America.

Source: University of Illinois, College of Agriculture, Office of Agricultural Communication. Used by permission.

females are destined to become full-time homemakers, and males to become wage earners (Maccoby and Jacklin, 1974, pp. 277–285). Generally, girls get better grades in school than do boys, while boys are rowdier than girls. Where do such gender differences come from?

There are some innate, biologically-determined differences between the sexes. Male infants seem to be more active than females, while female infants are more sensitive to taste, smell, and touch than males. Boys are more aggressive than girls (Maccoby and Jacklin, 1974, pp. 351–352). Research evidence indicates that socialization has a more profound influence on gender-role behavior than do any inborn differences between the sexes.

A *gender role* is the pattern of behavior expected of a male or a female in a society. Traditional gender-role behavior for American women included making themselves as physically attractive as possible, wanting a husband and children, and putting their families' needs before their own. Traditionally, men in U.S. society have been expected to assert themselves, to be emotionally controlled, to put their careers ahead of family concerns, and to compete vigorously for jobs, women, and prestige. In Iowa, boys' and girls' basketball are played by different rules; for example, girls are not allowed to cross the midcourt stripe, due to a presumed lack of the physical stamina that would be required to run full court.

The stereotyped gender roles conveyed by the mass media may be in part unintentional. For example, television coverage of college and professional basketball games implies that excellence in sports is an effective route to upward social mobility. Many ghetto boys thus spend long hours playing basketball, while ignoring their academic studies. Actually, the probability of an individual getting rich via pro sports is but one in many thousands (as some professional athletes outspokenly point out to their fans in the ghetto).

Male and female gender roles have begun to shift away from traditional patterns in recent years. For example, male secretaries and female welders are not unknown. But gender roles still exist, and teaching children to play their prescribed gender role continues to be an important part of socialization. In addition to learning gender roles from parents, teachers, and peers, children receive gender role socialization from books and television (Figure 3-5).

The average American teenager has spent more time watching TV (about six hours per day on the average) than he or she has spent in school. Television programs convey gender-role messages that are very biased and stereotyped. Males have three-fourths of the leading roles. TV heroes are men of action: doctors, reporters, policemen, cowboys. Most TV heroines care mainly about romance or pleasing their family or boss.

BOX 3-3   *CHILDREN AND TELEVISION VIOLENCE: RONNIE ZAMORA*

Many scientific investigations of children and television lead us to the conclusion that violent television programs have certain undesirable influences on at least some children. Some normal children become more aggressive as a result of their heavy viewing of television portrayals of violence.

The social problems resulting from watching violent television are illustrated by the case of Ronnie Zamora. In 1977, at age 15, Zamora shot to death an 82-year-old woman who lived next door to his family in Miami Beach. The neighbor had returned to her home unexpectedly and had caught Zamora in the midst of a burglary. Zamora took $415 and shot the woman in the stomach with a pistol that he had found in her home. At his trial, Zamora pleaded not guilty because he was legally insane. His attorney argued that Zamora had acted under the influence of excessive television viewing, and that he could not tell right from wrong. The night before the crime, Zamora had watched two "Kojak" episodes (which Zamora's crime had resembled closely).

However, the judge in this case ruled that there was not a causal relationship between television violence and violent behavior. Ronnie Zamora was tried as an adult, found guilty of first-degree murder, and sentenced to life in prison.

Many parents and teachers are not as certain about the effects of television violence as was the judge in Ronnie Zamora's trial. They notice that children often become hyperactive just after watching violent television programs. Violence on television is effective in attracting large numbers of viewers. That is one reason why the profit-minded television networks continue to broadcast programs with a high level of violence.

ADOLESCENCE

Adolescence is the stage in the life cycle extending from puberty to the early twenties. It is a time of awkwardness, as children rather suddenly become adults. Adolescence is a social creation that is peculiar to Western industrialized societies. In most other societies, individuals move directly from childhood into adulthood when they are physically mature, without an in-between stage. In the United States, the adolescence stage gets longer and longer. Adolescents are not regarded as adults: They are not expected to support themselves; they cannot vote or own a car until they are eighteen in most states; and they are discouraged from getting married and starting a family. But adolescents are not children. They have the bodies and intellectual abilities of adults, if not the experience.

Small children tend to segregate themselves by sex. A ten-year-old boy cannot be forced to play with girls. But fourteen-year-old boys are expected to seek every opportunity to be with girls. This change means that adolescent boys must unlearn their prior antagonism toward the opposite sex. This discarding of old roles in order to learn new ones is a process called *resocialization*.

Adolescents are expected to prepare for adult roles. Adolescence thus is a kind of "time-out" for such *anticipatory socialization:* learning and practicing a new role before one actually occupies it.

In childhood, family members are the most important agents of socialization. In adolescence, peers become as important as family; what happens in school becomes as important as what goes on at home. Many (although not all) adolescents deny that they care what their parents think about their friends, their clothes, and their hair styles. Rebelling against adults in general, and parents in particular, may be a necessary step for an adolescent to establish a personal identity. Yet the family remains an important agent of socialization through adolescence and beyond.

Many societies have *rites of passage,* ceremonies that mark the transition from one status to another. In coming-of-age rites (one type of rite of passage), adolescents are put through some test of strength or courage, and thereafter are treated as adults. Among the Old Order Amish, an unmarried young man is not allowed to wear a beard, while every married man must wear a beard. Thus an Amishman's adult status is highly visible. Among several East African tribes, female rights of passage traditionally involved clitorectomy, in which part of the female genitalia were removed. In recent years, there has been considerable pressure to end this practice.

For American youth today, the closest things to rites of passage are getting a driver's license, drinking alcohol, and graduating from college. However, none of these events is a sharp transition from youth to adult status.

ADULT SOCIALIZATION

The socialization process is not a smooth, uninterrupted course in which the individual internalizes culture at a uniform rate. And socialization does not end when an individual reaches adulthood. Rather, the adult undergoes *continued socialization,* the process of taking on new adult roles and the modification of old roles. For example a county extension agent learns the technical aspects of this role while in college. Later, on the job, the extension agent learns other expected roles, such as those of community leader, change agent in diffusing innovations, and youth counselor. If he or she is reassigned from a county in which cattle-growing is predominant to one in which wheat-raising is important, the extension agent must learn further new roles, undergoing continued socialization. *The process of personality socialization takes place over the entire course of an individual's life.*

One form of adult socialization is resocialization, defined previously as the discarding of old roles in order to learn new ones. An example of resocialization is experienced by a civilian who enters military service. A similar case of adult resocialization occurs for a Mexican rural peasant who migrates to the city. The peasant has been led by radio and television advertising to believe that urban life in Mexico City will be easy. But the reality is quite different, with almost 50 percent unemployment or underemployment, a shortage of adequate housing, and a smoggy, polluted environment. Suddenly, the illiterate rural-urban migrant must be able to read street signs and calculate how much change he or she should receive when purchasing food products.

Adult life in the United States also necessitates much resocialization, as the average individual changes careers five times during the lifespan. Even for Americans who do not change their careers, life in a rapidly changing society like the United States means that adult socialization must be underway almost continuously, in order to keep abreast of the fast-changing culture.

SUMMARY

Socialization is the process by which personality is developed through the transmission of the culture to the individual. *Personality* is the sum total of the attitudes, values, and habits of an individual, including both observable and unobservable traits, and both physical and mental qualities. The human is socialized in a different manner than other animals, primarily because of a lack of instincts and the presence of language. Each individual develops a concept of himself or herself through the process of personality socialization. *Self-concept* is a realization of one's own personality that is developed mainly through interaction with others. The individual comes to view himself or herself as others see him. *Continued socialization* is the process of taking on new adult roles and modifying old roles.

Interaction is the process of exchanging messages with other persons. We become socialized through interaction. Language, either verbally or through gestures and symbols, determines much of an individual's socialization.

REFERENCES

COOLEY, CHARLES HORTON. (1902). *Human Nature and the Social Order.* New York: Charles Scribner's Sons.

CROWLEY, WILLIAM K. (1978). "Old Order Amish Settlemen: Diffusion and Growth." *Annals of the Association of American Geographers, 68,* 249–264.

DAVIS, KINGSLEY. (1947). "Final Note on a Case of Extreme Isolation." *American Journal of Sociology, 52,* 432–437.

ERICKSEN, EUGENE P., JULIA A. ERICKSEN, AND JOHN A. HOSTETLER. (1980). "The Cultivation of the Soil as a Moral Directive: Population Growth, Family Ties, and the Maintenance of Community Among the Old Order Amish." *Rural Sociology, 45,* 49–68.

MACCOBY, ELEANOR E., AND CAROLE JACKLIN. (1974). *The Psychology of Sex Differences.* Stanford, CA: Stanford University Press.

MEAD, GEORGE HERBERT. (1934). *Mind, Self and Society.* Chicago: University of Chicago Press.

STOLTZFUS, VICTOR. (1973). "Amish Agriculture: Adaptive Strategies for Economic Survival of Community Life." *Rural Sociology, 38,* 196–206.

Chapter 4

Role, Status, and Social Class

F. Scott Fitzgerald: "The rich are different from us."
Ernest Hemingway: "Yes, they have more money."

—Hilda Scott (1984), p. 4

"The rich get rich, and the poor get children."

—Lee Rainwater (1960)

A recently married couple drove from their home in West Lafayette, Indiana, to Springfield, Illinois, in order to visit some rarely seen relatives from the wife's side of the family. One relative owned a combination bar and pizza restaurant, which formed the natural gathering place for the other relatives that evening. Their occupations included carpenter, nurse, truck driver, and grocery store clerk. After they had consumed several pizzas and pitchers of beer, and shared reminiscences and stories, the relatives turned their attention to the husband, whom they had not met previously. The truck-driver in-law asked: "What do you do to put bread on your table?" The reply, "I'm a college professor," was met with the truck driver's exclamation: "No kidding! You sure seem like a regular person."

The truck driver's definition of the expected behavior of a university professor differed from his observations of his new in-law. The truck driver has defined university professors as people who are not "regular."

In Chapter 2 culture was shown to define expectations about the actions of the members of society. These expectations guide the behavior of individuals as they interact in various situations. Many of society's culturally defined expectations center on how people are supposed to behave based on their occupations (that is, what they do to "put bread on the table").

The present chapter reviews sociological concepts that help us understand how culturally defined expectations are developed. These concepts include status, role, and social class.

STATUS

In society, every member occupies a series of positions, and associated with each position is a set of specific responsibilities (Horton and Hunt, 1984, p. 105). These positions include parent, doctor, student, police officer, truck driver, university professor, and so forth. The socially defined position of an individual relative to other positions in society is called *status*. Like many terms in sociology, status becomes meaningful only when two or more specific individuals are compared; our status depends upon who we are and with whom we are compared.

The sociological definition of status is not to be confused with its popular usage. In everyday conversation, we use the word status to mean *prestige,* that is, the rank or amount of respect associated with a status or position.

A status or position may be either temporary or permanent. Each of us occupies many temporary statuses. Some are based on a specific situation, such as the status of doctor and patient. We go to a bank and occupy the status of customer, and transact our business with someone who holds the position of bank teller. Later in the same day, we may have a conversation with the same person, who now has the status of neighbor. Other positions are temporary because we make a transition from one status to another. For example, we formerly occupied the status of high school student, but have now graduated to the status of college student (Johnson, 1986, p. 88).

In modern societies, many positions or statuses are temporary. In more traditional societies, the positions occupied by members generally are more permanent. The difference between temporary and permanent status is related to the two basic ways by which members of a society acquire status: ascribed and achieved. *Ascribed status* is the assignment of status based on inheritance, birth, physical traits, or other characteristics over which the individual has no control. *Achieved status* is based on the individual's own effort and achievement.

Ascribed Status

In the Yanomano society, males and females are ascribed or assigned a set of statuses based solely on their gender. In American society, status is more often achieved, such as through educational attainment or through performance. In baseball, earning the position or status of first-string shortstop is based on a player's fielding and batting skills, a matter of achievement. However, even within American society, where achievement and equality are highly valued, some statuses are ascribed. For example, there are no female major league baseball players. In tennis and golf, there are separate men's and women's professional circuits.

Two important forms of ascribed status are gender and age (Horton and Hunt, 1984, pp. 109–115). Every culture has different sets of expectations for its female and male members. These contrasting expectations are often expressed through the different socialization experiences of children (Chapter 3).

In some cultures, such as those of the Eskimos' and the Yanomanos', tasks are clearly differentiated on the basis of gender. For example, in both of these cultures, men are the hunters and women are the child-rearers (Sanders et al., 1956, p. 454; Stewart, 1976, p. 148). In most modern societies, sex-linked differences have diminished, although they are still much in evidence. In American society, girls are most likely to play with dolls, and boys tend to play with guns, robots, and chemistry sets. Toy advertisements perpetuate this gender difference. These contrasting socialization experiences later develop into sex-linked differences in occupational and educational aspirations and achievement between females and males. For example, male airline pilots far outnumber female pilots, and there are few male flight attendants (Chapter 3).

Ascription by age is common in every society, and age differences are often expressed in a culture through its laws. For example, in American

Figure 4-1
The socialization experiences of girls and boys differ, leading to gender differences in social status and prestige. Some positions in U.S. society are predominantly occupied by males (doctors, carpenters, and U.S. Senators), while others are predominantly composed of females (secretaries and nurses). Today, however, most of the distinctions between male/female oriented occupations are being erased.

Source: Office of Agricultural Communications, University of Illinois.

society, the criminal courts treat juvenile delinquents differently from adult offenders. A juvenile offender is less likely to be sent to jail than his or her adult counterpart for committing the same crime. The criminal justice system has devised many ways of "diverting" juvenile offenders into parole, probation, and rehabilitation programs. However, in most states, once offenders have turned 18 years of age, their status changes, and they are thereafter treated as adult criminals and are more likely to be given a jail sentence for the very same offense. Other examples of age ascription in American society include laws prescribing the minimum age for driving, voting, and drinking.

In many traditional cultures, elders are highly respected. Chinese culture bestows great respect upon the elderly, who are seen as wise because of their age and experience (Atchley, 1980, p. 94). Confucianism stresses respect for parents by their offspring. Confucius advised: "A man may gently remonstrate with his parents. But if he sees that he has failed to change their opinion, he should maintain an attitude of deference and not oppose them."

The Industrial Revolution changed the status of the elderly in U.S. society to one of greater dependence on others and lessened prestige and respect. Modern societies have developed the mandatory retirement age and established social security, medicaid, and other forms of welfare to take care of their aged dependents. The Gray Panthers and the American Association of Retired Persons are organizations that fight the problem of ageism which often relegates the elderly to the rank (prestige) of second-class citizens.

In many traditional societies, status change associated with age is accompanied by a ceremony or ritual referred to as a rite of passage (Chapter 3). The ceremony marks a publicly recognized passage from adolescence to manhood or womanhood. Among the Arunta aboriginal tribe in Central Australia

> the boy child is of the woman's side. . . . The elaborate and protracted initiation ceremonies of the Arunta therefore snatch the boy from the mother, dramatize his gradual repudiation of her. In a final ceremony, he is reborn as a man out of the men's ceremonial "baby pouch." The men's ceremonies are ritual statements of . . . masculine solidarity, carried out by fondling one another's churingas, the material symbol of each man's life, and by letting out blood drawn from their veins. After this warm bond among men has been established through the ceremonies, the boy joins the men in the men's house and participates in tribal rites. (Wilson and Kolb, 1949, p. 229).

There are many other forms of ascription in societies: by race, ethnicity, nationality, family/kinship, religion, and by social class. Often the process by which status is ascribed forms a basis for conflict within societies. Violence, riots, and wars between ethnic groups and nations often may be traced to differences that developed from culturally defined patterns of ascription. For example, at the center of the violence in South Africa is the racial policy of apartheid. In India, conflicts arise between members of the religious Sikh minority and the majority Hindu population. The conflict in Northern Ireland is based in large part on differences between Protestants and Roman Catholics. The United States experienced a civil war over the issue of slavery, and urban riots during the 1960s and 1970s resulted from racially based social class differences between blacks and whites. Lebanon's turmoil is a combination of religious and ethnic differences between the Christian phalangists, White Muslims, and Palestinians displaced from their homeland by the formation of the Israeli state.

Achieved Status

The young of ancient Egypt were advised that the skill of writing was important so "that you may protect yourself from hard labor of any kind and be a magistrate of high repute. That is what makes the difference between you and the man who handles an oar" (Stewart, 1976, p. 228). In every society, norms specify status based on accomplishments. However, achieved status is relatively more pervasive in modern, industrial societies. Most positions within modern corporate and industrial enterprises are based on the acquisition of skills and the success of their application to specific tasks. Promotion is based on merit, which in turn is based on performance.

The position of farmer in most societies represents a mixture of ascribed and achieved statuses. For example, in U.S. society it is difficult to become a farmer unless the operation is inherited from parents. Sons are more likely to be socialized (Chapter 3) into the occupation of farmer than daughters, in part because it is more traditional for sons to inherit the farm (Lyson, 1981, p. 97). However, farming is also based on achievement. In order to maintain the operation and avoid bankruptcy, a series of responsibilities must be skillfully employed by the farmer, including cultivation, harvesting, management, and marketing. These skills are acquired through education and experience. They cannot be inherited, nor are they due to genetic differences between males and females, nor to race. Some farmers achieve greater economic success than others through their more effective utilization of these skills.

ROLE

A *role* is a set of socially defined expectations about the beliefs, values, attitudes, and behavioral norms associated with a distinctive status. A rural male in American society may play many roles, each associated with a different status which he occupies, such as farmer, father, husband, member of the county extension service advisory committee, and part-time school bus driver. The roles he plays depend upon the other people with whom he interacts.

A socially defined role, like status, is meaningful only when two or more individuals are compared. The status of doctor carries with it a set of expectations about behavior, as does the status of patient. Physicians are evaluated on the basis of how they fulfill the socially defined roles associated with the status of doctor. This concept is *role performance*. Whereas the concept of role refers to expectations, role performance is the actual behavior of the individual who occupies a particular status. Personality and many other factors determine how closely the performance of the individual matches the role expectations of a status.

Evaluation of individual role performance includes two principal dimensions: actual performance and role style. One occasionally hears the remark that, "He can do the job, but he's not the right type." An individual is judged by more than objective indicators of performance; the attitude brought to a role may be even more important. This difference leads to such expressions as "To be an expert, you must sound like an expert," and "You must look the part." Hence, behavior associated with one status may be judged by society as inappropriate for a different status. For example, a business executive who is unfaithful in marriage to her husband would not be as severely condemned as an equally unfaithful minister's wife. Gender and racial stereotypes (Chapter 2) contribute to our expectations about the appropriateness of some people in certain statuses and about our evaluations of their role performance.

Rural-urban differences may still be found in the severity of sanctions applied against individuals who violate local community norms relative to specific statuses. Statuses involving service to the public, such as teacher, extension agent, and minister, are examples where role style more greatly affects the evaluation of performance in small towns and rural areas than in urban settings.

ROLE STRAIN

Role strain is the term used to describe the difficulties encountered in meeting expectations associated with roles. For example, in filling the role of father, a man must work to make money to provide for his family's needs. He must also devote time and physical energy to father-child and husband-wife interactions. An individual may perform more effectively in one role than in another, or the roles of one status may not be compatible with the roles of another status.

Recent research indicates that the duties associated with housekeeping and child rearing are not more evenly shared between husband and wife when the wife has a full-time job. In most cases, the wife has simply added a set of additional expectations, which in turn often causes feelings of guilt when she is unable to devote enough time to her children or to managing household chores (Schooler et al., 1984, pp. 118–121).

Role strain is caused by inadequate role preparation, technological and social change, and role conflict. In Chapter 3, we noted the importance of socialization in the development of skills necessary for children to successfully compete in society. Family and education are especially important in such role preparation. Often role strain is caused by inadequate preparation for expectations associated with a status. For example, many farm youth aspire to the occupation of farming and have grown up learning many of the skills necessary to become farmers. However, the decreasing number of farms in U.S. society necessitates that many farm youth will migrate to urban areas and work in nonfarm employment. Inadequate preparation may decrease their chances to successfully compete for these nonfarm jobs.

Sometimes role strain may result from difficulties in performing roles associated with the transition from one status to another. The life history of an individual is a series of changing roles associated with changing status. The child adopts roles dictated by parents. Successful child rearing is measured by the degree to which the child accepts the role definitions and expected behavior patterns of society. Role behavior for a child is relatively fixed; he or she is expected to obey parents and other adults, to learn manners, toilet training, and certain basic do's (prescriptions) and don'ts (proscriptions). During adolescence, there is greater freedom in role behavior. A teenager can make decisions on dress and on friends, but control of moral behavior is still generally monitored by parents.

By the time the individual reaches adulthood, he or she is expected to have internalized the expected roles of society. Role performance at this stage must be very close to role expectations. The individual must act like an adult. Following the stage of adulthood is old age. Many individuals do not make a smooth transition from the status of gainfully employed to the status of retired. A retired dentist who experienced much role strain stated: "You're nothing if you're not working." Studies of older rural and farm males have found the transition to retirement status especially difficult because they place a high value on the work ethic and the sense of independence associated with work (Goudy and Dobson, 1985, p. 60–64).

Often rapid societal change may cause role strain through inadequate role preparation. In Sri Lanka during the 1930s, many parents raised their children as Christians because at the time Christianity was the religion embraced by the British colonial rulers. However, soon after gaining independence in 1947, the nation experienced a resurgence of nationalism that caused Christianity to fall out of favor. Children raised as Christians were identified with the colonial regime. Inadequate preparation in the Buddhist or Hindu religions became a handicap.

Many manufacturing workers have been displaced from their jobs due to the shift from an industrial to an information economy in the United States. These workers lack the skills necessary to compete for information on work. Bankrupt farmers face the same difficult prospects.

A third type of role strain is known as *role conflict* and occurs when an individual occupies two incompatible statuses at the same time. For example, a high school teacher may personally like a student who is failing the course.

Figure 4-2
Law enforcement is considered a high-stress occupation due in part to the role conflicts and expectations associated with the job.

Source: Office of Agricultural Communications, University of Illinois.

Out of friendship, the teacher wants to give the student a good grade, but as a teacher, he or she must fail the student. People minimize role conflict by avoiding many life situations that might produce it, a behavior called *conflict avoidance*. For example, the teacher could transfer students that he or she knows personally to another teacher's class, thus avoiding a potential role conflict.

As a society becomes more modern, the opportunity for role conflict increases because of the multiple roles that each individual must play. For example, a book publisher must rely on professors for classroom adoption of the publisher's books. These professors must also submit manuscripts for publication as books. If the publisher is too strict with the writers, publication opportunities and subsequent book sales may be lost. Opportunities for role conflict increase as one is required to make decisions affecting other persons' lives.

The excessive role conflict inherent in certain occupations has caused them to be labeled high stress jobs in which the potential for burnout is great. The role of police officer illustrates this situation. The officer is caught between the role expectations of public service and law enforcement. Often the police officer must shift from the physically and psychically demanding role of arresting a law violator to the role of courteously giving directions to a lost motorist. Officers are taught the lesson in police training school (which is later reinforced by their peers) to "keep your guard up or one day you'll get shot" even in situations where a citizen is requesting assistance and appears to pose no threat (Wilson, 1972, pp. 60–72).

BOX 4-1   *RURAL BANKERS AND THE FARM CRISIS: AN EXAMPLE OF ROLE STRAIN*

In many small towns of the American Midwest, banking executives are burning the midnight oil. Their computers and calculators, their spread-sheet programs and their own intuition often tell them a truth they would rather avoid—

their banks will have to foreclose on local farmers whose debt has gone well beyond their capacity to pay back the loans.

These are not easy decisions for small town bankers. Most operate without the bureaucratic buffers that protect big-city bankers. Small town bankers are often caught between angry farmers who blame them for much of their troubles, and federal bank regulators who are more interested in the solvency of banks than farmers. The children of these bankers go to school with the children of farmers who may soon lose their operations.

Small town bankers feel the pressure of a farm financial crisis almost as much as the farmers themselves. For some bankers, the pressure becomes too much. A 39-year-old South Dakota banker killed himself, after first shooting to death his wife and two children. Similar suicides have occurred in Minnesota, Iowa, and other farm belt states (Chapter 10). Many small town bankers simply quit under the pressure of making decisions about foreclosing on the operations of farmers whom these bankers often have known for many years, and who may even be close friends.

Source: Richards, *The Wall Street Journal,* April 4, 1986, pp. 1, 10.

STRATIFICATION AND SOCIAL CLASS

Geologists study layers of rock, or strata. We also find this layer-upon-layer pattern existing in society.

Social strata in society are organized on the basis of status and role. Individuals occupying certain positions in society have more wealth, power, and prestige than do individuals holding other statuses. *Social stratification* is the process by which positions in society are differentiated into layers with resultant inequalities. As with our definitions of status and role, social stratification only becomes meaningful when comparing individuals and groups. A *social stratum* includes individuals occupying statuses associated with approximately the same level of wealth, power, and prestige. Some social strata are at the top, some in the middle, and others are at the bottom (Babbie, 1982, p. 191).

There are three major types of social stratification. The first is called the *caste system.* It has three major features: (1) membership in a social stratum is based entirely on birth so a child born to a family in the lowest stratum of a caste system will remain in that stratum for the remainder of the child's life; (2) there is little mobility or movement from one stratum to another, hence, status is completely ascribed; and (3) there is a high degree of stratification, that is, the lines of demarcation between each stratum are easily recognizable. Interaction between members of different strata are clearly defined by the norms of the society, which limit contact to specific situations.

The Hindu caste system of India is perhaps most widely known, although these castes were never completely stratified, even in ancient times. Ancient Hindu literature described five castes. At the top were the Brahmans or priestly caste, followed by the warrior caste known as the Kshatriya. Below them were the trader caste or Baisya, and the Sudras or servants. At the bottom of the caste system were the outcasts, or untouchables, who were assigned the most menial and least desirable tasks, such as burning the bodies of the dead and skinning dead cattle. The caste system in contemporary India is illegal, and under the weight of modernization and social change, it has gradually declined. However, it still greatly influences Indian society (Stewart, 1976, pp. 256–258).

The second type of stratification system is known as the *estate system,* in which status remains largely ascribed, but there is a greater chance of social mobility through achievement. Estate systems are based on land ownership. Europe during the Middle Ages was governed by an estate system known as feudalism, in which were three major strata: (1) lords who owned the land and served as military leaders and their vassals; (2) the clergy; and (3) peasants or serfs who worked the land. Peasants were provided protection and allowed to farm in exchange for providing food and other services. Peasants also provided manpower for the lord's army. Mobility out of the peasantry was possible by taking religious vows or through outstanding military service (Duberman and Hartjen, 1979, p. 407).

Social class represents the third type of stratification system. Social class differences have been found in societies throughout history. The ancient Egyptians, Greeks, and Romans had a type of social class structure. Karl Marx (1977) divided capitalist societies into two basic strata: The bourgeoisie, who owned the means for the production of goods and services, and the proletariat, or workers, who sold their labor to the bourgeoisie in exchange for wages. Saul Alinsky (1971, pp. 19–20), a labor union organizer in the 1950s, divided "mankind" into three social class strata: (1) "the haves," or upper class, who have "power, money, food, security, and luxury"; (2) the "have-nots," who are "chained together by the common misery of poverty, rotten housing, disease, ignorance, political impotence, and despair"; and (3) the "have a little, want mores," that is, the middle class.

Do Social Classes Really Exist?

People in the United States are generally inconsistent when remarking about the existence of social classes in their community. They sometimes deny that social classes exist. In the same breath, however, they are likely to describe the characteristics of the upper and lower classes as if they *did* exist.

In a sociological study of Plainville, a small Missouri rural community, James West (1945, p. 115) was told by local people: "This is one place where everybody is equal. You don't find no classes here." Other Plainville residents said, "We're all just a plain old class of common average working people here. You don't find no very rich people here, and no very poor people, like you find lots of places" (West, 1945, p. viii). The sociologist soon realized, however, that this commonly voiced expression of equality was a myth. Although the study of Plainville is over 40 years old, the same denial of social class may be found amidst obvious class differences in contemporary U.S. society.

A similar type of contradiction was reported in the study of Elmtown, an Illinois community of about 6,000 people. Although Elmtowners did not believe in classes, during the course of conversations it became obvious that they were aware of many social class differences. Consider the following comments from a citizen of Elmtown (Hollingshead, 1949, p. 83):

> The top class is what we call the Four Hundred or society class. This whole business is based on two or three things. First, I'd say money is the most important. In fact, nobody's in this class if he doesn't have money; but it just isn't money alone. You've got to have the right family connections. . . . And if you lose your money, you're dropped.
>
> There is a really low class here that is a lulu. It is made up of families who are not worth a . . . damn, and they don't give a damn. They simply don't have morals. They have animal urges and they respond to them. Have you ever heard of the Sopers? They don't have any common decency. They shell out kids like rabbits, and they never go any place in school. They're always getting in jams. The kids have been problems for years. There are dozens of families like the Sopers in this town.

The myth of equality exists in the United States because of the large middle class, and the high degree of social class mobility (individuals moving up or down the social class ladder). In the United States, many people say they belong to the middle class when asked whether they are upper, middle, or lower class (Centers, 1952, p. 301). It is not socially acceptable to admit that one is lower class. However, when the more neutral term of working class is suggested, fewer respondents place themselves in the middle class (Horton and Hunt, 1984, p. 344).

Components of Social Class

The concept of social class itself includes several components. Income and wealth are the most obvious. Money buys the accoutrements (housing, dress, and other material goods) identified with the lifestyles of distinctive social classes. Equally important status factors are occupation and education, for they influence the amount of income and wealth that are accumulated. A final component of social class is lifestyle, which refers to an individual's day-to-day pattern of living. Wide differences in lifestyle are evident between the upper, middle, and lower classes in the United States. Members of the upper class belong to special service and social clubs and are more influential in local, state, and national issues.

Together these components define *prestige,* or *social class rank.* Previously we defined prestige as the rank or amount of respect associated with a status. The factors that provide social rank usually go together in a consistent fashion. However, some persons possess certain of these prestige-giving characteristics, but not others. A high school teacher is generally accorded fairly high status in most rural communities. However, teachers receive a relatively low salary compared with others in occupations of the same status. These *status inconsistencies* occur when an individual possesses a series of high ranking status factors combined with one or more low ranking status factors.

An example of status inconsistency is the case of lottery winner Milton Murduck, who had difficulty adjusting to the sudden change in status (and rank) associated with the acquisition of wealth. Former neighbors and friends no longer treated Milt in the same way. They were either asking for money or giving him advice on how to spend it. He missed the daily discussion with coworkers from his former job and he felt uncomfortable during contacts with his new upper-class neighbors.

Social rank, or membership in a specific social class, is more than just economic level, although income and wealth are important aspects. An upper class person is not simply a poor person with more money. Given the same income, a poor man would still not behave like the aristocrat. In addition to differences in income and wealth, lower class persons differ from upper class persons in values, attitudes, and many other characteristics (ie., role style). The lower class lottery winner may not be accepted by the upper class. The winner's children, however, may learn the upper class lifestyle and join the ranks of the elite.

Social Class and Lifestyles

What are outstanding social characteristics of each social class in America? Figure 4-2, adopted from studies of social class in American communities, shows five social classes. The upper classes (classes I and II) represent only a small proportion of the total population. The middle classes (classes III and IV) make up the bulk of the population in most communities.

Occupation, Income, and Wealth   Family income decreases consistently from Class I to Class V. Members of Class I are more likely to have inherited their wealth and position. Their upper-class rank is more likely to be ascribed than to be achieved (MacNamara, 1972, pp. 105–107). The banks, large industries, business buildings, and the large farms are likely to be owned by Class I individuals.

Class II families more frequently have achieved their social rank through their own efforts. The Class II's are not likely, however, to become Class I's if their upward social mobility has been too sudden, although their children may

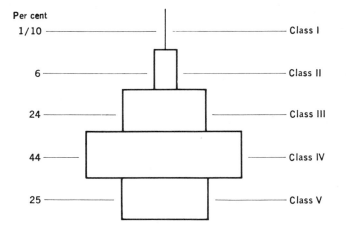

Figure 4-3   Percentage of community population in each of the five social classes in Elmtown.

Hollingshead divided the continuum of social status in Elmtown—a community with a population of about 6,000—into five social classes which he labeled I to V. He utilized community "judges" as a method of placing individuals on the social-class structure. Different portions of the population have been placed in each social class by other sociologists; most surveys, however, have resulted in a similar, diamond-shaped structure.

reach that status. Occupationally, Class II members are lawyers, doctors, engineers, college professors, operators of family-owned businesses, salaried executives in large industries, or salaried public servants such as school superintendents. Great emphasis is placed upon the career, and it is central to Class II lifestyle (Trillin, 1972, pp. 122–124).

Family incomes for Class III's are lower than the incomes of the II's and I's. Perhaps half of them own their own small businesses or farms. Other Class III's work for salaries in offices and factories or as minor public officials. Most have mortgages on their homes.

Class IV members are aware of their inferior status and resent it, but they are proud that they are not Class V's. The Class IV's are viewed by other people as "poor but honest." They work for wages on farms and in factories, shops, and in other blue-collar occupations (Miller and Riessman, 1968, p. 29).

Class V members are at the bottom of the class structure. Most are unskilled or semiskilled laborers, or unemployed.

Large income differences exist in U.S. society. In the United States, the top 10 percent of income earners receive about 30 percent of all reported income. In contrast, the bottom 10 percent earn less than 2 percent of all reported income (Tumin, 1985, p. 54).

Family   The Class I family is small and stable. Children are desired, but only one or two. Too many children break family estates into too many portions. For the same reason, marriage to other Class I's is desirable and achieved in many cases. Divorce or broken homes are rare. Family size increases moving from Class II through Class V families. The familiar saying at the beginning of this chapter is that "The rich get rich and the poor get children."

Sociologists have recently noted that some Class IV and many Class V families across the United States have become "feminized." That is, in contrast to the other classes, lower-class families are more likely to have a female as the head of household. In most instances, they are single females whose children are born out of wedlock, or women who have been divorced or abandoned by their spouses (Scott, 1984).

Education   Practically all of the Class I's have graduated from college, most from a "good" small college (MacNamara, 1978, p. 113). The Class II's believe that education is the key to success. This class is the most highly educated group and places the highest value on education. Class III's are not as well educated, but also value education as a way of "moving up." Class IV's rarely go beyond high school, and many never graduate. Class IV's place less value on education. Educational levels are even lower for the class V's. Many quit school, and little value is placed on education as a vehicle for social mobility.

The chances of going to college are closely related to social class. Over 60 percent of children from upper- and upper-middle-class families go to college, compared to about 40 percent for middle-class families and 25 percent for lower-class families (Tumin, 1985, pp. 93–95).

Religion   Almost all Class I families claim membership in some church, but few attend regularly. However, the Class I's contribute generously to the church budget. Class I memberships are concentrated in a few high prestige denominations—Episcopalian, Presbyterian, and Congregational. The class II's are very active in church work. Attendance is more regular than for the Class I's. The Class II's tend to belong to about the same churches as the Class I's. The Catholic and Lutheran churches claim large blocks of Class III people. Other churches attended by the Class III's are the Methodist and Baptist. The Class IV's either shun religion or else embrace it with enthusiasm. Church membership is largely in the Lutheran, Catholic, Baptist, and the more fundamentalist Protestant denominations, such as the Pentecostal, Free Methodist, and Church of God. Class V religious ties are generally very weak. However, Class V families are the most likely to belong to sectlike, fundamentalist denominations, and to "store-front" churches, as outlined in Chapter 8.

Recreation   Leisure, not labor, is regarded as dignified by class I's. The wealthier families hire a manager to run their businesses, so that they can devote more time to recreation. Practically all the Class I families belong to a private, exclusive country club. Travel is an important leisure pursuit, with trips to warmer climates during the winter months (Horton and Hunt, 1984, p. 360). Class II families have less time and money for extended trips. Family trips are often associated with travel to professional meetings and other activities related to their work. Occupational pursuits often delay or cancel vacations, and week-end leisure time is ignored in favor of work. Class III's and Class IV's take many vacation trips by automobile, visiting parks and recreation areas in their own or adjacent states. Both classes pursue much of their leisure time locally, joining baseball, bowling, football, or other sports leagues. The social life of Class V families consists of informal visiting between neighbors, drinking in public taverns, and other locally oriented pursuits.

Community Power   *Power* is the degree to which an individual can influence or control the actions of others. Persons who have a higher social rank are more likely to possess a relatively larger share of power. For example, Class I family member sit on the boards of directors of local industry and banking institutions. Class I persons tend to work "behind the scenes." Although they have much power, it is rarely visible or conspicuous. Members of Class II are often the visible leaders in community affairs. Class III's and IV's are not politically powerful, but are the strata from which volunteer workers for various community projects are recruited. Finally, Class V's are not politically active and display little interest in local community projects.

Lifestyles and Attitudes   *Aspiration* is the desire to get ahead. In terms of social class, aspiration is the desire to "climb the social ladder."

Class I individuals already have a high social status, usually acquired by being born to Class I parents. This lack of aspiration by Class I persons is partly reflected in their attitude toward education. The Class II's receive more education because undergraduate and advanced graduate training is viewed as essential if they are to improve their social rank. Class III's are similar to Class II's in their aspirations for high social standing. They likewise value education as a tool for getting ahead. Class IV's value education less, but parents of Class IV families still encourage their children to finish high school and are supportive of vocational training and college.

The social classes also differ in their political beliefs and behavior. More conservative political opinions are generally held by persons in classes I and II. Members of classes I and II are strongly pro-business and generally not in favor of government regulation. Class III's and IV's are more likely to approve of strong labor unions. They also favor an extension of the role of government in economic affairs and prefer closer regulation of large businesses. If Class V individuals hold political opinions, they resemble those of classes III and IV.

Class V's are the least likely to vote and are the least interested in both international affairs and local politics. Class I's and II's not only vote, but are actively involved in political affairs. Increasingly, individuals who run for state and national office in the United States are from classes I or II.

Individuals use various means to achieve their goals or ends. The achievement of these desired ends results in satisfaction or gratification. In many situations, an individual may choose between immediate or short-range rewards on one hand, and more long-range goals and their resulting satisfaction on the other hand (Mills, 1972, p. 129). *Deferred gratification* is the postponement of short-range rewards in order to secure long-range goals and the resulting satisfaction. An example of a person's deferring gratification is the college student. The college student postpones going to work immediately after high school graduation with the hope of a better job later. He or she hopes that this deferment of immediate gratification will result in a better job after college graduation.

In general, lower-class persons are not characterized by the deferred-gratification pattern. They prefer to have their satisfaction here and now and worry about the future when that time comes.

SOCIAL MOBILITY

Social mobility is the movement of individuals up or down the social class structure. When a person is socially mobile, the individual changes his or her social rank by gaining more education or a business promotion, marrying a person from a high social class, or by other means. Likewise, an individual may lose social rank and slip into a lower social class by going bankrupt or being arrested. Often rapid social mobility is accompanied by status inconsistency, as defined earlier.

Social mobility does not necessarily entail geographical movement. A person may continue to reside at the same location and yet increase or decrease social rank. The movement of persons geographically is referred to as *migration* by sociologists, rather than as mobility.

Will it be easier or more difficult for you to get ahead than it was for your father? Several sociologists have asserted that society is becoming more castelike and rigid, decreasing the chances of upward social mobility. Other sociologists believe that social classes are becoming less rigid.

The transition from the industrial age to the "information age" may change the nature by which social rank is determined in U.S. society, and therefore opportunities for upward social mobility. The Silicon Valley in California resembles in spirit a frontier gold-rush town, with stories of sudden wealth made through the development of computer or other electronics technology. TV advertisements for home computers stress to parents the "get ahead" advantages of computer experience for their children. Class II families are most likely to encourage their children to learn computer languages.

Increasing rates of divorce, separation, and teenage pregnancy have adversely affected the social class rank of many women in U.S. society, creating downward social mobility (Scott, 1984). Recently divorced women with children are often not prepared to compete for higher paying jobs, and in many occupations discrimination against women persists. Median incomes for males are greater than for females in all major occupational categories, including managerial, professional, clerical, domestic service employees, and craft and factory workers (Tumin, 1985, p. 90). Often promotions are more difficult for women. Added costs of child care and problems with after-school-hours supervision of children increase the burdens on single, working women. In contemporary U.S. society, women now account for two-thirds of all adults who live below the poverty line, hence prompting the phrase "the feminization of poverty" (Scott, 1984, p. 19).

SUMMARY

This chapter reviewed the sociological concepts of status, role, and social class. *Status* is the position of an individual relative to his or her position in society. Status may be either ascribed or achieved. *Ascribed status* is the assignment of status based on inheritance, birth, physical traits, or other characteristics over which the individual has no control. *Achieved status* is the acquisition of status based on effort and achievement of the individual.

A *role* is a set of socially defined expectations about the beliefs, values, attitudes, and behavioral norms associated with a distinctive status. *Role performance* is the actual behavior of the individual who occupies a distinctive status. *Role strain* is the difficulty encountered in meeting expectations associated with a role.

Social stratification is the process by which positions in society are differentiated into layers and the resultant inequalities. *Social strata* in society are organized on the basis of status and role. A *social stratum* includes individuals occupying statuses associated with approximately the same levels of wealth, power, and prestige.

Social rank or *prestige* is the position of an individual in a social class system. Social rank in U.S. society is determined primarily by wealth, occupation, and education.

Status inconsistency occurs when an individual possesses a series of high (low) ranking factors combined with one or more low (high) ranking factors.

Social classes in U.S. society differ in wealth, income, occupation, family size, education, religion, recreation, community power, and lifestyle.

Social mobility is the movement of individuals up and down the social class structure. It is also referred to as *vertical social mobility* and is different from geographic mobility or *migration*.

REFERENCES

ALINSKY, SAUL. (1971). *Rules for Radicals: A Practical Primer for Realistic Radicals.* New York: Random House.

ATCHLEY, ROBERT C. (1980). *The Social Forces in Later Life.* Belmont, CA: Wadsworth.

BABBIE, EARL. (1982). *Understanding Sociology: A Context for Action.* Belmont, CA: Wadsworth.

CENTERS, RICHARD. (1952). "The American Class Structure: A Psychological Analysis." In Guy E. Swanson et al., eds. *Reading in Social Psychology.* New York: Holt.

DUBERMAN, LUCILE, AND CLAYTON A. HARTJEN. (1979). *Sociology: Focus on Society.* Glenview, IL: Scott, Foresman.

GOUDY, WILLIS J., AND CYNTHIA DOBSON. (1985). "Work, Retirement, and Financial Situations of the Rural Elderly." In Raymond T. Coward and Gary R. Lee, eds., *The Elderly in Rural Society: Every Fourth Elder,* pp. 57–78. New York: Springer.

HOLLINGSHEAD, AUGUST B. (1949). *Elmstown's Youth.* New York: Wiley.

HORTON, PAUL B., AND CHESTER L. HUNT. (1984). *Sociology* (6th edition). New York: McGraw-Hill.

JOHNSON, ALLEN G. (1986). *Human Arrangements: An Introduction to Sociology.* San Diego: Harcourt Brace Jovanovich.

LYSON, THOMAS A. (1981). "Sex Differences in Recruitment to Agricultural Occupations Among Southern College Students." *Rural Sociology, 46,* 85–99.

MACNAMARA, CHARLES H. (1972). "Social Register, Philadelphia, 1969." In Saul D. Feldman and Gerald W. Thielbar, eds., *Life Styles: Diversity in American Society,* pp. 105–110. Boston: Little, Brown.

MARX, KARL. (1977). *Capital: A Critique of Political Economy.* Volume One. New York: Vintage Books.

MILLER, S. M., AND FRANK RIESSMAN. (1968). *Social Class and Social Policy.* New York: Basic Books.

MILLS, C. WRIGHT. (1972). "The Status Panic." In Saul D. Feldman and Gerald W. Thielbar, eds., *Life Styles: Diversity in American Society,* pp. 129–142. Boston: Little, Brown.

RAINWATER, LEE. (1960). *And the Poor Get Children.* Chicago: Quadrangle Books.

RICHARDS, BILL. (1986). "Troubled Lenders: Many Rural Bankers Face Intense Pressure in Farm-Credit Crunch." *Wall Street Journal* LXVI, pp. 1, 10.

SANDERS, IRWIN T., RICHARD B. WOODBURY, FRANK J. ESSENE, THOMAS P. FIELD, JOSEPH R. SCHWENDEMAN AND CHARLES E. SNOW, eds., *Societies Around the World.* New York: Henry Holt and Company, Inc., 1956.

SCHOOLER, CARMI, JOANNE MILLER, KAREN A. MILLER, AND CAROL N. RICHTAND. (1984). "Work for the Household: Its Nature and Consequences for Husbands and Wives." *American Journal of Sociology, 90,* 97–124.

SCOTT, HILDA. (1984). *Working Your Way to the Bottom: The Feminization of Poverty.* London: Pandora Press.

STEWART, ELBERT W. (1976). *Evolving Life Styles: An Introduction to Cultural Anthropology.* New York: McGraw-Hill.

TRILLIN, CALVIN. (1972). "Phoenix . . . Practice, Practice, Practice." In Saul D. Feldman and Gerald W. Thielbar, eds., *Life Styles: Diversity in American Society,* pp. 122–128. Boston: Little, Brown.

TUMIN, MELVIN M. *Social Stratification: The Forms and Functions of Inequality.* 2nd ed. (Englewood Cliffs, NJ: Prentice-Hall, 1985).

WEST, JAMES. (1945). *Plainville, U.S.A.* New York: Columbia University Press.

WILSON, JAMES Q. (1972). "The Police in the Ghetto." In Robert F. Steadman, ed., *The Police and the Community,* pp. 51–90. Baltimore: Johns Hopkins University Press.

WILSON, LOGAN, AND WILLIAM L. KOLB, eds. (1949). *Sociological Analysis.* New York: Harcourt, Brace, and World.

Chapter 5

Groups and Organizations

- Since the first edition of this book was published in 1960, the U.S. federal government has become much larger. Almost 250 agencies were added to its structure, and the total federal payroll has expanded proportionately.
- The number of successful small businesses has declined by about 10 percent each year, and the trend in almost every U.S. industry is toward fewer and larger companies. The general trend is to bigness.
- The 500 largest corporations in the United States earn about 90 percent of all profits.
- Productive agriculture is increasingly centralized in corporate farms, or through contract farming and vertical integration.
- *Holiday Inns* provide nationwide video-conferencing by satellite hookup.

Most countries like the United States have become nations of organizations: big business, big industry, big education, big religion, big agriculture, and big government. A theme of this chapter is how individual satisfaction and productivity are maintained while society becomes organized in larger social units that strive for increased efficiency. The following case history of Harold the Bureaucrat is an extreme example of how large-scale organizations restrict individual initiative in order to emphasize rational decision making.

BOX 5-1   *PORTRAIT OF A BUREAUCRAT*

Harold joined the federal civil service at an early age. He was out of school and needed a job, and he had heard of the advantages of federal work: good pay, liberal vacations and sick leave, and early retirement. The impossibility of getting fired was also an advantage. Harold was overcome with the idealism of youth and longed to do something to serve his country. Harold's idealism was fired up by films and pep talks in the orientation program at the federal agency that hired him. Then he began his apprenticeship as a bureaucrat.

One of his first tasks was to learn how to write "federal English." He used vague subjects and passive verbs exclusively ("it is regretted"), and avoided committing himself or his office by any kind of definite statement. Soon he was able to write such statements as: "Files in this office do not appear to indicate that the document requested by you is unavailable at this time."

Harold's career advanced rapidly, due mainly to his ability to get along with others and his desire to do everything expected of him. Harold soon learned that the acquisition of status symbols is vitally important to bureaucrats. He could tell by a glance at a person's office how far up he or she was: by the carpet, or lack of it; the presence or absence of a filing cabinet, bookcase, and couch; and whether the desk was made of wood or metal. Sometimes, while in a colleague's office, Harold would crane his neck to observe whether his colleague's calculator was new and of a certain expensive make.

Harold acquired a reputation for doing everything the right way. He had a deep and thorough knowledge of the Manual of Administrative Procedures, and could quote provisions that no one else knew existed. Harold went to great lengths to straighten out a ten-cent accounting discrepancy that was reported by his agency's field office in Yakima. The correction cost the agency thousands of dollars in man-hours, paper, and postage, and there were mild protests, but Harold was firm. "I don't care how much it costs," he declared, "it's the principle of the thing. If we don't treat ten-cent items according to the Manual, pretty soon we'll be letting ten-dollar errors get by, and where will it all end?" Where indeed?

Harold did not stay with the agency quite as long as he had planned. It was his own fault. He had been told, ten years previously, to burn his rash proposal to abolish part of his own work. But like any true bureaucrat, Harold could not bring himself to destroy a typed report, so he filed it. His proposal was eventually discovered by one of those cold-blooded opportunists who seeks ways of cutting costs regardless of the human consequences. This efficiency expert carried the suggestion further than Harold had intended. He convinced the Top Management Committee of the agency to abolish Harold's entire division (of which he was now the director) in the name of efficiency. This event was a blow, but his $50,000-a-year pension consoled Harold somewhat. He summarized his career at his retirement luncheon, when he wisely stated: "This expression of your esteem is greatly appreciated. All that I did, well, really it was nothing."

Our example of Harold the Bureaucrat incorrectly implies that all bureaucracies are inefficient, and that all their individuals have bureaucratic personalities. Later in this chapter, we shall discuss the relative efficiency of bureaucratic organizations.

Source: Adapted from Joan Zola, "Portrait of a Bureaucrat," *National Review*, April 18, 1967, pp. 410–412. Used by permission.

WHAT ARE GROUPS AND INSTITUTIONS?

Groups

We defined *sociology* as the scientific study of people in group relationships. Group relationships are the building blocks of sociology. What is a group?

A *group* is (1) composed of people (2) in interaction or communication and (3) together physically (4) with common interests or goals.

To test your understanding of this definition, ask yourself which of the following are groups and which are not?

1.   All of the females in India aged 30 to 35.
2.   The members of a student governing council on a university campus.
3.   The people living in Brazos County, Texas.
4.   The ten peasant families living in the El Camino Real neighborhood.

The first example is not a group. Females aged 30 to 35 are what sociologists call a category. A *category* is a number of individuals who share one or more characteristics such as age or occupation but who are not in interaction with each other. Other examples of categories are the wine growers in California, sociologists in the Netherlands, and peasant farmers in Colombia.

Our second example is a group. The members of a student governing council are in communication with each other, they are together physically at their meetings, and they have common interests.

Example number three is not a group. The residents of a Texas county are what sociologists call an *aggregate,* a number of individuals held together in a physical sense, but not interacting with each other.

Our fourth example is a group. The ten families living in the El Camino Real neighborhood fulfill our definition of a group because these neighbors are in interaction and share similar occupational and residential interests.

These examples show that our classification in groups, categories, and aggregates is somewhat arbitrary, but the reader by now should have a clear idea of what sociologists mean by the concept of group. This chapter shows ways to classify groups as primary or secondary, and formal or informal.

Institutions

An *institution* is an abstraction referring to the aspects of a culture that satisfy the fundamental welfare of a society. Most institutions are *cultural universals* and in some form are found in every culture. For example, all societies need to provide for rearing children. The institution responsible for child rearing is the family. The family institution is an abstraction, although our conception of the Mexican family is certainly based on real life. While the Juan Martinez family is a group, the Mexican family is an institution.

Likewise, while the Singh Carry-Out Restaurant is not an institution, the Indian economy is. In addition to the family and the economy, most cultures have institutions for religion, education, and government. The community is also sometimes regarded as an institution. We devote separate chapters in this book to the rural family, the church, rural industries, government agencies, and the rural community.

Primary Groups

Carolus Linnaeus, the biologist, classified all forms of life into kingdoms, phyla, orders, families, genera, and species. Sociologists have similarly attempted to classify human groups into different types, such as primary or secondary. The Australian students described below have migrated from a rural, primary-group background to a secondary-group life in a major city.

BOX 5-2

In most of rural Australia, population densities are so sparse that secondary schools are seldom nearby. Students who want to enroll in secondary school must live as boarders in a regional city. A typical student might be a 15-year-old girl from an isolated rural background and away from home for the first time.

Each February (which is mid-fall in the southern hemisphere), thousands of new students in Australia move from their "stations" (that is, farms) to secondary schools in urban areas. Most find city life quite lonely at first. The school situation seems strange. They are referred to as "Miss Jones," rather than "Fiona." As one rural student in Australia put it, "School is much more business-like." Because these students are boarders, they differ from other students, who return after school each day to live with their families. As a result boarders develop strong primary-group friendships with other boarding students. Individuals with these strong bonds are more likely to be successful in schools, and to later enroll in a university.

The concept of primary group was developed 80 years ago by an American sociologist, Charles Horton Cooley, who taught at the University of Michigan. He regarded the neighborhood, the family, and the child's play group as primary. He chose the term "primary" for this kind of group (1) because these groups are the first in which a child finds membership, and (2) because of their great importance in the socialization of personality (Cooley, 1909, pp. 23–24).

Although Cooley did not use the concept of "secondary groups," later sociologists developed this idea to describe the opposite type of group from the primary group. The specific characteristics of primary and secondary groups are (Horton and Hunt, 1984):

PRIMARY GROUPS

1. They are small in size: Less than 20 to 30 persons are members.
2. Personal and intimate relationships exist among the members.
3. Much face-to-face communication takes place.
4. They have great permanency: Members are together over a long period of time.
5. Members are well acquainted and have a strong sense of loyalty or "we-feeling"; strong group pressure is present.
6. Informality is more common; the group usually does not have a name, officers, or a regular meeting place.
7. Group decisions are more traditional and personally centered.

SECONDARY GROUPS

1. They are large in size.
2. Impersonal and aloof relationships exist among the members.
3. Little face-to-face communication takes place.
4. They are temporary: Members spend relatively little time together.
5. Members are not so well acquainted, and anonymity is prevalent.
6. Formality prevails: The group often has a name, officers, and a regular meeting place.
7. Group decisions are more rational and goal directed and the emphasis is on efficiency.

The characteristics of a primary group are illustrated by a coed's account of her dormitory friendship clique at Ohio State University.

> One group to which I belong is composed of my five best friends who live in my dorm. We were all freshmen last September and most of us were very homesick. I think that helped our group become more tightly knit. We are almost as close now as a family might be. We probably spend three or four hours every evening in bull sessions and we have a lot in common.
>
> Last week at the dorm meeting, we selected our dorm's nominee for campus Homecoming Queen. Carol, who is one of my five friends, was in the running. All of us voted for her because she's our friend. However, she isn't as attractive as several of the other girls in our dorm who were nominated. Our group felt we just had to vote for Carol, even though she wouldn't represent our dorm as well as the other girls.

This case illustrates the nature of decision making in a primary group. It is often less rational than in a secondary group. People make decisions in primary groups on the basis of emotions, opinions, and personal attitudes.

The primary group may act as a barrier to the adoption of new ideas. For example, farmers who have very strong ties with neighborhood groups and relatives are often reluctant to adopt innovations. A farmer is influenced by the opinions of other individuals in the primary group. A rational argument from a county extension agent for adoption of a farm innovation would play less part in the decision.

A more rational and efficiency-minded type of thinking occurs in secondary groups. An example is the U.S. Army general who publicly remarked that he would rather lose 50 of his troops than one of his tanks. As far as this general was concerned, his job was to win battles. His decisions were based on the most efficient methods of accomplishing this goal.

Most secondary groups place a major emphasis upon the ends rather than the means of attaining goals. In the Chicago Board of Trade grain pit (an extremely secondary group) on a Monday morning, anything goes. The end is to buy or sell grain at a profit, and any way of accomplishing this goal within legal bounds is acceptable. A shopkeeper in a small village also wishes to achieve the goal of financial profit. However, the methods utilized to reach this end are closely observed by the local community, a more primary group than the Chicago grain pit. The shopkeeper's reputation will suffer if family business methods are questioned.

The Continuum of Primary-Secondary Groups

A tool that will be used throughout this book is the *continuum*, which is especially useful in the analysis of social change to show the degree to which some characteristic is present. Continua are illustrated in Figures 5-1 and 5-2.

A continuum may be marked off in units or degrees like a ruler, thermometer, or scale. It is useful for comparisons; for example, Figure 5-1 shows that Sam is more intelligent than Jose and less intelligent than Chin.

FIGURE 5-1   Example of a continuum of intelligence.

A *continuum* shows the degree to which some characteristic is present. For example, this diagram shows at one end of the scale low IQ, and at the other high IQ. Any individual's intelligence can be located somewhere on this continuum of human intelligence. One may say that Sam is more intelligent than Jose and less intelligent than Chin. Thus, continua make comparisons possible even when exact measurement is not possible.

I.Q. Scores

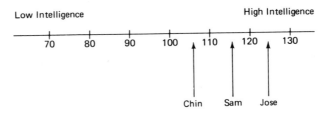

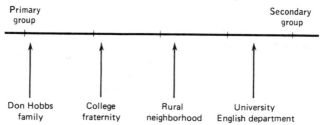

FIGURE 5-2   Different groups compared on the primary-secondary group continuum.

The location of a specific group on this continuum of primary-secondary groups may be determined on the basis of its characteristics, such as its size and the type of relationship among its members. For example, the rural neighborhood is more primary than the university English department but less primary than the college fraternity. The Don Hobbs family is more primary than any of the other three groups.

The types of data that are appropriately located on continua are called "continuous variables." For example, size of family is a continuous variable and may be plotted on a continuum. It is a continuous variable because it can assume any value from two up to perhaps 25, and any value in between these extremes. Rural families in the United States may be compared to urban families on this continuum of family size. Rural families today are larger in size than urban families. However, the direction of change is for smaller families for both urban and rural populations in the United States. Thus, a continuum is not only a way to make comparisons, but also a method of illustrating and showing the direction of change.

A *dichotomy* is a device that illustrates an "either-or" (or discrete) type of data. For example, a person is either male or female. Sex is not a continuous variable, and for this reason it cannot be placed on a continuum. Some sociological data are dichotomous or trichotomous (three discrete categories). For example, residence is sometimes viewed as a trichotomy of urban, rural nonfarm, and farm.

We have perhaps implied that primary-secondary groups constitute a dichotomy. They do not. A group is seldom either primary or secondary. Rather, most are somewhere between an extreme primary group and an extreme secondary group. The primary-secondary group dimension is continuous, as is illustrated in Figure 5-2.

Rediscovery of the Primary Group

Charles Horton Cooley and other early sociologists felt that the general trend was for secondary groups to displace primary groups in First World countries like the United States. This trend from primary to secondary groups may be observed in U.S. rural society today. Most rural groups are becoming larger in size and more complex in structure. Cooperatives, businesses, health care facilities, and schools are merging and consolidating. Examples of these trends are noted throughout the book.

Sociologists found that primary groups often play an important role in the functions of the larger secondary group of which they are a part. We saw in the example of Harold the Bureaucrat that even in the agency, primary groups were responsible for many of the decisions that were made.

Primary groups were, and still are, more common in rural areas than in urban places. Recent research has shown that primary group affiliation has been a major reason for the survival of the rural church (Chapter 8). The "new" rural residents of the 1970s and 1980s hold rural industrial or service jobs and have little in common with their new neighbors, who are commercial farmers. Fundamentalist or sectlike rural churches provide primary group shelter for the new residents who are adjusting to rural life (Hassinger and Holik, 1985). As societies become more urbanized, there is a corresponding change from primary to secondary groups. Even in rural areas, however, the expansion of travel and mass media communication has caused the gradual breakdown of many traditional primary groups. However, in Third World countries many social relationships are still on a primary group basis.

Even the primary groups of neighborhood and community are becoming less primary. Group affiliations of rural people are now more likely to be on the basis of their special interests than on where they live. A farmer today may belong to a cattle breeders' improvement association (a secondary group) on the basis of a special interest, beef production. Sixty years ago, the farm family would have been involved in a threshing ring with neighbors (primary). A sociological study of such farm work groups in the state of Washington showed that they were breaking down in the face of increased mechanization. About 40 percent of the respondents did not exchange any farm work. Increasing mechanization and the use of contract machines and hired labor decrease neighborhood cooperation and lead to the demise of this type of primary group (Slocum et al., 1958)

Adjustment problems are caused by a sudden change from living in a rural, primary group to an urban, secondary-group environment. An example is the young person who migrates from a farm background to an urban center in search of a job. Ninety-five percent of U.S. young people reared in farm areas today migrate to urban jobs by the time they reach 25 years of age. Other farm-urban migrants are rural young persons who attend a large state university. They experience sudden change as they move from a rural community, where primary-group relationships prevailed, to a large, secondary-group environment at college. The student becomes a number on a dormitory door, a seat in a large lecture hall, and a coded number on a registration card.

Importance of Primary Groups

The general trend in most societies today is toward increasing numbers of secondary groups. However, primary groups have not lost their importance.

Sociologists have generally found the primary group to be very important in determining the productivity of factory workers. For example, in the Western Electric Company's Hawthorne Works near Chicago, the employee who underproduced or overproduced (a "ratebuster") was ridiculed by fellow workers. The guilty individual might be punished by the force of group opinion or by being hit on the arm (Roethlisberger and Dickson, 1939). The primary groups within the larger industrial plant are difficult to observe. They do not appear on organizational charts. Nevertheless, their influence on worker satisfaction and production is very important.

The primary group also motivates troops in combat situations (Stouffer et al., 1949, p. 136). A soldier's buddies constitute a very primary group, based on mutual dependence. Veterans of the Vietnam War agree (and the Academy Award winning movie "Platoon" demonstrated) that the primary group was important in keeping them fighting. Their friendship bonds were tightened as they daily faced danger. A wounded U.S. infantry soldier remarked: "You know the men in your outfit. You have to be loyal to them. The men get pretty close-knit together. They like each other. They depend on each other and wouldn't do anything to let the others down. They'd rather be killed than do that. It's the main thing that keeps a guy from going haywire, going to pieces." In terms of motivating men to fight, officers and enlisted men attached little importance to such idealistic motives as patriotism and global political concerns (Stouffer et al., 1949, p.111).

The primary group is important in keeping men in combat because the group is committed to the fight. Therefore, anything that tied the individual to the group also kept him in combat. The U.S. Army used these sociological research findings to improve combat effectiveness by overhauling its replacement procedures. Because these "buddy groups" were so primary in nature, it was very difficult for replacement troops to become full members of an existing squad or platoon. Sociologists accordingly recommended to Army authorities that they make replacements of squads or platoons rather than on an individual basis. This strategy increased combat efficiency. In the Korean War, many staff and support troops were rushed into combat to stop the North Korean invasion. These troops had not been trained together, and most were complete strangers. Primary group relationships had not developed. These troops had a very poor combat record. Troops entering the Korean War who had trained together performed much better, with fewer casualties and with almost no losses due to capture (Kincaid, 1959).

Group Influences

An important way in which individuals accept or resist change is through the influence of group pressures. The Old Order Amish exert strong group control over their members. Someone who violates a group norm is socially banished. For example, a man who attends a movie might be punished by "shunning," a practice in which the individual's Amish friends refuse to speak to him. His wife does not allow sexual intercourse, and his family ignores him. For the Amishman with few acquaintances outside of the Amish community, this form of group pressure is particularly effective.

Group pressure may operate to encourage individuals to adopt deviant behavior, such as the use of drugs. Many university students who use drugs or alcohol would not do so but for peer pressure. The following example indicates the cross-pressures operating on students from the family and peer groups regarding drinking and smoking.

> Marie came from an average middle-class family. Both parents worked in order that money would be available for housing, nice clothes, a family holiday, and education for their three children. Marie did well in school, was popular, and participated in many activities including the church. Neither parent smoked or used drugs. The father sometimes drank wine with evening meals. On holidays and special occasions the children might be offered a drink at home.
>
> Marie was invited to many parties. At first she drank only soda, although many girls in her class were drinking beer. She was seen as out-of-place for not smoking or drinking, and her friends said she put a damper on the party. Finally, the pressure of her classmates was so great that she took a drink and began smoking, not only at parties, but in cars and at her friends' homes. Her parents were against smoking (for health reasons) under any circumstance and disapproved of drinking away from home. Marie's father offered to buy her a car if she had not smoked by age 21.
>
> Now that she smoked and drank, Marie felt peer pressure from her church and from scholarly friends who opposed her new behavior. These students were committed to healthy lifestyles. Marie, like many teenagers, was caught between two peer groups that shared different values and lifestyle priorities.

Secondary groups lack strong group influence. An example is the behavior of individuals at a large convention. The convention is usually held in a hotel in a large city where the convention delegate is free from the usual primary-group control. College professors attending professional meetings might drink to excess or in general be rowdy, a type of behavior impossible in the more primary campus community. Even the convention antics of clergymen sometimes offer an interesting contrast to their back-home behavior.

Primary Groups Within Secondary Groups

Many examples in this chapter illustrate the existence of small primary groups within larger secondary organizations. The coed's bull-session group within the college dormitory and the work groups within the industrial plant are examples.

While the larger secondary group, such as a factory, may have formally established goals and procedures, it is often within the primary group that these goals and procedures are either modified or carried out. Because these primary groups are small and not very visible, they are often overlooked in large-scale organizations.

Some large organizations make important use of primary groups within their structure. An example is the discussion councils that are the smallest local unit in the Ohio Farm Bureau Federation: Each is composed of about twelve families who gather monthly to discuss the state of agriculture, the economy, the family, environmental issues, and other concerns that are outlined in discussion guides prepared by the Farm Bureau state office. These councils meet in members' homes and the social aspects are an important part of the meeting. Members sit in easy chairs in the host's living room, and often enjoy refreshments after the meeting.

Members are well acquainted and may have met with each other over a period of many years. Discussion is intense and friendly disagreement is encouraged. When a council arrives at a stand on some issue, it sends a written statement to the state Farm Bureau office. These resolutions give the state organization a monthly report on their members' opinions on current legislative topics.

More than 1,400 discussion councils, representing 20,000 families, operated in Ohio in 1986. The discussion councils are primary groups and perform an important function in providing a highly personalized communication within the loosely integrated secondary organization. About one-fourth of all Ohio Farm Bureau members participate in discussion councils.

A similar illustration of primary groups at the local level are the radio forums and teleclubs in Third World countries. The typical forum is a primary group of 12 to 15 villagers who meet each week to listen to or watch an agricultural program, and then to discuss its contents. They may send questions of clarification about the weekly program to the radio or TV station, which are then answered on the next week's program.

Informal Groups

Informal groups are small primary groups that are based on friendship and mutual interest. Families, friends, neighbors, relatives, work associates, and others may constitute informal groups. These informal groups do not have any of the trappings of a formal association, such as written purposes or procedures, selected and titled officers, and a common meeting time and place.

Rural sociologists have found that informal groups are a very important influence in convincing farmers to adopt new agricultural ideas. Mass media such as farm magazines, bulletins, radio, and TV are important in creating knowledge about the idea, but interpersonal communication with a farmer's neighbors and friends is most important in persuading the farmer to adopt it.

Informal groups may be classified on the basis of attraction for members: (1) neighbors or locality groups, (2) relatives or kinship groups, and (3) friendship or clique groups.

Locality groups are informal groups in which the basis of membership is that the members live near each other. The general trend in First World countries has been for neighborhoods, communities, and other locality groups to become less important, although neighbors are still a more important informal group in rural life than in urban life. Many urban apartment dwellers are not acquainted with their "neighbors" who live across the hall from them, even after several years of residence.

Families and relatives are one type of informal group for most persons. On a day-to-day basis, relatives and kinship groups are becoming less important reference groups, due to increased job mobility and the barrier of geographical distance to informal contacts with relatives and kin. Kinship groups are more important to rural than to urban people. Many farmers, for example, exchange work and visit regularly with their relatives. This contact is less likely to happen in the city, where family members usually do not share the same job. Despite the barrier of distance, urban families often maintain strong ties through extensive phone calls, frequent writing, and visiting on Sundays and holidays.

Friendship cliques often replace other types of informal groups. *Cliques* are informal groups in which the basis of membership is common interest or friendship. Cliques are very tight-knit and have a strong primary-group feeling.

The members of a friendship group may have a common interest in home computers, in beef cattle raising, in discussing politics, or in some other topic. The members of informal groups in general, and cliques in particular, are usually similar in age, social status, and other personal characteristics. Friendship is *homophilous* (see Chapter 14); we select friends who are like ourselves.

VOLUNTARY ASSOCIATIONS

Sociologists also study groups that are more formal in nature, called *voluntary associations*. These are formal groups that usually have a name or title; selected and titled officers; a written purpose, constitution, bylaws, or charter; and a regular common meeting time and place. Informal groups seldom have any of these characteristics, except in some cases a name or title.

Examples of voluntary associations are: PTA, Farm Bureau, Lions Club, American Legion, the Sierra Club, 4-H Club, Dairy Herd Improvement Association, and the League of Women Voters.

Participation in Voluntary Associations

There is a strong tendency in the United States to organize and maintain voluntary associations. One European visitor said that whenever two or more Americans with similar interests get together, they soon start an organization, choose a name, elect officers, appoint a committee, and start to work. A woman in a small midwestern town listed the names of formal groups as they appeared in the town's newspaper. She found that her community of about 5,000 population had over 100 formal groups, 10 of which had been formed within the previous year. We define *voluntarism* as participation in the activities of an organization without monetary pay.

One reason for low participation in a voluntary association is that the organization does not serve the individuals' needs (Warner, 1965). Many rural organizations spend considerable time preoccupied with matters of maintaining the organization. It often takes much effort to prevent small informal groupings from becoming formal organizations.

> Our latest neighborhood activity started by chance when one of the children was urged by her parents to sing for us after dinner one night. She was reluctant until we agreed to sing with her. Suddenly we found ourselves, four adults and six children, trying another song. Some of us started to harmonize. It was such fun that we telephoned another neighbor, and we spent the whole evening singing.
>
> Now we all get together regularly to sing, and other friends join occasionally. I heartily recommend to others the rediscovery of group singing. In fact, our songfests have become so popular that I'm a bit worried about them. We are inclined, in the typical way of suburbia, to have a regular night to sing.
>
> Then we probably will move to a next step: election of officers and adoption of bylaws. Within a year, we probably will not be singing at all. We will be meeting and *talking* about singing. (Adapted from "The Man Next Door," *Better Homes and Gardens*. September, 1969).

Although Americans are usually regarded as joiners, there is a considerable number of adult citizens (about one-third) who belong to no voluntary association (Gallup, 1981).

Reasons for Participation

There are many motivations for the formation of voluntary associations. Some observers of U.S. society believe that as certain types of primary groups like neighborhoods have become less important, individuals join formal associations in order to secure the feeling of primary group belongingness.

Another reason that individuals belong to formal organizations is to secure the type of legislation they desire, which can be obtained more effectively through a group than through individual effort. Voluntary associations that attempt to influence the passage of favorable legislation, called "pressure groups," are discussed in Chapter 11. Legislative goals are most important for such formal organizations as the American Farm Bureau Federation, the American Medical Association, labor unions, and the National Association of Manufacturers. Many formal associations, such as PTAs, churches, and Chambers of Commerce, maintain legislative lobbyists and carry on pressure group functions. As the role of government increasingly affects each citizen's life, individuals will become more interested in pressure groups.

In some cases, a voluntary association may outlast the original purposes for which it was organized. An example is the Daughters of the American Revolution, which was initially established by the female relatives of Revolutionary War veterans in order to provide assistance for the wounded and needy. Membership in the D.A.R. is restricted to persons who can prove they are direct descendants of veterans. Translated, such membership criteria mean individuals of white, anglo, Protestant ancestry. The last Revolutionary War veteran has by now been dead for a century and a half, but the D.A.R. has become a high-prestige group to which some women aspire to belong. Its goals have obviously changed from those originally stated.

In recent decades, voluntarism has been elevated to the status of a full-time activity. For example, persons with independent financial support and university students work in voluntary organizations without pay. A University of Wisconsin extension specialist found for each day that a county extension agent spent with a volunteer, the volunteer worked 51 days. This research showed that in a recent year there were 2.9 million days of volunteer work for the extension service, estimated to have a cash value of $4.5 billion (Steele, 1985). The National Park Service replaces a large portion of its paid temporary staff during summer months with volunteers who maintain trails, conduct campfire and nature interpretation programs, direct traffic, collect fees, maintain records, and greet park visitors. In return these volunteers receive the status of being a Park Service staff member, a place to sleep, and free meals. They pay their way to and from the park at which they work. Why do people pay for the privilege of doing work? The Park Service has more applicants than it can process.

The popularity of the neighborhood crime watch program (Titus, 1987) demonstrates the importance, and the peculiarities, of voluntary associations in developing primary group relations. Throughout the United States, neighborhood crime watches have sprung up as a partial solution to the problem of increased property crime. A few citizens join neighborhood watches out of fear, and others because they recognize the limits of their police system in controlling crime.

Today about six million Americans participate actively in crime watch programs. They tend to be middle class, and are concerned with maintaining the neighborhood quality of life. They are 'joiners," socially integrated homeowners with children. Lower-class neighborhoods where mutual suspicion exists among families are less likely to have crime watch groups, even though these families must cope with higher crime rates than their middle-class counterparts (Fems, 1983).

Do neighborhood crime watch groups reduce property crimes? Yes, in the neighborhoods where the watch groups are organized; but property crimes then tend to be displaced to areas of a city (such as lower-income neighborhoods) without such watch groups.

As society becomes more complex, associations act as mediators between the individual and the larger society. Feelings of alienation and frustration come from the inability to influence the larger society. An important function of voluntary associations is to link the individual to the political, economic, and social processes of the larger society.

BUREAUCRACY

Bureaucracies are extreme secondary groups. The trend from primary group to secondary group in U.S. society is reflected in the bureaucratization of many aspects of contemporary life. This change is especially prominent among rural people today. Agriculture and other rural industries are now highly dependent upon such government agencies as the Soil Conservation Service, the Agricultural Stabilization and Conservation Service, the Bureau of Land Management, and the Forest Service. These are bureaucracies. So are farmers' organizations and cooperatives. So are the commercial concerns from which the farmer and the rancher buy and sell. These agricultural and land management organizations are later topics in this book (Chapters 10, 11, and 13), and the analysis of them as bureaucracies is an important theme.

Most universities are bureaucracies. Student activities such as residence groups, campus publications, and church groups are bureaucratically organized. The typical student will probably seek employment in a bureaucracy after graduation. It is necessary to understand more completely the nature of bureaucracies, what they are, and how they work.

What Is Bureaucracy?

A *bureaucracy* is a secondary, formal type of organization designed, ideally, to coordinate the work of many individuals in the pursuit of large-scale administrative tasks. Many people regard all bureaucracies as inefficient, and point to the government or the military as typical examples. On both counts, a sociologist would disagree. A bureaucracy may be inefficient, but it is not necessarily so. In fact, if there were a more efficient method of organization than bureaucracy, it would be in use. Many government agencies are bureaucracies, but so are many other organizations. Examples are churches, corporations, universities, and hospitals.

Characteristics of Bureaucracies

How can one tell if an organization is a bureaucracy? Max Weber, a German sociologist writing in about 1900, identified the important characteristics of bureaueracies (Weber, 1922/1958).

1. The offices are arranged in a *hierarchy;* each lower office is under the control and supervision of a higher one (Figure 5-3). This hierarchy is called the "chain of command" in military service.

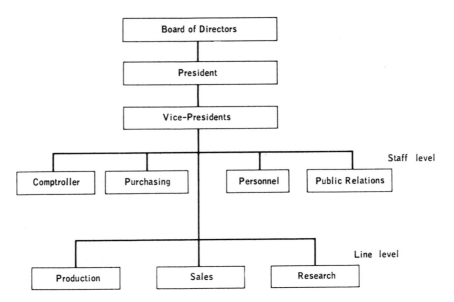

FIGURE 5-3   Simplified organizational chart of a farm machinery company.

This diagram shows the organizational chart for a fairly typical industrial bureaucracy. Most industrial companies, government agencies, and farmer organizations are bureaucratically organized. In the bureaucracy shown here, the line executives are in a direct chain of command under the supervision of higher levels. The staff levels receive instructions from higher levels and make recommendations to these levels without directly supervising the line levels. If the director of personnel wishes to communicate with the director of sales, that person may be required to route the communication through a vice-president.

2. All activities of the bureaucrat are governed by a system of *abstract rules* or procedures. These rules are devised so as to cover almost every possible situation that might arise. They are to be applied consistently in every case, so that all activities will be standardized.

3. Candidates for bureaucratic positions are usually selected on the basis of their *technical qualifications*, determined by examinations such as Civil Service exams, or educational achievement as indicated by a college degree in a certain field.

4. Being a bureaucratic official constitutes a *career*, with a system of promotions usually based on seniority in office or on achievement. Bureaucracies offer vocational security to the individual that reduces individual risk-taking, and often guarantees a job. The salary of bureaucrats is fixed and enables the average individual to live modestly but seldom luxuriously.

5. A bureaucracy requires *specialization*. Each bureaucrat has one special job to perform at one time. Someone else has another specialized job. Each position has a job title that describes the work performed. Job specialization has made possible the modern assembly-line method of mass production. The organiza-

tional chart in Figure 5-3 illustrates the high degree of job specialization in a bureaucracy. One division of the company is solely in charge of production, another is responsible for sales, and another for research.

6. Bureaucracies are *impersonal* and are secondary groups rather than primary groups in nature. Positions and job titles are important and permanent, although the persons filling these positions may come and go. The bureaucracy is not concerned with the emotional or personal life of its employees. One of the objectives in many bureaucracies is to take human fallibility out of the daily activities.

Bureaucratic Inefficiency

Bureaucracies are not necessarily inefficient, but there are certain aspects of bureaucracies that may lead to inefficiency. These inefficiencies seem to be almost built into the bureaucratic structure itself.

Inefficiency may arise from the circumvention of rules and regulations. For example, one agricultural chemical company allows its traveling salespeople to be repaid only for meals and lodging on their expense accounts. A salesperson could not be reimbursed for parking in a downtown parking lot. So the sales staff simply add parking fees on to their expense accounts as part of the cost of dinner, thereby circumventing the company regulations against paying parking fees. It was common practice to "eat up" parking lot fees. Thus we see how a norm of evasion arose to replace the bureaucratic regulation (see Chapter 2).

Another government bureaucracy had strict regulations covering the firing of incompetent secretarial help. The office in which the incompetent individual was employed had to conduct a major investigation of the individual, file detailed complaint reports, and submit these reports up through channels. This complex procedure required about two years before action could be taken to fire an incompetent employee. As a result it was much easier to *promote* the incompetent individual to a higher level position in another office, where the incompetency was not yet known. The authors knew of one particularly incompetent individual who was promoted three times in one year as a means of being "fired."

Rules and regulations are generally accepted as necessary in a bureaucracy. Inefficiencies result, however, when there is overconformity to these rules. The purpose of the regulations and procedures is usually to obtain standardized treatment of all similar cases. There is a tendency for the bureaucrat, however, to apply the rules to *all* situations, whether or not they are entirely appropriate. The rules may be applied literally and not in the sense in which they were originally written. Thus, regulations that were developed to promote general efficiency often produce inefficiency in particular situations.

One sociologist has argued that this happens, in part, as a result of the personality of the bureaucrat (Merton, 1956). Such rewards of the bureaucratic system as seniority, promotions, and pensions (illustrated previously in the example of Harold the Bureaucrat) are designed to encourage disciplined conformity to official regulations. But these factors also induce timidity, conservatism, and technicism. Regulations gain great symbolic significance in themselves. As a result, the bureaucrat often overconforms to them. We see how bureaucracies socialize their employees' personalities to inefficient behavior.

Bureaucracies are resistant to change. New procedures require greater effort for the bureaucrat and may cause disturbing consequences. Old rules and methods become institutionalized and firmly imbedded in habit. In a society that is undergoing rapid social change, it is also necessary for many bureaucracies to make appropriate changes. There is often a lag between the need for a change in the bureaucratic regulations and the actual change itself. The larger an organization becomes, the more difficulty it has in obtaining feedback from its own operation. Hence, the bureaucracy is increasingly less able to correct its own errors (Crozier, 1984; Gardner, 1962).

A bureaucracy is a highly secondary group. The emphasis is on impersonal relationships. Yet there are certain situations within the bureaucracy where primary group relations are necessary. An example is the social relationship between the bureaucracy's clientele or customers and the low-level bureaucrat. The bureaucratic regulations specify how the client is to be handled. But the client is not a formal part of the bureaucracy, and impersonal treatment of the client may result in a loss of business. The customer who has been mistreated simply walks away and does not come back.

The following quotation from a receptionist in a (U.S.) Production Credit Association local office illustrates this point:

> The farmers who come in here the [PCA office] like to be called by their first name and greeted in a friendly fashion. And they love to talk. Especially on rainy days, when farm people are in town, this office is crowded with loungers. It takes real tact to let a client know when the business is concluded and they should leave.

In dealing with government agencies, farmers are likely to refer to the high-handed fashion in which they were treated or to complain that the bureaucrat with whom they dealt was too businesslike. The secondary nature of most bureaucratic relationships is a sharp contrast to the more primary bureaucratic-client situation.

Real and Ideal

Bureaucracies offer a contrast between the ideal (what is shown on organization charts) and the real world of individuals trying to accomplish a job. A basic assumption in a bureaucracy is that an official policy will be faithfully carried out by subordinates. But sociological studies have shown that this policy is often modified or nullified in its passage through the bureaucracy. Even though the rules and regulations may specify ideal behavior for the bureaucrat, real activity may be quite different. As one sociologist has said, "A bureaucracy in operation appears quite different from the abstract portrayal of its formal structure. Many official rules are honored in the breach. The members of the organization act as human beings, often friendly and sometimes annoyed, rather than like dehumanized impersonal machines" (Blau, 1952, pp. 13–14).

Informal communication in bureaucracies is very important; in many cases the grapevine is more important than formal communication in bulletins, memos, letters, and orders. In fact, one study suggests that the main function of formal communication in bureaucracies is to confirm what people have already learned from informal channels.

A bureaucrat's informal activities may provide far more power than the formal position would imply. An example is the army sergeant who effectively controls far more individuals—including several officers—than the position as sergeant indicates. Bureaucrats build up reciprocal obligations or "social capital" through informal dealings. Consider the statement of one bureaucrat: "Sure, I can get Jim Banks over in printing to run this off for us ahead of his other work. I sent one of our mechanics over there last month to fix one of his presses when it broke down, and he owes me a favor."

Why Have Bureaucracies?

In spite of their limitations, bureaucracies are necessary. In many situations, a bureaucracy is probably the only known form of social organization that could accomplish certain desired goals.

If you alone had the job of collecting the dues in a small fraternity, you could proceed at your own discretion. But if five persons had this job in a large club, they would find it necessary to organize their work lest some members were asked for dues repeatedly and others never. If hundreds of persons have the assignment of collecting dues from millions of persons, then work must be very systematically organized; otherwise chaos would reign and the assignment could not be fulfilled. The type of organization designed to accomplish large-scale administrative tasks by systematically coordinating the work of many individuals is called a bureaucracy.

Telecommuting and Bureaucracy

Nothing has changed the routine of the workplace more than the introduction and widespread use of the personal computer. The introduction of the mainframe computer in the early 1960s led to advances in record keeping and data analysis. However, the user had to be linked directly to the computer. In the early 1980s, microcomputers with a memory capacity as large as mainframe computers of the previous decade were introduced. In short, the personal computer uncoupled work from a specific workplace. Thus was born *telecommuting,* the practice of employees working in their homes (or another location) while linked to their place of employment with a microcomputer or a computer terminal.

The advantages of telecommuting accrue to employees, as well as to employers (Gordon, 1983, pp. 58–64). Financial management, automotive design, and the preparation of textbooks in rural sociology can be done on a personal computer. Individuals can be employed who otherwise could not go to an office, such as young mothers with children. A valued employee can be retained, if he or she moves to a new location. Workloads can be balanced and part-time persons may be employed. The employer does not maintain costly office space. Workers have greater freedom in where they live and may be able to avoid commuting. As one indicator of the impact of microcomputers, notice the number of persons walking through an airport with two briefcases. One is often a portable computer.

However, not all individuals can work away from an office (Kroll, 1984, p. 19). Some people miss going to work and do not have the self-discipline to work in an unsupervised setting. They need interaction with persons in their work setting as they seek primary group relationships. An "out-of-sight-out-of-mind" syndrome may prevent individuals from getting promoted to new positions. So the widespread adoption of the personal computer in nontraditional work environments may be inhibited by the need for primary-group relationships.

Bureaucracy in Third World Countries

Bureaucratic organization is not peculiar to First World countries. The fundamentals of bureaucratic structure were introduced to Third World countries by colonial administrations, missionaries, and others. Most major institutions have become thoroughly bureaucratized. In India, government rules are often so cumbersome that one must use bribes in order to obtain desired services from governmental officials. The practice of bribing is so common that even it has become standardized. It costs two rupees (about 15 cents US) to get a folder past a low-level secretary to the boss, and ten rupees to get a folder on to a high-level boss. One observer estimated that in order to start a small business, 26 "official permissions" are necessary, that means 26 times 10 rupees in bribes.

In some Third World countries, government and other bureaucracies represent a strange amalgam of local values versus Western administrative forms. An illustration is the ministry of education in Thailand. Efficiency, rationality, productivity, and innovativeness are not highly valued by Thais. Prior to Western influence the Thai governmental structure demonstrated such values as personalism, politeness, and extreme respect for status. The result is an amalgam in which the form and appearance, but not the substance, of Western bureaucratic organization is adopted. For example, the minister of education ordered all high schools in Thailand to have a school library. But 10 years later, only a small number had this facility, and many of these were in locked rooms, so that students could not read the books. Ministry officials could not determine how many schools really had libraries, because school reports to superiors indicated complete adoption. Most record keeping by Thai governmental officials is only an attempt by subordinates to report compliance with directives (Rogers et al., 1967).

Types of Bureaucracies

Most sociologists distinguish between two types of bureaucracies, according to their basic organizational structure: the centralized approach and the participative approach.

In *centralized* organizations, there is a high concentration of power, and members or employees are generally limited to carrying out orders and decisions transmitted from higher levels. This centralized approach involves a one-way announcement coming from an individual (or a small group of persons) with high formal authority. This announcement of procedure or standardization of regulations must be adhered to by those in lower positions. Maximum centralization exists in an organization when one individual makes all the decisions.

In a *participative* (or decentralized) approach, power and decision making are widely shared by the members or employees. Leaders in a participative organization make decisions about change by consulting those affected by the change. Centralized change is faster than the participative approach. However, the change may not be as permanent as with the participative approach. Organizational members may resist announcements or innovations when they have not participated in the decision making. Neither of these two basic approaches excel in all situations. The particular situation should always be the first consideration, and then, the appropriate approach adopted. This typology of centralized and participative bureaucracies will be used in analyzing types of churches, farmer organizations, and government agriculture and land management agencies.

During the 1980s, competition from the Japanese automobile industry severely damaged the Detroit auto industry. Sociologists and management scholars traced the Japanese success to "Type Z" organizational decision making (Ouchi, 1981, p. 79). Instead of a top-down bureaucratic style as outlined by the great German sociologist Max Weber, employees in Japan are encouraged to contribute ideas on how to enhance productivity and improve the quality of the product. Persons closest to a process often know best how to make improvements. Workers are involved in making company policies. The work environment tends to be informal, with people dealing on a first name basis . . . it is Ken rather than "Mr. Crider." There is broad concern for the welfare of employees. This environment enhances communication, improves problem solving, and leads to innovation in the workplace.

The Japanese model of bureaucratic structure can be followed in the United States with good results. Ford Motor Company attempted to install such a work environment in its Louisville, Kentucky, truck plant. Employees were involved in issues from product design to quality control to work hours; morale and productivity have improved (*Fortune,* April 18, 1983, p. 6). Type Z management is really the application of psychological and sociological research findings that show that individuals seek primary group relations and respond best when supported and not coerced.

RELATIONSHIPS AMONG LARGE-SCALE ORGANIZATIONS

Competition means that two organizations are pursuing a similar goal or resource which both cannot have. A classic example in the United States was the competition between the Tennessee Valley Authority (Chapter 13) and the Cooperative Extension Service (Selznick, 1966). Both were competing to improve soil conservation practices among Tennessee Valley farmers. TVA, realizing it could not compete with the state extension services, simply bought their time. TVA hired extension agents to demonstrate soil conservation practices and chemical fertilizer to farmers.

Accommodation is the process by which two organizations retain their own identity in pursuing similar goals. The National Park Service and the U.S. Forest Service both have the important goal of providing outdoor recreation facilties to the American public. Both compete for federal funds to expand their present programs. They have reached an accommodation whereby each provides different types of outdoor recreation experiences (Clark and Stankey, 1979). Accommodation is possible because the number of recreationists is so large.

Cooperation is agreed-upon action by two or more organizations that is directed to similar goals. In Australia, a decline in the number of rural people means that in most communities the Protestant denominations could not support separate churches. The problem was solved cooperatively by combining all Protestant denominations into The Uniting Church. Now one church stands in place of the separate Methodist, Episcopal, or Presbyterian congregations.

Sometimes, particularly among government agencies, cooperation with another agency is specified by legislation. The Fish and Wildlife Service in cooperation with the post office, collects money for duck hunting permits because waterfowl are migratory. The funds are then given to departments of natural resources and conservation in the individual states to improve waterfowl habitat.

SUMMARY

We define the social *group* as people in interaction or communication and together geographically with common interests or goals. An *institution* is an abstraction referring to the aspects of a culture that satisfy some fundamental need of a society. Examples of institutions are the family, religion, education, government (polity), the community, and the economy.

Primary groups are smaller, more intimate, more face-to-face, relatively more permanent, better acquainted, more informal, less rational, and more relationship oriented than *secondary groups*. Groups may be compared on a primary-secondary group continuum.

There is a rapid growth of formal organizations in industrialized nations, but this trend does not mean that primary groups will become extinct. Within many of the large secondary groups there are numbers of smaller primary groups. An example is the primary group of buddies within the formal organization of the army. Primary groups are generally more common in rural than in urban areas.

Voluntary associations usually have a name, selected officers, a written constitution or bylaws, and a regular meeting place and time. On the other hand, *informal groups* seldom have these characteristics. They are usually more primary than formal groups. North Americans have been widely characterized as joiners of associations. And there is research evidence that more than half of the adults spend nonpaid hours in these organizations. *Cliques* are informal groups in which membership is based on common interests or friendship. Small informal groups influence an individual's behavior and sometimes different groups compete for the conformity of the individual.

A *bureaucracy* is a secondary, formal type of organization designed ideally to coordinate the work of many individuals in the pursuit of large-scale administrative tasks. Ideally, bureacracies are organized with a hierarchy of authority, governed by written procedures, and staffed by personnel selected on their technical qualifications, who are encouraged to be career minded, specialized, and impersonal. Bureaucracies are not necessarily inefficient, yet there are certain built-in aspects of bureaucracy that often lead to inefficiency. These are: overcompetition, circumvention of rules, overconformity, institutionalization and resistance to change, and the conflict of primary and secondary relationships. The trend in the United States is toward implementing small groups in large-scale organization. Bureaucracies in Third World countries are generally more rigid than in First World countries.

Two types of bureaucracies can be distinguished: *participative,* in which the major decisions are shared by the members or employees, and *centralized,* where the members or employees are generally limited to carrying out the orders and decisions transmitted from higher levels. *Competition* means that two organizations are pursuing a similar goal or resource that both cannot have. *Cooperation* is agreed-upon action by two or more organizations that is directed to similar goals. *Accommodation* is the process by which two organizations retain their own identity in pursuing similar goals.

REFERENCES

BLAU, PETER M. (1952). *Bureaucracy in Modern Society.* Glencoe, IL: Free Press of Glencoe.
———. (1955). *The Dynamics of Bureaucracy.* Chicago: University of Chicago Press.
BROOM, LEONARD, et al. (1984). *Essentials of Sociology,* 3rd edition. Itacca, IL: Peacock Publishers.
CLARK, R.N., and G.H. STANKEY. 1979. *The recreation opportunity spectrum: A framework of planning, management, and research.* USDA Forest Service General Technical Report PNW-98. Portland, Oreg.: Pacific Northwest Forest Experiment Station.
COOLEY, CHARLES H. (1909). *Social Organization.* New York: Scribner.
CROZIER, MICHAEL. (1984). *The Bureaucratic Phenomena: An Examination of Bureaucracy in Modern Organizations and Its Cultural Setting in France,* University of Chicago Press.
FEMS, JUDITH D. (1983). *Partnership for Neighborhood Crime Prevention.* Washington, DC: Office of Development, Testing, and Dissemination, National Institute of Justice, U.S. Department of Justice, U.S. Government Printing Office.
GALLUP ORGANIZATION, INC. (1981). *Americans Volunteer: 1981.* Conducted for the Independent Sector, Princeton, NJ. (As cited in Broom et al., 1984.)
GARDNER, JOHN. (1962). *Self-Renewal: The Individual and His Organization in an Innovative Society.* New York: Harper.
GORDON, GIL E. (1983). "Community by Computer." *Best's Review,* pp. 58–64.
HASSINGER, EDWARD W., and JOHN S. HOLIK. (1985). "The Church in Rural Missouri." Unpublished paper, Department of Rural Sociology, University of Missouri, Columbia.
HORTON, PAUL B., and CHESTER L. HUNT. (1984). *Sociology.* New York: McGraw-Hill.
KINKAID, EUGENE (1959). *In Every War But One.* New York: Norton.
KROLL, DOROTHY. (1984). "Telecommuting: A Revealing Peek Inside Some of Industries First Electronic Cottages." *Management Review,* pp. 18–23.
MERTON, ROBERT K. (1956). "Bureaucratic Structure and Personality." In Robert K. Merton et al., eds. *Reader in Bureaucracy.* New York: Random House.
OUCHI, WILLIAM. (1981). *Theory Z: How American Business Can Meet the Japanese Challenge.* New York: Addison-Wesley.
ROETHLISBERGER, F. J., and W. J. DICKSON. (1939). *Management and the Worker.* Cambridge, MA: Harvard University Press.
ROGERS, EVERETT M., et al. (1967). *Diffusion of Innovations: Educational Change in Thai Government Secondary Schools.* East Lansing: Michigan State University, Institute for International Studies in Education and Department of Communication.
SELZNICK, PHILIP. *TVA and the Grass Roots. A Study in the Sociology of Formal Organizations.* NY, Harper & Row Torchbook, 1966.
SLOCUM, WALTER L., et al. (1958). *Extension Contracts, Selected Characteristics, Practices and Attitudes of Washington Farm Families.* Pullman, Washington Agr. Exp. Sta. Bull. 584.
STEELE, VIRGINIA, L, "The Contribution of Volunteers to Cooperative Extension Programs," (1985) Wisconsin Cooperative Extension Bulletin, No. 27, Univ. of Wis. Madison.
STOUFFER, SAMUEL A., et al. (1949). *The American Soldier: Volume II, Combat and Its Aftermath.* Princeton, NJ: Princeton University Press.
TITUS, RICHARD M. (1987). "Residential Burglary and Community Response." in Ronald Clarke and Tim Hope (eds.) *Coping with Burglary: Research Perspectives on Policy,* Boston, Kluwer-Nishoff. (Date nor price set (ISBN 0-89838-151-7)
WARNER, W. KEITH. (1965). "Problems of Participation." *Journal of Cooperative Extension,* 1, 219–228.
WEBER, M. (1922/1958). "Bureaucracy." In H. H. Gorth and C.W. Mills, eds. and trans.. *From Max Weber: Essays in Sociology.* New York: Oxford University Press.

Chapter 6

Communities

One does not have to be a particularly astute observer to detect that contemporary life in New York City and Los Angeles is still quite different from that in Bug Tussle, Oklahoma, or Gravel Switch, Kentucky.

—Thomas R. Ford (1978), p. 3

Thousands of communities, both large and small, form the places where we live. Each settlement has a name which we use when responding to that universal question: "Where are you from?"

Not long ago almost everyone lived a substantial portion of his or her life in one community. It was home. But times have changed. We may be born in one town, attend school in two or three other locations, and look forward to working at numerous jobs in as many cities. The United States was once a nation of small communities and close personal ties. As noted in Chapter 5, these tight-knit relationships of the small town are increasingly being replaced by the depersonalized relationships of urban life.

Important changes are taking place in community life in U.S. society and around the world. There is a shift from small neighborhoods to towns and cities. Some rural areas are losing population. As farms grow larger and become more mechanized, farm population declines. Small towns lose their economic viability as businesses shut down and people move away.

Other rural areas are gaining population as suburban areas, industry, and recreational facilities expand into nearby farmland. Housing developments are springing up where livestock recently grazed. Shopping centers are appearing in the midst of cornfields.

The purpose of this chapter is to describe the changing pattern of rural community life. Special emphasis is placed on how rural areas have declined or grown, based on trends in migration of people, economic factors, and technology.

WHAT IS A COMMUNITY?

A *community* is a group. It possesses all the characteristics of a group as defined in Chapter 5. It is composed of people in communication who have common interests or ties. What makes a community different from other kinds of human groupings is that membership is based on locality. You are a member of Zig Zag rather than Boring, Oregon, for example, because that is where your residence (or address) is located. Theoretically, one need not form any kind of emotional attachment, loyalty, or other feelings to maintain membership, although most of us do. As long as your residence is at that particular place, you are a member.

Another way to define community is that it is the place where we live our lives on a day-to-day basis, and it is the locality from which we experience the events of the larger world around us.

For our purposes, community may be defined as that combination of people and social groups which performs the five major functions relevant to a locality. These five functions are: production/distribution/consumption; socialization; social control; social participation; and mutual support (Warren, 1978, p. 9).

Production/distribution/consumption includes economic functions. For example, some rural communities have their economic base in farming. Businesses on Main Street provide various goods and services for farmers in the surrounding hinterland. Other rural communities survive on the tourist trade, the timber industry, mining, manufacturing and service businesses, or as bedroom/commuter towns for nearby metropolitan areas. Although most local rural economies include a mix of economic activities, because their base is smaller, they are more likely than urban communities to be dominated by only one type.

In addition to economic activities, production/distribution/consumption includes educational services, local government services, religious activities, and recreational/leisure pursuits. For example, in a community based on farming, vocational agriculture is likely to be an important part of the local high school curriculum. Local radio stations and newspapers cater to the farm audience with special reports on weather, farm commodities prices, and farm legislation.

The second major function of a community is socialization. The major socializing agencies of society (see Chapter 3), including the family, schools, peer groups, mass media, and religion are present in most communities. It is on the local level that individuals encounter and learn about the culture and the society in which they are raised and live out their lives.

It is also on the local level that the beliefs, values, attitudes, and behavior of individuals are rewarded and punished through society's sanctions. This is referred to as social control. The same groups that perform the function of socialization likewise are involved with social control, plus such agencies as law enforcement, the health department, and other parts of local and state government. Together they enforce the norms of society, and their enforcement is expressed at the local level.

The fourth function of community is social participation. We are distinctively human through our participation in human groups, and most of these associations are with neighbors or friends from the same community. Many of the professional, civic, and social organizations to which we belong are local or have local chapters. For many people, residence in a local community determines to a considerable degree the nature of their social life.

The final community activity is mutual support. Mutual support refers to more than the normal types of assistance provided among neighbors and friends, such as borrowing a ladder or trading recipes (Chapter 5). Mutual support also refers to help provided during times of crises, such as emergency medical services and disaster relief. In an Amish community, a farmer who loses his barn to a fire will soon find it replaced through a tradition called "barn raising."

The self-sufficiency of communities varies by how well the five functions are performed. For most communities in U.S. society, however, the religious, educational, economic, and other services that its members desire are met at the local level. Most individuals in a community are aware of their membership in it; nearly all communities have a name, and the majority of people living in them identify with this name.

THE NATURE OF RURAL COMMUNITIES

As the quotation at the beginning of this chapter illustrates, even in societies like the United States, with advanced communication and transportation systems, there remain differences between the culture and social life of Bug

FIGURE 6-1 Mutual support is important in Amish communities. These Amishmen are helping to rebuild a barn which had burned down. The men started building the walls at 6:45 A.M. By 1:00 P.M. the same day, donated hay was being stocked in the nearly completed barn.

Source: Joel. A. Troyer, *The Wooster Daily Record.*

Tussle, Oklahoma, and New York City. Despite the size of its urban population, less than 3 percent of the land in the United States today is used for
urban settlements (Zimolzak and Stansfield, 1979).

In Chapter 1, rural was defined as any incorporated or unincorporated
area of less than 2,500 in population. However, in reality most communities
contain both rural and urban elements. Different types of U.S. communities
may be arranged along a continuum or line, from a purely rural type to a
purely urban type. Although some rural sociologists question whether the
continuum accurately portrays reality, the rural-urban continuum remains a
useful concept for understanding differences between communities. This
rural-urban continuum is diagramed in Figure 6-2. The rural-urban continuum
is a device showing that rural and urban differences are a matter of degree.
The location of a particular community on the continuum seems to depend
mainly upon the size of the population, the density of the population, and the
relative strengths of rural and urban norms. It is obvious that real communities are neither completely rural nor completely urban. Most small towns,
rural-urban fringe communities, and suburbs occupy a position midway on
this continuum.

Rural Settlement Patterns

A newcomer to the Midwest and the Great Plains states will notice a
regularity to the physical arrangement of buildings and other man-made structures in rural areas. Traveling through farm areas, the sojourner finds that
most farm homesteads are dispersed or separated from each other. Farmers
normally work the fields behind and to the sides of their homesteads. The
homesteads is usually set near a public road. Occasionally interspersed be-

FIGURE 6-2   The rural-urban continuum of community organization.

Although differences between rural and urban subcultures are often viewed
as a dichotomy, in real life the different types of communities range on a
continuum from extreme urban to extreme rural. Most suburban and rural-
urban fringe communities occupy some midway position on the continuum.
The exact location of a particular community on this continuum depends
mainly upon the population size of the community, the population density of
the community, and the degree to which the community members observe
rural or urban norms.

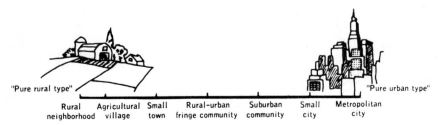

"Pure rural type"   "Pure urban type"

Rural   Agricultural Small   Rural-urban   Suburban   Small   Metropolitan
neighborhood village   town   fringe community community   city   city

tween farm homesteads are a cluster of houses (sometimes mobile homes), whose residents commute to nonfarm jobs in a nearby town. Upon entering the outskirts of town, the discerning traveler may notice a farm implement and supply dealer, a livestock auction house, and perhaps an array of new fast-food franchise restaurants or a recently constructed shopping center. Along the main street going toward the center of town on both sides are large, older homes, with spacious front porches and gabled windows. The main street is lined with tall trees that form a canopy during the summer. Along the side streets are smaller, less spacious residences. In the center of town is the courthouse. Usually the tallest structure in town, the courthouse is surrounded by a park, and in this area may often be found an artillery piece or statue of a soldier (normally a former native who rose to the rank of general). Facing the courthouse across the street on all four of its sides is the main business district, with its usual array of stores, banks, law offices, restaurants, movie house, and perhaps a bar or saloon. Unlike larger cities, the parking spaces are often positioned at a 45 degree angle from the curb.

The settlement pattern described here may be found throughout the rural United States, but the pattern is most common in the Great Plains and

FIGURE 6-3 Business districts of many small towns in U.S. society have declined due to improved transportation systems and the attraction of big shopping malls.

Midwest. It is referred to as the *scattered farmstead community*. The scattered farmstead community is the most prevalent settlement pattern in the United States and Canada. Towns developed as service centers for the surrounding farms, and the distance between towns was a day's ride by horse or wagon. The geographic separation of homesteads in the open country produced social isolation. The town became more than a place to buy supplies and conduct business; a visit to town was also an occasion to "catch up" on news. Visitors to farm homesteads were welcomed for the news they brought, thereby developing the image that rural people and communities are more friendly and neighborly (Horton and Hunt, 1984, p. 448).

Sociologists note two other major types of settlement patterns. One, the *cluster village,* is common in most parts of the world but particularly in Asia and most of Latin America and Africa. Farmers live in the village and are within walking distance of their land. Examples of this type of rural community organization also are found in New England, the Mormon villages of Utah, and some dry-wheat farming areas of the Great Plains. Although the cluster village is the most common type of rural community organization in the rest of the world, it is not as common as the scattered farmstead community in the United States and Canada.

The *line village* is the third type of settlement pattern. Homesteads are strung along highways, lakeshores, or rivers. Some sections of southern Louisiana and Europe have line villages on the banks of bayous and rivers. Farm homes are most often located in rows along both sides of the river or highway, and the farmland extends back in long, narrow strips.

Community Boundaries

Although it may be relatively easy to determine the political boundaries of a community, it is more difficult to determine its social boundaries. The geographic boundaries of towns, cities, counties, and townships are clearly marked on maps; but these boundaries do not necessarily coincide with the areas in which we interact relative to the five community functions mentioned earlier. For example, a study in central Michigan found that social boundaries rarely corresponded with political boundaries (see Figure 6-6).

In 1911, Charles Galpin, a founder of rural sociology, conducted a study of Belleville, New York (Jefferson County). He devised the following "lane turning" method:

"What is the extent and bounding line of this community?" This was the first question that faced me. I finally settled it this way: Take the village as the community center; start out from here on any road into the open country; you come to a home, and the deep wear of the wheels out of the yard toward the village indicates that this home naturally goes to this village for trade, doctor, post office, church, lodge, entertainment, high school; the next home the same, the next and next, until by and by you come to a home where the ruts run the other way—and you find that this home goes to an adjoining town for its major

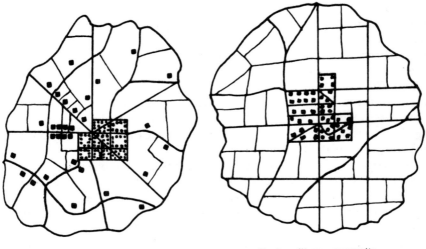

Scattered farmstead community   Cluster village community

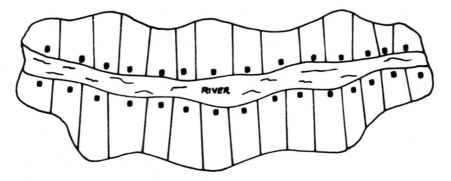

Line village community

FIGURE 6-4 **Types of rural community organization.**

There are three major types of rural community organization: the scattered farmstead community, in which the farmers reside on their farms; the cluster village, in which farmers' homes are located in the center; and the line village, in which farm homes are located in rows along a river or highway. The scattered farmstead community is the most common in the United States, but the cluster village is more common in the rest of the world.

associations; between these two homes is the bounding line of the community. (Larson, 1986, p. 198)

Of course, automobiles and asphalt roads have made the measuring of lane-turnings in the road an impractical method of locating community boundaries; but the principle remains sound. One approach is to ask local

FIGURE 6-5   **Aerial view of a cluster village in the Netherlands.**

The farmers who live in this Dutch cluster village travel each day to surrounding fields to work. Both homes and farm buildings for livestock are located in the village, along with churches, schools, and businesses. Dutch rural sociologists have studied the optimum number of cluster villages which should be established in farmlands reclaimed from the North Sea and found that as methods of transportation improve—from bicycles to motorbikes, for example—fewer and larger cluster villages are needed in a given area (Chapter 1).

residents where they purchase certain products, attend church, send their children to school, and obtain other community services. As one travels out from the center and approaches the community boundary, local residents become more likely to go in a different direction for their community services. This method is breaking down in the face of a continuing trend toward obtaining different community services in several different community centers. However, it is still possible to map out grocery trade communities, church attendance communities, and other communities on the basis of specific services.

Another method of locating community boundaries is to ask knowledgeables in the community where the boundaries are. Grocers, bankers, teachers, ministers, and others can often draw in the boundaries on a map with little trouble. This method is much quicker than asking local community residents, and may be almost as accurate.

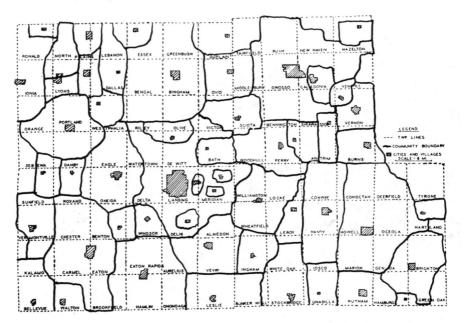

FIGURE 6-6   Township boundaries seldom correspond closely to community boundaries.

Some people accept such legal boundaries as school districts or county and township lines as community boundaries. But this figure graphically shows that there is very little correspondence between townships lines and community boundaries in central Michigan. There is an increasing tendency in rural North America to plan new school districts on the basis of existing community boundaries. One result may be a greater overlap between school districts and community boundaries.

Community Types

Communities can be often characterized by the nature of the local economy. This may appear easier for smaller rural communities which are more likely to be dominated by one type of industry or company. However, even large metropolitan areas can be distinguished on this basis. For example, Detroit is dependent on the automobile industry, the Houston economy rests on the oil industry, and Washington D.C. is dominated by the federal government and thousands of lobbyists. The San Jose, California, area is referred to as "silicon valley" because a large amount of its employment is based on computer industries.

Many small towns are dependent upon the farm economy; however, there are other types of rural communities. Fishing villages line the coastal areas. Mining towns may be found throughout the Appalachian and Western states. During the 1970s sudden increases in oil prices caused many isolated communities in the Rocky Mountains area to be characterized as "energy boomtowns." Their populations grew in response to growth in the coal and oil industries. Lumbering towns are scattered throughout Idaho, Oregon, Washington, and northern California (Carlson et al., 1981, pp. 86–95).

Geographic mobility has created other types of rural communities. The economies and way of life of many rural communities in Florida and Arizona are dominated by the influx of older, retired persons. The Ozarks region of southern Missouri and northern Arkansas, as well as central Michigan, have also experienced population growth due to the in-migration of retired households (Zuiches and Brown, 1978, p. 62).

Tourist towns are located near national parks and recreational areas. For example, Gatlinburg, Tennessee, developed into a tourist town with dozens of hotels to accommodate visitors drawn to the beauty of nearby Great Smoky Mountains National Park. Lake and mountain areas are ideal locations for vacation or "second homes." Some rural communities are so entirely dominated by the summer tourist trade that they may be best described as "transitory" settlements. For example, one community in Hildalgo County of southern Texas has fewer than 100 people during the summer. However, winter brings several thousand mobile homes and camper-vans. Suddenly the population swells, and so does traffic, crime, trash, and noise.

Other rural communities are dominated by a single industry or a college/ university. In the United States, rural areas have often been the location for various "utopian" and religion-based communities. One recent example comes from Antelope, Oregon. For several years, the religious followers of the Rajaneesh were so dominant that the name of the town was changed to Rajaneesh, and most of the original inhabitants lost control of community power.

Rural west-central Ohio is the location for a religious sect (see Chapter 8) known as The Way International. The sect was founded by George Wierwille and the major county road leading into the religious complex is appropriately named "Wierwille Road." The headquarters includes several dozen buildings comprising a large biblical research center, educational facilities, and dormitories. Its own security force patrols the roads. Every August about 15,000 Way International followers trek to the headquarters for a week-long religious celebration, jamming all the hotels for miles around. Many local residents and businesses resent the intrusion. Even some hotel owners refuse accommodations to The Way followers.

Neighborhoods and Neighbor-Groups

Within a community there may be several neighborhoods (Figure 6-7). A *neighborhood* is a locality group that is not as self-sufficient as a community in that it does not fulfill all the major community activities. A rural neighborhood may often center around one service, such as an open country church, a crossroads general store, or a grain elevator. Neighborhood members go to a

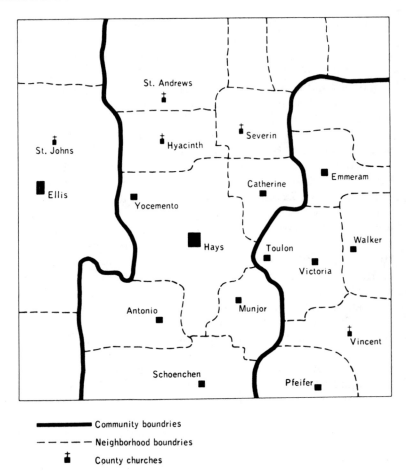

— Community boundries
— — — — — Neighborhood boundries
✝ County churches

FIGURE 6-7   **Map of Ellis County, Kansas, showing rural communities and neighborhoods.**

A community is a locality group which contains the major social institutions. It is relatively self-sufficient; the residents secure most of their community services from stores, churches, and schools in the community center. A neighborhood is not as self-sufficient as a community; it contains fewer of the social institutions. Several neighborhoods are often contained within one community. Some of the rural neighborhoods shown above offer a few services, such as a church or store; others do not, and some do not even have names.

community center for other community services not provided by the neighborhood. Rural neighborhoods are generally primary in nature and small in size, and sometimes have a name. There is a trend for rural neighborhoods to disappear in the face of improved transportation and the consolidation of churches, schools, and stores.

Rural sociologists use the concept *neighbor-group* to explain the dynamics of community action programs (see section on community power and action) (Slocum and Case, 1953, pp. 52–59; Bertrand, 1954, p. 176). A neighbor-group is composed of a network of primary relationships (Chapter 5) with no definite membership boundaries; often five to ten rural families are included (Mayo and Barnett, 1952, pp. 371–373). These families are friends and informal acquaintances. They may be a primary group or perhaps just a pattern or network of primary relationships. The members of neighbor-groups do not necessarily live on adjoining farms, as would the members of a neighborhood.

Rural-Urban Fringe

Some of the fastest growing rural areas are those on the fringe of large urban centers. This is often referred to as the *rural-urban fringe*. The rural-urban fringe is the area containing mixed rural and urban land uses. It is where the city and farm meet. Ranch houses and housing developments are scattered among farmlands.

Sometimes conflicts arise. For example, a farmer may suddenly be the target of a complaint (or even lawsuit) about the "odor" emanating from the hog operation, or the method by which farm chemicals are applied. The source of the conflict is the differing values and attitudes about the uses of land between the farmer and nonfarm neighbors.

COMMUNITY POWER STRUCTURE

Why do some community projects succeed, while others fail? Why do some persons have more power to influence local issues, and how do they maintain their power?

The importance of studying the community power structure is obvious to anyone who has attempted to consolidate or reorganize a school district, start a new service club, head a community fund drive, or secure the construction of a swimming pool, hospital, fire station, or other community facility. In fact, sociological studies of American communities, both large and small, have found that no community project can succeed without using the community power structure, especially if it involves large sums of money.

Power Structures

A *community power structure* is a network of persons and groups that influence decisions about local issues and projects. There are three major types of power structures. The first is *pyramidal* and consists of a small number of people at the top who hold most of the power. Pyramidal power structures are found in towns dominated by one industry or family, and in communities where a small closely knit group of influential people form a *clique* (Figure 6-8) (Mitchell and Lowry, 1973).

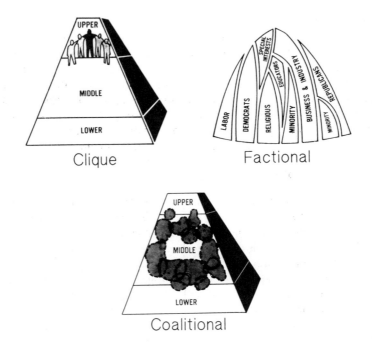

FIGURE 6-8   Types of power structures include pyramidal—only a few persons at the top; factional—many special-interest groups; and coalitional—a series of temporary alliances.

Source: Mitchell and Lowry (1973).

The second type of power structure consists of factions or special-interest groups who struggle against each other for influence over community decisions. Usually there are several *factions,* one representing business interests, another representing labor interests, a third representing the interests of farmers, and so on. The Democratic Party and the Republican Party represent examples of political factions. At the local community level, both parties compete to get their members elected to public office. Compared to a pyramidal type, the factional power structure is marked by a greater sharing of influence among many persons.

A *coalitional* power structure is characterized by the development of temporary alliances between individuals and groups relative to specific projects and issues (Mitchell and Lowry, 1973). Coalitions form temporary factions. Coalitions emerge, dissolve, and re-emerge in differing forms as issues and projects arise. Often community power holders in a coalition are managers and directors of organizations who have a specific stake in the issue at hand. For example, the building of a new wing to the local hospital is likely to see the involvement of local medical groups.

Power Holders

Sociological research has shown that community power is in the hands of a small group of persons. These persons are often referred to as *power holders* or legitimizers (Polsby, 1959 pp. 232–236). An investigation of "Springdale," a rural town in New York, disclosed that important local decisions were made by a political machine consisting of four power holders who worked behind the scenes to control the affairs of the town. Yet Springdalers claimed that one of the advantages of their small town life over city life was "equality" and "neighborliness" (Chapter 4) (Vidich and Bensman, 1958).

Power holders exist in large urban centers as well. A sociological study of Atlanta disclosed that 40 key power holders were influential in important community decisions, such as expanding city limits and starting a community fund. Decisions and instructions often passed down from the top power holders to their lieutenants, much as happens in the levels of management in a company. The 40 top power holders operated as a large friendship clique; each was influential in some sphere of city life, and cooperated with the others to run the city (Hunter, 1953).

A restudy of Atlanta by the same sociologist nearly 30 years later reached similar conclusions. Top power holders, or *influentials,* operate in primary friendship cliques. Most power holders are from the top social classes (Chapter 4). Many are executives and owners of large industrial and commercial concerns. They have high incomes and are well known and respected in the community (see Figure 6-9).

Below the top power holders are the *lieutenants.* Lieutenants provide leadership in the carrying out of decisions made by the top power holders.

FIGURE 6-9
Different power holders perform different functions. Influentials are the top power holders and make policy decisions. Lieutenants supervise the carrying out of these decisions, and doers are responsible for the execution of tasks and activities.

Source: Mitchell and Lowry (1973).

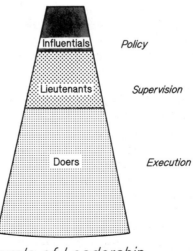

Levels of Leadership

Further down the ladder of influence are the *doers*. They are responsible for the actual execution of tasks and activities associated with decisions made at the top.

Altogether, the three types of power holders described above are predominately from the upper and middle classes (Chapter 4). Power holders comprise a minority of the population in a community. Many community members, over a long period of time, do become temporarily active (normally as doers) on a specific type of action. However, in most cases, a single issue or project will only involve a small percentage of the total community.

Community Decision Making

Community decision making is the process by which a community chooses a plan or idea that affects the community (Figure 6-10). The decision-making process is generally viewed as a series of steps or stages. These stages represent the general chronological order in which decisions are made; a given action project, however, may be interrupted or modified, in which case the decision-making process may start over again (Holland, 1958, pp. 149–155; Sower and Freeman, 1958, pp. 25–44).

Stimulation   The first stage in the process of community decision making is stimulation. This occurs when an idea or problem is judged to be important enough to merit community action. The community recognizes a new idea or the existing problem and so is motivated to take action.

An antiquated school building in a rural community may not be perceived by local citizens as a problem because it has deteriorated gradually. However, if the school building burns, the whole community realizes the need for a new school, and directs its efforts toward this goal.

Often an influence from outside the community provides the stimulation. For example, a new school superintendent may come into a community and realize that the old school building is a firetrap. This school administrator is a stimulator if he or she calls the problem of the school building to community attention.

Initiation   Action to solve the community problem soon follows stimulation. The individuals who perform the action at this stage are called initiators. Initiation involves a search for alternative means to solve a community problem, a narrowing of the possible alternatives, and consideration of the consequences of these alternatives.

Initiators are made aware of the importance of a community problem by the stimulators. There is usually some communication between the two groups, and it is not uncommon for some of the initiators to have been stimulators at the previous stage in the decision-making process. There are usually more people, however, involved at the initiation stage than at the stimulation stage.

Initiators possess many of the same social characteristics as the stimulators, but are more likely to have lived in the community a longer time. Both stimulators and initiators would primarily be the type of power holders known as lieutenants. One of the important roles of the initiators is to secure information about various decision alternatives.

Legitimation   At the legitimation stage, certain key power holders in the community give their approval or sanction to the proposed solution of the community problem. These legitimizers often change or alter the plans proposed to them by the initiators, sometimes quite radically. Seldom do legitimizers actively promote an idea or plan after giving their approval; they play a more passive role in the community decision-making process. Legitimation is a further narrowing of alternatives by the selection of one solution or plan.

Legitimizers possess considerable social resources, such as wealth and social rank. Legitimizers have usually resided in the local community for a number of years. They usually do not hold visible political or appointed positions, but instead operate "behind the scenes" through a small network or clique. Often the legitimizers can kill an idea if they are not consulted.

The decision to act   The fourth step in the process of community decision making is the public selection of a plan for the solution of the group problem and the means to accomplish this goal. Public opinion is determined

FIGURE 6-10   The community decision-making process.

Community decision making is the process by which a community chooses a plan or idea that affects the community and puts this idea into action. The stages in this process are: stimulation, initiation, legitimation, decision, and action. Examples of community decisions are construction of swimming pools and hospitals, school and church reorganization, and fund-raising drives for the Community Chest.

Stimulation of interest in the
need for the new idea (by stimulators)

    Initiation of the new idea in
    the social system (by initiators)

        Legitimation of the idea
        (by power holders or legitimizers)

            Decision to act (by members
            of the social system)

                Action or execution
                of the new idea

or expressed in a variety of ways. A survey can be taken, a referendum may be called, petitions may be circulated, or a public hearing or meeting may be held. It is usually desirable to involve as large a portion of the community as possible in the choice process—this contributes to a better decision and a greater willingness to carry it out on the part of the doers, and avoids the feeling on the part of community members that they are simply rubber-stamping a decision already made by a small, elite group. Sometimes community members may choose not to go along with the decisions made during the stimulation, initiation, and legitimation stages. For example, citizens may vote against a bond issue to finance the new school.

Action   After the public decision to act comes the action to correct the community problem. This action or execution step may take a number of years to complete. Individuals who carry through with the action are the doers, involving even more community members than previous stages of action.

Ideally, when the action stage is completed, an attempt to evaluate the community decision-making process should be made. Evaluation also takes place at each stage of community decision making, which may modify, slow down, or even permanently halt the process.

The case of the founding of the Sandusky County Crime Prevention Association and how it later became inactive shows clearly the dynamics of community power and local power structures.

BOX 6-1   *SANDUSKY COUNTY FIGHTS CRIME*

A rapid increase in vandalism during 1980 and 1981 stimulated the organization of a citizen's group to fight crime in Sandusky County. Crime had been rising since 1970 (see Chapter 7) in Sandusky County, an agricultural and manufacturing county of 60,000 in northern Ohio. Despite growing citizen concern, there was little public outcry. Then one evening a group of vandals sprayed paint on the front side of the *News Messenger* offices, the county's only newspaper. The publisher of the *News Messenger,* a man of considerable wealth and influence, was outraged. Over coffee the next morning, he and the president of a local bank made the decision that something must be done or "our town will turn into a little Cleveland."

The publisher and the banker (both community influentials) visited local law enforcement officials, and the community resource development cooperative extension service agent for Ohio's northwest district (the lieutenants). A decision was made to hold a series of four public meetings in order to discuss the problem and possible solutions. The extension agent was central to the planning and organization of the meetings. However, the publisher was designated chairman for each meeting. News of the public meetings was prominently displayed on the front page of the *News Messenger,* along with additional stories (with pictures) of other local vandalism incidents. Hence, the local initiative was legitimized.

Over 90 persons attended the first meeting, filling the local Chamber of Commerce conference room. County commissioners, law enforcement officials, judges, school superintendents, and the district farm bureau operational director, among others, were in attendance. All agreed that something had to be done. The second meeting included a presentation on rural crime and its prevention by a state specialist for the Ohio Cooperative Extension Service; and the third meeting included representatives from the governor's Office of Crime Prevention. Attendance, and presumably enthusiasm of the citizens remained high, and so by conclusion of the fourth public meeting, a decision to act had been made.

The Sandusky County Crime Prevention Association was founded, and the publisher of the *News Messenger* was named chairman. Three subcommittees were formed: one to work on fund-raising, one to plan a neighborhood crime watch program (Chapter 5), and one to plan a reward program.

Nearly $12,000 from local businesses and individual donors was raised, matched by a $6,000 allocation from the County Commissioners. Finally, the big day came; it was time for action. Crime prevention educational brochures were hung on the doorknobs of thousands of homes in Sandusky County by dozens of volunteers (the doers). Hundreds signed up for the neighborhood crime watch program, and received from the sheriff's department a confidential identification number to be used when calling suspicious activities in to the police. A "crime of the week" column was started in the *News Messenger* and citizens with information about the described incident were encouraged to contact law enforcement. If the information helped the police make an arrest, the citizen was to receive a small cash award.

For about six months, the Sandusky County Crime Prevention Association was very active. Everything was going well, in large part because the local community power structure was supportive.

However, within another six months the Association was defunct. Why? Because key leaders were no longer actively involved. A labor dispute involving local law enforcement resulted in neglect of the neighborhood watch program. A police officer who had spent many hours organizing the citizen volunteers left his job for a better paying position in another county. The area community development extension agent was transferred to the southeast district. The local publisher simply lost interest and the *News Messenger* no longer printed stories about the Association's activities. Altogether a significant share of the local leadership (both influentials and doers) was gone, and so was the crime prevention program. Without continued support from key leaders, most social action programs will die.

The death knell occurred one year later when the *News Messenger* ran a story that asked: "What happened to the the Sandusky County Crime Prevention Association?"

Source: Raymond Schindler and Joseph F. Donnermeyer (1984).

THE CHANGING RURAL COMMUNITY

Rural Population Change

When the first census of the population was conducted in 1790, the total population of the United States was 3.9 million. Over 95 percent of the population was rural, and nearly all of these were farmers. Community life was centered around agriculture. Today, the population of the United States exceeds 235 million, and less than 3 percent of the population lives on a farm. Although the rural population numbers nearly 60 million, rural community life is determined by factors reaching far beyond fields and pastureland.

Chapter 2 noted that rural culture in recent times has experienced a revival in popularity. Researchers find that most people, whether rural or urban, prefer to reside in rural areas. Throughout nearly every decade of the twentieth century, more people moved from rural to urban areas than from urban to rural locations. During the 1970s, this trend reversed itself, and more people began relocating from urban to rural areas than moving in the opposite direction (Beale and Fuguitt, 1986 p. 48). The 1980s have seen a balance of geographic mobility, with approximately equal numbers moving into and out of rural America.

Rural Population Growth   Five rural growth areas have been identified.

1. The Florida peninsula: Retirees moving from the North and Midwest have caused rapid growth in many small towns and open-country areas.
2. The Piedmont area of Virginia, North Carolina, and South Carolina: Population increases here are based on the growth of industry and business.
3. The Pacific Coast and the Southwest: The factors of climate, retirement, and spillover of population growth from Los Angeles, San Francisco, Portland, Seattle, and other metropolitan areas combine to cause rural population growth.
4. Scattered energy boom (and bust) towns of the Great Plains and Rocky Mountain states: Rising oil price increases encouraged the development of oil and gas energy sources and touched off a population boom among rural communities near mining sites.
5. Rural areas adjacent to large metropolitan areas of the Great Lakes and Northeast states: A series of metropolitan areas stretch from Milwaukee east through Chicago, Detroit, Toledo, Cleveland, and Pittsburgh, and from Boston south through Hartford, New York, Philadelphia, Baltimore, and Washington D.C. Other metropolitan areas of the Midwest are likewise included. Rural counties near these urban centers gain population as suburban developments spillover into land formerly used for farming.

Rural Population Decline   Rural population decline primarily has occurred in four areas.

1. Agricultural regions of the Great Plains and North Central States: Growth of farm size, farm consolidation, and farm insolvency have reduced the farm

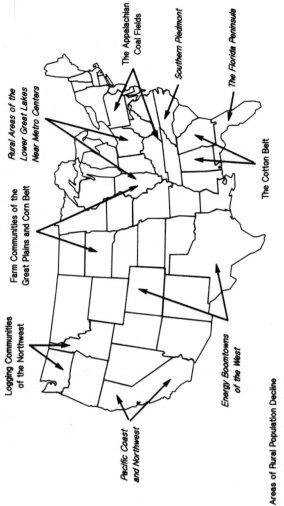

Logging Communities of the Northwest

Farm Communities of the Great Plains and Corn Belt

Rural Areas of the Lower Great Lakes Near Metro Centers

The Appalachian Coal Fields

Southern Piedmont

The Florida Peninsula

The Cotton Belt

Pacific Coast and Northwest

Energy Boomtowns of the West

Areas of Rural Population Decline

Areas of Rural Population Growth

FIGURE 6-11 While some rural areas have experienced persistent population decline, other areas have grown. Rural population decline is generally in agricultural areas and the Appalachian Coal Fields. Long-term population growth is associated with energy boomtowns, industrialization, suburbanization and the growth of retirement communities.

Source: Beale (1978), p. 41.

129

population. Small towns no longer function as service centers for a declining base of farm operators. Businesses close, jobs are lost, and the cycle of decline continues.

2. The old Cotton Belt region: The decline of sharecropping and the movement of Southern blacks out of farming have caused many rural communities of the South to lose population during the previous 30 years.

3. Appalachian coal fields: The cyclical price of coal and the lack of other employment opportunities have made Appalachia a chronically depressed region. Many highlanders have relocated to northern cities in search of jobs (Beale, 1978, pp. 43–48).

4. Logging communities of the Northwest: The decline of timber resources and automation of lumber mills have reduced jobs.

Factors affecting rural population growth and those causing decline stand in sharp contrast. Population decline is associated with the continued downward trend in farm population. Population growth is related to the nonagricultural factors of industrial relocation, energy development, and urban to rural migration.

The Consequences of Rural Population Growth and Decline

Many rural community leaders assume that population growth is always beneficial. However, social impact assessment studies (Chapter 1) have demonstrated that the consequences of growth can be both positive and negative. Growth can place severe strains on a community's ability to perform its functions. For example, a study of energy boomtowns in the West found that the influx of new students outpaced the ability to construct new schools, hire teachers, and acquire books and other learning aids. Hospitals became overcrowded. Local roads deteriorated, sewage systems were inadequate for the growing size of the population, and the quality of other governmental services declined (Murray and Weber, 1982, p. 97).

Population growth does increase the volume of local business, but even this is a mixed blessing. Long-established, family-run businesses cannot compete with the influx of chain stores (Leistritz et al., 1982, pp. 45–46).

Sometimes the values and attitudes of newcomers conflict with those of long-term residents. The power structure of the community may change as newcomers gain influence. However, it is difficult to pinpoint this as a benefit or cost of growth.

The positive benefits of rural population growth are found side by side with the costs. New businesses and homes increase the tax base and allow local school systems and government to improve service quality and local service organizations increase membership rolls (Leistritz et al., 1982). Rural sociologists have generally concluded that gradual population growth is not as disruptive to local community life as rapid growth.

FIGURE 6-12   Population growth has occurred in rural areas next to urban centers. Persons seeking the quiet of suburban living often resent noisy farm machinery and a smelly barnyard.

Population decline brings a different set of problems to rural communities. The local tax base erodes and local services suffer. Businesses close. Schools and churches can no longer be supported and are consolidated with those in communities farther away (see Chapter 7). Families of child-bearing age are most likely to leave in search of communities where there are jobs, leaving behind older, retired families (Beale, 1974, p. 16). Civic and social organizations lose members and eventually close their doors (Erickson, 1974, pp. 72–75).

SUMMARY

Community is unique among human groups because membership is based completely on locality. *Community* is defined as that combination of people and social groups which perform the major functions having relevance to a locality. The five functions of a community are: (1) production/distribution/consumption, (2) socialization, (3) social control, (4) social participation, and (5) mutual support.

The *scattered farmstead community* is the predominant community type in the rural United States. Other types of rural communities include the *cluster village* and the *line village. Community boundaries* can be determined by identifying the limits where people go for shopping and other services.

Besides the farm community, rural North American communities include other types, such as fishing villages, mining and lumbering towns, retirement communities, tourist and college towns, as well as utopian religious communities.

Neighborhood was identified as a locality group which is not as self-sufficient as a community. However, neighborhood groups are important in determining patterns of social interaction in a community.

Community power structure is a network of persons and groups who influence decisions about local issues and projects. There are three types of power structures: *pyramidal, factional,* and *coalitional. Power holders* are members of the power structure. They include *influentials* at the top, plus *lieutenants* and *doers. Community decision making* includes five stages: *stimulation, initiation, legitimation, the decision to act,* and *action.*

Some rural communities are growing and others are declining. Factors associated with growth are relocation of industry, energy development, migration of retired households to rural environments, and spillover from nearby urban centers. Rural population losses are associated with the declining farm population.

Population growth has both benefits and costs for rural communities. Growth can outpace the ability of communities to provide essential services. The values and attitudes of newcomers may conflict with those of long-term residents. The traditional power structure may change due to growth. However, growth increases business volume, the local tax base, and membership rolls of churches and civic organizations.

Population decline reduces the tax base and may force schools, churches, and other community services to be consolidated with those in other communities.

REFERENCES

BEALE, CALVIN L. (1974). "Quantitative Dimensions of Decline and Stability Among Rural Communities." In Larry R. Whiting, ed. *Communities Left Behind: Alternatives for Development,* pp. 3–21. Ames: Iowa University Press.

BEALE, CALVIN L. (1978). "People on the Land." In Thomas R. Ford, ed., *Rural U.S.A.: Persistence and Change,* pp. 37–54. Ames: Iowa State University Press.

BEALE, CALVIN L., AND GLENN V. FUGUITT. (1986). "Metropolitan and Nonmetropolitan Population Growth in the United States Since 1980." In *New Dimensions in Rural Policy: Building Upon Our Heritage,* pp. 46–62. Studies prepared for the Subcommittee on Agriculture and Transportation of the Joint Economic Committee, Congress of the United States. Washington, DC: U.S. Government Printing Office.

BERTRAND, ALVIN L. (1954). "Rural Locality Groups: Changing Patterns, Change Factors, and Implications." *Rural Sociology, 19,* 169–181.

CARLSON, JOHN E., MARIE L. LASSEY, and WILLIAM R. LASSEY. (1981). *Rural Society and Environment in America.* New York: McGraw-Hill.

ERICKSON, EUGENE C. (1974). "Consequences for Leadership and Participation." In Larry R. Whiting, ed. *Communities Left Behind: Alternatives for Development,* pp. 67–81. Ames; Iowa University Press.

FORD, THOMAS R. (1978). "Contemporary Rural America: Persistence and Change." In Thomas R. Ford, ed. *Rural U.S.A.: Persistence and Change,* pp. 3–16. Ames: Iowa State University Press.

HOLLAND, JOHN B. (1958). "A Theoretical Model for Health Action." *Rural Sociology, 22,* 149–155.
HORTON, PAUL B., AND CHESTER L. HUNT. (1984). *Sociology* (6th edition). New York: McGraw-Hill.
HUNTER, FLOYD. (1953). *Community Power Structure.* Chapel Hill: University of North Carolina Press.
JOHNSON, ALLAN G. (1986). *Human Arrangements: An Introduction to Sociology.* New York: Harcourt Brace Jovanovich.
LARSON, OLAF F. (1986). "On Galpin's Wheel Ruts Technique: An Answer to Merwyn Nelson's Inquiry." *The Rural Sociologist, 6,* 197–199.
LEISTRITZ, F. LARRY, STEVE H. MURDOCK, and ARLEN G. LEHOLM. (1982). "Local Economic Changes Associated with Rapid Growth." In Bruce A. Weber and Robert E. Howell, eds. *Coping with Rapid Growth in Rural Communities,* pp. 25–62. Boulder, CO: Westview Press.
MAYO, SELZ C., and WILLIAM E. BARNETT. (1952). "Neighbor Groups—An Informal System of Communication." *Rural Sociology, 17,* 371–239.
MITCHELL, JOHN B., and SHELDON G. LOWRY. (1973). *Power Structure, Community Leadership and Social Action.* North Central Regional Extension Publication No. 35. Columbus, OH: Ohio Cooperative Extension Service, Ohio State University.
MURRAY, JAMES A., AND BRUCE A. WEBER. (1982). "The Impacts of Rapid Growth on the Provision and Financing of Local Public Services." In Bruce A. Weber and Robert A. Howell, eds. *Coping with Rapid Growth in Rural Communities,* pp. 97–114. Boulder, CO: Westview Press.
POLSBY, NELSON W. (1959). "The Sociology of Community Power: A Reassessment." *Social Forces, 37,* 232–239.
SCHINDLER, RAYMOND, and JOSEPH F. DONNERMEYER. (1984). *Sandusky County Crime Prevention Association and Its Efforts in Block Watch and Crime Solvers Anonymous.* Columbus, OH: National Rural Crime Prevention Center. NRCPC 22.
SLOCUM, WALTER L., and HERMAN M. CASE. (1953). "Are Neighborhoods Meaningful Social Groups?" *Rural Sociology, 18,* 52–59.
SOWER, CHRISTOPHER, and WALTER FREEMAN. (1958). "Community Involvement in Community Development Programs." *Rural Sociology, 23,* 25–44.
VIDICH, ARTHUR J., and JOSEPH BENSMAN. (1958). *Small Town in Mass Society.* Princeton, NJ: Princeton University Press.
WARREN, ROLAND. (1978). *The Community in America* (3rd edition). Chicago: Rand-McNally.
ZIMOLZAK, CHESTER E., and CHARLES A. STANSFIELD, JR. (1979). *The Human Landscape: Geography and Culture.* Columbus, OH: Charles E. Merrill.
ZUICHES, JAMES J., and DAVID L. BROWN. (1978). "The Changing Character of the Nonmetropolitan Population, 1950–1975." In Thomas R. Ford, ed. *Rural U.S.A.: Persistence and Change,* pp. 55–69. Ames: Iowa State University Press.

Chapter 7

Rural Community Services

Rural local governments have a special difficulty. Because they usually comprise small towns or sparsely settled areas, they face problems of economies of scale. That is, it is much more expensive on a per capita basis to provide a service over a widely dispersed area for a few people.

Kenneth D. Rainey and
Karen G. Rainey (1978,
p. 127)

According to the 1982 Census of Government, there are approximately 52,500 units of local government in nonmetropolitan areas of the United States. These consist of 12,000 municipalities, an equal number of towns and townships, nearly 2,500 counties, over 9,000 school districts, and almost 17,000 special or single-purpose districts (Sokolow, 1986). Taken altogether, these units of government provide essential community services, including law enforcement, emergency and medical services and education.

Often services provided by local governmental units overlap and are duplicate; but too often rural community services are barely adequate to do the job, and many times services fall below acceptable levels.

The purpose of this chapter is to describe the current status and changes in several basic rural community services, including local government, education, and public safety and health.

LOCAL GOVERNMENT

Rural governmental units consist of two basic types: those that provide a single service and those that provide multiple services. Single service units include school and hospital districts. Multiservice districts are county (parish) and town (borough) governments whose responsibilities include public safety, fire and emergency medical services, street and bridge repair, and trash collection (Sokolow, 1986, p. 375).

Whether the unit of government is single or multipurpose, and whether it serves an open-country or small town population, the problems of local government officials are aptly summarized by the following analysis.

BOX 7-1   *WANTED; DEDICATED PERSON FOR A THANKLESS JOB*

If the following employment opportunity were to appear in the classified section of the local newspaper, do you think anyone would respond? "Looking for an industrious person. Must have full-time job elsewhere to supplement low salary. Must be willing to devote long hours. Must follow complex rules and regulations. Must place self and family under the threat of harassment and public ridicule. Must be willing to accept phone calls at all hours. Will be faced with demands that are impossible to fulfill. Should have aptitude for dog catching, public speaking, financial planning, grant-writing, dispute resolution and personnel management. Apply now!"

It seems incredible that anyone would want to hold such a job, yet all small towns and villages in America have at least one such individual. They are called mayors.

A recent survey of Ohio's rural mayors found the typical small town mayor is about 50 years old and has had more than 10 years of public service. Most are male, but an increasing number of women are being elected to the mayoral post. Ninety percent are married. Most have some education beyond high school and 70 percent have had managerial experience before being elected to office. Yet these individuals earn less than 10 percent of their family income from public service.

Most mayors felt that (1) their duties were too time-consuming, (2) serving in office disrupted their family life, (3) their public salary was inadequate and (4) they were less than successful in securing federal grants for their communities. . . . Almost 40 percent of those surveyed said they did not intend to seek re-election.

Major community problems identified by these mayors included: (1) finance of local government services, (2) finding capable people to run for public office, (3) lack of citizen participation in government, (4) problems of compliance with federal regulations, (5) problems of compliance with state regulations, (6) loss of legal immunity for public officials, (7) lack of long-range planning, and (8) decline in community pride.

The mayors also evaluted a list of possible approaches to problem-solving, identifying those which they considered to be useful. Attracting new industry was the highest rated approach. Other approaches included: (1) making state agencies more accessible, (2) encouraging population growth, (3) improving management efficiency, (4) entering in joint purchasing agreements with other jurisdictions, (5) keeping expenditure rates below the inflation rate, (6) obtaining additional intergovernmental revenue, (7) sharing services with other jurisdictions, and (8) implementing training programs designed for small town mayors. In addition to these approaches, a surprising one-fifth of the mayors thought that simply ignoring state regulations would be a good approach.

Source: Hines (1985), pp. 11–14.

Small-town mayors in Ohio reflect the same concerns and opinions as county commissioners, township trustees, school board members, and thousands of other small town and rural government officials. Local government is caught between the rapidly rising demand for community services and a rising inability to pay (Rainey and Rainey, 1978), p. 127). A large part of the problem is the relatively higher per capita cost of providing services in rural areas due to a smaller population base. In contrast to cities, service provision in rural communities cannot take advantage of "economies of scale" (Rainey and Rainey, 1978, p. 128).

Another problem for rural governmental units is that most depend upon property taxes to finance services. Despite increased reliance on the sales tax, income taxes, user fees, and intergovernmental transfer of public funds, such as federal revenue-sharing, property taxes remain the largest income source. The decline of farmland prices has eroded the tax base of many rural governments in the midwest. Additionally, rural people are slow to approve property tax rate increases. The only solution, as expressed by the mayors of small towns in Ohio, is to generate additional revenues through sales and income tax, but both are not possible without the growth of industry and an increased population base. Although some rural communities have gained population during the 1970s and 1980s, many have not (Chapter 6). Congress recently abolished federal revenue sharing, which already had been declining in response to the trend toward less intervention in local government affairs by the federal government. The loss of revenue sharing will require local governments to either maintain current services by increasing other sources of income, or reduce the quality and or amount of these services.

A third part of the financial problem is the growth of state and federal mandates on local government programs. For example, national clean water standards, established by the federal government, are implemented through state government requirements that local municipalities upgrade or build new wastewater treatment plants. Construction of these facilities is an expensive proposition for local governments even when most of the costs are paid for by state and federal funds (Sokolow, 1986, 377).

Historically, local rural governments have provided less service, hence tax rates are lower. Lower local taxes represent an attraction for many urban householders to relocate to the countryside and escape the higher taxes of big cities. Once the newcomers arrive, they often are not satisfied with the amount or quality of services offered by local rural governments. Ironically, they will favor higher taxes to improve and expand services. Dissatisfaction spills over in the political arena, especially among rural communities experiencing population growth (see Chapter 6). The consequences are political conflicts between local residents who fear higher property taxes and newcomers who demand better community services.

Lower expenditures result in lower levels of service provided by local rural governments. For example, the per capita expenditure by rural governments for public welfare is only 35 percent of the per capita amount spent by urban governments. Similarly, per capita expenditures for fire protection are only 31 percent of the amount spent in urban areas; for sewer service, 42 percent; for parks and recreation, 27 percent; and for libraries, 50 percent. Road and bridge repair is one of the few areas where rural governments' per capita expenditures are higher (35 percent higher) (Rainey and Rainey, 1978, p. 129).

RURAL SCHOOLS

Education is the process by which a culture is formally transmitted to learners. As such, education is similar to socialization (Chapter 3). In a broad sense, education refers to any type of culture-learning, but its use is generally restricted to formal training that takes place in a classroom under the guidance of a trained teacher.

The *school* is the social organization in which education takes place. The major emphasis in this section is upon rural schools—those located in the country and small towns—and the schools rural children attend in larger communities.

Functions of Education

Transmission of knowledge   The most obvious function of education is the transmission of knowledge. Standard school curricula include physical science, mathematics, reading, spelling and grammar, art, social science, health, and physical education. Learning disability programs and computer science represent recent additions. Many school administrators, teacher organizations, and parent groups advocate increased emphasis on geography and the introduction of foreign language classes at the elementary school level. Still other groups, such as various religious denominations, seek to include instruction in basic values of morality. Some advocate inclusion of religion-based theories on the origins of the universe and the development of the human race, and oppose the exclusive teaching of evolutionary theories.

Controversy about what types of information should be transmitted in schools illustrates the importance of formal education in U.S. society. It is more than a set of facts that is learned, for there is also the formation of basic beliefs and values which determine to a large part the character of a society's culture.

Custody of the young   The second function of education is custody of the young. Schools represent a place where young people are provided shelter and food, and where they are under adult supervision. This function has expanded, since in the majority of U.S. households (and the households of most industrialized countries), both spouses work (Chapter 9). The trend toward dual-employed households followed the trend toward universal education through high school.

Social mobility   Social mobility is the third function of education. Researchers have found that middle-class children accept school better than lower-class children. One reason is that middle-class parents themselves have higher educational levels than lower-class parents, and their children are aware that they are expected to do the same or better (Toby, 1957, pp. 226–236). Middle-class parents value education highly. They pass on their values to their children both before they go to school and while they are in school. The parents support the views of the teacher, they praise the children for academic achievement, and they are able to help with difficult school work (see Chapter 4).

Lower-class students are not encouraged in school by their parents because these parents do not value education as highly as middle-class parents. They see no reason why their children should not quit school and add to the family income by securing their own job, or leave the parental home to live on their own. This is a vicious circle in which lower social classes tend to perpetuate themselves because of the relatively low value they place on education. This leads to fewer years of schooling and lower-paying jobs that maintain the individual in a lower-class position (Hyman, 1953).

Thus, while education remains the surest means of upward social mobility (Chapter 4), it often acts as a series of sieves which allow some individuals to pass through to higher levels of education and higher-income occupations. Other individuals are sifted out with less education, and they generally can

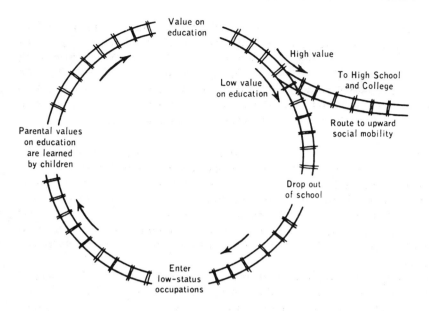

FIGURE 7-1 The "vicious circle" by which values on education tend to maintain individuals in lower social classes.

Education can serve as a means of upward social mobility by which persons climb to higher social classes. Likewise, lack of education can act to maintain individuals in a lower social class. In this diagram, parental values on education are learned by lower-class children; this value on education determines whether these youths stay in school or drop out to enter a low-status occupation. The cycle is repeated with the next generation. Values on education act as switches by which youth either stay on the vicious circle or become upwardly mobile.

only obtain low-income jobs. More education generally leads to more pay and higher social rank.

Self-identity   In Chapter 3, we discussed how significant others help develop an individual's sense of identity, that is, the "me." In some societies, such as in caste systems, self-identity is largely determined by the family into which the individual is born. The son of a carpenter was expected to become a carpenter, and much of his socialization was toward this end. In modern, industrial societies, the formation of an individual's identity becomes an important function of education. Schools today are large and complex, and are required to teach a large variety and amount of subject matter. From this developed the idea of grouping students according to their abilities. This is referred to as "tracking." The explicit function of tracking is to allow students to work at their own respective speeds, and within small groups of children with similar abilities. However, research has also shown that tracking results in the reinforcement of students' images about their own abilities from both teachers and their fellow students. Smarter students learn that they are smarter, while slower students learn that they are slower. The result during the elementary years can be that slower students lose motivation to achieve in school. Hence, they never get off the slow track (Coleman, 1966).

Creation of Knowledge   Creation of knowledge represents the fifth function of education. Throughout history, colleges and universities were places where knowledge in science and philosophy was developed. However, in modern, industrialized societies, the creation of knowledge, especially in the realm of technology development, grew in importance. The academic prestige of an institution of higher learning in contemporary U.S. society is frequently judged according to the number of scientific publications produced by its faculty.

One important area where creation of new knowledge has affected rural society is research conducted in the Colleges of Agriculture at the land-grant universities. This research is financed through the U.S. Department of Agriculture to the College's research arms or "experiment stations." Agricultural research has historically been focused on ways of improving farm productivity. Chapter 15 discusses agricultural experiment stations and research in more detail.

Rural-Urban Differences in Educational Attainment

School attendance in the United States has increased dramatically in the past 50 years. Between ages six and fifteen, school enrollment is over 90 percent, due to mandatory attendance laws. A more important reason is the general awareness that education is required to get ahead. More education generally brings good jobs which provide status and money. Even the U.S. military does not enlist persons unless they have a high school diploma.

Urban persons are better educated than rural persons. In 1980, urban adults averaged 13 years of school compared with less than 12.3 for rural nonfarm and 10.8 for farm adults.

Rural Schools and Rural Communities

There are approximately 11,000 rural school districts, comprising about 70 percent of all districts in the United States (Parks et al., 1982, p. 187). The school plays an important integrative role in rural communities because the school is often the center for many of the available social and recreational activities.

Since World War II, one of the most significant trends in rural education has been the consolidation of small-size school districts into larger units. This process is variously named consolidation, reorganization, or merger. Rural school closings have threatened the viability of some rural communities. Because schools are operated by the authority of a local school board, the decision to consolidate with other school districts is usually made at the local level. States have usually encouraged school consolidation, but have seldom forced it on local communities. There has often been intense conflict between local citizens and the state-level educational authorities or between different factions within the local rural community on this issue.

A historical review of rural education in the United States shows why school consolidation has become so common in rural communities. The first rural schools were usually planned so that children could walk to them. In some parts of the United States a rural school was located in the middle of every four-square-mile area. These one-room schools offered the elementary grades (one through eight), and one teacher instructed all grades in all subjects. This was the famous little red school house.

However accurate this nostalgic image may have been, it is hardly a valid characterization of most rural schools today (Folkman, 1961, p. 126). There are still some one-room schools in operation, but their numbers have decreased greatly. Modern school buses and the greater efficiency of larger schools have made these small school districts increasingly obsolete. Delaware County, Ohio, for example, had 12 rural high school districts in 1950; in 1960 there were 5 and by 1980 there were only 3. Cerro Gardo County, Iowa, had 103 elementary and high school districts in 1935; however, by 1986 they had consolidated to only 4.

In 1932, there were nearly 233,000 elementary schools in the United States, of which 143,400 had only one teacher. In 1972, the number of elementary schools had declined to less than 65,000, and only 1,475 were one-teacher schools. Paralleling the decline of elementary schools was the decrease in school districts due to consolidation. From 127,500 districts in 1932, only 15,900 were operating in 1979 (Gilford et al., 1981, p. 100).

One major reason for school consolidation is the increased efficiency of larger schools in cost per pupil. For example, a study in Nebraska found that the per pupil cost in rural school districts was 53 percent higher than in urban school districts (Carlson et al., 1981, p. 307). Fewer students per teacher and transportation costs were the principal differences. Another reason for consolidation is the financial difficulties of some small schools resulting from an inadequate property tax base. Nearly half the states have devised special funding formulas for rural school districts since many lack the economic base to support local schools (Edington, 1981, p. 362).

There is considerable resistance to school consolidation in rural communities. Most rural people view their schools as symbols of local pride and solidarity, hate to lose them, and feel the loss will result in a dying community. However, a recent study by rural sociologists of 61 rural communities in

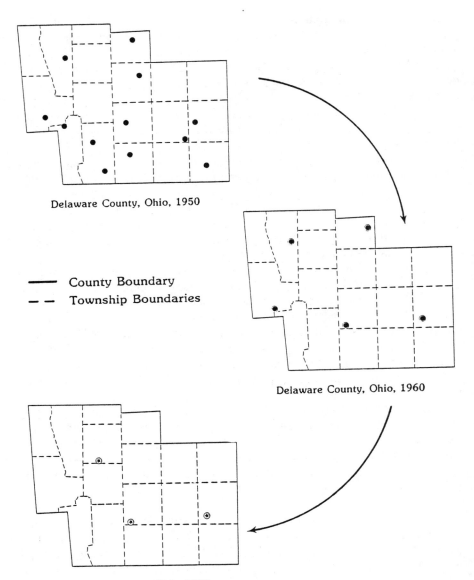

Delaware County, Ohio, 1950

Delaware County, Ohio, 1960

—— County Boundary

– – Township Boundaries

Delaware County, Ohio, 1980

FIGURE 7-2 The experience of Delaware County, Ohio, shows a typical pattern of rural school consolidation. Consolidation reduced the number of rural high schools from 12 to 3 in less than 30 years.

Source: Donald Thomas, rural sociologist, Ohio State University.

southern Illinois found that school consolidation and decline in local businesses did not go hand-in-hand (Voth and Danforth, 1981, p. 364).

There is also fear of less personal attention given to students in larger schools. Pride is often developed in local athletic teams; there is reluctance to see the local school merge with a traditional rival.

Another reason why consolidation is often opposed is the multiple functions performed by the rural school. The school is the focal point for the local social and recreational life of the community. Additionally, the power structure of a rural community may be threatened by school closings. Much of the financing of rural schools comes from local property taxes, and school finance is often the most expensive budget item. The prospect of school consolidation brings with it the fear the local community will lose political power and influence.

Growing concern over control of school curriculum also illustrates why rural school consolidation is opposed. Many rural people believe that they have greater opportunities to influence the content and style by which their children are taught. They fear that additional consolidation will increase the power of professional teacher organizations and the state and federal governments to control local curriculums. A recent Gallup poll shows that most people in U.S. society believe that local school boards should have more influence in determining school curricula and that the federal government should have less (*Salt Lake Tribune*, 1986, p. A3).

Despite the continuing trend toward consolidation, the one-room school still flourishes in some rural areas and remains a vital community institution.

FIGURE 7-3   One drawback to rural school consolidation is long bus rides for students.

Source: University of Illinois Agricultural Experiment Station.

BOX 7-2   *THE ONE-ROOM SCHOOL IN AUSTRALIA AND SOUTH DAKOTA*

Jill Perkins drives 44 kilometers each day to teach in the one-room school located in Wollomonbi, New South Wales. There are 16 children ranging in age from 5 to 12 years and drawn from a radius of 10 miles. After graduating from the one-room school, the children will go for secondary education to Guyra (some 55 kilometers to the West) or to a primary (private) boarding school. Children of the large property owners will go to the private schools and then on to tertiary education (college or university). The children of small property owners and workers will go on to the state school and likely return to jobs similar to those of their parents.

The location of the one-room school appears isolated and remote—the quality of education is first rate. The Parents Club has purchased a video recorder and two computers. One of the parents acts as librarian and all take their turn at teaching a special lesson (ranging from literature to natural science). They go to Guyra twice a year to learn lifesaving and swimming. The school is the center of community involvement and pride. It provides a focus for attention and considerable identity for local people in the 100-square-mile area. It is the last rural institution in the Australian "outback" where the towns are small and far apart. Regardless of whether they have any children in the school, it is the center of community identity and pride.

As one parent said, "You get a lot of community involvement and interest by parents . . . maybe because we are small. Parents tend to overcompensate for the isolation. When we lived in the city (Brisbane), the children went to a school of 1,200. The teachers were very good and the facilities excellent, but I think they have learned as much, or more, in this setting."

A similar view is offered by Donna von Lehe, the teacher of a one-room school in western South Dakota. Her Greenwood school is one of 144 one-teacher schools in South Dakota that has *not* been consolidated.

South Dakota is a large rural state with relatively few people, and one-teacher/one-room schools are an important part of the educational system. State officials used to think the same way as officials in other states—consolidation saved public monies and resulted in more efficiently operated school systems. However, today the one-room school is no longer considered a rural anachronism. Bigger is not necessarily better, and for many of South Dakota's most rural areas, the one-room/one-teacher school is considered the best way to go about education.

Many of South Dakota's teachers, especially those who themselves were educated in one room schools, like the close personal one-on-one relationships they develop with their students. Some teachers in the larger city schools of South Dakota now yearn to return to the one-room school.

The one-room school survives in South Dakota, and will not soon become extinct. Local residents are proud of their schools, and the schools continue as the focal point of local community activities.

Source: Carlson et al. (1978), p. 309.

PUBLIC SAFETY

Studies show that most members of U.S. society prefer to live in rural rather than urban areas. One reason identified by city dwellers is a lower incidence of crime. Urban crime rates soared during the 1960s and 1970s, contributing to the flight of many urban households to the suburbs, the rural-urban fringe (Chapter 6), and open-country areas (Federal Bureau of Investigation, 1986).

Historically, rural crime rates were lower than urban crime rates. National statistical studies have shown the per capita rate of violent and property crime used to be as much as ten times higher in the city (Federal Bureau of Investigation, 1984; Bureau of Justice Statistics, 1985). The image of rural crime was of occasional incidents of cattle theft and stagecoach robberies.

However, the same social forces and trends that have changed the nature of rural community life and farming (Chapter 1) have likewise contributed to the growth of rural crime.

Rural sociologists note that crime in the countryside grew faster than urban crime during the 1960s and 1970s. While the national urban crime rate increased 350 percent, the rural crime rate jumped 420 percent (Phillips, 1975, p. 51).

The pattern of rural crime is different from urban crime. Rates of violent crime such as armed robbery, personal assault, homicide, and rape remain low in most rural areas. Rural people often fall victim to crimes of violence when they are in urban locations, such as when they travel to a downtown business district or a shopping mall. Although rural people are relatively safe from violent crime, changing lifestyles bring them to places that increase their risk of encountering crime (Donnermeyer, 1982, p. 47).

Rates of property crime such as burglary, theft, and vandalism are nearly as high in some areas as they are in urban areas. For example, a study in Ohio among medium- and large-scale farm operators found burglary rates to exceed those for residents of large cities. Nearly 10 percent of the farmers reported at least one breaking and entering into farm buildings during the previous year. In comparison, a typical residential burglary rate for city dwellers is about 5 percent (Donnermeyer, 1984).

The most frequently occurring crime in rural areas is vandalism, which is largely committed by teenagers. Dollar damage from a single incident of vandalism is generally very low, hence most arrests for vandalism are misdemeanors rather than felonies. Favorite targets include mailboxes, farm equipment, crops and pastureland, and decorative front-yard lawn furnishings. Despite the seemingly minor economic damage of vandalism, research has found it to be extremely fear-provoking, especially among the rural elderly. Rural victims react to vandalism as an example of society's changing norms with regard to property. Respect for property is an example of an important rural norm or mores, (Chapter 2). Incidents of vandalism are perceived as acts of malicious violence directed at the victim's property, and therefore serious violations of society's norms (Donnermeyer and Phillips, 1984, pp. 155–156).

Various forms of con and fraud are increasing, especially against farmers and ranchers. For example, many farm operators who advertise the sale of their livestock in farm journals find the purchaser to be someone who wrote them a "bad check." The farm financial crisis has spawned a new twist on an old trick. Many farmers have paid thousands of dollars to con artists in the form of fees for false promises of finding low interest loans from "secret sources." One con artist boasted that she was the representative of a wealthy Saudi Arabian family sympathetic to the financial problems of American farmers, and promised to provide tens of millions of dollars in 20-year deferred interest loans. In order to prove one's "honest desire" to remain in farming, the farmer was required to make a $2,500 "earnest money" deposit.

Perceptions of crime are changing among rural people. A longitudinal study in Ohio found that the proportion of rural residents concerned about crime doubled during the 1970s. The rate of increase in concern about crime was higher among the rural elderly (Donnermeyer et al., 1983, pp. 98–113). In Illinois, residents from nonmetropolitan counties ranked public safety higher than city dwellers as a community problem (Burdge et al., 1979). A study of crime perceptions among older persons in the state of Washington found that farmers were as fearful of crime as city residents (Lee, 1982).

Rural Offenders

Another way to examine crime is to look at arrests made by law enforcement agencies. Per capita arrest rates in rural areas are generally lower than in urban locations, although rapidly catching up. The total arrest rate was 20 percent lower in rural law enforcement jurisdictions in 1983. However, as recently as 1970, arrest rates were 60 percent less in rural jurisdictions. Rural arrest rates are higher for specific offenses, including crimes against the family and children, fraud, and murder (Warner, 1982). Mental health specialists and family counselors have noted an increase in the number of spouse and child abuse cases among financially stressed farm families (*Wall Street Journal*, 1985:20) (Chapter 10).

Arrests for murder in rural areas reflects strong regional variations. Arrest rates for violent offenses in the rural South and West are higher than in the Midwest and New England. Violent crime rates in some rural Southern and Western states are higher than in the city. The reasons cited for this center on the development of a "culture of violence" associated with the absence of law enforcement in sparsely populated areas, poverty, and a "frontier mentality" to the resolution of conflicts (Warner, 1982).

Rural arrest profiles show that most offenders are young males. A study of arrests made by sheriffs in Ohio found that females accounted for less than 10 percent of all offenders. Persons below the age of 24 represented nearly 80 percent of all those arrested (Phillips, 1975).

Studies have recently noted the increased tendency of rural youth involvement in such delinquent activities as shoplifting, drug abuse, and vandalism. Although rural youth lag behind their urban counterparts in the seriousness of delinquent activities, studies show the many changes in U.S. rural society (see Chapter 1) that have contributed to rising rural delinquency rates. These factors center on the partial transfer of the socialization function from the family institution to other institutions in society, including the peer group and mass media.

Not so long ago criminologists assumed that delinquent behavior was less likely among rural youth because they were not exposed to gangs and gangster delinquent role models (Chapter 3) found in large urban centers. However, rural and urban youth are equally exposed to television and other mass media sources that often portray delinquent role models. Rural youth increasingly orient outside their neighborhoods due to the consolidation of rural schools. These trends have contributed to the development of a youth subculture (Chapter 2) in rural areas. Normative expectations among rural youth relative to activities such as vandalism, drugs, and shoplifting differ from expectation of parents and adult authorities (Donnermeyer and Phillips, 1984, pp. 155–156). These activities are rationalized by many rural youth today as normatively appropriate, as they often are among urban youth. The result is an increased participation of rural youth in activities considered "criminal" by society, and this trend is reflected in higher rates of crime among rural residents and higher rates of arrest by rural law enforcement (Natalino, 1982; Sagarin et al., 1982).

Expenditures for police, jails, and courts in rural areas are below national averages. For example, per capita spending for rural law enforcement is less than half the dollar amount for urban areas (Rainey and Rainey, 1978, p. 129). The average number of law officers per 1,000 persons is 2.1 nationally. However, for sheriffs' departments, the average number of deputies is 1.3 per 1,000 persons (Ward, 1982). Rural law enforcement agencies face other obstacles as well, including geographically large jurisdictions, lack of specialized training and investigative equipment, and comparatively low salaries. In isolated villages in the Alaskan bush country, emergencies were called in to law enforcement officers over shortwave radios. Sometimes it took days for help to arrive at the scene of the reported crime (Angell, 1978).

Most sheriffs' departments are required to maintain jails. Rural jails are faced with problems of staffing and antiquated facilities. Enforcement of sanitary and medical standards often require costly repairs. In rural counties of Alabama, most jails lack round-the-clock staffing. Only 17 percent of rural jails in Kansas comply with federal and state standards (Miller, 1982).

Legal assistance in many rural areas is inadequate. The per capita number of lawyers in rural counties is only one-fourth that of urban counties. Rural judges often lack adequate legal training (Ward, 1982).

All things considered, rural areas remain safer from crime than urban areas. However, trends in crime rates, arrest rates, and increased rural juvenile delinquency among rural youth foreshadow increasing problems of public safety in the countryside. The response of the police and courts may be inadequate given problems of funding and staffing. Societal trends changing the character of rural society in the United States (Chapter 1) are diminishing the importance of one major reason why most people prefer to live in the country: a crime-free environment.

RURAL HEALTH SERVICES

One indicator of quality of life is the health of a society's people. Since the establishment of the U.S. Department of Agriculture in 1862, the health of rural people in the United States has been a subject of much concern. Dr. W. W. Hall, the first commissioner of agriculture, noted in a report to President Abraham Lincoln that rural areas exhibited higher rates of insanity and various physical ills associated with farm living (Roemer, 1976, p. 3).

Over a century later, concern about rural health remains. Rural sociologists, in a review of rural health studies, concluded, "Widely dispersed populations, lower average incomes, lower educational levels, and a generalized failure to design health care systems to fit the unique attitudes of rural regions, each contribute to inadequate health care for rural people." (Carlson et al., 1981, p. 112).

This view was supported by the findings of two rural health specialists who pessimistically concluded: "Contrary to popular opinion, rural America, land of fresh air and unharried lifestyles, is not necessarily a picture of health, nor is country-living a panacea for longer life. Recent evidence suggests that equating ruralness with good health is a myth" (Wright and Lick, 1986, p. 461).

Some health concerns are special to farm areas, such as deaths or loss of limbs due to tractor accidents. Improper use of farm chemicals and contaminated water supplies may lead to environmentally related health problems (see Chapter 13). More recently, stress associated with financial and other problems of farming has been recognized.

Rural-Urban Differences in Health Status

A comparison of several measures of health indicates that rural residents are less well-off. For example, each year 13.9 percent of the farm population suffers from an illness or injury sufficiently serious to restrict activities, compared to 13.0 percent of the rural nonfarm population and 10.9 percent of the urban population. The farm population has a much higher rate of work-related injuries—129.6 injuries for every 1,000 workers. The rural nonfarm rate of work-related injuries is 96.8 per 1,000 workers; the urban rate is 87.2 per 1,000 workers.

The rate of motor vehicle accident deaths is 28.4 per 100,000 persons among the rural population. The urban rate of motor vehicle deaths is 17.1. Deaths among newborn infants is 24.9 per 1,000 live births, compared to a rate of 22.0 per 1,000 live births for the urban population (Carlson et al., 1981, p. 113).

Rural-Urban Differences in Health Care Services

Access to health care services is difficult for many rural people. For example, a visit to the doctor's or dentist's office can be a long and difficult trip. Many rural counties do not have hospitals. Most medical specialists practice out of large medical complexes in urban centers because rural hospitals can afford little in the latest in medical technology.

The per capita number of medical and health care specialists is considerably lower in rural areas. For example, in urban areas there are 1.5 physicians per 1,000 persons. In rural areas, the number of physicians is less than half the urban total: .67 per 1,000 persons. The differences are even more pronounced when comparing the most urbanized with the most rural counties. The number of physicians in counties with a city of 50,000 or above is 2.7 per every 1,000 persons. In counties without a city of more than 2,500 in population, the number of physicians is .39 per every 1,000 persons. Similar shortages of dentists and nurses in rural areas also exist (Miller et al., 1982, pp. 638–639).

Fewer rural people have medical insurance to help defray the costs of hospital stays and long-term illnesses. Only 62 percent of the farm population is covered by a hospitalization plan, compared to 74 percent of the rural nonfarm population and 81.3 percent of the urban population. While 80 percent of the urban population also has insurance to cover the costs of surgery, only 73 percent of the rural nonfarm and 60 percent of the farm population are covered by surgical insurance (Carlson et al., 1981, p. 113).

FIGURE 7-4
Many rural areas suffer from shortages in health care professionals. For example, there are twice as many physicians per capita in urban than in rural areas.

Source: Carlson et al. (1981), p. 113.

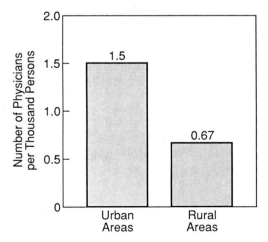

Mental Health Services

The rural population has greater problems of access to professional mental health services for reasons similar to those cited above. Psychologists, psychiatrists, and social workers tend to be concentrated in urban centers.

Psychological problems associated with financial stress illustrate the shortage of mental health services in farm areas. Studies of financially strapped farmers in Iowa and Missouri listed a number of stress-related problems, including marital difficulties, depression, loss of appetite, increased smoking and drinking, insomnia, withdrawal from family and friends, feelings of worthlessness, and increased physical aggression against spouse, children, and acquaintances (Hargrove, 1986, p. 88; Heffernan and Heffernan, 1986, pp. 276–277).

Economic problems on the farm affect more than the farm operator. The whole family, especially children, also feel the strain.

BOX 7-3   *FARM PROBLEMS AFFECT THE CHILDREN TOO*

One day she walked out behind a grove of trees in the back of the house and placed her father's shotgun to her head. She stood there silently, debating whether she should pull the trigger.

Aleta grew up on a farm near Spirit Lake, Iowa, and during her childhood she did what most farm children do. She helped her family with the chores, fed the newborn calves, and completed many a 4-H project.

Things changed for Aleta Kuhnman her senior year, because she felt the tension and the stress from her parents as they struggled to cope with the threat of foreclosure on the family farm.

Aleta Kuhnman did not commit suicide. She put the gun down and went back to the classroom. She graduated from high school, but the dream of someday being a farmer herself was gone forever.

The story of Aleta Kuhnman is repeated throughout the farm belt. As the financial situation of more and more farmers turns bleak, spouses and children often suffer, too. Sometimes the suffering is expressed in a spate of violence, resulting in rising rates of child and spouse abuse, and even homicide and suicide.

Because farming is by nature a "family affair," a bad economic situation dominates the day to day living of the whole family. Sometimes the farm has been in the family for three or more generations, making its financial ruin especially difficult on the family. When the farm fails, the parents lose confidence and become ineffective parents.

In Mitchell, South Dakota, a small farming community, there were 14 suicides during a recent two year period. Teenage alcoholism is also on the rise in Mitchell.

The movie *Country* is a vivid portrayal of the psychological side-effects of farm financial difficulties. The father becomes listless, and at one point vents his anger by striking his son. His confidence destroyed, he does nothing for days, neglecting ordinary farm chores.

Source: Wall, 1985, pp. 1, 20.

SUMMARY

There are over 50,000 units of local government in rural areas of the United States. Many are unable to provide adequate services due to problems of *economies of scale* and overreliance on the property tax as the primary source of public funds.

Rural government officials face difficult management problems. Most are part-time leaders who receive little remuneration from their public service. Many find the work frustrating and do not plan to run for office again.

Education is the process by which a culture is formally transmitted to learners. *School* is a social organization in which education takes place. Education has five major functions. These include transmission of knowledge, custody of the young, offering of a means of social mobility, formation of self-identity, and creation of knowledge.

Educational attainment of the rural population continues to lag behind that of the urban population.

Rural schools are integral to community life, and for this reason, school consolidation is often vehemently opposed. Despite widespread opposition, consolidation has greatly reduced the number of rural schools. However, in very sparsely populated areas, such as the outback areas of Australia and South Dakota, the one-room school remains a vital rural community institution.

Crime is a growing problem in many rural areas of the United States. During the past 15 years, rural crime rates have risen faster than urban crime rates. The most frequently occurring crimes in rural areas include vandalism, burglary, and larceny.

Arrest rates by rural law enforcement officers likewise have increased. *Delinquency* among rural youth also has increased, and for some types of violations, there are few differences in rural-urban delinquency rates.

Despite a growing problem of rural crime, expenditures for police, jails, legal assistance, and courts lag well behind expenditures in urban areas.

The *health status* of the rural population has long been of concern among health specialists. Compared to the urban population, rural people have higher rates of restricted activities due to illness, work-related injuries, motor vehicle deaths, and infant deaths.

Health care services in rural areas are below urban averages. The *per capita* number of physicians, dentists, and nurses is much lower in rural areas. Rural people are also less likely to have medical insurance.

The lack of mental health care services is a problem, especially in farming areas where severe financial stress can have serious effects on family well-being.

REFERENCES

ANGELL, JOHN. (1978). *Alaskan Village Police Training: An Assessment and Recommendations.* Anchorage: Criminal Justice Center of the University of Alaska.
BURDGE, RABEL J., RUTH M. KELLY, HARVEY J. SCHWEITZER, LINDA

KEASLER, and ANITA RUSSELMAN. (1979). *Crime Victimization in Illinois: The Citizen's Perspective.* Urbana: University of Illinois, Cooperative Extension Service, Special Series 4.

BUREAU OF JUSTICE STATISTICS, U.S. Department of Justice. (1984). *Sourcebook of Criminal Justice Statistics.* Washington, DC: U.S. Government Printing Office.

CARLSON, JOHN E., MARIE L. LASSEY, AND WILLIAM R. LASSEY. (1981). *Rural Society and Environment in America.* New York: McGraw-Hill.

COLEMAN, JAMES. (1966). *Equality of Educational Opportunity.* Washington, DC: U.S. Government Printing Office.

DONNERMEYER, JOSEPH F. (1982). "Patterns of Criminal Victimization in a Rural Setting: The Case of Pike County, Indiana." In Timothy J. Carter, G. Howard Phillips, Joseph F. Donnermeyer, and Todd N. Wurschmidt, eds. *Rural Crime: Integrating Research and Prevention,* pp. 34–49. Totowa, NJ: Allenheld, Osmun Publishers.

DONNERMEYER, JOSEPH F. (1984). *Property Crime Victimization Among Farm Operators: An Executive Summary.* Research Report Prepared for the National Institute of Justice. Columbus, OH: National Rural Crime Prevention Center, Ohio State University.

DONNERMEYER, JOSEPH F., and G. HOWARD PHILLIPS. (1984). "Vandals and Vandalism in the USA: A Rural Perspective." In Claude Levy-Leboyer, ed. *Vandalism: Behavior and Motivations,* pp. 149–161. Amsterdam, The Netherlands: North-Holland.

DONNERMEYER, JOSEPH F., G. HOWARD PHILLIPS, GEORGE M. KREPS, and MARY JO STEINER. (1983). *Crime, Fear of Crime and Crime Prevention: An Analysis Among the Rural Elderly.* Research Report prepared for the Andrus Foundation, American Association of Retired Persons. Columbus, OH: National Rural Crime Prevention Center, Ohio State University.

EDINGTON, EVERETT D. (1981). "Change in Rural Schools." *The Rural Sociologist, 1,* 359–364.

FEDERAL BUREAU OF INVESTIGATION. (1986). *Crime in the United States: Uniform Crime Reports.* Washington, DC: U.S. Government Printing Office.

FOLKMAN, WILLIAM S. (1961). "Rural Problem Areas Need Better Schools." *Agricultural Economics Research, 13,* 126.

GILFORD, DOROTHY M., GLENN L. NELSON and LINDA GRAM, eds. *Rural America in Passage: Statistics for Policy.* (Washington, D.C.: National Academy Press).

HARGROVE, DAVID S. (1986). "Mental Health Response to the Farm Foreclosure Crisis." *The Rural Sociologist, 6,* 88–95.

HEFFERNAN, WILLIAM D., and JUDITH BORTNER HEFFERNAN. (1986). "Impact of the Farm Crisis on Rural Families and Communities." *The Rural Sociologist, 6,* 160–170.

HINES, ROBERT L. (1985). "Ohio's Village Mayors Speak Out." *Ohio Cities and Villages, 10,* 11–14.

HYMAN, HERBERT H. (1953). "The Value System of Different Classes: A Social Psychological Contribution to the Analysis of Stratification." In Reinhard Bendix and Seymour Martin Lipset, eds. *Class, Status, and Power.* Glencoe, IL: Free Press of Glencoe.

LEE, GARY R. (1982). "Residential Location and Fear of Crime Among the Elderly." *Rural Sociology, 47,* 655–669.

MILLER, MICHAEL K., DONALD E. VOTH, and DIANA M. DANFORTH. (1982). "The Medical Care System and Community Malady: Rural, Urban, and Suburban Variations in Impact." *Rural Sociology, 47,* pp. 634–654.

MILLER, ROD. (1982). "A Needs Assessment for Small Jails in the United States." In Shanler D. Cronk, Joanne Jankovic, and Ronald K. Green, eds. *Criminal Justice in Rural America,* pp. 205–230. Washington, DC: National Institute of Justice, U.S. Department of Justice.

"Most Believe Education Is State, Local Responsibility." (1986, August 31). *Salt Lake Tribune,* p. A3.

NATALINO, KATHLEEN. (1982). "Family, Peers and Delinquency: A Rural Replication of Urban Findings." In Timothy J. Carter, G. Howard Phillips, Joseph F. Donnermeyer, and Todd N. Wurschmidt, eds. *Rural Crime: Integrating Research and Prevention,* pp. 66–96. Totowa, NJ: Allenheld, Osmun Publishers.

PARKS, GAIL ARMSTRONG, PEGGY J. ROSS, and ANNE E. JUST. (1982). "Education." In Don A. Dillman and Daryl J. Hobbs, eds. *Rural Society in the U.S.: Issues for the 1980's,* pp. 185–195. Boulder, CO: Westview Press.

PHILLIPS, G. HOWARD. (1975). *Crime in Rural Ohio.* Report ESO 363. Wooster, OH: The Ohio Agricultural Research and Development Station, Ohio State University.

RAINEY, KENNETH D., and KAREN G. RAINEY. (1978). "Rural Government and Local Public Services." In Thomas R. Ford, ed. *Rural U.S.A.: Persistence and Change,* Chapter 8. Ames: Iowa State University Press.

ROEMER, MILTON I. (1976). "Historical Perspective of Health Services in Rural America." In Edward W. Hassinger and Larry R. Whiting, eds. *Rural Health Services: Organization, Delivery, and Use,* Chapter 1. Ames: Iowa State University Press.

SAGARIN, EDWARD, JOSEPH F. DONNERMEYER, and TIMOTHY J. CARTER. (1982). "Crime in the Countryside—A Prologue." In Timothy J. Carter, G. Howard Phillips, Joseph F. Donnermeyer, and Todd N. Wurschmidt, eds. *Rural Crime: Integrating Research and Prevention,* pp. 10–19. Totowa, NJ: Allenheld, Osmun Publishers.

SALT LAKE TRIBUNE. (1986). "Most Believe Education Is State, Local Responsibility," August 31, A3.

SOKOLOW, ALVIN D. (1986). "Local Governments in Rural and Small Town America: Diverse Patterns and Common Issues." In *New Dimensions in Rural Policy: Building Upon Our Heritage,* pp. 372–379. Studies prepared for the Subcommittee on Agriculture and Transportation of the Joint Economic Committee, Congress of the United States. Washington, DC: U.S. Government Printing Office.

TOBY, JACKSON. (1957). "Orientation to Education as a Factor in the Social Maladjustment of Lower-Class Children." *Social Forces, 35,* 226–236.

VOTH, DONALD E., and DIANA M. DANFORTH. (1981). "Effect of Schools upon Small Community Growth and Decline." *The Rural Sociologist, 1,* 364–369.

WALL, WENDY L. (1985). "Farm Crisis is Taking Subtle Toll on Children in Distressed Families." *Wall Street Journal,* LXCI pp. 1, 20.

WARD, STEVEN M. (1982). "Rural Crime and Law Enforcement: A Perspective." In Shanler D. Cronk, Joanne Jankovic, and Ronald K. Green, eds. *Criminal Justice in Rural America,* pp. 49–68. Washington, DC: National Institute of Justice, U.S. Department of Justice.

WARNER, JOHN R., JR. (1982). "Rural Victimization in a Southern State." In Shanler D. Cronk, Joanne Jankovic, and Ronald K. Green, eds. *Criminal Justice in Rural America,* pp. 29–40. Washington, DC: National Institute of Justice, U.S. Department of Justice.

WRIGHT, J. STEPHEN, and DALE W. LICK. (1986). "Health in Rural America: Problems and Recommendations." In *New Dimensions in Rural Policy: Building Upon Our Heritage,* pp. 461–476. Studies prepared for the Subcommittee on Agriculture and Transportation of the Joint Economic Committee, Congress of the United States. Washington, DC: U.S. Government Printing Office.

Chapter 8

The Rural Church

In an era of lost services such as schools, medical facilities, and businesses, rural churches may have greater importance as rural community institutions.

—Edward W. Hassinger
and John S. Holik (1985), p. 150.

Mind you, we do not say there have been no changes in organized religion during the past half-century. That would be absurd. . . . There are enough new things under the sun in Middletown's religion to amaze and delight a curious observer. But we have not been able to find much trace of the great massive trend that was supposed to be carrying us irresistibly out of an age of faith into an age of practical reason. What has happened instead—the persistence and renewal of religion in a changing society—is more interesting than the secularization that never occurred.

—Theodore Caplow,
Howard Bahr, and Bruce
A. Chadwick (1983), p. 26.

The above statement by Theodore Caplow and his colleagues was made on the basis of a 50-year follow-up to the classic sociological study of Middletown, a small city in Indiana. In a 30-year follow-up study of the rural church in Missouri, two rural sociologists, Edward Hassinger and John Holik, reached the same conclusion. Before we investigate why rural churches have been resistant to change, let us consider certain basic ideas surrounding religion and the church in society.

WHAT IS RELIGION?

Religion is a belief in a supernatural power which helps people to distinguish between right and wrong and which provides answers to some of life's ultimate problems. A *church* is an organization of believers having a common faith and a common creed. In other words, a church is a group of people with a religion of some form. Religion is a *cultural universal:* All cultures have some kind of religion. One reason for this universality is humankind's anxieties concerning death and other crises of life. All peoples seem to feel a need for belief in life after death. Religion and the church exist to answer some of these ultimate questions about life and death.

Specific religious practices vary widely among different cultures, but they are usually closely related to each society's way of life. For instance, a tribe that lives in a desert area may worship water holes or springs. To certain Inuit tribes in Alaska, Hell is a very cold place. The Hopi Indians of Arizona and New Mexico depend on dry-land farming for their existence. They worship the sun and perform an elaborate snake dance to pray for rain for their crops. Many societies with patriarchal (father dominated) families worship father-image gods, and societies with matriarchal (mother dominated) families often worship mother-image gods (see Chapter 9).

In many cultures, including First World countries, people often resort to religion, superstition, magic, and other nonempirical explanations of phenomena when more rational and scientific approaches fail to answer important problems completely. There are differences between religion and magic, but individuals tend to resort to them in similar types of situations, as is illustrated by the following example of agricultural magic in the United States.

BOX 8-1   *AGRICULTURAL MAGIC*

When are superstition and magic ritual most often used in the United States? They are associated with certain occupations and activities in which a high degree of risk and uncertainty are involved. Examples are the soldier in combat who carries a rabbit's foot, the baseball hitter who taps the plate before each pitch, and the gambler who blows on his dice. Magic is one means for reducing anxiety about important decisions.

U.S. agriculture is typified by rapid technological changes and increasing efficiency. One thinks of the North American farmer as a modern businessman who has rejected the more traditional beliefs of previous generations. But even the new farmer is dependent upon magic ritual in certain situations. *Agricultural magic* is defined as those farming beliefs and practices that lack scientific explanation. These magical beliefs are accepted because they seem to work rather than because they have any scientific basis.

Examples of agricultural magic are special times for planting crops, castrating or dehorning livestock, and cutting or spraying weeds. Some farmers believe that if corn is planted in the Zodiacal sign of the Twins, more ears will grow on each stalk. They believe that root crops such as potatoes, onions, and beets should be planted in the dark of the moon and grains and other nonroot crops, such as corn, tomatoes, and beans, in the light of the moon.

Agricultural magic is also involved in the practice of witching for wells and other sources of water. Water witching, a practice that has been used for centuries, entails the use of a Y-shaped branch, called a dowsing rod, to locate underground water supplies. The forked branch is grasped so that it points upward while the water dowser walks back and forth over an area. The dowsing rod twists and points downward at the point where underground water is located. The dowser then instructs well drillers to sink a shaft at that point.

Water witching is not a reliable method for locating underground supplies of water (Vogt, 1952; Meinzer, 1944). The percentage of dry wells is just as high for those that have been witched as not witched. Nevertheless, the North American Association of Diviners lists its 1987 membership at 900. Early research by sociologists found that water witching in the United States was most likely to occur when water was difficult to find and to maintain in a steady, adequate supply. They concluded that witching persisted where the search for water was characterized by anxiety and uncertainty and was a method of coping with nature where the outcome was important, but uncertain (Hyman and Cohen, 1957; Vogt and Hyman, 1959).

It may be difficult to believe that water witching persists in modern-day U.S. agriculture. However, one of the authors was recently asked to come to a large farm and witch for a new well. The farmer was a former student in a rural sociology class who had seen the instructor witch for water (as a classroom demonstration of agricultural magic), was convinced, and now wanted help to locate a well on his farm.

Magic is generally used when decisions are risky and the outcomes are uncertain. For example, the Trobriand Islanders in the South Pacific possessed technical knowledge that they used in growing yams or in catching fish, but their techniques were seldom so effective that results were certain. Even when yams were properly planted and cultivated, a drought might destroy the crop. It is in such situations of uncertainty and anxiety that magic rituals are most likely to be used, an anthropologist named Bronislaw Malinowski (1948) found.

The largest of the Trobriand Islands consists of a ring of land surrounding a central lagoon. Individuals living on the inner lagoon used poison as a method of fishing; the results were absolutely reliable. Individuals living on the outside shores of the island ventured forth in the Pacific Ocean in pursuit of schools of fish; the results were uncertain and the method of fishing was dangerous. Magic did not exist in the lagoon fishing where the islanders relied completely upon their knowledge and skill, and where the food supply was plentiful. However, extensive magic rituals were used in the open-sea fishing to ensure a good catch and a safe return of the fishing boats (Malinowski, 1948).

Agricultural magic is commonly used in specialized agriculture. Kentucky horse breeders rely extensively on the signs of the Zodiac. The accepted rule is to wait until the sign is below that part of the body to which the horse breeder wants to give attention. So weaning should be done during those few days per month when the sign is below the knee. Once the sign returns to the head, for example, weaning might cause the foal to become a mental case. Weaning in the sign in the heart and lungs could result in a short-winded horse. The expected consequences of going against magical custom are serious (Stone, 1964). The signs of the Zodiac are printed in every issue of the *Blood Horse,* a magazine for thoroughbred breeders. Many breeders follow the signs "religiously," while others profess to not really believe them, but admit that they follow the signs when it is convenient. The horse-breeding industry is a high-risk, high-payoff business, with no assurance that a particular horse will be a winner. So agricultural magic is widespread among horsebreeders.

Agricultural magic will probably be practiced for many years in rural areas of the U.S. These folk beliefs will be shared by fewer persons, however. Science, magic, and religion are all present at times of uncertainty. The practice of agricultural magic, such as planting by the signs of the moon, weaning foals by the Zodiac, and participating in rain dances is an individual and collective attempt to reduce uncertainty.

WHY IS RELIGION IMPORTANT?

What does religion do for people? Why do we have it?

1. *Relief of fear and anxiety.* All individuals have experienced fear for their life or the life of a close friend or relative. A soldier in combat may promise to devote his life to religion if he returns home safely. When we are uncertain about the outcome of a particular event, we look to religion for an explanation. In this sense, religion serves a need similar to that served by agricultural magic.

2. *Self-justification and moral identity.* We seek order out of chaos. Each individual looks for some rationale or justification for personal or group suffering. Religion and belief in a life hereafter provide such meaning and help people develop explanations and justifications for individual life situations.

3. *Explaining the unknown.* Religion may explain what cannot be explained by science. Religion and science are not necessarily at odds because where scientific knowledge ends, religion often takes over (at least for many individuals). "The less we know, the more magic we invent to explain it" (Malinowski, 1944 p. 14). Religion provides an answer for unknowns, and through these answers provides a rationale and a justification for life.

4. *Agency of social control.* The church has traditionally supported other established social institutions in which it operates (such as government and the economic system). Religion serves as a mechanism of social control, as a means of

enforcing norms. The organized church usually supports the status quo and opposes radical change. However, in Third World countries like Iran, the Islamic faith supported revolutionary social change.

5. *Other functions of the church.* What specific services does the church provide to its members? It teaches religious doctrine, encourages its members to follow this doctrine, provides a physical structure for religious activities, carries on welfare and recreational activities, provides counseling services to its members, and influences the larger society in religious and moral beliefs (Durkheim, 1912/1965). In recent years, the church in the United States has become involved in certain social issues, such as nuclear disarmament, abortion, and apartheid.

RELIGION AND SOCIAL VALUES

Major religions are important in determining the basic attitudes and values of individuals. An example occurred when Protestantism split off from the Catholic Church in Europe 450 years ago. Max Weber, a German sociologist who also studied modern-day bureaucracies (Chapter 5), hypothesized that the Protestant revolt and the rise of capitalism (which occurred at the same time, during the Renaissance) marked important, basic changes in such values as the emphasis on hard work, economic initiative, competition, acquisition of wealth, and individualism. The new ideology, commonly referred to as "the Protestant ethic," was part of the teachings of Martin Luther, John Calvin, and other Protestant leaders. Individual communion with God was stressed as a means of repentance and salvation. Early Protestant theology taught that the way to salvation was through one's efforts while on earth, emphasizing hard work and personal striving. Individuals engaged in business and industry who worked hard and accumulated wealth were favored by the early Protestant religions and tended to be attracted to Protestantism.

The Protestant religious values were functional for economic development. "National or religious minorities which are in a position of subordination to a group of rules are likely, through their voluntary exclusion from positions of political influence, to be driven with peculiar force into economic activity" (Weber, 1904/1958). Examples were the Jews in Central Europe, the Huguenots in France, and the European Protestants of the Middle Ages.

"As of 1960, Protestant countries were economically more advanced on the average, even taking their differences in natural resources into account, than were Catholic countries" (McClelland, 1961, p. 53). Religious beliefs encourage different social values, which in turn contribute to economic development. In some respects, Jewish people in the United States represent the original Protestant values of individual striving and pecuniary success better than do most Protestants. The Jains and Parsees in India, the Lebanese in Africa, the Chinese in Thailand, and the Vietnamese in Australia are modern-day examples of the sort of work-orientation found in the tenents of the "Protestant ethic."

The contemporary work ethic is being replaced gradually by a leisure ethic that emphasizes security and leisure rather than work. Individual initiative is replaced by group problem solving. Rural people, and particularly farmers, still hold the work ethic in America. In a survey of attitudes toward work, one of the book's authors found that Ohio farmers were more likely than urban persons to agree that work was important; in fact, many believed that work was a reasonable end in itself. Many farmer respondents felt particularly guilty when they did not spend most of their time working; some even felt guilty when they were on vacation (Burdge, 1961). Persons in higher-status occupations, with more formal education and higher income, and those who belonged to mainline churches (rather than fundamentalist churches), adhered less strongly to the Protestant ethic. They more likely supported a leisure ethic (Burdge, 1961). The work ethic seems to be declining in First World nations (even including Japan), but it lingers on among farmers in most nations.

The examples just discussed illustrate the influence of religion on social values and through these values on economic and other aspects of society.

PARTICIPATION IN THE RURAL CHURCH

A *rural church* is an organization of believers with rural people among its membership. In various other countries, a rural church is called a temple, a mosque, a pagoda, and so forth. In this book, we shall call all of these religious organizations churches.

Rural churches may be located in the open countryside or in villages, towns, or small cities. A Missouri study indicated that about 40 percent of rural churches were located in towns and villages and about 60 percent in the open country (Hassinger and Holik, 1985).

The importance of the church as an institution in the United States is indicated by its large membership. In many states, four times as many people belong to churches as to any other single formal organization. This ratio is generally higher in rural than in urban communities, perhaps because the church has less competition with other activities in rural areas (Samson, 1958). In many declining rural communities, the church is the only institution that has not yet left the community.

While church membership is increasing, North Americans are not necessarily becoming more religious. Nevertheless, the numbers of persons claiming church membership has tripled in the last century. In 1890, 22 percent of the U.S. population were church members. In 1986, 69 percent claimed to be church members (Figure 8-1). Americans have the highest rate of church membership of any of the First World Protestant-dominated countries (Salisbury, 1958, *Yearbook of American Churches,* 1985).

Most rural churches are small. For example, a Missouri study found that

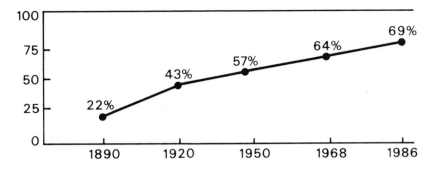

FIGURE 8-1   The trend toward greater church membership in the United States.

Even though the percentage of persons who are church members increased from 22 percent in 1890 to 69 percent in 1986, there is little evidence that people are necessarily more religious in their everyday behavior.

one church in three had less than 50 members (Hassinger and Holik, 1985). The average membership in Missouri rural churches was only 127, with a range from 10 to over 500. In comparison to its urban counterpart, the rural church is generally smaller and more primary in its group relationships (Chapter 5). Church membership is generally higher in rural areas, in part because fewer organizations compete for available free time.

Despite their small membership size, rural churches are an important part of the U.S. church picture. All major religious denominations maintain a "town and country" or "rural" division. About half of all seminaries have rural church departments. The rural church often serves as a training ground for a young minister, who begins his or her career in a rural church and then moves to larger churches. Proportionately more priests and ministers enter the profession from rural than from urban backgrounds. Most rural church pastors serve in the same state in which they were born.

Certain denominations have a greater percentage of rural members than do others: Baptists, Methodists, and Lutherans are examples in the United States. In contrast, about 98 percent of U.S. Jews live in cities, and 80 percent of Roman Catholics are urban (Figure 8-2).

Prior to World War II almost all members of U.S. rural churches were farm families. Today rural nonfarm members dominate. These members work in industrial, service, and information jobs and often have views on many religious issues that are different from those of farmer members.

Women are more active in rural churches than are men. Participation in the rural church is also more characteristic of older people. In a Kentucky study, persons over 65 years of age made up 34 percent of church members but only 23 percent of nonmembers; individuals under 35 years of age made up 19 percent of church members and 33 percent of nonmembers (Kaufman, 1948). In contrast, older persons are much less active in nonchurch formal

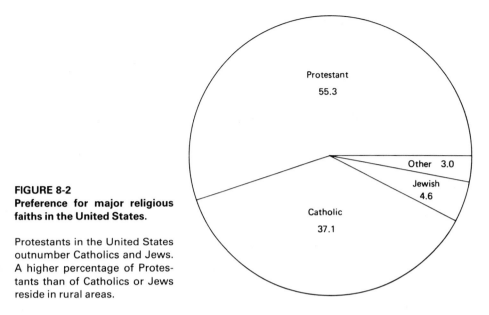

FIGURE 8-2
Preference for major religious
faiths in the United States.

Protestants in the United States
outnumber Catholics and Jews.
A higher percentage of Protestants than of Catholics or Jews
reside in rural areas.

organizations than younger people. Why are older people more active in rural churches? Possible reasons are a growing concern with life after death, the availability of older persons to participate in the daytime activities of the church, special efforts by many churches to appeal to older people, and the lack of involvement of older people in nonchurch activities.

THE ROLE OF THE RURAL CLERGY

The rural clergy, the professional leaders of the church, play a key role in the changes taking place in the rural church (Blizzard, 1956). For many people, the cleric represents the church. What church members think of their church is largely affected by the personality and behavior of their religious leader. The rural cleric plays at least six roles in the community. First is the preacher role, which involves leading the people of the congregation. Second, the pastoral role, counseling members when they need or request it. Third, the role of priest, administering religious rites. Fourth, the role of administrator, insuring order, unity, and efficiency in church affairs. Fifth, the role of pastor, ministering to the needs of the people. Sixth, the role of model family member and leading citizen in home and public life, setting a good example for the rest of the community.

The clergy in rural Missouri churches spent most of their time in the preacher, priestly, and pastor roles (Hassinger and Holik, 1985). Like many farmers, most rural ministers are part-time clerics with another full-time job.

The time spent on administrative and on external activities increased for the clergy who served full time.

In order to be successful, rural clerics must be able to get along well with people and must be part of community life. They must be able to deliver an effective sermon with only a short time for preparation. Rural ministers are often criticized more for the length of their sermon than for its content. The spouse of the rural cleric must be active in the affairs of the church but should not be perceived as running the church (Vidich and Bensman, 1958).

Here is a description of how two rural ministers carry out their duties, based on a Missouri study:

> "*Preacher Ed*" is a minister of a mainline congregation in a county seat town. His congregation recently built a new church building on the outskirts of town. Although Ed is a seminary graduate and theologically sophisticated, he maintains social closeness to the community in dress and behavior. On a summer day, he wears a seed company hat and poplin work trousers, his transportation is a pickup truck, and he affects country-style speech pattern. Although his church members know where he stands on most social and moral issues, Preacher Ed tries not to antagonize his parishioners. He conducts funerals and weddings for nonmembers of his church.
>
> "*Reverend John*" is also a minister for a mainline congregation church in the same town, but does not blend so well into the community's lifestyle. He has recently been assigned by his denomination to the three-congregation parish, and he expects to be moved within a few years. Reverend John's manner is more formal than that of Preacher Ed. A seminary graduate, he gives much of his time to sermon preparation, to the supervision of three church buildings, and to denominational matters. His normal dress is a coat and tie, which sets him apart from most townspeople. Reverend John spends most of his day in his well-equipped church office, or calling on hospital patients and on church members in their homes. (Adapted from Hassinger and Holik, 1985, pp. 124–125. Used by permission of the authors.)

Improved training for rural ministers can contribute to their greater success. Many future clergy receive preseminary training in rural sociology. These students concentrate their course work in both technical agriculture and in sociology (Bertrand, 1959, p. 251). Many state universities and seminaries provide in-service training to rural ministers through short courses, seminars, and conventions. A study of 224 U.S. clerics indicated their greatest need was for training in the social sciences. Over half felt their college training in the social sciences was insufficient.

CHANGES IN THE RURAL CHURCH

Compared to other rural social institutions, the church has been the least likely to change, but some alterations have occurred due to the decline of farm population, and the influx of nonfarm people to rural areas. Among

FIGURE 8-3 **The rural church has been slower to change than other rural institutions.**

This open-country church was built about 1890, when its members traveled to church by horsepower. The modern highway and high-speed automobile are symbolic of the changes in rural life that are affecting the rural church. One of the reasons this open-country rural church remains active is the members' strong attachment to the church graveyard, where many of their relatives are buried.

these changes in the church is the rise of the electronic church, the shift from theological to social functions, and the slowing of church consolidation.

The Electronic Church

No change has influenced the U.S. religious landscape in the 1980s more than the rise of the electronic church. The *electronic church* is an identifiable group of believers who do not meet physically but who receive religious messages through the mass media, especially television. The Reverend Charles Coughlin conducted the first religious programs on radio in the 1930s, and Bishop Fulton J. Sheen commanded a large prime-time television audience in the 1950s. Billy Graham followed in the 1970s. In the 1980s, the Reverends Pat Robertson, Jim Bakker, Jerry Falwell, and Oral Roberts, among others, raised the electronic church to become a powerful influence in

religious, political, and social activities. One consequence is that fundamentalist religious values coupled with right-wing, conservative politics have gained
increased attention.

1. Who watches religious programs on TV?   A 1985 study of TV
ratings by the A. C. Nielsen Company showed that 40 percent of U.S. and
Canadian households with television sets watched one or more of the top 10
syndicated religious broadcasts per month (*Los Angeles Times,* 1985). The
audience for this religious broadcasting was older, poorer, less educated, and
more likely to be a blue-collar worker, black, and from the South than the
average North American. The electronic church audiences are also church
members; they participate in other religious activities, tend to be evangelical
Protestants, and are conservative in their religious beliefs and values (Gaddy
and Pritchard, 1985, p. 124).

2. What is the growth rate of the electronic church?   In 1981 electronic preachers for the top four television programs grossed $240 million
through contributions in response to over-the-air appeals, with the Reverend
Jimmy Swaggart collecting $60 million (Abelman and Neuendorf, 1985, p.
110). The Christian Broadcast Network (CBN) own four television stations,
five FM radio stations, and uses a twenty-four-hour-a-day transponder on the
Satcom III R satellite and the latest in computerized production facilities. In
1983 there were 65 religious television stations; two years later, the number
had increased to 92 (Dart, 1985). The Mormon Church has purchased its own
cable TV channel, and Catholic and Jewish programs are now regularly fea-
tured on religious stations.

The growth and continued success of the electronic church depends
upon a steady flow of money from the public. In addition to the broadcast,
appeals for money are made through mail solicitation campaigns. One researcher analyzed 45 letters from different religious broadcasting organizations and found that only four mentioned the religious conversion experiences, while 44 asked for money (Horsfield, 1985, p. 96).

*3. What impact has the electronic church had on rural congrega-
tions?*   A 30-year study of the Missouri rural church showed little change in
the total number of rural churches. However, the number of fundamentalist
congregations had increased, while the number of mainline churches declined, due primarily to merger (Hassinger and Holik, 1985, p. 39). The
religious values espoused by the fundamentalist churches were in line with the
electronic preachers. The increase in U.S. rural fundamentalism has paral-
leled the increase in the number of electronic religious programs.

The electronic church is taking the place of regular church attendance.
Mailings from the electronic church seldom encourage local church attendance or give the name of a specific church (Horsfield, 1985, p. 96). Only one

in eight of the top 30 religious TV programs mentioned local church attendance (Abelman and Neuendorf, 1985, p. 106). Electronic programs were directed at building up their own organization, rather than encouraging attendance at a local church. So, to a certain extent, the two religious approaches are in competition.

4. How are political values mixed with religious content?   The most profound change caused by the electronic church of the 1980s is the mixing of political and religious issues. A Virginia sociologist pointed out, "The pace at which religious broadcasters have moved to define the public agenda is astounding . . . the underlying conservative mood of American culture owes much of its sustaining, driving focus to the electronic evangelists" (*Los Angeles Times,* October 26, 1985). A content analysis of religious television showed that 26 per cent of the content was devoted to political and social issues (Abelman and Neuendorf, 1985, p.110).

The Politicalization of Religion

In recent decades the church in America has increasingly taken stands on social and political issues. One example is the role of the Catholic Church on birth control and abortion. Some priests and other Catholic Church leaders feel that birth control must be permitted in order to limit population growth rates in Third World countries, but the Vatican remains firm in its opposition to contraception. The church increasingly takes a stand on certain social and political issues, although the Pope feels this activity is an inappropriate role for the Catholic Church. Racial integration is favored by most rural churches, even when they have an all-white membership (Hassinger and Holik, 1985). A content analysis of religious television programs found that 74 percent of the air time was devoted to religious themes, with 24 percent concerned with such social issues as abortion, school prayer, and family planning. Two percent of television time was devoted to direct political appeals to support a particular issue (Abelman and Neuendorf, 1985).

In the past, the separation of church and state meant that churches generally avoided direct involvement in U.S. politics. However, clergy became involved in social and political issues during the civil rights movement of the 1950s and 1960s. The Reverends Jesse Jackson and Pat Robertson have conducted national presidential campaigns. In the election of 1980, the Moral Majority claimed to have defeated five influential U.S. senators who were liberal Democrats, mainly through hate campaigns. Reverend Jerry Falwell's Moral Majority (and its sequel, the Liberty Foundation in the mid-1980s) represents a direct attempt by the electronic church to promote conservative political issues (Young, 1982, p. 95). "People for the American Way" was founded to act as a watchdog over the new religious right, and specifically as a countermeasure to the Moral Majority (People for *the American Way,* 1980).

In part due to television broadcasting, the U.S. church has become directly involved in political issues.

Trends In Church Consolidation

The trend in the United States and Canada had been toward consolidating several small churches into one larger church. However, in the 1980s, consolidation has slowed. A Missouri study found that in many rural areas, the church is the only social institution left. Schools, health facilities, and businesses have consolidated into larger units. Despite the importance of the church to rural communities, there are too many churches in rural areas for the number of people. Improved transportation and farm depopulation caused a chronic oversupply of churches in many areas. An important factor for rural overchurching is competition among different religious denominations (Blume and Hepple, 1960).

The rural church is often the local institution most resistant to social change in society. The religious institution retains past values. The cemetery where grandfather was buried holds great sentimental value, and rural church cemeteries often act to slow church consolidation. Rural churches do not consolidate as rapidly as other rural institutions. In one Midwestern U.S. county, there were 87 schools and 85 churches in 1900 (Hassinger and Holik, 1985). Sixty years later, there were only three schools, but there were still 73 churches. The typical school is a much more centralized organization than the typical church, which is relatively more participative. Strong pressure for consolidation have seldom come from high-level church authorities, and when it has, local churches have sometimes ignored it.

Some denominations are relatively more centralized in their church organization than are others. The Lutheran, Episcopal, and Roman Catholic churches are more centralized than the Quakers, Baptists, and most fundamentalist churches. Congregationalists, Methodists, Mormons, Presbyterians, and other denominations fall somewhere between the extremes on this centralized-decentralized continuum. More centralized denominations have progressed further in church consolidation than have more participative denominations. For example, the average Roman Catholic and Lutheran rural church has a larger church membership than does the typical Methodist or Baptist rural church.

Types of Church Consolidation

Between 1952 and 1982, about one-fourth of the original Missouri rural churches ceased operations. Forty percent went through some type of merger. Church consolidations are of four types (Samson, 1958):

1. The *larger parish* is a plan of cooperation and joint activity among several churches in an area in order to have a mutually approved religious program. Each of the participating churches maintains its own building and treasury, but

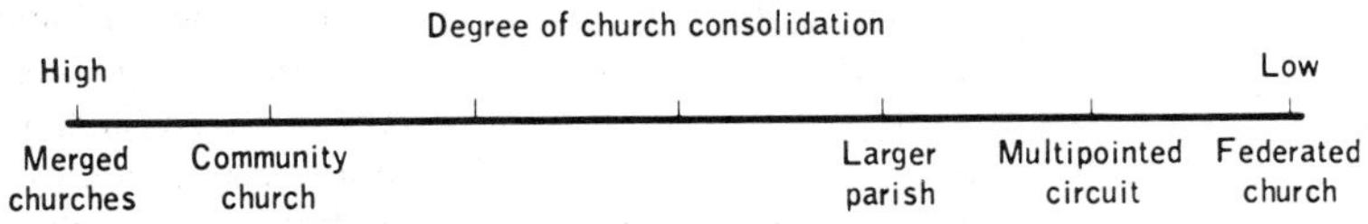

Degree of church consolidation

High   Low

Merged	Community				Larger	Multipointed	Federated
churches	church				parish	circuit	church

FIGURE 8-4   Different types of church consolidation.

> In a federated church, the member churches give up a little of their previous
> autonomy and independence; they only cooperate in hiring a cleric and in
> sharing a common church building. At the other end of the continuum is the
> merged church, in which complete consolidation has occurred. Sometimes
> two separate local churches may form a federation, then after many years
> become a community church, and finally merge. Thus, over a period of
> years, several local churches may gradually move on the continuum in the
> direction of a higher degree of consolidation.

each also contributes to a larger parish budget and sends representatives to a
larger parish council. Clergy and other professional religious workers are employed by the larger parish. Church services are usually held at each of the local
church buildings; youth activities and women's auxiliary meetings, however,
may be on a larger parish basis. All of the local churches involved in a larger
parish are usually of the same denomination.

2. A type of church consolidation requiring somewhat less integration of member
   churches is the *multipointed circuit*, which is also called the *yoked field* by
   certain denominations. The multipointed circuit plan enables one cleric to
   serve two or more churches; each of these local churches maintains its own
   independence and only cooperates in the hiring of clergy. This individual is like
   the circuit-riding ministers of the past. The member churches are usually of the
   same denomination.

3. The *federated church* consists of two or more congregations of different denominations which usually share the same church building, employ a single pastor,
   and carry on a mutual religious program. However, each congregation maintains
   its separate identity and its denominational connection. Each of the congregations has its own church board and treasury; separate collection plates are usually passed for each of the congregations, even when they meet in the same
   church services. In one area of rural Australia, the Catholic priest conducts mass
   once a month in the Protestant Anglican church.

4. The *community church* or *nondenominational church* is a local church that is not
   affiliated with any particular denomination. The membership of the community
   church previously may have been members of various denominations, but there
   may not be enough members of any one denomination in the community to
   support a church of that faith. A frequent problem for community churches is to
   secure a pastor and to select hymn books and other materials, which usually are
   of a denominational nature (Figure 8-4).

BOX 8-2   *HOW DO NEW RELIGIONS BEGIN? THE SHAKERS*

The case of how the Shaker religion was founded helps us better understand
how a new denomination is formed. The Shakers, an off-shoot of the Quakers,
were founded by Ann Lee in Manchester, England, in about 1774. Ann Lee and

eight followers migrated to the United States because of her visionary experience. The name "Shakers" is a shortened version of "Shaking Quakers," appropriate because wild singing and frantic dancing characterized Shaker meetings. The Shakers began as a protest movement that objected to certain social problems in England. This protest movement soon became more formally institutionalized, acquired a name, and held regular services.

The Shakers reached a membership peak of about 6,000 in 18 communities at the time of the Civil War. Shakers did not believe in sexual intercourse. Ann Lee, in a vision while she was in an English jail, became convinced that sex was the cardinal sin. To minimize the mingling of the sexes, Shaker houses had separate doors and stairs for men and women. New members were acquired only by conversion. If, somehow, a Shaker boy and girl fell in love, they were put on probation for six months. Then, if they still wished to marry, they were sent into the "world" with a sack of flour, a horse, $100, and a blessing. "Brothers" and "sisters" ate in the same dining room, but at separate tables, and they never touched, even during the spirited Shaker dances which provided a recreational outlet in addition to having religious meaning.

The Shakers are credited with such innovations as the clothes pin, the flat broom, and the buzz saw. Today, only one Shaker community with eight members exists. The women live quietly, enjoying television and such old-fashioned pleasures as sorting cranberries and gossiping. A Shaker community has been restored near Lexington, Kentucky, as a historical curiosity.

The case of the Shakers shows that many churches begin as a social movement, led by a charismatic leader.

What Is a Sect?

In addition to religious denominations, there are religious sects. What are sects?

Sects are expanding rapidly in the United States. A *sect* is an uninstitutionalized church. Table 8-1 lists several characteristics that distinguish a sect from a church. The sect is generally at odds with its social environment (Johnson, 1963). In this textbook, we use the term *sect* to refer to an uninstitutionalized church in which most members share a fundamentalist view.

Fundamentalist churches are very important in rural areas. In rural Missouri from 1967 to 1982, the number of fundamentalist congregations increased from 27 to 32 percent (Hassinger and Holik, 1985). Fundamentalist clergy have much less formal religious training and lower salaries than do clergy in more institutionalized churches.

Who Belongs to Sects?

About 20 million people belong to fundamentalist religions in the United States and Canada. An estimated 60 million people belong to fundamentalist churches in the rest of the world. Members of sects have lower social

TABLE 8-1   Characteristics of Mainline and Fundamentalist Churches

FUNDAMENTALIST CHURCHES	MAINLINE CHURCHES
1. Untrained, part-time clerics	1. Trained, professional clerics
2. Lower class members	2. Generally middle-class members
3. Spontaneous and fervent participation of members in church services	3. Restrained and passive participation of members in formalized church services
4. Evangelism of adults as the source of new members; a feeling that one must be saved	4. Education of children in Sunday schools as the source of new members
5. Simple church organization, occasional Sunday school	5. Most administrative decisions made by a hierarchy of church officials or lay leaders
6. Appeals mainly to the emotions of members	6. Appeals more to the intellects of members
7. Acceptance of fundamentalist social values	7. Acceptance of dominant social values

status than members of mainline churches. Sect members attend services more often than do other church members, and are more likely to watch electronic religion programs. The closest friends of sect members are usually found within their religious group (Dynes, 1957).

The sect may serve as a kind of cultural cushion for individuals who move from urban to rural areas; the fundamentalist church provides a responsive primary group to ease the shock of personal adjustment.

THE INSTITUTIONALIZATION PROCESS: FROM FUNDAMENTALIST TO MAINLINE

Many of today's established denominations began as pentecostal sects with an untrained but zealous ministry and a lower-class following. Gradually, a sect moves toward becoming a church as it climbs the ladder of respectability, develops seminaries and a trained ministry, and sets up youth training (such as Sunday schools) to provide future membership (Hassinger and Holik, 1985). Survival becomes a dominant goal. In short, the sect may become institutionalized into a church (Figure 8-6). As defined in Chapter 5, *institutionalization* is the process through which a relatively simple, informal grouping becomes a recognized and formalized institution.

The Methodist Church in the United States is an example of a religious sect that became institutionalized into a church. Methodism began as a radical dissenting sect in England. When leaders of the sect came to the United States, they wished to gain converts. They needed to coordinate their efforts, and to raise funds for their work. This emphasis caused a shift from spiritual

FIGURE 8-5 A Pentecostal religious sect in Kentucky includes the handling of poisonous snakes in its services.

Despite the outlawing of snake-handling in several states, this practice continues. Worshippers believe that handling snakes, usually rattlesnakes and copperheads, demonstrates their religious faith. The man in the picture was bitten, but recovered. When a snake-handler is bitten, it is considered as due to a momentary lapse of faith. The snake-handling cult shown here is in the hill country of Appalachia; services are extremely emotional; members shuffle, hop, skip, and sing while praying.

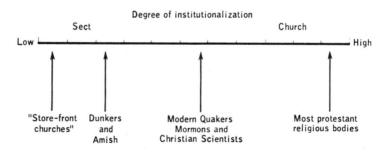

FIGURE 8-6 Continuum of institutionalization of religious bodies.

Institutionalization is the process through which relatively simple groupings become recognized institutions. Many denominations began as sects, with a zealous but untrained ministry and a lower-class membership. They gradually climbed the ladder of respectability, developed seminaries and educated clergy, and set up Sunday schools to provide future membership.

enthusiasm to more worldly concerns. Efforts to organize were successful, and the Methodist Church grew large and powerful. The growing institutional- ization of the Methodist Church shifted its appeal to higher social status individuals. Thus Methodism became institutionalized into a church.

FUTURE OF THE RURAL CHURCH

Further mergers may be required if the rural church is to continue as a viable institution. Although a major block to church mergers is their graveyards, the U.S. Corps of Engineers, in relocating people for reservoir construction, has found that rural people will generally accept the idea of bringing all the cemeteries together in one area (Korsching, et al., 1980). Rural churches may be able to merge if their cemeteries are consolidated.

Better-trained clergy are needed for rural churches but cannot be justi- fied on the basis of small congregations competing with other small congrega- tions for members from a static population base. It is also difficult to convince clergy to remain in rural areas.

The rural church has persisted and survived in an otherwise rapidly changing rural society. Local schools have consolidated and moved out of the community. Local medical services have been largely displaced by larger service centers and are now highlighted by an occasional visit of a doctor to the community. So, too, community businesses have closed due to their slump- ing sales. In an era of so many lost services, rural churches may be assuming greater importance as rural community institutions. They have remained lo- cally oriented and dependent because they are organized in a time of change to meet local needs. Because they exhibit primary group activities for local people, they will persist. Long-term studies show that rural churches are as popular as ever (Hassinger and Holik, 1985).

SUMMARY

Religion is a belief in a supernatural power which helps people to distinguish between right and wrong and which provides answers to some of life's ulti- mate problems. A *church* is an organization of believers having a common faith and a common creed.

Agricultural magic is composed of those farming beliefs and practices that lack scientific explanation. Examples are witching for water and planting crops by the signs of the moon. Agricultural magic is used when decision are important but uncertain.

Important changes taking place in the rural church include the politicalization of religion through the institutionalization of the electronic church, increased politicalization of the church, and the gradual slowing of church consolidation. The number of rural churches in North America has not declined appreciably in recent years. Rural churches are generally slower to adjust to social changes than are schools, businesses, and other social institutions. Forms of partial church consolidation are the community church, the larger parish, the multipointed circuit, and the federated church.

Major problems of the rural church include small membership, lack of financial support, unqualified clergy, and inadequate church programs. The rural church will continue as one of the most important, if not the most important, institution in many' rural communities.

REFERENCES

ABELMAN, ROBERT, and KIMBERLY NEUENDORF. (1985). "How Religious Is Religious Programming" *Journal of Communication*, pp. 98–110.

BERTRAND, ALVIN L. (1959). *Rural Sociology*. New York: McGraw-Hill.

BLIZZARD, SAMUEL W. (1956) "The Role of the Rural Parish Minister," *Christian Century,* April 25, pp. 508–509.

BLUME, GEORGE T., and LAWRENCE M. HEPPLE. (1960). Part VI, *Spatial and Social Relationships,* Columbia, MO: Agr. Exp. Sta. Bull. 633F, p.?

BURDGE, RABEL J. (1961). "The Protestant Ethic and Leisure-Orientation." Paper presented at the Ohio Valley Sociological Society, Cleveland.

CAPLOW, THEODORE, HOWARD BAHR, and BRUCE A. CHADWICK. (1983). *All Faithful People: Change and Continuity in Middletown's Religion.* Minneapolis: University of Minnesota Press.

COUGHENOUR, MILTON, and LAWRENCE M. HEPPLE. (1957). *The Church in Rural Missouri.* Columbia, MO: Agr. Exp. Sta. Res. Bull. 633B.

DART, JOHN. (1985, February 9). "Growth of TV Ministries Translates into Clout." *Los Angeles Times,* Part II, p. 5.

DURKHEIM, E. (1965). "The Elementary Forms of Religious Life." New York: The Free Press. Originally published in 1912.

DYNES, RUSSELL R. (1955). "Church-Sect Typology and Socio-Economic Status." *American Sociological Review, 20,* 557–560.

DYNES, RUSSELL R. (1956). "Rurality, Migration and Sectarianism." *Rural Sociology, 21,* 25–28.

DYNES, RUSSELL R. (1957). "The Consequences of Sectarianism for Social Participation." *Social Forces, 35,* 331–334.

ELLIS, ARTHUR J. (1917). *The Divining Rod: A History of Water-Witching.* Washington, DC: U.S. Geological Survey, Water Paper 416.

GADDY, GARY D., and DAVID PRITCHARD. (1985). "When Watching Religious TV Is Like Attending Church." *Journal of Communication*, pp. 123–131.

HASSINGER, EDWARD W., and HOLIK, JOHN S. (1985). "The Church in Rural Missouri." Unpublished manuscript, Department of Rural Sociology and Missouri Agricultural Experiment Station, Columbia.

HASSINGER, EDWARD W. and JOHN S. HOLIK. (1985). "Changes in the Rural Church in Missouri", Unpublished Manuscript, University of Missouri-Columbia. A 30-year-update of *The Rural Church in Missouri,* published in seven parts with various authorships. Columbia, MO: Missouri Agricultural Experiment Station Research Bulletins 633a (1957); 633b (1957); 633c (1958); 633d (1959); 633e (1959); 633f (1960).

HORSFIELD, PETER G. (1985). "Evangelism by Mail: Letters from Broadcasters." *Journal of Communications,* 89–97.

HYMAN, RAY, and ELIZABETH G. COHEN. (1957). "Water-Witching in the United States." *American Sociological Review, 22,* 719–724.

JOHNSON, BENTON. (1963). "On Church and Sect." *American Sociological Review, 28,* 539–549.

KAUFMAN, HAROLD F. (1948). *Religious Organizations in Kentucky.* Lexington, KY: Agr. Exp. Sta. Bull. 524.

KORSCHING, PETER F., JOSEPH F. DONNERMEYER, and RABEL J. BURDGE. (1980). "Perception of Housing and Property Settlement Among Displaced Persons." *Human Organization, 39,* 332–338.

LANDIS, BENSON Y. (1967). "Trends in Church Membership in the United States." In Richard D. Knudten, ed. *The Sociology of Religion.* New York: Appleton-Century-Crofts, p. 528.

LOS ANGELES TIMES, (1985, October 26), p. 9.

MALINOWSKI, BRONISLAW. (1948). *Magic, Science and Religion and Other Essays.* Boston: Beacon House, p. 14.

MCCLELLAND, DAVID C. (1961). *The Achieving Society,* Princeton, NJ:?p. 53.

MEINZER, O.E. (1944). "U.S. Ground Water Geologist Warns Against Water Diviners." *Waterworks Engineering, 97,* 571.

People for the American Way. (1980). Untitled brochure. Washington, DC.

ROOF, WADE CLARK. (1976). "Traditional Religion in Contemporary Society." *American Sociological Review, 41,* 197.

SALISBURY, W. SEWARD. (1958). "Religion and Secularization." *Social Forces, 36,* 197–205.

SAMSON, A'DELBERT. (1958). *Church Groups in Four Agricultural Settings in Montana.* Bozeman, MT: Agr. Exp. Sta. Bull. 538, p. 3.

STONE, CHARLES H. (1964). "The Sign." *The Blood-Horse, 87,* 432.

VIDICH, ARTHUR, and JOSEPH BENSMAN. (1958). *Small Town in Mass Society.* Princeton, NJ: Princeton University Press.

VOGT, EVON Z. (1952). "Water-Witching: An Interpretation of a Ritual Pattern in a Rural American Community." *Scientific Monthly, 75,* 185–186.

VOGT, EVON Z., and RAY HYMAN. (1959). *Water Witching, U.S.A.* Chicago: University of Chicago Press.

WEBER, MAX. (1958). *The Protestant Ethic and the Spirit of Capitalism.* New York: Scribner, p. 39. Originally published in 1904.

WILSON, JOHN F. (1979). *Public Religion in American Culture.* Philadelphia: Temple University Press.

YEARBOOK OF AMERICAN CHURCHES, 1985. % Information Services, American Council of Churches, NV, NY.

YOUNG, PERRY DUANE. (1982). *God's Bullies: Native Reflections on Preachers and Politics.* New York: Holt, Rinehart and Winston.

Chapter 9

Rural Families

- Single person households account for nearly one-fourth of all households in U.S. society.
- One study estimated that 20 percent of children in U.S. society live in single parent households. About half of all children today have a chance of living in a single parent household before they reach the age of 18 years.
- Another study concluded that the average daily time parents and children spend communicating has declined to less than 15 minutes.
- Average life expectancy for a person born in 1900 was 47 years. Today average life expectancy is over 73 years.

The sociological nature of the family is important to understand because virtually every person in the world is a member of a family group, and because in most cultures, the family is a small primary group (Chapter 5) that plays a key role in socialization. The family teaches children a culture's beliefs, norms, values, and attitudes. Even in modern societies like the United States, where the family has lost many of its traditional functions, it is mainly responsible for socialization and personality development. Early lessons on personal values and attitudes are still taught in the family.

In Chapter 2, we identified the family as a *cultural universal* because it has existed in some form or in every culture throughout history. There have always been standard or expected ways of reproducing the next generation and of caring for and rearing children. However, specific human arrangements for fulfillment of these basic functions varies greatly between societies.

DEFINITION OF THE FAMILY

Before defining what a family is, consider first the concept of a *household*. In the United States every ten years, the U.S. Department of Commerce (through its Bureau of the Census) conducts a census or complete enumeration of the nation's population. However, the U.S. Bureau of the Census does more than count every member of U.S. society. Information on age, occupation, ethnicity, household characteristics, and many other types of information are collected.

According to the most recent census, there were over 80 million households out of a total population of nearly 227 million in the United States. The U.S. Bureau of the Census defines a household as "all persons who occupy a housing unit," such as a house, apartment, or any other living arrangement in which "separate living quarters" are maintained.

A household may include only one person, and in fact one person households are on the increase. Another type of household consists of two or more people who are not related by marriage or kinship but share the same living quarters. These include both heterosexual and homosexual living arrangements. Households of this type also are increasing in U.S. society.

FIGURE 9-1 The traditional concept of the American family—husband, wife and children—represents less than one-third of all households in the United States today.

Source: Horton and Hunt, 1984, p. 244.

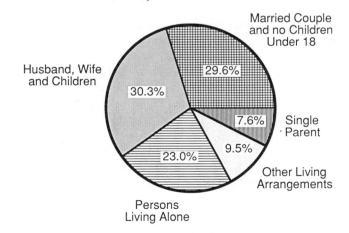

The traditional concept of the family—parents and children—represents a minority of American households today. Married couples without children, single parent households, and married couples with children are most prevalent in U.S. society.

The *family* is unique among all the social institutions because it is both a social unit and a biological unit. The U.S. Bureau of the Census defines a family household as "one or more persons living in the same household who are related by birth, marriage, or adoption." As a social unit, the family is that human group responsible for socializing and rearing the young. It is a primary group in which the members interact on a face-to-face basis, and whose members are tied together by virtue of marriage, common parentage, or adoption.

The family may range from a single member to many members; from a "young urban professional" (yuppie) who purposely pursues a single lifestyle, to households with three generations of parents, grandparents, children, and a host of other kin or relatives, all living under the same roof. The family in U.S. society and other cultures displays great diversity.

FUNCTIONS OF THE FAMILY

The family performs six basic functions. The first and most obvious function of the family is replacement of members through reproduction. Although the reproduction function remains firmly in the grasp of the family, many futurists suggests that this responsibility will one day shift to the state. Advances in medical technology and genetic research have already produced "test-tube" babies and "surrogate mothers." Futurists see a time when children are scientifically bred, and the fetus developed totally outside the mother's womb. How will these technological possibilities affect the family and society (Horton and Hunt, 1984, p. 238)?

A second important function is the regulation of sexual behavior. Every culture has a series of *prescriptive* and *proscriptive* norms (Chapter 2) associated with sexual relations, and it is normally through the family as a small primary group that these norms are expressed and enforced. In most Western societies, sexual relations are considered to be proper only between a husband and wife. Adultery and premarital sex are not considered proper, although our attitudes about these have changed in recent decades.

A third function of the family is economic. In primitive societies, the family is the sole economic unit, that is, through families, all food, goods, and services necessary for survival are produced, and the well-being of dependents (children, the elderly, the ill, and the disabled) are provided for. In more complex societies like the United States, much of the economic function has been taken over by other institutions. Goods and services are produced by businesses and factories, and government has assumed a large part of the responsibility for the welfare of dependents.

FIGURE 9-2   The nuclear family is the predominant type in Western societies. Extended families are most frequently found in other parts of the world.

Yet, even in more complex societies, the family has some economic responsibility. Husbands and wives work, receive wages, and purchase goods and services necessary for daily living. The modern family is a consumer rather than a producer.

A fourth function of the family is the ascription of status. Ascribed status was defined as status assigned on the basis of inheritance, birth, and physical characteristics over which the individual has no control (Chapter 4). In certain societies, like Great Britain, social class standing is largely inherited. One's social rank is determined by the social standing of the family into which one is born. Even in the United States, where social mobility is highly valued, the offspring of lower class parents are less likely to "rise to the top" than are the offspring of upper class parents. The relative income or wealth of a family affects the opportunities available to the offspring by affecting where they go to school, who they know, and of course, their inherited wealth (Horton and Hunt, 1984, p. 242).

Within the rural sector of U.S. society, ascription of status is very important in selection of farming as an occupation. Research has consistently found that only sons and daughters of farmers have strong aspirations to farm. The high capital costs of entering farming and the economic uncertainty of farm prices deter many farm youth from farming. The prospects of inheriting a farm or marrying into one allow some farm youth to enter agriculture (Lyson, 1981; Molnar and Dunkelberger, 1981).

The fifth function of the family is socialization of the young. In modern societies, the family shares the function of socialization. Schools, day care centers, the peer group, the mass media, among others influences, are also

FIGURE 9-3 Many sons and daughters become farmers themselves because they learn life roles by being with their parents each day. Family sociologists maintain that farm families are closely knit.

involved. Some social scientists even would argue that the family has lost its preeminence as a socializing agency. For example, one study indicates that in U.S. society the amount of time spent by parents and children together each day has fallen precipitously, from more than three hours to less than one hour. A large share of "quality" time is spent passively watching television in the same room, leaving the actual amount of time parents and children spend in conversation to as little as 15 minutes (Glenn, 1980).

In contemporary U.S. society, socialization is the shared responsibility of several institutions. However, the beliefs, values, norms, and attitudes that they transmit may not always be compatible. For example, in Chapter 2 we discussed "norms of evasion" and the difference between "ideal" and "real" patterns of culture. Very often, what is transmitted by the family (as well as educational and religious agencies) is in conflict with what is transmitted by the peer group or by the mass media. Norms having to do with such activities as drug use, premarital sex and alcohol consumption represent some of these issues. In each case, what is proscribed by the adult culture is often prescribed by the peer culture.

The final function of the family is emotional support. In U.S. society, as the family became less important for many functions, it has grown in its importance for emotional support. Chapter 5 described the social changes in U.S. society and in local communities from primary group relationships to secondary group relationships. This shift is part of the transformation from an agricultural to an industrial society. The family today remains one of the few social institutions mainly functioning to provide long-term, intimate, and emotional relationships.

FAMILY CONCEPTS

A wide variety of family behavior is found in different societies ranging from wife sharing among the Koryak Eskimo tribe to the couvade (a practice in which the father remains in bed with a newborn baby while the mother resumes her usual duties) in several American Indian tribes. Here we shall look at family behavior in various cultures to illustrate important family concepts.

Family Composition

In contemporary U.S. society, the predominant composition of the family is *nuclear*. The word nuclear in reference to the family means *core* or *nucleus*. Hence, the *nuclear family* is a family made up only of parents and their offspring (until they marry). The *conjugal* family is related by marriage, blood, or some legal form of adoption. The conjugal family is similar to the nuclear family. It consists of one or two generations. The nuclear family does not include either aged relatives or married children.

The usual type of nuclear family in U.S. society is a husband, wife, and one or more children. However, the latest census found that this type of nuclear family represented only 30 percent of all households. Other types of nuclear families include the husband and wife with no children (29 percent of all households), and one parent with one or more children (7 percent of all families). This latter type is called a single parent family. Persons living alone make up 23 percent of all households.

Single parent families have been increasing over the past 25 years. One study estimated that 20 percent of children in U.S. society live in single parent households. Half of all children today have a chance of living in a single parent household before they reach 18 years of age. Increasing also in U.S. society are *compound families,* in which the children are not related by blood to one of the parents. Compound families are the result of divorce or death of a spouse and remarriage (Horton and Hunt, 1984, p. 240).

About 8 percent of all contemporary U.S. families are not nuclear in composition. These *extended families* consist of the husband, wife, and offspring, plus additional relatives such as grandparents, aunts, uncles, cousins, and so on, who share the same residence. Most Amish families (Chapter 2) are extended in that the grandparents live with one of their married sons. The Hopi Indians in Northeastern Arizona also have extended families, but with a different arrangement than the Amish. The Hopi extended family is arranged along maternal lines and consists of the grandmother and her married daughters, their husbands, and their children.

The United States has made the transition from an agricultural society to an urban, industrial, service-oriented society. This transition was accompanied by a change in the predominant type of family composition from extended to nuclear. In contrast to colonial times, most U.S. families today consist only of one or two generations.

FIGURE 9-4
Traditional weddings remain popular among U.S. families. The family has survived many changes and continues as a basic unit of social organization.

Marriage Patterns

In most societies, marriage patterns are *monogamous:* one woman married to one man. However, many cultures allow multiple marriage partners. This is called *polygamy.*

The practice of polygyny (in which one man is married to two or more women), once common in the Mormon Church, has long since been banned (it is also illegal in all 50 states); however, a few polygamous settlements remain. Colorado City, Arizona, an isolated desert town of 1,700 population near the Utah border, is a community of conservative Mormons who still practice polygyny. The founder and leader of the town, LeRoy Johnson, who died in 1987, married for the sixteenth time at the age of 98. Thirteen of his wives still are living. Some scholars estimate that perhaps as many as 50,000 people in the United States practice polygamy (mainly polygyny); they live primarily in rural areas of Arizona, California, and Utah (*Wall Street Jornal,* 1985, pp. 1, 15).

In a few societies the wife has two or more husbands. This cultural practice is called *polyandry.* The Toda tribe who live in the Nilgiri Hills of southern India is one such example. The arrangement is that when the eldest brother marries, his wife is considered to be the wife of all his brothers. These marriages, usually arranged during childhood by the parents, are often between cousins. Of the few cases of polyandry known to exist in the world today, most are arrangements in which the woman marries the eldest brother and all of his younger male siblings (Steward, 1976).

With either polygyny or polyandry, an excess number of unmarried adults occurs. The excessive number of unmarried females among the Toda was balanced in the past by the practice of female infanticide (similar to the Yanamano tribe described in Chapter 2). Now the practice of female infanticide has declined and it is customary for the younger brothers to marry and bring their wives into the household. This modification of the traditional polyandrous arrangement results in a group marriage.

Group marriage, in which several men and women are married without a consistent or definite pairing up, is very rare today. The Koryak, an Eskimo tribe, has an unusual practice of wife-sharing. When a guest visits a Koryak home he may be invited to have sexual intercourse with the host's wife. Failure to do so is considered an insult to the wife, and may result in the beating of the "impolite" guest to death by the "outraged" husband.

One *cultural universal* in connection with the family is the *incest taboo,* which prohibits marriage or sexual intercourse between certain relatives, such as brothers and sister, parents and children. A taboo is a proscriptive norm, and violating its expectations brings the most serious consequences. The marriage of first cousins in the United States is permitted in about 20 states, but is generally discouraged even in those states where it is permitted. The Amish, on the other hand, frequently marry their cousins.

Beyond norms restricting marriage and sexual relations between close relatives, there are norms that regulate which persons are eligible marriage partners for a given individual. In some cultures, eligible partners are limited to persons inside a specified group. This is *endogamy*.

U.S. society is endogamous in marriage across racial, religious, and social class lines. For example, marriage between blacks and whites, or between Jews and Protestants, or between the scion of a multi-millionaire and the offspring of a sanitation worker, generally do not happen. On the other hand, U.S. laws forbidding marriage among blood relatives, the high geographic mobility of most individuals, and the ethnic diversity of the population leads to many *exogamous* marriages.

Lineage

In every culture are norms that specify how lines of descent are traced within the family, and how kinship or relations are defined. This is known as *lineage*. The Hopi family is *matrilineal*. The line of descent is traced through the mother; kinship ties through the father are ignored. In a *patrilineal* family, kinship is traced only through the father. Descent traced through both the father and mother is called *bilateral*. In U.S. society, lineage is bilateral, although some aspects are patrilineal since in most families offspring are given the father's surname.

Residence

There are cultural differences that dictate where the newly married couple will live. The Hopi family is matrilocal: The couple moves in with the bride's parents after the wedding ceremony. The Amish represent an example of *patrilocal* residence: the newlyweds reside with the groom's parents. Eventually, the son takes over the farm from the father. The older grandparents then live in a separate-but-connected house on the farmstead, which is called the grandfather house. Most married couples in the United States are *neolocal* (neo = new): They set up a separate residence and live with neither the wife's nor the husband's parents. This new residence reflects the break between the parental families and the newly formed family. Most U.S. couples want independence and separation from their parents.

Authority

Families in different cultures also vary as to who has the family authority. The Amish family is *patriarchal* (archal = ruling); the father makes most of the decisions in the family. The Hopi family is *matriarchal;* the mother is boss. At one time, most U.S. families were more patriarchal, but the trend is toward a more "democratic" or *equalitarian* family in which both mother and father share decision making. Another trend in U.S. society is to allow offspring to have some influence on family decisions. This trend in part reflects the growing number of single parent families.

In most industrial societies, family composition is nuclear, the marriage relationship is monogamous, and the selection of marriage partners is largely exogamous. In many nonindustrialized societies, the family composition is extended, the marriage relationship is more frequently polygamous (but still largely monogamous), and the selection of marriage partners is more endogamous.

Likewise, line of descent, residence, and authority are generally either all mother-centered or else all father-centered. For example, the Hopis are matriarchal, matrilocal, and matrilineal. The Amish family is both patriarchal and patrilocal. The U.S. family is becoming equalitarian, and is neolocal and bilateral.

Cultures also vary in their methods of rearing children. In some cultures, the father plays an important role in the birth of children. Among the Arapesh tribe of New Guinea, both the mother and father must participate in childbirth. The husband lies down at his wife's side and is said to be in bed having a baby. The husband also helps in caring for the young children. If one comments upon a middle-aged male as good-looking, the people will answer, "Good-looking? Yes? But you should have seen him before he bore all those children" (Mead, 1935, p. 39).

A different adult often serves as a role model (Chapter 3) for the growing child in different cultures. In the United States this adult model and disciplinarian is most often the mother. As industrialization and suburbanization increase, the father tends to be gone from the home during most of the hours when children are awake. As more and more mothers enter the work force, the adult model is transferred to school authorities, the employees of day nurseries, and baby-sitters.

One rural-urban difference which remains in force today is that in rural areas the father serves as the adult model to a greater degree, especially in farm families. However, the trend toward part-time farming and suburbanization is changing even this pattern.

FAMILY CHANGES AND TRENDS

The family has undergone vast change in modern society. There are changes in family functions, family composition, family roles, mate selection, and the status of the elderly.

Changes in Family Functions

The family is a cultural universal, as we mentioned earlier. Every known culture has some type of family organization and every family performs the six activities of reproduction, regulation of sexual behavior, economic functions, status ascription, socialization of the young, and emotional support.

The family is losing certain of its functions while gaining others. In most Western societies, as well as most of those making a transition from an agricultural to an industrial society, the family is losing its functions as an economic unit and for socialization of the young. Replacing the family in certain functions are schools and day-care centers, the peer group, police and courts, and television. Paralleling the loss of several functions by the American family is its increasing importance for emotional support.

Changes in Family Composition

The size of the typical family in the United States has decreased considerably in the past 200 years. In 1790, the average number of household members was 5.9. This average decreased to 5.0 in 1890. By 1940, family size was 3.8 and by 1980 had slipped to 2.9 persons.

The reasons for the decrease in family size are many. More people now defer marriage and children in order to establish careers. In U.S. society, most older people no longer live with their adult children. They live independently or are institutionalized in nursing homes. More married couples utilize birth control methods in order to limit their family size. Children are no longer valued as an economic asset, that is, as labor or contributors to the family income. Finally, married couples now prefer fewer children (Babbie, 1982).

The size of the farm family is larger than its rural nonfarm or urban counterparts. Offspring are valued as labor for the farm operation, and farm children are generally assigned chores and various responsibilities at an early age. Cultural expectations of American farm families are that one of the children will take over the farm from the parents.

A rural sociological study in Illinois found that planning for the transfer of responsibility for the farm from one generation to the next also included the extended kinship system. Brothers, sisters, and other relatives (who also are farmers) sometimes provide financial and other forms of assistance in transfer decisions. For instance, if neither sons nor daughters prefer to take over the farm, a nephew, niece, or even a cousin may assume the responsibility. Generally, there is considerable planning in order to make sure that the farm stays in the family (Salamon, 1982).

As family size has decreased, its composition has changed from the extended to the nuclear type. In contemporary U.S. society, the typical family consists of only one or two generations. In 1790, when U.S. society was more agricultural, a family usually included aunts, uncles, grandparents, and other relatives. Today, less than 10 percent of U.S. households are of this extended type, and fewer than one-third contain two generations (one or more parents and children).

Changes in the American family have accelerated in the past two decades. The proportion of children who live with both parents has decreased from 85 percent in 1970 to lower than 75 percent today. In 1970, only 11 percent of all children lived with their mother only. Today it is more than 20 percent. These social changes in the family reflect the growing rate of divorce (and its growing acceptance), as well as the increasing number of American women who are single parents.

An illustration of the change in the American family is provided by contrasting the lifestyle of the farm family of 1800 with the farm family of the 1980s.

BOX 9-1   *TWO FAMILIES: A DIFFERENCE OF TWO CENTURIES*

This is the story of two families. Neil and Jan Christiansen typify the farm family of 1800, while Bill and Judy Hightower represent the contemporary farm family.

Neil and Jan and their five children and Neil's parents live on an eighty-acre farm in western Pennsylvania. Their place is up a winding dirt road that is often impassable during the winter snows and spring rains. Although the Christiansen family is only 12 miles from the county seat town, most of their shopping is done in a once-a-week trip to a nearby crossroads store. It is there that they purchase the necessities: nails, flour, rifles and bullets, and other essential manufactured goods.

Bill and Judy Hightower and their two children live on an 800-acre grain farm in east-central Missouri. The farm is conveniently located a mile from a state highway, only 15 miles from Interstate 70, the major four-lane highway running east/west through Missouri. The Hightowers are about equally distant from two large trading centers which serve as sales points for farm products and where most of the family's groceries are purchased. Clothing and larger household items are purchased in the Kansas City area, about 80 miles away. They also visit Bill's parents, who retired from the farm and now live in a senior citizens' high-rise in a suburb of St. Louis.

While the Hightowers produce very little for their own consumption, the Christiansen family was its own best consumer. Only an occasional drove of hogs or a few head of cattle were sold off the farm. The Christiansen family was geographically isolated, economically self-sufficient, and socially self-contained.

Because the Christiansen family was semi-isolated, it was dependent upon its own members for recreation, economic endeavor, education, and religious worship. The Christiansen family spent almost every evening together. The children's most popular pastimes were reading and playing checkers with their father. Family Bible readings supplemented a once-a-month church service when the circuit-riding preacher came through the neighborhood. Visits to kin and relatives in the neighborhood were a popular responsibility.

The Hightowers sometimes hardly see each other all week. The children are involved in baseball, soccer, swimming, dance lessons, the computer science

FIGURE 9-5 Improved technology has changed the nature of family living in the U. S. Kitchen equipment, prepackaged food, and other innovations lighten the labor needed in the home. The past eighty years have seen much change in the typical U. S. farm kitchen.

club, watching television, and hanging out with their high school friends. Lori, the oldest, started to fatten a few pigs as a 4-H club project, but soon became more interested in other pursuits. Her current goal is to earn a college degree in business or accounting, and then gain admission to "the best" Master's of Business Administration program. Lori would prefer to go to college in another state, rather than "stay in Missouri."

Michael, the youngest Hightower, only has a mild interest in farming. He knows that since his older sister does not want the farm, he is the only other possibility. However, for now young Michael wants to be a veterinarian. Aside from a few chores, and helping mom and dad during the "busy times," neither Lori nor Michael work regularly on their parents' farm.

In contrast to the Hightowers, the Christiansens' eldest son, James, 17, performed the work of a man. All the children had regular tasks to perform on the farm or in the home. Even Ann, age five, had eggs to gather and chickens to feed.

The Christiansen home is large; a rambling wooden structure with five bedrooms. Grandma and Grandpa Christiansen live in the home and help with family tasks. Grandpa is regarded as an excellent source of advice on both agricultural and family matters. He is consulted as to when to start planting corn, whether to whip son Paul for disobedience, and where to locate the new henhouse.

The Hightowers' grandparents only see their children during holidays and special occasions, such as birthdays. These are special events for them; a time to catch up on family news. In fact, they are not told everything: such as the time Lori was arrested for drunk driving with her friends, and the police found some marijuana under the seat of the car. Once Bill Hightower caught young Michael and some friends behind a barn with a copy of *Hustler* magazine. Bill chuckled to himself to think of the uproar his mother would have raised if she had ever caught him with a "nudy" magazine.

In the Christiansen household, there was no question that Neil was the boss. That is the way it was in the nineteenth century. Each morning at the breakfast table, he issued orders to his family for the day's work, and arbitrated all family disputes. Back then, wives were expected to be obedient, faithful, and subordinate. Jan Christiansen's influence was based on her persuasive abilities with her husband, but he had the final say in all matters. Jan prided herself on the neatness of her home and was noted throughout the neighborhood for her peach cobbler. She was in charge of educating the younger children in the three Rs; at the same time she performed the midmorning kitchen chores. Spinning wool and weaving cloth for the family's clothes were also her responsibility.

Judy Hightower's roles and responsibilities are much different from Jan Christiansen's. She shares in most decision making, although she does defer to Bill's opinion on matters related to the farm. Judy's day is filled up with her job as assistant manager for a local branch of a nationally franchised fast-food restaurant, chauffeuring Michael around (Lori has her own car), her book club, and PTA activities. Her income is important to the economic survival of the farm.

Despite the Hightowers' modern kitchen appliances, the house is often "a mess." The kids occasionally make their beds, and rather inconsistently complete what few chores are assigned them. As far as Bill and Judy are concerned, their rooms are the childrens' own so "they can live in them that way" if they want. Mr. Hightower tried to make Mike tear up the "Motley Crue" poster on the wall of his room because of its sexual suggestiveness and satanic symbols, but Mike pleaded that he would be laughed at by his friends. Mr. Hightower relented with the admonition that when the grandparents visited, the poster would come down for a day.

Bill Hightower worries about what to do with his farm when he retires. The kids are not very interested in carrying it on, and given the financial uncertainties of farming, he does not blame his son. Bill had always wanted to farm. He worked on his father's operation during high school, and by the time he left for two years in the military, he owned a 180-acre farm that has been expanding ever since.

He is a grain farmer with no livestock and so has some free time during the winter months. Last year he worked as a carpenter for a local construction company. He also maintains his tractors, combines, and other farm machinery in the winter. He has recently enrolled in night classes on futures marketing and other farm business management strategies in order to better utilize the agricultural video-text home computer system to which he has subscribed. Unlike his counterpart from the past, Neil Christiansen, there are no elderly parents around for advice and assistance.

Changes in Family Roles

Role is the set of expectations associated with a specific status held by an individual within society (Chapter 4). In the family, statuses include spouse, parent, and children. Associated with these statuses are roles or expectations of behavior. Over time, these roles have changed.

The rural family once was of the patriarchal type; the father had virtually all the authority. The example of the Christiansens and Hightowers shows that farm families in contemporary U.S. society are becoming equalitarian, which means that all family members have approximately equal voices in family affairs.

In suburban areas, a further realignment of family authority is emerging. Here we find the matricentric family. *Matricentric* means that the mother exercises most of the control and authority in the family. In suburban areas the father is often required to commute long distances to work. He may leave in the morning before the children are awake and return just as they are ready for bed. It is a home with a weekend father. The wife is not only responsible for the child rearing, but makes most domestic decisions for the family.

The mother is the only adult in most single parent families. Not only does she assume all domestic and child-rearing responsibilities, but she also must fill the role of breadwinner and father.

In some families the father is the only adult regularly present, so the man takes on the status of a "house husband." However, only a small fraction of households in U.S. society are of this type.

The roles of children in contemporary U.S. society are also changing. Young people are exposed to an increasingly complex set of cultural messages as the family's socialization function is transferred to other units of society. There is increasing autonomy for young people. School and recreational activities are increasingly perceived as preparation for lifelong career interests. Conflicting normative standards, increased autonomy, and the pressures of school and sports, have contributed to rising rates of alcohol abuse, drug abuse, suicide, and crime among youth.

Although the roles of men and children are changing in U.S. society, nowhere has role transformation been more dramatic and more comprehensive than in the cultural expectations for women. A major factor has been their entry into the labor force.

Between 1960 and 1980, the number of rural women working outside the home more than doubled. By 1979, 44 percent of farm women and 48 percent of rural nonfarm women were employed outside the home—only slightly less than the rate for urban women (McKenry, 1986, pp. 24–25).

The nature of employment for working women has also changed, from temporary to permanent jobs. Historically, rural women supplemented family income by home food production and the sale of garden products. Nonfarm income has become as important to farmers in recent years in part because farm wives have become the largest source of nonfarm income.

The full-time employment of women outside the home has affected family life, creating role strain and conflict (Chapter 4). Performing the roles of employee, wife, mother, and homemaker is difficult. However, despite their often low-paying, unattractive jobs and their general lack of support from their traditional husbands, more rural women are continuing to find full-time jobs.

Changes in Mate Selection

The mate selection process in modern society has changed greatly in the past two or three decades. The trends today emphasize the goals of love and personal happiness in marriage, with mate selection by dating a number of prospective partners and choosing among them. Mate selection on the basis of love is a fairly recent innovation. Previously, parents were a major factor in mate selection. Parents screened eligible candidates and had veto power in approval or disapproval of their offspring's possible marriage partners.

A contrast to contemporary patterns of mate selection in U.S. society is provided by an Indian student studying at a U.S. university, who describes the mate selection process in his country.

BOX 9-2   *MOHAN MEETS MEERA*

In Indian society, personal ads advertise for a marriage partner. In *The Times of India,* a Bombay newspaper, a typical ad would read: "Beautiful, talented, tall, educated homely (translated—good-looking) girl of around 20, from respectable family, for handsome, smart, graduate Punjabi (Arora) businessman, 24 years/170 cms (translated—170 centimeters in height) income very high four figures. Wealth tax assessee. Affluent status family of Kanpur. Write Box Z 281—S. Times of India, Bombay—400 001."

In India, when a young man reaches marriageable age, about 20 to 24 years old, his parents start looking for a wife for him. Similarly, parents with a girl of marriageable age (18 years old) start looking for a husband. Two such families may be friends, they may reside in the same community, or they may be brought together by a common friend or "go-between." The parents may begin deliberations by having tea together, going to lunch together, or meeting at the home of a common friend. Many Indian families place a newspaper advertisement like the one described earlier, and then receive applicants. If the families are well-acquainted, there' is not much need for an extensive inquiry into the other family. Otherwise, each family begins investigating the other to determine its social status, wealth, and general reputation. Further steps are taken only after both families have fully investigated each other.

In the Indian mate-selection process, the main objective is to get the "best buy" possible. Parents consider several possible mates for their offspring, and the best among them is selected.

Consider a marriage between Mohan, a boy, and Meera, a girl, in India. Meera's father is the principal of a school in the city. He approaches Mohan's father, who is a businessman. Both Mohan and Meera are students at the time their wedding is arranged. The marriage negotiations start through a common friend. Before Mohan's father agrees to accept Meera as his future daughter-in-law, he and his wife and the go-between arrange to see Meera at her father's residence. In honor of the visit Meera's father arranges for a sumptuous tea. Meera joins them for a short time and the visitors get a chance to talk with her. The marriage is settled after much haggling. Meera's father agrees to pay a dowry in rupees of one thousand dollars. Paying the dowry is prevalent in India, although it is officially considered a social evil. The size of the dowry in money, clothes, and other presents depends upon the social status of the boy and of his future in-laws.

After the completion of the marriage rituals, which last for three days, the bridegroom and bride are brought together, where they see each other for the first time. A few days later Meera is brought to Mohan's house.

Thus we see that Mohan and Meera have little to say in their marriage. However, Indian marriages are usually quite stable; divorces are legal but rare, and are generally socially disapproved. This stability is partly because Indian women are trained to treat their husbands as their "lord and master." However, as India gradually changes from an agrarian to an industrial society, the role of the woman within Indian society changes also.

In U.S. society, dating is a process of selecting a suitable and desirable mate. One dates many people, perhaps associating steadily with several for a longer time, and may be engaged once or twice, before finally deciding to marry. Especially during adolescence, features associated with highly desirable dates are dependent on the whims of popular culture, that is, current fashions and fads (Chapter 2).

Dating was quite different back in the horse-and-buggy days. It was then called "keeping company," "walking out," or "sparking." When most of the U.S. population lived on farms or in rural communities, boys and girls and their families were well-acquainted. A lengthy period of getting to know each other was then unnecessary. If a couple were seen together more than once, they were considered to be courting. If a boy took a girl home from church, they were considered to be practically engaged.

Today, dating has purposes other than the selection of a marriage partner. Many people purposely choose to remain single. "Hitting the singles' bars" is an end in itself; it is an expression of a preferred lifestyle.

Dating is also different in contemporary U.S. society because it is not solely restricted to the young. The increasing number of single parent families and the increasing rate of divorce has produced a large number of middle-aged and older people who go "sparking."

Marriage, Divorce, and Remarriage

Two of the most important changes in an individual's family status are marriage and divorce. In contemporary U.S. society, divorce occurs nearly as often as the former.

The U.S. trend since 1900 was to marry at a younger age; however, this trend reversed after 1970, as marriage is now being deferred in favor of a career. The median age of first marriage among women born in 1910 was about 23 years of age. For women born thirty years later, in 1940, the median age was less than 21 years. However, for women born in 1955, the age of first marriage had once again increased to over 22 years. This trend reflects the growing entry of women into the labor force and the resultant conflict between the role demands of a career and the role demands of marriage (Population Reference Bureau, 1984, p. 2).

Divorce is also on the rise in contemporary U.S. society. In 1860, the annual rate of divorce was about 2 per 1,000 existing marriages. Gradually the divorce rate increased by about tenfold, so that today the rate of divorce is 22 per 1,000 marriages. In 1981, the number of divorces reached an all-time high of 1,121,000. Given the present rate, nearly half of all first marriages will end in divorce. In 1970, for the first time, divorce exceeded death of a marriage partner as the most frequent reason why a marriage ended.

The impact of divorce is directly felt by both partners and their children. Each year about one million children are in families where their parents file for divorce. This represents about 2 percent of all persons below the age of 18 during any given year. Divorce rates are slightly lower among the rural population, but reflect the general trend of U.S. society (Population Reference Bureau, 1984, pp. 2–3).

The reasons for divorce in U.S. society include the changing norms of society. Divorce is today more acceptable than in the past. Divorce laws in many states have been liberalized, making divorce easier and less expensive. Job opportunities for women make them less financially dependent on their husbands. Couples today have fewer children, hence custody and child support is less problematic.

Women usually receive custody of children after a divorce, which often requires women to enter or reenter the labor force. The ex-wife's job may be a low-paying clerical or service position, which is inadequate for maintaining a separate household. In only about 27 percent of all cases is full payment of court-ordered child support made by the father (and in about 26 percent of all cases of court-ordered child support, none is made) (Horton and Hunt, 1984, p. 251).

Most divorced people will remarry a second (or more) time, especially younger people. Remarriage creates a whole new set of statuses (and related roles) among family members (Chapter 4). These include the relationships of stepparents and stepchildren, and half-brothers and half-sisters. Couples with children from previous marriages must also consider the compatibility of their two sets of children who will now be part of the same household.

Status of the Rural Elderly

Recent estimates from the U.S. Bureau of the Census show that 27 percent of the nation's population 65 years of age and older live in communities of less than 2,500 residents. An additional 13 percent live in towns of fewer than 10,000 persons. Altogether, over 8.5 million elderly people live in small towns, villages, and on farms. A higher percentage of the rural population (when compared to the urban population) is old. Farming itself is an occupation of older people. In Ohio, the average age of a farmer is almost 50 years.

The number of older persons in U.S. society is increasing yearly, both in absolute numbers and as a share of the total population. The elderly are the fastest-growing age group, and will continue to expand more rapidly than both the young and the middle-aged through the year 2015. Since 1900, the absolute number of Americans over 65 years of age increased eightfold, from 3 million to 24 million. If current trends prevail, the over 65 population will increase to 32 million by the year 2000. Both urban and rural areas will share in the increase of the elderly population. Some rural areas, such as the Ozarks region, central Michigan, and rural Florida, are presently experiencing population growth due to the in-migration of retired households.

The basic biological reason for the increase in the elderly population is increased life expectancy. A child born in 1977 is expected to live to the age of 73. Comparatively, the life expectancy of a child born in 1900 was only 37.

The social implications of the "graying of America" are tremendous. Problems include the maintenance of an adequate income for an individual throughout the retirement years, and the cost of medical care. Social security and private pension programs have helped. Today, about 8 percent of the elderly live with a married child, and 10 percent with an unmarried child. In 1900, over half of the elderly lived with their adult children, both married and unmarried (Population Reference Bureau, 1984, pp. 7–8).

Although many elderly families are plagued by poverty, older people on average have slightly higher per capita incomes than other age groups. After-tax per capita income of the elderly in 1980 was $6,300, compared to $6,000 for the population as a whole.

Other problems include declining physical agility and increased health problems, the quality of housing, and fear of crime. However, the most serious problem of the elderly is social. With advanced age comes a process of "disengagement," or role-loss (Chapter 4), from society. Older persons retire and lose their identity as productive members of the economy. Children leave home to attend college, pursue careers, and marry.

The transition from married to widowed status is one of the most difficult problems for the elderly, especially older women. The life expectancy of U.S. women is several years higher than for men. For every 100 men over the age of 65 today, there are 146 women. Loss of friends and relatives also means the loss of social roles. Gradually, an older individual's network with family and friends shrinks (Atchley, 1977).

In addition to role-loss, the elderly live in a society that is constantly

FIGURE 9-6
The elderly population in the United States is increasing much faster than the general population. Population projections indicate a continuation of this trend into the twenty-first century.

Source: U.S. Department of Health and Human Services, Administration on Aging, 1979.

Number of Persons Over 65 Years in the United States

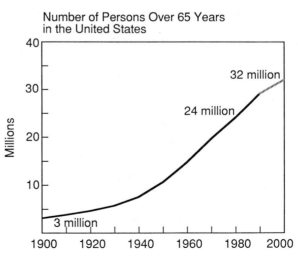

changing. Often they find their most cherished cultural standards in conflict with new, emerging standards. For example, there are large attitudinal differences between older and younger people on such issues as marijuana use and the permissibility of premarital sex.

Certain problems of growing old are more acutely felt by those who live in rural areas. Older rural families have lower income than their urban counterparts, and are more likely to live below the poverty line (Goudy and Dobson, 1985). The rural elderly are more likely to live in substandard housing. The rural elderly are as fearful of crime as the urban elderly, in part because of their geographic isolation (younger rural and urban people are less fearful).

The rural elderly have more frequent and chronic health problems, due to greater difficulties in gaining access to specialized medical care, than do urban aged. Transportation is also a greater problem for the rural elderly than for the urban because of the greater distances involved. Poorer health and lower incomes often restrict the elderly's use of the car, which to them is symbolic of their ability to live an independent existence (Lassey and Lassey, 1985, pp. 90–91).

The image of the rural elderly surrounded by the wealth of their land and family is incorrect. All things considered, the aging process is especially difficult for the rural elderly.

SUMMARY

The family is a *cultural universal* because it exists in every culture. The *family* is that human group responsible for socializing and raising the young. The family performs major functions including reproduction, regulation of sexual behavior, economic activities, status ascription, socialization, and emotional support.

Family composition may be *nuclear* or *extended*. A nuclear family is made up only of parents and their offspring. Extended families include other relatives living in the same household.

One man married to one woman is a *monogamous* family. *Polygamy* refers to one partner married to multiple partners. One husband and two or more wives is polygyny. One wife and several husbands is *polyandry*. *Endogamy* is the restriction of eligible marriage partners to persons inside a specified group. *Exogamy* is marriage to someone from outside immediate kin.

In some cultures, lineage is traced through the wife's side of the family. This is a *matrilineal* family. A *patrilineal* family traces ancestry through the husband's side.

The cultural pattern that establishes the residence for a newly married couple with the bride's parents is called *matrilocal*. *Patrilocal* is the newlyweds moving in with the groom's parents. In contemporary U.S. society, the established pattern is *neolocal* in which the married children reside at a place separate from both sets of parents.

Family decision-making patterns vary among cultures. Some are *patriarchal*, that is, the male makes most of the decisions. Others are *matriarchal*, in which the female makes most of the decisions. Still others are *equalitarian*, in which decision making is shared.

The family in modern society has undergone many changes. The family's function as a productive economic unit has declined, as has its socialization function. However, the function of emotional support has increased. Family size has steadily declined as the United States has evolved from an agricultural to an industrial society. Traditional and modern families differ in decision making and many other roles played by family members. Trends in mate selection emphasize love and personal happiness in marriage. Divorce rates have steadily increased, creating problems of child rearing and support.

Elderly families in U.S. society have lower incomes and fewer social contacts than younger families. The rural elderly have special problems associated with transportation and health needs.

REFERENCES

ATCHLEY, ROBERT C. (1977). *The Social Forces in Later Life: An Introduction to Social Gerontology.* (2nd edition). Belmont, CA: Wadsworth Publishing Company.

BABBIE, EARL. (1982). *Understanding Sociology: A Context for Action.* Belmont, CA: Wadsworth Publishing Company.

GLENN, STEPHEN H. (1980). "Common Ground." Part 1 of "Developing Capable People" videotape series. Columbus, OH: National Rural Crime Prevention Center, Ohio State University.

GOUDY, WILL J. and CYNTHIA DOBSON. (1985). "Work, Retirement, and Financial Situations of the Rural Elderly." Chapter 3 in T. Coward and Gary R. Lee, eds., The *Elderly in Rural Society.* New York: Springer Publishing Company, Inc.

HORTON, PAUL B., and CHESTER L. HUNT. (1984). *Sociology* (6th edition). New York: McGraw-Hill. '

LASSEY, WILLIAM R. and MARIE L. LASSEY. (1985). "Life Conditions of the Elderly in Rural Society." Chapter 4 in Raymond T. Coward and Gary R. Lee, eds. *The Elderly in Rural Society.* New York: Springer Publishing Company.

LYSON, THOMAS A. (1981). "Sex Differences in Recruitment to Agricultural Occupations Among Southern College Students." *Rural Sociology, 46,* 85–99.

MCKENRY, PATRICK C. (1986). "Rural Women Fill Changing Roles." *Buckeye Farm News, 64,* 24–25.

MEAD, MARGARET. (1935). *Sex and Temperament in Three Primitive Societies.* New York: William Morrow.

MOLNAR, JOSEPH J., and JOHN E. DUNKELBERGER. (1981). "The Expectation to Farm: An Interaction of Background and Experience." *Rural Sociology, 46,* 62–84.

Population Reference Bureau. (1984). *The American Family: Changes and Challenges.* Washington, DC: Population Reference Bureau.

SALAMON, SONYA. (1982). "Sibling Solidarity as an Operating Strategy in Illinois Agriculture." *Rural Sociology, 47,* pp. 349–368.

STEWART, ELBERT W. (1976). *Evolving Life Styles: An Introduction to Cultural Anthropology.* New York: McGraw-Hill.

WALL STREET JOURNAL, "Polygamous Communities in the West." (1985, October 15). pp. 1–15.

Chapter 10

The Nature of Farming

The farmer is endeavoring to solve the problem of a livelihood by a formula more complicated than the problem itself.

—Henry David Thoreau

Farming was once synonymous with rural life in the United States. Perhaps this is still true in many Third World countries, but in the United States the occupation of farming can no longer be equated with rural values and rural life. Farming is now a business, and differences between it and other businesses are rapidly diminishing. The theme of this chapter is that farming in First World countries such as the United States has emerged as an occupation, complete with its own system of statuses, rights, privileges, and obligations. Sociologists now study farmers much as they study doctors: as an occupational group. The unique personality of the farmer has been explained in part by residential isolation, but this dimension is changing. Those who are in farming to make money differ from their urban cousins only by the fact that they apply technology to a different kind of production system.

A second theme of this chapter is the emergence of distinctive sectors within the farm population with a widening gap of social backgrounds, values, economic orientations, and size and scale of the farming operations. These categories include the commercial/industrial farms, the more traditional family farms, the growing number of part-time and hobby farms, and the remnants of the once large number of subsistence farms.

MAJOR CHANGES AND TRENDS IN FARMING

We know that the job of farming has changed considerably in recent decades. What specific changes have taken place? The trend has been to more technology and formal education and increased emphasis on commercialization, specialization, and capitalization, which in turn has brought about increased efficiency, larger farm size, and fewer farmers.

Emerging Technologies

Mass production techniques have provided farmers with a variety of new farm technologies. Most innovations in farming come from state agricultural experiment station research or from the private industry that sells farm products and implements. At the heart of the changes in agriculture are the applications of science to farming, and the necessity of available and reliable information for all aspects of the farming operation.

BOX 10-1   *THE INFORMATION AGE: THE FARMER AS INFORMATION WORKER*

A few years ago, while one of this book's authors was interviewing a Kentucky farmer about his use of a new electronic information service, a postal employee delivered the daily mail to his door. On that particular day, our farmer-respondent received about 35 pieces of mail: A local newspaper, the *Louisville Courier-Journal;* the *Wall Street Journal;* 13 magazines; a dozen first-class letters (this farmer was a seed grower, and several of the letters were related to his business); and several pieces of junk mail. That day's mail was a foot-high stack that would not fit in the farmer's mailbox, which was why the postman brought it to his door. This farmer told us that he spent an average of three hours each evening reading his daily mail. He felt this information work was the most important profit-making part of his farming role. The respondent said that his grandfather had believed that hard physical work was the key to farming success. His father had believed that close attention to the marketing of his farm products was fundamental to success as a farm businessman. Our respondent argued that today's agriculture exists in the context of an information society, and so the gathering, processing, and outputting of information is one of the most important roles for a modern farmer. In fact, the Kentucky farmer expressed a strong need for satellite weather maps of the Ukraine (this farmer raised wheat, and bought and sold wheat futures on the Chicago Board of Trade).

FIGURE 10-1   Personal computers provide farmers with quick and reliable information. With increased sophistication of farming technology and practices, today's farmer needs highly specialized information, often on short notice, to make management decisions for the farm enterprise. The micro-computer allows the farmer to collect, process, store, and retrieve information about the farm operation as well as access to more specialized management programs and information at remote locations through telephone linkage.

Computers for Farm Decision Making

The personal computer provides farmers with timely and reliable information for farm management decisions. Its use is slowly increasing. A 1983 study of farmers in Iowa showed that about 10 percent had adopted a personal computer (Bultena and Hoiberg, 1984, p. 21). Many farmers who do not have personal computers have access to a computerized information system through the County Cooperative Extension Office, or through agricultural equipment, chemical, and farm supply stores.

The potential of the personal computer for providing farmers with relevant information was demonstrated through the Green Thumb Project in Kentucky (Clearfield and Warner, 1984). This demonstration project provided farmers with access to information on marketing, weather, and agricultural production, plus family-oriented and emergency information. Farmers received their information through a telephone hookup of a micro computer with a computer in their County Extension Office, which in turn was connected to a large mainframe computer at the University of Kentucky. Information was stored in the computer, and then could be viewed on the farmers' television set on request. Thus Kentucky farmers could access relevant information on weather, crop pests, and market prices almost instantaneously.

The model established by the Green Thumb project is now generally used by several commercial computerized information services. One of the most successful is called "Grassroots." With this growth in the availability of computerized information services, the Kentucky farmer discussed above, perhaps in a few years, will receive much of his daily print mail in electronic form via a computerized information system.

Biotechnology for Increasing Production

One of the newest high-technology fields is *biotechnology,* any technique to improve plants or animals by changing their genetic structure, or the use of living organisms to make or modify products. It has the potential of greatly increasing plant and animal production. Biotechnology actually includes several technologies: the artificial production of enzymes necessary for mass producing hormones, vaccines, and feed additives; artificial reproduction or growth of cells such as cloning or growing tissue cultures; and genetic engineering, altering the genetic structure of the cell. The latter has led to the possibility of a "supercow" that can produce several times the amount of milk of present dairy cattle.

Although much public attention has focused on genetic engineering, actual efforts have been more limited (Buttel et al., 1984). Crop plant research conducted in a genetic engineering context has dealt with nitrogen-fixation capability, drought resistance, stress tolerance, disease and pest resistance, and increased photosynthetic efficiency. Animal research includes growth hormones and other feed additives, embryo transfer and in-vitro fertilization, cloning, and gene transfer or splicing to select for desired livestock traits. A novel but economically important application for California vegetable growers is the development of a strain of bacteria that helps lettuce and other vegetables withstand a mild frost.

As discussed in Chapter 13, not all impacts of technological change are necessarily good. The impacts of biotechnology are of particular concern for Third World countries. The U.S. goverment has established regulations to safeguard against most major catastrophes of biotechnologies, but they may not prevent undesirable social consequences. U.S. laws do not prevent the exportation of biotechnologies to countries that have no protective laws. As an example, a scientist working in a major U.S. corporation saw the answer to the world hunger problem in the development of an organism through genetic engineering that could degrade cellulose (Krimsky, 1983). By replacing the intestinal bacteria of people living in famine-persistent areas of the world with the cellulose-degrading bacteria, indigestible vegetation would attain some food value. Unfortunately, the bacteria would also eliminate the roughage in the digestive tract, and increase the rates of such low-fiber diet conditions as obesity and bowel cancer.

Robotics for Reducing Farm Labor

Robotics is the development and use of self-controlled machines through a combination of engineering automation and computerized artificial intelligence. The automobile industry, which instituted the then revolutionary assembly line production process, has in turn been revolutionized recently through robotics. Much of the work formerly carried out by human labor in the assembly line is now accomplished by robots. The Robotics Industry Association estimated that about 6,300 robots were in use in U.S. industry in 1983.

Currently the use of robotics in agriculture is at a very early stage, such as farmer North's operation described in Chapter 1. Because of the high capital investment required, application of robotics is likely to be in high-value, labor-intensive crops (Office of Technology Assessment, 1986). Many futuristic depictions of farming show the entire farm being operated by the farmer from a remote location through use of computers and radio control. Plowing, planting, cultivating, and harvesting would be computer controlled. Electronic sensors would provide information on soil moisture, needed nutrients, weeds and pests, and crop maturity. Livestock would automatically be fed proper amounts based on nutrient needs.

Although this futuristic example is now possible, actual applications of robotics to agriculture in the near future probably will be limited. Research is now being conducted on automatic apple harvesters that will use ultrasonic sensors to detect tree trunks and steer around the trees (Office of Technology Assessment, 1986). Tomato harvesting, one of the first mechanized production processes, has more recently utilized an automatic electronic color-sorting device (Thompson and Scheuring, 1984).

Changes in Other Technologies

The dominant trend for most agricultural technologies has been "bigger is better." Tractors, cultivators, harvesters, and other machinery have grown in size, capacity, and sophistication. The 1970s saw the advent of the eight-wheel tractor which nearly doubled the horsepower of earlier tractors, and a combine which could harvest 12 rows of corn or soybeans (a swath 36 feet wide with normal 36 inch row planting). The size of center-pivot irrigation systems increased, with some covering one square mile. Fertilizers and pesticides are applied through the irrigation water (chemigation).

Impacts of Technology

New technological developments in farm production have eased the work of the farmer, increased the amount produced, improved the quality of the food, and maintained low food prices for the consumer. But there are also

FIGURE 10-2 Center-pivot irrigation systems can each irrigate automatically an area covering nearly one square mile. The Condon Ranch near Sterling, Colorado, has 15 center-pivot sprinklers. They are operated by a master computer; each sprinkles water onto 200 or more acres of cropland, and they automatically apply fertilizer and pesticides through irrigation water.

Source: U.S. Department of Agriculture Agricultural Research Service.

undesirable results, as shown by the following example of vacuum cooling applied to lettuce production.

BOX 10-2   *THE VACUUM COOLING OF LETTUCE*

The introduction of vacuum cooling, a process that chills lettuce in airtight chambers to 33 degrees in 30 minutes, represented one of the first major technical breakthroughs of the lettuce industry. In 1949, Lester "Bud" Antle met the inventor of the vacuum-cooling process, endorsed the invention, and had the first vacuum-cooling plant built on his property in Watsonville, California. Railroad cars of vacuum-cooled lettuce left Antle's fields in spring, 1950. Vacuum cooling was a crucial step in the history of Antle's phenomenal growth, and it paved the way for a complete transition from traditional shed packing of lettuce to field packing.

A major impetus behind the innovation of vacuum cooling was the lettuce industry's agricultural labor situation. In the era of packing sheds, employees worked in permanent operations with some degree of job stability. They were organized under the auspices of the United Packinghouse Workers of America (UPWA) and received top wages. In contrast, the field workers in the lettuce industry were not in unions. Field workers were relegated to a subordinate role in the industry. California's packing sheds were reserved for Anglo workers; Mexican and Filipino workers worked in the fields.

The fact that packing-shed labor was organized in unions gave growers an economic interest in packing lettuce in the fields and in substituting field labor for packing-shed labor. With the inauguration of vacuum cooling in 1950, California growers began to shift their packing operations into the fields, and packing-shed workers lost their economic importance and union strength.

Though the majority of lettuce growers were at first resistant to vacuum cooling, due to the capital required, "Bud" Antle was convinced it was the wave of the future. He was right: Almost 80 percent of the industry switched to vacuum cooling within three years.

In terms of reducing labor and shipping costs, vacuum cooling technology was unprecedented. Growers replaced wooden crates with cardboard cartons, and moved all of their packing procedures into the fields. They were able to hire lower-paid field workers, which expedited the decline of the packing-shed workers' union.

The introduction of vacuum cooling eliminated up to 75 percent of the packing-shed laborers. While not in itself laborsaving, vacuum cooling was extremely cost-effective. Growers and shippers escaped union domination and could control field workers' wages; though labor requirements were 7 percent to 42 percent higher than for shed-packing labor.

Source: Anne Fredricks (1984), "Technological Change and the Growth of Agribusiness: A Case Study of California Lettuce Production." In Gigi M. Berardi and Charles C. Geisler (eds.), *The Social Consequences and Challanges of New Agricultural Technologies,* Boulder, CO: Westview.

New farm technology has sharply reduced the amount of labor required and greatly increased yields, resulting in an exodus of the farm population to the cities throughout this century in the United States and in other First World countries. In 1920 the U.S. farm population was 32 million, or 30 percent of the total population of 106 million. By 1985 the total U.S. population had increased to 239 million, but the farm population had decreased to just over 5 million, or 2.2 percent of the total population. The exodus received impetus from the advent of the gasoline tractor in the 'Teens and was augmented by the development of chemical fertilizers and pesticides and hybrid plants and animals in the 1930s and 1940s.

Typically, new farm technology also requires a substantial capital investment. Innovative farmers are the larger-sized operators with a cash flow to support the technology. Those who do not have the income to purchase or maintain the technology soon find they cannot compete with their more efficient neighbors. As they retire or sell out, their land is absorbed by the larger or expanding farms. These trends to increasing farm size, commercialization, specialization, capitalization, and concentration, are discussed in more detail in the following sections of this chapter. The overall result is declining farm population, fewer, but larger farm operations, and less farm labor.

Decline in the farm population (Chapter 6) has a direct impact on the vitality of rural communities. With fewer people to shop in local stores, attend schools and churches, use doctors and banks, rural communities decline and some die. A classic study conducted by Goldschmidt (1978) in California showed that a community with a large number of small farmers was a much more viable community in terms of support for local businesses, organizations, and institutions than another community with large corporate farms. Beyond the local community, the problems of poverty, unemployment, and congestion in cities are in part due to the migration of farmers who have lost their previous means of livelihood.

Farm Size

Since 1930 the number of farms in the United States has declined from 6.3 million to about 2.4 million in 1983. During this same period, the average farm size increased from less than 150 acres to almost 450 acres. The trend is toward fewer but larger farms. Mechanization and new technology make it possible to farm more cropland with less labor. The 1970s and 1980s, however, have seen a change in this trend. As shown in Figure 10-3, between 1974 and 1982 for farms with sales of at least $2,500, the number of small farms (less than 50 acres) increased by 25 percent, the number of large farms (1,000 or more acres) increased by 5 percent, but the number of middle sized farms (50 to 999 acres) declined by 13 percent. Many middle-sized farms do not provide the farm family sufficient return on labor and capital investments (income) to survive financially. A farmer with 500 acres must invest nearly as much in equipment as a farmer with 1,000 acres, but the 500-acre farm will produce only one-half the crops of the 1,000-acre farm. Small farms can survive because most are part-time farming operations with the farmer having a second, off-farm job.

The trend of a growing number of small and large farms and a declining middle is known as the bimodal or dual structure of agriculture. The two growing categories in this dual structure have different needs in terms of farm

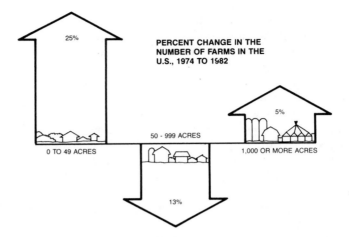

FIGURE 10-3   The decline in the number of middle- or family-sized farms is resulting in a dual structure of agriculture. For farms with sales of at least $2,500, the number of very small farms (less than 50 acres) and the number of very large farms (1,000 or more acres) both increased. The trend is toward a small number of very large farms that produce most of our food and fiber, and a large number of small farms that require some off-farm income to survive.

Source: Paul Lasley, Iowa State University

financing, machinery, marketing of products, and farming information. Both influence policies and programs for rural areas, but for different reasons. Small farms represent the largest number of farmers but the smallest amount of agricultural production. The large farm category represents the largest volume of agricultural production but the fewest farmers. Farms with sales over $200,000 represent only 5 percent of all farms but, have 48 percent of cash income. Farms with sales under $20,000 represent 60 percent of the farms but receive only 7 percent of the total cash income. Large farmers are concerned about the traditional agricultural policies and programs such as price supports for farm commodities, regulation of chemical pesticides, and the importing of farm products. Small farmers are more concerned about local off-farm job opportunities and wage rates, social welfare programs, and food prices.

Commercialization

Farm commercialization is the production of agriculture products for exclusive marketing off the farm. Commercialization implies farming for the purpose of profit, with the implication that an operator will not continue farming without receiving a fair return for labor and capital investment. Farm operators who follow this rational business orientation make up an increasing percentage of farmers.

The increased number of corporation farms heightens the trend to commercial farming. Corporation farms (discussed later in this chapter) place emphasis on efficiency and rational decision making.

Specialization

U.S. farms have become specialized. Instead of producing a little of everything for the family's needs, as in 1800, the modern farmer concentrates on a smaller number of farm enterprises. Farmers increasingly put "all their eggs in one basket." Most farm families must now drive to town to purchase such products as eggs, vegetables, meat, or milk for their family's use.

Reasons for the trend to specialization lie in farm mechanization, gains in efficiency due to size and location, and the difficulty in keeping up-to-date on recent innovations unless one specializes. Farmers today are not generalists. They are grain growers, broiler producers, beef feeders, or dairy producers (who may resent being called dairy "farmers"). The 1982 Census of Agriculture showed that only 4 percent of all farms were classified as general farms, compared to 7 percent in 1969. Instead of belonging to a general farmer organization such as the National Farmers Organization, they increasingly join a specialized commodity organization, like the National Cattlemen's Association or the National Turkey Federation (Chapter 11).

Capitalization

Farming is not only becoming more specialized, it is also becoming more heavily capitalized. One of the most striking changes in farming since 1940 is the substitution of money for labor. Sweat has been replaced increasingly by dollars. At one time, labor was the primary input in farming; success or failure depended to a great degree upon being a hard worker and a careful spender. The contrast with modern times is provided by the following data on the labor and nonlabor cost of raising one acre of corn over the past 50 years (Duffy, 1985):

	1933	1986
Amount of labor required	25 hours	3.6 hours
Cost other than labor	$6	$290

This trend to increasing capital and decreasing labor is found in most other farm enterprises. High-cost farm machinery and equipment have become more widely adopted in recent years: tractors, combines, hay balers, crop dryers, automatic feeders, irrigation systems, and sprayers.

Increased Efficiency

Efficiency and productivity characterize farming in First World nations like the United States. This trend is illustrated by the fact that between 1950 and 1980, average yields per acre have increased from 16.5 to 33 bushels for wheat, from 38 to 91 for corn, and from 22 to 27 for soybeans (Rasmussen, 1982). Modern farm technology has largely been responsible for this dramatic increase in agricultural productivity.

Because of this increased efficiency there is little alarm about the loss of farmland in the United States. Over the period of 1950 to 1980, about 160 million acres of U.S. farmland went out of production, and about 3 million acres more will be gobbled up each year by future suburban development, industry, airports, and highways. Even if it all comes out of cropland, there is little cause for worry about our lack of room for agricultural production. The slight decrease in total amount of farmland is more than offset by more productive farming methods.

Concentration

As the number of farms declines and the size of farms becomes larger, concentration of agricultural production continues. The U.S. government estimated that by the year 2000 about 95 percent of total food and fiber production will come from farms with sales over $100,000 (Rasmussen, 1982). The 50,000 largest farms, those with sales over $500,000, will produce 75 percent of all U.S. farm products.

Ownership of land is also becoming more concentrated. A U.S. Department of Agriculture report showed 5 percent of cropland owners control 48 percent of the cropland, and 13 percent control 59 percent of the land (Office of Technology Assessment, 1986). Western rangeland ownership is even more concentrated. Nine percent of the owners control 59 percent of the rangeland, and 17 percent control 83 percent of the rangeland.

Intensification

Intensification is increasing the amount of food or fiber produced on a given parcel of land by increasing the density of plants or animals on that land or by increasing the number of production cycles for that land in a given period of time. Two of the most common practices of intensification are multiple cropping and intercropping, practices that are widely used in many parts of the world. Intercropping, a system where two crops are grown on the same land simultaneously is little used in the United States. Multiple cropping, the production of two or more crops in sequence on a piece of land during one year, is more common. In the warmer states such as California and Florida, multiple cropping of vegetables makes maximum use of expensive irrigated land (Thomas, 1983). Double cropping is used for field crops in some of the warmer areas of the United States, with the usual crops being winter wheat followed by soybeans.

Other intensification practices include planting field crops in rows with narrower spacing (normally, row spacing less than 30 inches is considered narrow), and closer spacing of individual plants. Citrus growers are experimenting with higher density tree plantings and shorter trees. It may be possible to develop over-the-row equipment for production and harvesting. Cattle and hog confinement operations are also intensification technologies.

The major problem with intensification technologies is that they have a higher potential for environmental degradation. Multiple cropping provides less opportunity for the soil to restore its natural fertility and also increases the potential for soil erosion because the soil has more exposure to wind and water. Livestock confinement operations present problems of waste disposal and water pollution from runoff.

Vertical Integration and Contract Farming

For many years, the trend in the United States has been toward fewer self-employed persons. This is not true of agriculture. In fact, one of the few remaining occupations where one can work for oneself is farming. But this last remaining island of economic independence seems to be shrinking. And one reason for the loss of farmer independence is called "vertical integration."

Vertical integration. What is vertical integration? There are two types of integration: horizontal and vertical. *Horizontal integration* is simply the combining of two or more similar businesses into one larger business. A local feed dealer can integrate horizontally by purchasing another feed business in the community. Likewise, two farms can be horizontally integrated under one management.

Vertical integration is the coordination under the control of one management of two or more steps in the chain of supplying materials, producing, processing, and distributing a product. Notice that the word is "control" and not necessarily "ownership" by one management. "Management" is also a key word; unless some management is taken over by the controlling firm, vertical integration has not taken place.

Contract farming. *Contract farming*, a type of vertical integration, is an agreement between a farmer and a business operator to partially coordinate the supplying, production, processing, and marketing of a farm product under one management. An example is found in the broiler industry, where over 95 percent of broilers are raised under contract (Heffernan, 1984). The typical broiler contract gives much of the management power to the nonfarm business; in exchange, the farmer receives a guaranteed price for the poultry. At one time the contractor was often a hatchery operator or feed dealer who agreed to supply the chicks, feed, medicine, capital, electricity, heat, and supervision; the farmer supplied labor and buildings in exchange for a certain price guarantee. Today, the contractors are large food-processing corporations such as Con-Agra or Holly Farms which are in turn subsidiaries of large conglomerates. In 1981, the four largest contracting firms controlled one-fourth of all broiler production and the eight largest firms controlled over 40 percent of the production (Heffernan, 1984).

Contract farming is most common in the broiler industry, in vegetable and sugar beet growing, and in timber and egg production. The latest enterprise to move in this direction is hog production. The advent of controlled environment confinement operations has helped to facilitate vertical integration of hog production. Some swine operations are large enough to produce half a million hogs in a year and farrow 30,000 sows (Strange and Hassebrook, 1981).

One farmer's motivation for accepting contracts is a desire to reduce risks. The farmer is willing to exchange some independence for this security, although the farmer's independence, with the contract in the hands of a large corporation, may be even less than in earlier years when the contractor was a local entrepreneur. A study of poultry producers in Union Parrish, Louisiana, found that producers had to sign an agreement which gave the contracting firm the right to make all major production decisions (Heffernan, 1984). When asked why they signed the contract, one-fourth said it reduced their risk, one-fourth said there was no market for independent producers, and one-half stated they could not raise enough capital in any other way.

Changes in Farm Tenure

In the United States, farmers may be classified into six tenure classes:

1. *Farm owners* are those who have title to all of the land they operate. In 1982, about 59 percent of all U.S. farms were fully owner operated, and about 35 percent of all farmland was farmed by full owners. Full owners tend to operate smaller-sized farms than they are capable of managing. Owners have freedom in their farming decisions; on the other hand, they have to be satisfied with relatively smaller-sized farms.

2. *Part owners* are those who own some land and rent additional land in order to enlarge their farming units. In 1982, they made up about 29 percent of all U.S. operators and farmed about 54 percent of all U.S. farmland. In general, part owners have larger farms in acres and in terms of value in land and buildings than do either full owners or tenants.

3. *Tenants* are those farmers who rent all of the land that they farm. In 1982, only 12 percent of all farmers were tenants; they operated 11 percent of all U.S. farmland. There are several different types of tenants; for example, sharecroppers are tenants who pay a particular type of rent: a share of the crop. Other tenants are on livestock share leases, cash rent, and other types of renting arrangements.

4. *Farm laborers* are those who work for wages in agriculture. They are even more mobile than tenants. Although historically the number of farm laborers has declined in number but increased as a percentage of all farming occupations, 1974 to 1982 saw a 33 percent increase in the numbers of workers on farms with sales equal to or greater than $2,500. Migratory workers constitute a sizable portion of the farm laborers. Other farm laborers are neighboring farmers' sons and daughters who are not needed to work on the home farm, and hired laborers who have never been able to enter farming for themselves.

5. *Farm managers*, professional salaried employees, belong to the newest of the tenure classes. Their numbers are dramatically increasing. While some farm managers are hired by large food-production corporations, others are employed by farm-management firms. These firms contract with absentee landowners, such as outside investors or retired farmers, to operate their farmland at a profit. Farm managers have the highest level of education of farm occupational categories as well as the highest incomes (Coughenour, 1984).

6. *Corporation farms* are the large agriculture operations owned by groups of stockholders. The corporation farm generally is limited to a few commodities produced on a very large scale. Corporation farms are most common in the large cattle and grain areas of the Great Plains and western United States. They also share many similarities to the large farms (haciendas) of Latin America and Africa. The corporation farm is often a model of business efficiency. The amount of farmland under corporate control will likely increase in the future.

Of course, the distinctions are not always so clear. Progressive family farmers may incorporate the business for financial purposes. Nearly 90 percent of all corporate farms are family held, that is, the shareholders are related (Albrecht and Ladewig, 1982). Some extremely large farms may also be considered family operations. For example, the "superfarm" described below is a family-owned operation.

BOX 10-3   *THE LIFE OF A SUPERFARMER*

Harris Country. It looks like it stretches forever. Just here, on the west side—the popular term for that ubiquitous expanse of San Joaquin Valley land west of Highway 99 from about Bakersfield to Fresno—the Harrises have 20,000 acres in farmland and maybe that much more in grazing land. They have another 10,000 acres of farmland in Arizona, and of the total 30,000 farming acres, about one-third is planted in cotton. They own a third of a crop-dusting service; built and own the cotton gin and a meat-packing plant and restaurant complex; grow 10 percent of the world's supply of garlic (which is even more than the garlic capital of the world, Gilroy); raise cattle; breed and raise horses for racing; also grow canning tomatoes and 15 other crops. Their feedlot is the second largest in the world.

The Harrises, and it's just John and Carole, are big. Not as big as Boswell or Salyer, of course. J. G. Boswell Co., with more than 145,000 acres in California alone, is generally considered the largest farming operation in the nation. Its headquarters are in Los Angeles. Just next door to the Boswell properties in

FIGURE 10-4   Commerical farms in the United States are increasing in size. Displacement of labor through new mechanization and technological innovation has allowed even family-operated farms, such as this one, to become substantial business corporations. Almost 90 percent of all corporate farms are family operations.

Source: University of Illinois, College of Agriculture, Office of Agricultural Communications

Corcoran is Salyer American, usually referred to as the nation's second-largest corporation farm, with around 84,000 acres.

John and Carole Harris, both in their late thirties, are probably typical of large-scale commercial farmers. Their operation is a little more diversified than most perhaps, but their lifestyle—sophisticated, yet rooted in the farmers' classic conservative values—is right on target.

Carole Harris acknowledged this. "Sometimes," she said, "I feel like I'm standing on my grandmother's shoulders." She looked around her airy living room, all blue and white printed cotton, a mixture of country English and the pretty porcelain pieces she brought back from a trip to Japan. So much of the life she's enjoying came about because of her grandmother's pioneering efforts, she reflected. And her husband, where would he be without the hard work of his father and grandfather?

Their life, both say, is fast paced. A weekend house at San Malo Beach; fast flights (in their eight-passenger King Air) to Los Angeles or San Francisco for shopping, Sacramento or Monterey for meetings (he has been active in Republican politics); an occasional week in New York where she likes to shop at art auctions; occasional entertaining at home. When it's just the two of them for dinner, they usually head down the road to the Harris Ranch restaurant. "Unless we pick up something there and bring it back here," Harris teased his wife.

Life on the land. No matter how well you're doing, you never forget that it wasn't always like this. Even for the young Harrises, "We went through some tough times. Agriculture is not always so marvelous. It's hard when you've expanded and things reverse. Early in our marriage, the price of cotton dipped to 25 cents a pound. Polyester leisure suits. That's what did it." All the time he was growing up, said John Harris, "I always thought I was going to do this. It was just a question of if I wanted to specialize. And, as it turned out, I am more of a specialist. But I always liked it (agriculture)."

There were a few years off. After graduation from the University of California at Davis, Harris volunteered for the Army Air Defense Artillery and was eventually assigned to Korea. Upon his return he and Carole (who had been working for the Fresno Welfare Department during this period) lived briefly in an apartment in Fresno before moving to a small white trailer on the ranch. Fifteen years ago they moved into the original house built in the mid-1930s by Jack Harris and John's mother, Teresa. And, said Carole Harris, they've been remodeling ever since.

"I like having a large farm," he reflected. "You can keep people busy year-round. It's a good efficient use of people. We have four who do nothing but repair people's houses. We have our own building company for the houses we construct for our managers. Large things, of course, we bid out."

Harris likes talking about farming. "We own 25 percent of the land we farm. It's like a checkerboard. We lease 75 percent of the land, half from Southern Pacific, half from private individuals."

"It's a tough business. You have to diversify. There's an economics of scale to getting bigger. You've got more people, but only one president. I think it would be hard to be a small-sized operation. I mean, we can repair our own tractors."

He laughed, "I think farmers feel it's their destiny to farm as much land as they can."

It's easy to understand a small farmer being awestruck at an operation like Harris Ranch. John and Carole Harris are in a different league. For one thing, along with the usual agricultural and civic involvements, he's a member of the Young Presidents Organization, the prestigious nationwide organization of men who became presidents before their fortieth birthday of a business grossing more than $4 million annually and with more than 50 employees.

Source: Based on Tia Gindick, "It's a Wonderful Life in Agriculture," *Los Angeles Times,* February 5, 1984.

CHANGING ATTITUDES AND VALUES OF FARMERS

As the nature of farms and the occupation of farming is changing, so are the values and attitudes of farmers. U.S. farmers are often characterized as individualistic, conservative, supporters of the status quo, and ardent defenders of the rural way of life. In Chapter 2 we defined values as a symbolic statement of what is right and important. Marginal and subsistence farmers tend to support traditional rural values more strongly than do commercial farmers, who more closely share the values of their urban cousins. The following rural values remain important to many farmers, but their importance is decreasing.

INDIVIDUALISM

The rugged farmer arrayed against the forces of big business, railroads, and the weather represents an outdated and romantic portrayal. We now have price supports, the farmer relies on state experiment stations for new research findings, few farm supplies are produced on the farm, the farmer is now covered by social security, and crop insurance is available. Any resemblance of the modern-day commercial farmer to the individualistic farmer of the past is largely an illusion. As farmers become more business oriented, they place more value on cooperation and less on individual independence.

CONSERVATISM

The farmer generally has been aligned with conservative political forces which support laissez faire economic policies, that is, little or no government interference in the economy, and autonomous local government with minimal federal interference. A conservative position might not seem appropriate for the commercial farmer, who needs stricter economic controls for production and marketing, who exports about 40 percent of the yearly farm production, and who needs federal support of research programs, federal controls on the quality of marketed items, and transportation facilities to move goods from farm to the market. Farmers actually support government involvement in certain programs such as soil and water conservation (Korsching and Nowak, 1983). They also want the federal government to enter into more long-term trade agreements with other countries (Lasley, 1984).

RURAL LIFE

Rural people place a high value on rural living, and feel their life is generally superior to that of the city dweller despite the fact that many rural areas do not have the amenities found in urban areas. In fact, many farm people place rural living "next to godliness." One of the reasons many farm families are willing to operate their farms part time while working a full-time off-farm job is because there is no place for a child to grow up like the farm (Barlett, 1986).

WORK AND LEISURE

Farmers also differ from urban persons in attitudes toward work and leisure. A recent survey showed that 26 percent of farmers said they had the best job in the world. Only 17 percent of persons in other occupations said they had the best job in the world (Pins, 1986). No farmers said they disliked their jobs.

Farmers tend to hold to a work ethic that puts great emphasis on work. The saying "Idle hands are the Devil's keeper" is taken seriously. A high value is placed on work as an end in itself. Ohio farmers generally agreed with such statements as, "I don't feel right about my leisure unless I have worked first," and, "I feel uneasy when I am on vacation because I am not working."

ROUTES TO FARMING

It is now more difficult to get into farming. Types of tenure arrangements are changing, and the steps to full farm ownership are different. The occupational desires and aspirations of rural youth are oriented to urban jobs. Changes in socialization and entrance into agriculture, changes in tenure classes, and land tenure relationships have hastened the trend to large-scale agriculture in the United States, while land fragmentation is a problem in Third World countries.

The New "Agricultural Ladder"

A popular saying among farmers today is that a boy must either inherit or marry a farm. Recent estimates indicate that 80 percent of all farmers 20 to 64 years of age have a farming background. The inheritance of a farm has taken the place of several rungs on the agricultural ladder. The "agricultural ladder" was traditionally used to describe the process whereby a farm boy was first a nonpaid laborer on his father's farm, then became a hired man, then a tenant, then the operator of a mortgaged farm, and finally a farm owner. The objective of most farm operators has been to attain full ownership of their land and then to live from rental income in their declining years. The high cost of owning land has made emphasis on total ownership less realistic.

Several changes have occurred in the agricultural ladder for entering commercial farming. The first change was replacement of the unpaid family laborer rung by 4-H and Future Farmers of America (FFA) projects or other agriculturally related high school experiences. More recently, a college education has become a prerequisite for entering farming. The hired man rung is replaced by a formal agreement in which the son or daughter becomes a partner in the father's (or father-in-law's) farm. This is followed by a transfer agreement by which the new generation gradually earns control of the farm.

It is more difficult to enter farming even with family help; without family help it is almost impossible (Lyson, 1984). One other option is entry through part-time and/or small-scale farming. The part-time farmer can use off-farm income to build a farming operation. Can the part-time farmer accumulate the necessary capital, given current inflation and tax policies, to enter commercial agriculture? Male students at agricultural colleges may continue to disregard a coed's physical measurements; they are more interested in whether she's a three-hundred-acre woman or a twelve-hundred-acre woman.

Another way to start farming may be as a manager of a corporation farm or working for a farm-management corporation. Almost any agricultural college bulletin board is filled with job openings for farm managers. Such a career route is like climbing the organizational ladder of a large corporation.

FFA is a high school association composed of high-school-aged students enrolled in vocational agriculture courses. Technical agriculture is taught in the classroom and practiced on each student's home farm. 4-H Clubs are youth organizations sponsored by the Cooperative Extension Service. It features a variety of farm-related projects for boys and girls. The results of these projects are generally displayed at state and county fairs.

These youth-oriented agricultural organizations function to socialize farm children into the norms and expectations of the farming occupation. However, they tend to idealize certain positive aspects of farming. The 4-H Clubs and the FFA provide a recruitment function for the farming occupation.

CHANGES IN FARM-FAMILY RELATIONSHIPS

In no other occupation is the interdependence between family and business so strong as in agriculture. Farming and living are more nearly identical in agriculture than working and living in nonagricultural occupations. The farm family contains both the production unit—the farm—and the consumption unit—the family household; the two are completely intertwined. This close relationship between farm and family has some novel advantages; it also has some important disadvantages.

The family farm has long been an ideal which both rural and urban people valued highly. Pressure groups and politicians know they can usually rally the voters to preserve the family farm even though people understand that most of the food grown in this country is produced on large farms (Resource Conservation Act, 1980). Is the family farm good? Is the family farm in danger? How many farms are actually family farms?

The U.S. Department of Agriculture has four separate classification schemes for family farms (Vogeler, 1981).

AMOUNT OF HIRED LABOR

Family farms are family-operated businesses that use no more than 1.5 man-years of hired labor or management. This definition includes 95 percent of all farms under family farms.

LAND TENURE

Family farms are owned either fully or partly by the operators. Tenants and hired managers are not included. Full or part owners constitute 80 percent of farms.

LEGAL STATUS

Ownership of the farm is by an individual, family, or partnership with ten or fewer shareholders. Nonfamily partnerships and corporations account for less than 2 percent of all farms.

WORK FORCE

No decline in the proportion of family labor to the total farm labor. Between 1930 and 1967 this remained constant at about 75 percent.

From these data we can conclude that "(1) approximately 95 percent of all farms are family farms, (2) family farms dominate food and fiber production, (3) the proportion of family farms relative to total number and sales of farms is not decreasing, and (4) corporate farms are an insignificant percentage of total farm numbers and sales" (Lemons, 1986, p. 76).

Part-Time Farming

There is an increasing trend to part-time farming. About 45 percent of all U.S. farm operators are classified as part-time farmers. A *part-time farmer* is a farmer who spends part of his or her time in farming, and spends part of it (at least 100 days per year according to the U.S. Census Bureau) in off-farm work. Among part-time farmers are important distinctions based on reasons for farming parttime. One researcher has classified part-time farmers into transitional farmers, standard farmers, and investors (Barlett, 1986).

Transitional part-time farmers are former full-time farmers experiencing downward social mobility (Chapter 4) by being forced to take off-farm work. The transition into part-time farming is made to save the family farm or to increase family income. Some reduce the size of the farm operation to compensate for time spent in off-farm work while others maintain the full-size farm, relying on help from the family or a hired hand. Some have aspirations to return to full-time farming.

At one time, most part-time farmers were in the transitional group. Today, the majority of part-time farmers are *standard* or persistent part-time farmers. Because of the difficulty of entering farming full-time today, they first established themselves in a nonfarm, full-time job and then moved to a farm. Farming part-time is their route into farming. Although many standard part-time farmers aspire to farm full-time, few will be able to accumulate enough resources to actually become full-time farmers.

A common trait of *investors* is that they have always had full-time, off-farm jobs. Many investors inherit their farms. They farm, in part, to keep the land in the family. Other investors are urban professionals with fairly high incomes who want to enjoy certain aspects of agrarian life. Often called hobby farmers, they do not need income from their farms. Indeed, any financial loss from the farm may represent a tax deduction. Another group of part-time farmers that may be included with investors is the back-to-the-landers. These are well-educated, affluent urbanites with a strong commitment to simple, rural-based lifestyles (Jacob and Brinkerhoff, 1986). They practice part-time semi-subsistence agriculture on small parcels of land, but most of their income is from a nonfarm occupation.

Research has shown that most part-time farmers are similar to full-time farmers in their attachment to the local communities and their reasons for wanting to live in rural areas (Heffernan et al., 1981). The mix of crops and livestock produced on part-time farms also tends to be similar to that of full-time farmers. The major difference is the size of the operation, with the part-time farm being a miniature version of the larger farm (Barlett, 1986). Additional differences are that part-time farmers have higher incomes than their full-time counterparts, and that they tend to identify more closely with their off-farm than their farm status.

Why Part-Time Farming?

Important motivations for off-farm employment are a desire for economic security and the strong values attached to rural life. A study in Georgia identified some additional income and life-style reasons for part-time farming (Barlett, 1986). These include the data for additional income through a sideline business, an investment for a retirement nest egg or a bequest to the children, a job after retirement from the off-farm occupation, the recreation of working the farm, being your own boss, and the benefits of rural living for the children.

But part-time farming also has disadvantages. The farmer is often in a stressful situation, being forced to perform farm operations on weekends or after dark because the farming is in addition to a regular forty-hour-per-week off-farm job. This results in a loss of companionship for the spouse and a general decline in family interaction. Part-time farming also involves a heavy burden of work for farm women who assume an increasing share of the housework and perhaps also have an off-farm job (Chapter 9).

Part-time farming has become a permanent, institutionalized feature of U.S. agriculture. There are both desirable and undesirable aspects to part-time farming. Part-time employment gives farm people higher incomes. Farming is a difficult occupation to enter or leave, but part-time farming provides a means by which millions of U.S. farmers can enter, increase, or decrease their farming operation in a relatively short time.

Farm and Family Labor and Decision Making

A family farm largely remains a labor-intensive enterprise. Family labor is especially suited for the farm. The production of most crops and livestock includes times when there is a high demand of labor, such as planting and harvesting grain or farrowing hogs, and other times when little labor is needed such as in the winter after the crops are in. Furthermore, because family members are tied by affection and kinship they are willing to submit to greater

FIGURE 10-5   Off-farm income is a major component of the total income of farm households. More than 45 percent of farmers work off the farm more than 100 days a year. In 1984 net farm income (profit after expenditures) was just over $25 billion, whereas off-farm income for farm households was nearly $41 billion. Off-farm income is often the difference between a negative or positive cash balance for the farm household.

Source: *NADO News*, May 6, 1986.

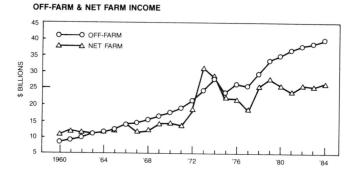

OFF-FARM & NET FARM INCOME

control and expend whatever effort is necessary to complete the task at hand (Colman and Elbert, 1984). They know that family well-being is dependent upon each other's cooperation.

Women are involved in providing labor for the farm and in making management decisions, especially in the early years of the farm and family cycle. There is, however, a division of labor with women having responsibility for the housework and men having responsibility for the farming activities. The amount of women's involvement is related to the size of the farm (Sharp, Gwynne, and Thompson, 1986). Smaller farms cannot afford hired labor, so women and other family members provide the labor. As the farm expands and becomes more prosperous, hired labor is substituted for the labor of the farm women. Full-time hired farm labor is most often found in traditional situations in which the farm woman works neither on nor off the farm (Buttel and Gillespie, 1984). As the farm reaches this mature stage, one of the consequences is a loss of input and control by the women. As farm technology become more complex there may be a tendency for the male family members to become the experts and overtly or covertly work to keep the women out (Colman and Elbert, 1984).

The financial contribution women make to the farming operation is substantial, partly through the contribution to family income from off-farm work. Another part is savings from not having to hire farm labor. A major contribution is money that is saved from activities such as baking, canning, and sewing. By producing many of the goods that the family needs (bread, canned fruits and vegetables, clothing, and household articles such as drapes and rugs) purchase costs are reduced. Because the household and farm budget are not separate on most family farms, women contribute directly to the farm operations. One study showed that 35 percent of the women in farm households were involved in such activities compared to 11 percent of the women in nonfarm households (Reimer, 1986).

ORGANIC FARMING

In 1962, Rachel Carson published her book *Silent Spring* in which she quoted the following lines from John Keats:

> The Sedge is wither'd from the lake,
> And no birds sing.

The point of the quotation, and the book, was that the indiscriminate use of pesticides was poisoning the world. The book touched off the environmental revolution in the United States and led to the ban of certain pesticides such as DDT. Despite the concern and action initiated by the Rachel Carson book, pesticide use in the United States has more than doubled since its publication. The indiscriminate extinction of wildlife species, cancer in humans, and eventual development of immunity by the insect species that the pesticides are meant to control, have resulted in concerns about agricultural chemicals (Chapter 13).

One reaction to this concern is an increase in organic farming. A 1980 USDA report estimated that about 1 percent of American farmers, 25,000 to 35,000 in number, were organic farmers. *Organic farmers* avoid the use of chemical fertilizers and pesticides, as well as synthetically compounded growth regulators and feed additives. Organic farmers also are concerned about the future availability of water for irrigation and energy-related products (Geisler et al., 1984). The popular conception of organic farmers is that they are part of the back-to-the-land movement, have a metaphysical perspective, strive for self-sufficiency, use labor-intensive methods, are economically marginal, and sell largely through specialized channels to natural food stores. This description fits a segment of the organic farmer population.

The majority of organic farmers are not different from conventional farmers. They were brought up on a farm, began farming chemically, and then switched to organic farming. They have similar size operations, have a commercial orientation, are highly productive and efficient, use the latest in farming implements and use conventional market channels (Dalecki and Bealer, 1984; Harris, Powers, and Buttel, 1980; Lockeretz and Wernick, 1980). When asked why they adopted organic farming, three-quarters of a sample of farmers from the Corn Belt mentioned their health or that of their families or livestock; the cost or ineffectiveness of using chemicals; or problems with their soil resulting from chemical agriculture. About half mentioned contacts with proponents of organic farming, and only one-third mentioned philosophical or ideological reasons (Lockeretz and Wernick, 1980).

Del Akerland is a typical example of the commercial organic farmer. He has a 760-acre farm in the eastern Nebraska corner of the Corn Belt. He operates his farm with the latest machinery, has a 300-head cattle feedlot, and twin cement silos with a 1,200-ton grain capacity. The farm is 100 percent organic and has been for 11 years. The switch to organic farming had little to do with high ideals about raising organic food. Financial and ecological costs of conventional farming were driving him out of business (Zwerdling, 1978).

Organic farming is becoming institutionalized. After decades of neglect, the USDA has begun to investigate the best approaches to organic farming, such as crop varieties to be grown and the best marketing techniques. Pennsylvania State University has an Organic Gardening and Farming Research Center, and a model farm where organic foods are grown. The model demonstrates soil conservation and energy-saving devices that can be applied in organic farming. The Organic Foods Production Association of North America was formed in 1985. Its purpose is to set standards and certify whether or not a farm is truly organic.

Integrated pest management (IPM) uses fewer, but does not exclude chemical pesticides. The philosophy behind IPM is to manage, rather than control, pests through a wide variety of management techniques. IPM utilizes a combination of natural enemies, better methods of selective pesticide application, cultural controls, and genetics, resulting in a less energy-intensive, more environmentally compatible system that can reduce pesticide use by 35 to 50 percent (Battenfield and Haynes, 1983).

IPM is being taken another step to on-line pest management (OLPM), which adds biological and environmental monitoring to IPM. Using computer simulation with large data bases, including information on weather, pest infestation, effectiveness of previous control strategies, plant resistance, natural enemies, cultural practices, and planting schemes, OLPM provides forecasts that can be used for management decisions. OLPM is another example of the computer and information age of modern agriculture.

THE AGRICULTURAL TRANSITION

Since World War II, incomes in the United States for urban families have generally increased each year, but in the same time farm incomes have barely held their own, or dropped. Farm production has risen faster than population growth for First World countries, and the United States is competing with other First World countries in exporting surpluses. Many countries that once imported food from the United States are now growing much, if not all, their own food, and some also have become food exporters. The new technology practiced on large farms has widened the economic gap between large and small farms. The number of persons wanting to farm is larger than the number of profitable farms. These are all aspects of the *agricultural transition*, the change that is occurring in the nature of farming and all other parts of the agricultural industry (Chapter 12) in response to new technology and the changing world economy.

A major problem of the agricultural transition is the undesirable social and economic consequences for farm families and rural communities. Lower farm incomes, food surpluses, increasing farm-to-urban migration, dying rural communities, and ineffective rural institutions are direct and indirect results of technological changes in farm life and the impact of the world economy.

Problems of Superabundance

A nation can be wealthy only if a few of its people are required to produce food. For example, in many parts of the world around 80 percent of the population is required to raise the food and fiber for the remaining 20 percent, who are employed in industry or other occupations. About one-fifth of the Soviet Union labor force is estimated to be in farming, compared to

The U.S. Produced More Grain on Less Land in 1980

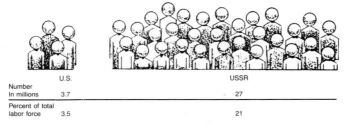

	U.S.	USSR
Area Million acres	177	315
Production Million metric tons	270	189

With a Much Smaller Farm Labor Force.

	U.S.	USSR
Number In millions	3.7	27
Percent of total labor force	3.5	21

FIGURE 10-6   U.S. agriculture is much more productive than agriculture in Russia. The amount of land in production in the United States is only about half that in Russia, yet the United States land produced over 40 percent more grain. One of five Russian workers is involved in agriculture, and each worker produces about seven metric tons of grain. In the United States one of 28 workers is involved in agriculture and each worker produces about 73 metric tons of grain.

Source: Barry Murray, "Soviet Agriculture Struggles to Grow," *Farmline*, July 1981.

about 3.5 percent in the U.S. The North American farmer produces nearly twice as much per acre for crops such as wheat, corn, barley, and oats, than the Soviet farmer.

But in the United States and other developed countries farm production has outstripped food consumption. Two major reasons for the problems of the agricultural transition are too much farm production in relation to consumer food needs and the inadequacy of the size of the average farm to permit many farm families to utilize their available labor and machinery efficiently. So the lack of adjustment exists at the two levels of individual farm size and a national food surplus. Behind both of these reasons is a common cause: new farm technology.

New technology is the major cause of both food surpluses and low farm incomes. Food output has increased too fast for either population growth or higher incomes to absorb it. By 1987 the U.S. government stored an amount of corn equal to 75 percent of a normal year's harvest (Muhm, 1986). This surplus continues to accumulate.

When the public does not wish to consume all of the food products that are supplied, it notifies the producers by paying a lower price. Some claim that the domestic demand for farm products can be increased by more advertising and promotion. This is doubtful; consumption patterns can be changed but probably cannot be increased. Furthermore, change in the type of food we eat can have a negative impact on farms. Decline in red meat consumption has had serious consequences for beef cattle and hog producers.

FIGURE 10-7 Continuing overproduction of food has resulted in low farm incomes. Through application of new technology the amount of food produced by each farm worker and each parcel of land continues to increase. Demand for food has not kept pace with production, and the accumulating surplus contributes to the downward spiral in prices paid for farm products. One solution is to remove marginal cropland farm production.

Source: Brian Duffy, *Des Moines Register*, August 14, 1986.

Problems of Agricultural Financing

The farm exodus discussed earlier in this chapter has continued through-out this century, but at certain times, due to the severity of the plight faced by the farmers, it has received much more attention by the media and the public. The 1980s have been labeled a farm crisis period. Farmers have been facing severe financial difficulty and are filing bankruptcy or are being foreclosed by banks and other lenders at unprecedented rates. The U.S. Department of Agriculture estimated that in 1985 about one-third of the commercial farmers were experiencing financial problems, with many being technically insolvent (Economic Research Service, 1985). The same year farm lenders saw delin-quency rates reach record highs (Easterbrook, 1985).

The financially failing farmers are not the marginal farms that might be expected to fail. Many are family farmers: members of the disappearing mid-dle in the emerging dual structure of agriculture. Some expanded their opera-tions in land and equipment by borrowing on the equity of increasing land values of the 1970s. When the land values and prices paid for farm products dropped, they were unable to repay their loans. A study comparing North Dakota and Texas farmers experiencing financial stress showed that the fail-ing farms were not marginal farmers with small, poorly managed operations (Leistritz et al., 1986).

Initial reaction to financial stress are adjustments in family living and farm expenditures (Lasley, 1985). In response to the types of adjustments made by farm families to the sagging farm economy, most families cut back on social activities and entertainment expenses, and postponed major household and farm purchases. But some had to take more serious measures such as using savings, selling possessions, cashing in life insurance or letting it lapse, not paying property tax, forfeiting a land contract or mortgage, and selling land.

BOX 10-4   *FARM CRISIS, MURDER, AND SUICIDE*

On the morning of September 29, 1983, the bank president of Ruthton, Minnesota, Rudy Blythe, and his chief loan officer, Toby Trulin, were gunned down on an abandoned farmstead on which their bank had foreclosed the mort-gage. These murders were the first in a series of violent outbursts across the Midwest, which were to take the lives of several farmers and bankers as the farm crisis of the 1980s deepened.

The Ruthton murders were to be the most famous outcroppings of a spread-ing farm depression caused by relatively high interest rates and depressed farm prices. Early indicators of the high level of social disorganization in Midwestern farm communities were divorce, spouse-beating, child-abuse, and a sharp in-crease in the number of farm bankruptcies. At many farm auctions, neighboring farmers protested the sale, sometimes by roughing up anyone who made a bid, until sheriffs were called in to restore order. A number of organized farm protests broke out in the Midwestern states, some of them advocating violence. Farmers' attitudes toward bankers grew more resentful as more farm mortgages were forclosed. And as more and more farms went under, so did many small-town farm implement dealers, seed and hardware stores, and, eventually even banks themselves.

Who killed Banker Blythe and his loan officer? Jim Jenkins and his teenage son lived alone on their ten-acre dairy farm near Ruthton after Jim's wife of 20 years left him for another man in 1980. Father and son were very close, working together on their small dairy farm for long hours every day. Steve learned how to farm from his father, as Jim Jenkins had from his father. Much of this learning was unspoken, as when Steve would silently hand his father a wrench while they struggled to repair their wornout farm machinery. Both Jim Jenkins and his son Steve were high school dropouts; they figured they did not need much formal education to be farmers. Jim did not like paper-and-pencil work, and he did not keep close control over his financial situation. He believed that when times got tough, he could just work a little harder and go a little deeper in debt. Jim Jenkins loved his dairy herd, and often drove his old pickup 50 miles one way to a vegetable processing plant to bring back a load of pea silage for his cows. Jim's neighbors pointed out that the free silage was not very nutritious, and anyway the transportation cost was more than the silage was worth. Jim Jenkins did not buy expensive fertilizers or pesticides or new machinery. But he was unusually capable in fixing up his rundown equipment. And he worked very hard.

As the economic recession got worse and his financial stress increased, Jim began to have wild fits of temper. Little things would set off a spark of fury. He ran his dog through a cornpicker on one such occasion. In another temper outburst, Jim cut off the tails of 20 of his dairy cattle because one swatted him in the face while he was milking, knocking his eyeglasses in the manure. Milk prices remained low, and Jenkins's interest payments increased. He could not meet his mortgage payments, despite working as a hired man for his neighbors. Meanwhile, his dairy cattle were starving. So were Jim Jenkins and his son. They usually ate all their "meals" at a restaurant in Ruthton: scrambled eggs and toast and a glass of milk, three times a day.

Rudy Blythe was born rich and raised on Philadelphia's Main Line. After being sent to good schools, Rudy went into big-city banking. He was successful. But he had a vision of buying a small-town bank and raising his small son in what he considered an idyllic setting. The Blythes moved to Ruthton in 1977 to fulfill Rudy's dream, but problems began immediately. Rudy's wife Susan, with her elegant silverware and Eastern ways, did not fit into rural life in Minnesota. Rudy's son was ostracized at school. The Blythes were not accepted by local folk, and when Rudy's bank began foreclosing on Ruthton's farmers, the local attitude turned surly. Rudy Blythe grew more and more depressed as the local economy floundered, leading his bank into a financial crisis. Blythe had purchased his bank on the assumption that interest rates were going to drop. At first, he had made loans to farmers (like Jim Jenkins) that were considered poor credit risks. Now his earlier optimism came back to haunt him. And interest rates slowly climbed. He could no longer meet the payments on his own loan, with which he had purchased the Ruthton bank. By 1982, Blythe was receiving anonymous telephone calls at night threatening to shoot his dog. His situation in Ruthton was becoming decidedly unpleasant.

When Rudy Blythe foreclosed on Jim Jenkins's little farm, Jim beat him to the punch by selling off his dairy cattle and skipping town with the money. Jim ripped out the plumbing fixtures, the sinks, tubs, and toilets, to make the farmhouse uninhabitable. Rudy was furious, and threatened legal action. But Jim Jenkins and his son fled to Texas, where they got work maintaining the trucks and other equipment for a school district. Steve, now 18 years old, began to act in strange ways. He wore only camouflage clothes, shaved his head, and strapped a knife on his leg. He purchased an M-1 carbine, and stalked rabbits and other small animals. Steve dressed a log in shirt and pants, with a bottle for a head. Then he shot this target over and over again. He dreamed of military service, but was rejected by the U.S. Marine Corps. Meanwhile, Jim Jenkins held down two jobs, slept in the maintenance garage, and gradually saved up several thousand dollars. In September 1983, Jim Jenkins and his son returned to Minnesota.

They rented a new farm near Ruthton and some farm equipment. Jim Jenkins tried to borrow money to buy dairy cattle. But time after time, when a cattle dealer would call Rudy Blythe's bank for credit reference on Jenkins, he would be turned down. Finally, on September 28, 1983, his last effort at securing credit was refused. It was then that Jim Jenkins decided to strike back.

He phoned Rudy Blythe at his bank, and using an assumed name, expressed interest in buying the 10-acre farm. Overjoyed at unloading this worthless property, Rudy set up an appointment to meet the next morning at the farm.

Rudy and his loan officer were greeted with a blast of M-1 carbine fire. The two bodies were left where they fell in a weed-filled ditch near their car. Jim Jenkins and his son drove south to Texas, pursued by police. Finally, near the small town of Peducah, Texas, Jim Jenkins decided to stop running. He got out of his truck, and told Steve to drive on alone. At age 46, a financial failure at farming, Jim Jenkins felt that he had run out of options. He put the gun in his mouth and pulled the trigger.

Steve Jenkins turned himself in to police authorities claiming that his father had killed the two bank officials. Taken back to Minnesota, he was found guilty when tried, and given a sentence of life imprisonment for his involvement in the murders.

The Minnesota tragedy in 1983 heightened public awareness of the farm crisis. But the farm foreclosures continued, as did bank failures.

Source: Based on Andrew H. Malcolm (1986), *Final Harvest: An American Tragedy*, New York: Times Books.

"Losing the family farm affects the social and emotional well being of farm families as profoundly as it affects their financial well being" (Heffernan and Heffernan, 1986, p. 29). A study of Missouri families that lost their farms found that almost every aspect of their lives was thrown into turmoil. Table 10-1 shows some stress-related reactions experienced by men and women who lost their farms. Because these reactions can lead to other problems within and outside the home, such as child or spouse abuse, most states established telephone hotlines and special assistance programs for these families.

A major complaint was lack of support from friends, relatives, and the church. This may be related to withdrawal from friends, relatives, and other social relationships. But it was this social-psychological support that was generally mentioned as being most helpful (Heffernan and Heffernan, 1986).

The impact of financial stress and failure by farmers does not stop at the farm gate. The loss of farm population and its effect on the local community was discussed earlier in this chapter. Bankrupt farmers may also leave behind many unpaid debts. Lending institutions may not be able to recover the debts or recoup the losses or bankruptcies as happened to banker Rudy Blythe. During the first two months of 1986, there were 38 agricultural banks across the United States that failed (Elbert and Ballard, 1986). Even if the banks don't fail, by having to use cash reserves to cover loan losses from defaults, banks have less credit to extend to nonfarm borrowers who might use the funds to create additional badly needed jobs. It becomes a vicious circle. "In many agriculturally dependent areas, however, nonfarm job opportunities are unlikely to grow as the impacts of reduced agricultural income are felt by the agribusiness sector and other local trade and service firms" (Leistritz et al., 1986, p. 17).

Possible Solutions for the Farmer and Society

During the period of agricultural transition, the farmer has several alternatives. *The farmer can acquire more land, allowing more efficient use of labor and equipment.* Expansion is most often accomplished by renting or purchas-

TABLE 10-1   **Stress-related Reactions Experienced by Men and Women Who Lost Their Farms**

STRESS-RELATED REACTION	HAVE EXPERIENCED		CONTINUE TO EXPERIENCE	
	Men	Women	Men	Women
	Percentage of Respondents			
Became depressed	97	100	56	72
Withdrew from family and friends	97	66	56	41
Experienced feelings of worthlessness	74	69	49	41
Increased drinking	18	12	10	6
Became more physically aggressive	49	31	26	9

ing adjoining farm land. This alternative is only available to part of the farm population; someone must leave farming in order to provide the land for other farmers to acquire.

The farm family can enter an off-farm occupation and continue farming part time, assuming off-farm jobs are available. There is a change of occupation but not a change of residence. Increasing numbers of part-time farmers view their combination of industiral and farm work as a permanent rather than a transitional status. They prefer part-time farming, and are not using it as a step into or out of full-time farming. Improved transportation and the development of industries in rural areas make it possible to shift from farm to industrial employment without moving from a rural home.

The farm family faced with economic problems can migrate to the city to seek employment. It has already been pointed out that the farm families most likely to migrate to cities are younger and better educated and have less invested in farming.

Families in low-income areas have the greatest need for new job opportunities, but also have the greatest barriers to opportunities. They have lower income and lower educational levels, are older, and are more tied to their homes by tradition. They possess little information about nonfarm employment opportunities and have few of the skills that employers desire. Even if these low-income farmers migrated to the city, they might lose more in security, residence, and subsistence than they would gain in wages.

The lack of occupational flexibility on the part of farmers is one barrier to farm-to-city migration. The punch-press operator in a factory can easily transfer his skills from tractors to automobiles, but the transfer from milking cows to microelectronics is not so simple.

Unfortunately, these measures treat only the symptoms of the problem and not the problem itself. The real problem is overproduction of agricultural products, and the solution is reduction in the acres of farmland used to grow crops, reduction in the numbers of dairy cattle, and reduction in the number of animals produced each year for meat consumption. Marginal cropland should be taken out of crop production and used for other purposes such as grazing or wildlife preservation. Government subsidies for certain commodities such as dairy products should be greatly reduced or eliminated. A recently proposed policy would eliminate overproduction by eliminating all commodity support payments. The money used for commodity support payments would be used instead for direct income support payments to farmers below the poverty level, and for job training and relocation programs (Tweeten, 1986).

The problem of the agricultural transition will not be solved within this century. Food surpluses will not disappear for some time: The backlog of new technology is too great. Nor do rural sociologists expect new farm legislation to provide answers, for the problem of the agricultural transition is much too complex.

SUMMARY

Farming in the United States is a business, and differences between it and other enterprises have largely diminished. Farm operations are characterized by an emphasis on sophisticated technology and information needs. The new technologies include computers for decision making; *biotechnology*, attempts to improve plants or animals by changing the genetic structure, or the use of living organisms to make or modify products; and *robotics*, the development and use of self-controlled machines through a combination of engineering automation and computerized artificial intelligence. New farm technology continues to displace farm workers, by reducing the amount of required labor, as do new practices, such as *intensification*. *Intensification* is increasing the amount of food or fiber produced on a given parcel of land by increasing the density of plants or animals on that land or by increasing the number of production cycles for that land in a given period of time. The trends toward fewer but larger farms, commercialization, specialization, capitalization, and concentration will continue. The only inconsistency in these trends is the development of a *dual structure of agriculture* with a growing number of small and large farms and a disappearing middle.

Vertical integration, the coordination under the control of one management of two or more steps in the chain of supplying materials, producing, processing, and distributing a product, is expanding into new areas, such as hog production. Many farmers in hog production are becoming vertically integrated through contract farming. *Contract farming* is an agreement between a farmer and his business operator to partially coordinate the supply, production, processing, and marketing of a farm product under one management.

Farmers may be classified into six tenure classes. *Farm owners* have title to all the land they farm. Full owners tend to operate smaller farms, and as a class are declining in number. *Part owners* own some land and rent additional land to enlarge their operations. They constitute the largest class and individually tend to have larger farms than full owners or tenants. *Tenants*, those farmers who rent all the land they farm, are only about 12 percent of all farmers. *Farm laborers* are those who work for wages in agriculture. *Farm managers* are professional salaried employees that operate farms for the owners, such as *corporation farms*, large agricultural operations owned by groups of stockholders.

New farmers are almost exclusively the sons and daughters of present farmers. FFA and 4-H projects provide the function of socialization for prospective farmers, and a college education is becoming a prerequisite.

As evidence of the increased commercialization in agriculture, we see an increase in the number of part-time farmers. *Part-time farmers* spend at least 100 days per year in off-farm employment. Part-time farming has become an institutionalized feature of U.S. agriculture.

The traditional role of women and other family members in farm work and farm decision making may be changing with increased use of sophisticated technology. New technology may reinforce a family division of labor that does not include a direct role for women in operating the farm. Women do, however, continue to make a major financial contribution to the farm operation by producing many of the goods consumed by the family.

Not all farmers are following the trend toward increased mechanization and chemical farming. Concerns about the effects of chemical farming on the land, animals, and people has resulted in the growth of organic farming. *Organic farmers* avoid the use of chemical fertilizers and pesticides, as well as synthetically compounded growth regulators and feed additives.

National and international trends are creating a transition in agriculture that is forcing many farmers out of farming and causing many rural communities to die. The *agricultural transition* is the change that is occurring in the nature of farming and all other parts of the agricultural industry in response to new technology and the changing world economy. Two major reasons for the problems of the agricultural transition are too much farm production in relation to consumer food needs, and the inadequacy of the size of the average farm to permit farm families to utilize their available labor and machinery efficiently. One solution to the problem is to reduce production by transferring cropland, especially marginal cropland, to other uses.

REFERENCES

ALBRECHT, DON, and HOWARD LADEWIG. (1982). "Corporate Agriculture and the Family Farm." *The Rural Sociologist, 2,* 376–383.

BARLETT, PEGGY F. "Part-time Farming: Saving the Farm or Saving the Lifestyle?" *Rural Sociology, 51,* 289–313.

BATTENFIELD, SUSAN L., and DEAN L. HAYNES. (1983). "Plant Pest Control Strategies." In Yao-chi Lu, ed. *Emerging Technologies in Agricultural Production.* Washington, DC. U.S. Department of Agriculture.

BULTENA, GORDON L., and ERIC O. HOIBERG. (1984). "Farmers Adopting Computers Bit by Bit." *Agri Marketing, 21.*

BUTTEL, FREDERICK H., and GILBERT W. GILLESPIE. (1984). "The Sexual Division of Farm Household Labor: An Exploratory Study of the Structure of On-Farm and Off-Farm Labor Allocation among Farm Men and Women," *Rural Sociology, 49,* 183–209.

BUTTEL, FREDERICK H., J. TADLOCK COWAN, MARTIN KENNEY, and JACK KLOPPENBURG, JR. (1984). "Biotechnology in Agriculture: The Political Economy of Agribusiness Reorganization and Industry-University Relationships." In Harry K. Schwarzweller, ed. *Research in Rural Sociology and Development, Vol. 1, Focus on Agriculture.* Greenwich, CT: JAI Press.

CLEARFIELD, FRANK, and PAUL D. WARNER. (1984). "An Agricultural Videotext System: The Green Thumb Pilot Study." *Rural Sociology, 49,* 284–297.

COLMAN, GOULD, and SARAH ELBERT. (1984). "Farming Families: The Farm Needs Everyone." In Harry K. Schwarzweller, ed. *Research in Rural Sociology and Development, Vol. 1, Focus on Agriculture.* Greenwich, CT: JAI Press.

COUGHENOUR, C. MILTON. (1984). "Farmers and Farm Workers: Perspectives on Occupational Complexities and Change." In Harry K. Schwarzweller, ed. *Research in Rural Sociology and Development, Vol. 1, Focus on Agriculture.* Greenwich, CT: JAI Press.

DALECKI, MICHAEL G., and BOB BEALER. (1984). "Who is the 'Organic' Farmer?" *The Rural Sociologist, 4,* 11–18.

DUFFY, MIKE. (1985). *Estimated Costs of Crop Production in Iowa—1986*, FM-1712. Ames: Iowa Cooperative Extension Service.

EASTERBROOK, GREGG. (1985, July). "Making Sense of Agriculture." *Atlantic Monthly*, pp. 63–78.

Economic Research Service. (1985). *The Current Financial Condition of Farmers and Farm Lenders.* Agriculture Information Bulletin 490. Washington, DC: U.S. Department of Agriculture.

ELBERT, DAVID, and STEVE BALLARD. (1986, August). "Iowa Falls Bank is 9th '86 Failure." *Des Moines Register.*

GEISLER, CHARLES C., J. TADLOCK COWAN, MICHAEL R. HATTERY, and HARVEY M. JACOBS. (1984). "Sustained Land Productivity: Equity Consequences of Alternative Agricultural Technologies." In Gigi M. Berardi and Charles C. Geisler, eds. *The Social Consequences and Challenges of New Agricultural Technologies."* Boulder, CO: Westview.

GOLDSCHMIDT, WALTER. (1978). *As You Sow: Three Studies in the Social Consequences of Agri-Business.* Montclair, NJ: Allenheld, Osmun.

HARRIS, CRAIG K., SHARON POWERS, and FREDERICK H. BUTTEL. (1980). "Myth and Reality in Organic Farming." *Newsline, 8,* 33–43.

HEFFERNAN, JUDITH BORTNER, and WILLIAM D. HEFFERNAN. (1986). "When Families Have to Give Up Farming." *Rural Development Perspectives, 2,* 28, 29.

HEFFERNAN, WILLIAM D. (1984). "Constraints in the U.S. Poultry Industry." In Harry K. Schwarzweller, ed. *Research in Rural Sociology and Development, Vol. 1, Focus on Agriculture.* Greenwich, CT: JAI Press.

HEFFERNAN, WILLIAM D., GARY GREEN, R. PAUL LASLEY, and MICHAEL F. NOLAN. (1981). "Part-time Farming and Rural Community." *Rural Sociology, 46,* 245–262.

JACOB, JEFFREY C., and MERLIN B. BRINKERHOFF. (1986). "Alternative Technology and Part-time, Semi-subsistence Agriculture: A Survey from the Back to the Land Movement." *Rural Sociology, 51,* 43–59.

KORSCHING, PETER F., and PETER J. NOWAK. (1983). "Flexibility in Conservation Policy." In David E. Brewster, Wayne D. Rasmussen, and Garth Youngberg, eds. *Farms in Transition,* Ames: Iowa State University Press.

KRIMSKY, SHELDON. (1983). "Biotechnology and Unnatural Selection: The Social Control of Genes." In Gene F. Summers, ed. *Technology and Social Change in Rural Areas.* Boulder, CO: Westview.

LASLEY, PAUL. (1985, June). "Family Living Changes." *Iowa Farm and Rural Life Poll: Summary,* pp. 7, 8.

LASLEY, PAUL. (1984, January). "Grain Agreement with Russia." *Iowa Farm and Rural Life Poll: Farm Policy Issues,* p. 5.

LEISTRITZ, F. LARRY, BRENDA L. EKSTROM, ARLEN G. LEHOLM, STEVE H. MURDOCK, and RITA R. HAMM. (1986). "North Dakota and Texas Farmers Who Are in Financial Stress." *Rural Development Perspectives, 2,* 14–17.

LEMONS, JOHN. (1986). "Structural Trends in Agriculture and Preservation of Family Farms." *Environmental Management, 10,* 75–88.

LOCKERETZ, WILLIAM, and SARAH WERNICK. (1980)."Commercial Organic Farming in the Corn Belt in Comparison to Conventional Practices." *Rural Sociology, 45,* 708–722.

LYSON, THOMAS A. (1984). "Pathways in Production Agriculture: The Structuring of Farm Recruitment in the United States." In Harry K. Schwarzweller, ed. *Research in Rural Sociology and Development, Vol. 1, Focus on Agriculture.* Greenwich, CT: JAI Press.

MUHM, DON. (1986, August 13). "Near-Record Corn Harvest Is Predicted." *Des Moines Register.*

Office of Technology Assessment. (1986). *Technology, Public Policy, and the Changing Structure of Agriculture.* Washington, DC: U.S. Government Printing Office.

PINS, KENNETH. (1986, September 1). "On the Whole, Farmers Enjoy Their Labors," *Des Moines Register.*

RASMUSSEN, WAYNE D. (1982). "The Mechanization of Agriculture." *Scientific American, 247,* 77–89.

REIMER, BILL. (1986). "Women as Farm Labor." *Rural Sociology, 51,* 143–155.

SHARP, CHARLOTTE, DOUGLAS GWYNNE, and ORVILLE E. THOMPSON. (1986). "Farm Size and the Role of Farm Women." *The Rural Sociologist, 6*, 259–264.

STRANGE, MARTY, and CHUCK HASSEBROOK. (1981). *Take Hogs, for Example: The Transformation of Hog Farming in America*. Walthill, NE: Center for Rural Affairs.

THOMAS, GRANT W. (1983). "Multiple Cropping, in Yao-chi Lu, ed. *Emerging Technologies in Agricultural Production*. Washington, DC: U.S. Department of Agriculture.

THOMPSON, O.E., and ANN F. SCHEURING. (1984). "From Lug Boxes to Electronics: A Study of California Tomato Growers and Sorting Crews, 1977." In Gigi M. Berardi and Charles C. Geisler, eds. *The Social Consequences and Challenges of New Agricultural Technologies*. Boulder, CO: Westview.

TWEETEN, LUTHER. (1986). "New Policies to Take Advantage of Opportunities for Agricultural and Rural Development." In Peter F. Korsching and Judith Gildner, eds. *Interdependencies of Agriculture and Rural Communities in the Twenty-First Century: The North Central Region*, Ames, IA: North Central Regional Center for Rural Development.

Resource Conservation Act Coordinating Committee. (1980). *Public Attitudes Revealed on Soil and Water Conservation*. Washington, DC: U.S. Department of Agriculture.

VOGELER, INGOLF. (1981). *The Myth of the Family Farm: Agribusiness Dominance of U.S. Agriculture*. Boulder, CO: Westview.

ZWERDLING, DANIEL. (1978, June). "Organic Farming Works." *The Environmental Journal*, 10–16.

Chapter 11

Farmer Organizations and Movements

Don't look now but the bumper crop being harvested on the nation's farms this year is a harvest of surly, disenchanted farmers who are fed up with producing more for less. . . . The farm problem, which is as perennial as the noxious weeds along the road, isn't going to die at the end of the year as those thistles. And, just like the thistles, the farm problem vegetates and flourishes each year.

—J.L. Brown (1956)

What you farmers need to do is to raise less corn and more Hell!

Elizabeth Lease, Farmers
Alliance Leader in Kansas
(1931)

One is likely to think of the typical farmer as a mild-mannered, conservative, and slow-to-act person with little interest in issues or events outside of the farm's line fences. Yet these seemingly mild-mannered and conservative farmers have been sufficiently provoked by farm conditions over the years to participate in numerous revolts against the authority of the U.S. government.

It is from a history of such early farmer movements as the Shays' Rebellion and Farmers Holiday Association that modern farmer organizations have evolved. Although these early social movements bear little resemblance to modern farmer organizations, it is necessary to understand them before we can understand present-day farmer organizations. The legacy of the early protest movements has not been lost. The American Agricultural Movement of the late 1970s with its Washington tractorcades demonstrated that the propensity for protest, as suggested in the quote by Elizabeth Lease, is still very alive among farmers.

In this chapter, we shall describe the four major farmer organizations functioning in today's society: the Grange, the Farmers Union, the Farm Bureau, and the National Farmers Organization (NFO). We also examine such recent farm protests as the American Agricultural Movement, the North American Farm Alliance, and Posse Comitatus. We begin with an illustration of a U.S. farmers' movement.

BOX 11-1   *FARM STRIKE!*

Denison, Iowa, Friday, April 28. . .

The battle started shortly after 1:30 P.M. [at a farm foreclosure auction]. The sheriff, surrounded by his officers, six of whom were state agents and the rest special deputies, had sold two cribs of corn when several truckloads of farmers rolled into the farmyard.

The farmers jumped from the trucks and rushed the officers, who were armed with clubs and axe handles. Men went down but more farmers entered the fray.

Clubs and fists thudded.

Men shouted.

The area between two large barns was filled with a swirling, swinging mass of men.

The battle lasted for 15 or 20 minutes. It ended when the sheriff and his deputies retreated, climbed into their cars and returned to Denison, where the sheriff announced the sale had been postponed until 10 A.M. Saturday.

This battle between policemen and farmers occurred when the sheriff attempted to hold a legal foreclosure sale. A similar scene was depicted in the popular movie *Country*. Farmers had had a decade of prosperity. Land values and farm mortgage debts skyrocketed. In Iowa, slightly more than half of all farms were mortgaged. Low farm prices and subsequent low farm incomes in an economic depression made it impossible for many farmers to meet their mortgage payments. When a bank foreclosed a farmer's mortgage and attempted to auction off the farm equipment and livestock, the farmer's friends would band together and set very low bidding prices. Then they would buy their friend's property for practically nothing, and after the auction return it to the farmer. If an outsider tried to bid a reasonable price at these auctions, the farmers would physically dissuade him. Such control of bidding at auctions is, of course, illegal. The battle at Denison, Iowa, occurred when the authorities attempted to stop such a "penny sale," as the auctions were known.

When did this farm strike in Denison, Iowa, occur? In 1978, 1980, or 1987? It actually occurred in 1933! It was part of the Farmers Holiday Association.

The Farmers Holiday Association was formed by irate Midwestern farmers as a protest against low farm prices in the Depression years of the 1930s. The frustration and anger of farmers caught in these severe economic straits exploded into violent incidents. While many of the farmers picketing at the Densison auction were probably members of the Farmers Holiday Association, the penny sales were not one of the Association's approved activities. The original purpose of the Association was to call a "farmers' holiday," a strike in which no food products would be marketed until farm prices were raised. One Association member composed this poem:

Let's call a Farmers' Holiday
A Holiday let's hold
We'll eat our wheat and ham and eggs
And let them eat their gold.

Interestingly, the original aims of the American Agricultural Movement in the early 1980s were almost identical. The Movement's followers wanted to shut down agricultural production sufficiently to create a scarcity of farm products and thus to drive consumer prices higher (Browne, 1983).

Three months after its beginning, the Farmers Holiday Association covered 24 states and claimed about 2 million members. Wisconsin dairy farmers were especially active in the Association. In one incident, 300 farmers spilled over 30,000 pounds of milk from trucks attempting to pass the strikers' roadblocks. Over 2,000 Wisconsin state troopers were called out to quell this rebellion. These were spontaneously organized blockades, not part of the activities that the Assocation had initially planned. The peaceful withholding action had little direct affect on farm prices. But such irrational, violent incidents brought national attention to the farmer's plight in the 1930s, and resulted in the creation of several government agencies to help the farmer, such as the Farmers Home Administration, the Agricultural Stabilization and Conservation Service, the Soil Conservation Service, and the federal farm loan agencies (Chapter 15). Farmers' movements in the 1980s have borrowed the tactics of farm strikes from the Farmers Holiday Association.

FIGURE 11-1   This farm auction scene is being repeated many times across rural America. With low prices for farm products, farmers who are deep in debt are unable to make their mortgage payments. When the banks foreclose, the farms are sold at public auction. Friends of the bankrupt farmer sometimes protest what they feel is unjust treatment by disrupting the auction or by setting very low bidding prices and physically threatening anyone who bids higher.

Source: Joy and Johnson Auction Company, Incorporated.

IMPORTANCE OF FARMER ORGANIZATIONS IN THE UNITED STATES

When agriculture in the United States was largely a self-sufficient family enterprise (as it still is today in many Third World countries), there was little need for farmer organizations. The farmer was his own boss. He had complete independence because his farm income was not dependent on a government farm program, favorable price supports, or even on cooperative economic ventures with neighbors. Early farm families were self-sufficient units.

This individualism of pioneer days has long ago been eroded, and the difficulties confronting the modern farmer can no longer be overcome by unaided efforts. Until this century in the United States, the economic factors that made for success or failure were largely in the control of the individual farmer. An industrious farmer who handled resources efficiently became a successful farmer. But as agriculture became commercialized, many other factors affected the success of the farm enterprise. The most thrifty and efficient farmer could fail through no personal fault. Forces had been set in motion over which the farmer individually had no control.

Farmers began to realize that farmer organizations were necessary to safeguard them against the interests of other pressure groups. Thus farmer organizations developed at the same time that the self-sufficient farming pattern began to break down. Farmer organizations in Third World nations are not yet so functional as in America and Europe, where farmers are more interdependent with nonfarm society.

FARM PRESSURE GROUPS

Politics is first nature to the farmer, and it has been used by farmers for many decades to bring about changes in the social system favorable to farmers. Politics was used to carve out satisfactory land laws and to get homesteads on the public domain. Through politics, the farmer went after the railroads and the elevators in the 1870s Granger legislation. Especially in this century, U.S. farmers have piled triumph upon triumph: agricultural credit, advantages for farmers' cooperatives, regulation of market and commodity exchanges, aids to conservation, rural electrification, and price supports and commodity loans. Indeed, when farmers are not playing politics with and against others, they pursue the art among themselves. The struggle for power within agriculture is something to watch.

Farmer organizations are important to farmers, but they also affect everyone else. One of the major legislative interests of farmer organizations is the federal farm program administered by the U.S. Department of Agriculture. The U.S. public has a very direct stake in this farm program, as they pay for it. In the mid-1980s, about $40 billion of the federal budget each year went to agriculture. If the public is interested in how its tax dollars are spent, it must be interested in the role of farmer organizations in influencing federal farm programs.

The farm vote continues to be important enough for the major political parties to court it in each presidential election; at least one platform plank consists of promises to the farmer. Because of the small size of the farm population, however, future elections will show a growing importance for the food vote rather than the farm vote.

FUNCTIONS OF FARMER ORGANIZATIONS

The goals of most farmer organizations may be categorized, in order of importance, as (1) legislative, (2) economic, and (3) educational. The Farm Bureau's symbol once was a "three-legged stool" of legislation, education, and economic services. The traditional emblem of the Farmers Union is a triangle, with the three sides representing "legislation, education, and [economic] cooperation, bounded by the circle of farm organization."

Legislative Functions

Farmer organizations start in periods of economic distress for farmers. The original purpose of these organizations was mainly centered around the solution of farmers' economic problems by legislative action. In the United States and in other nations, farmers formed pressure groups to solve their economic misfortunes. Most farmer organizations plainly state in their purposes that their major goal is to secure favorable legislation for their members.

A *pressure group* is a formal organization composed of people with common interests or occupations who seek to secure desired legislation by improving communication with their legislators. The main purpose of pressure groups is to exert influence upon legislators by communicating to them the wishes of their constituents or followers.

A citizen can increase control over elected representatives by joining with others of similar interests. Through activity in a pressure group, a citizen may have considerable influence over legislators during their term of office, rather than just at election time. A thousand letters from Farm Bureau members arguing for an issue are likely to have more effect on a harried legislator than a letter from one farmer. Pressure from an organized block of voters is more effective than individual action. And so farmer organizations provide an important function for their members by expressing their composite wishes to legislators in a systematic and effective manner.

Many public officials welcome the activities of pressure groups and are glad to receive an expression of public opinion about specific issues from a segment of their constituents. Undoubtedly there are some pressure groups that operate by undesirable methods, such as blackmailing, bribery, or threatening public officials. The average U.S. citizen probably views pressure group activities as shady, dishonest, and undesirable. However, most pressure groups fulfill an important role in a democracy by crystallizing public opinion into government policy and action.

Farmer organizations are not the only pressure groups to which farmers belong. For instance, the trend to part-time farming results in a higher percentage of labor union membership among farm people. In several highly industrialized states, more than half of all farmers work over 100 days per year in a nonfarm job, and many of these are union members. But most part-time farmers seem to belong to unions in name only; they retain their psychological identification with their farm occupation and with farmer organizations.

In addition to the general labor unions to which many part-time farmers belong, there are specialized labor unions that seek members among farm laborers. The United Farm Workers, one of the AFL-CIO unions, primarily concentrated in the fruit and vegetable regions of California, has about 100,000 members.

Economic Functions

One of the main goals of farmer organizations is to act as pressure groups, but this is not their only function. In the Depression days of the 1930s, the first thing an impoverished farmer did was to cancel farm magazine subscriptions, and the second was not to renew his farmer organization membership. Today, most farm pressure groups offer programs of economic services, so that farmers cannot afford *not* to renew their membership, even in hard times. The services are aimed at saving money for their farmer members by supplying them with fuel, fertilizer, insurance, and feed at a reduced cost. A statewide survey of Michigan farmers, for instance, showed that the most important single reason for belonging given by Farm Bureau members was to obtain such economic services as insurance, followed closely by legislative advantages (Hathaway et al., 1966). Economic services were relatively unimportant for Grange members, who belonged for fellowship reasons.

Many farm pressure groups also sponsor farmer cooperatives through which members may buy or sell at a saving. When there is a large number of small-scale sellers of some product, and a small number of large-scale buyers, the buyers have a decided advantage in bargaining for price. This concentration of buyers' power exists for most farm products. Farmer cooperatives provide the individual farmer with an effective means to counterbalance this power, and farmer organizations, since the days of the Grange, have played an important role in forming such cooperatives for their members.

If a farmer organization can show the farmer that $30 in annual dues can save $100 in economic services, it is not difficult to gain the farmer's continued loyal support. One criterion of a powerful pressure group is a large and stable membership. The economic purposes of farmer organizations attract this membership and contribute to its legislative power (Olson, 1971). Legislative benefits are sometimes difficult for a member to see, and all farmers benefit from favorable legislation even if they are not members. But economic savings are much easier to demonstrate and the savings are benefits only members receive. While it encourages a larger, stable membership in a farmer organization, the disadvantage of providing economic services is that these farmers are often members in name only.

One type of economic activity by farmer organizations is the farm strike, like the one by the Farmers Holiday Association described early in this chapter. In the 1960s, several such "withholding actions" were staged by the National Farmers Organization (NFO). This organization began in 1955 out of perceived grievances by Iowa farmers about low agricultural prices (Stofferahn and Korsching, 1986). After mass meetings and other pressure group activities failed to result in amelioration of depressed farm prices, the NFO hit upon the farm strike as a means of direct economic action. In 1962, an NFO holding action on livestock extended for 32 days. During this time, all cattle and hogs were held on members' farms, rather than sold, and attempts were made by the NFO to prevent livestock sales by nonmember farmers. This influence sometimes resulted in unofficial violence (officially deplored by NFO leaders) when nonmembers tried to market their animals.

The effect of the livestock marketing strike was difficult to assess. In its first weeks, the total numbers of livestock sold was lowered somewhat. Overall, only very small gains (if any) in livestock prices resulted. And the delay in time of marketing actually increased the meat supply because the livestock gained weight while being withheld from market. NFO leaders disagree with this analysis. NFO President Oren Lee Staley claimed (in the *NFO Reporter,* May, 1963, p. 1): "There is no question in anyone's mind that we raised the price on hogs and cattle $2.00 per hundredweight."

In 1967, the NFO called a holding action on a highly perishable food product: milk. This strike was better organized and its support was more widespread than the livestock strike of 1962. One result was favorable publicity for the cause. The 1967 milk strike undoubtedly gained more members for the NFO, as well as more NFO marketing contracts with dairy plants (who agree to buy specified amounts of milk from NFO members at a certain price.)

Educational Functions

The educational goals of farmer organizations may be fulfilled through a variety of activities. Some groups carry on regular educational programs at their local meetings through the use of speakers and group discussion. Several farmer organizations like the Farm Bureau have given direct and indirect financial aid to adult educational agencies such as the Cooperative Extension Service. The educational programs of some farmer organizations are mainly concerned with new agricultural technology, while other programs are about current public affairs or community issues. Most sociological studies of farmer organization members show that they do not belong mainly for educational reasons; nevertheless, almost all farmer groups carry on some type of educational activities for their members.

CHANGES IN U.S. FARMER ORGANIZATIONS

Early Farmer Protests

Shay's Rebellion took place in New England in 1785, soon after the Revolutionary War (which was in itself a farmer movement in the sense that it was composed almost entirely of farmers, and its goals dealt, at least in part, with the marketing of farm products). A majority of Daniel Shays' army of debtors were farmers, and his movement was primarily a farmers' protest against debts, taxes, and low farm prices. An unsuccessful attempt was first made to secure legislation that would benefit farmers. When these legislative endeavors failed, Shays' followers adopted more violent means: They forcibly prevented judges from trying debtors and foreclosing mortgages. Shays' army was finally defeated in a clash with federal military troops.

Agricultural Societies

Probably the earliest farmer organizations in the United States were the agricultural societies, which were established to improve agriculture by the exchange of new farm ideas. They were not organized as pressure groups. Most of the early members were gentlemen farmers. George Washington and Benjamin Franklin, for instance, were members of the first agricultural society, established in Philadelphia in 1785. By the time of the Civil War, over 900 agricultural and horticultural societies had been established in the United States.

Early agricultural societies promoted township, county, and state agricultural fairs. These fairs aided the diffusion of new farm ideas and, through competitive judging, spurred the development of improved crop and livestock varieties. Many state and county fairs in the United States today are still officially administered by agricultural societies.

The Grange

The typical Grange Hall was once described as "a hotbed of rural opinion, a community center where farmers gather to achieve social, economic and political integration. It is also a fraternal sanctum, full of top-secret rituals and symbolism. And . . . it's an outpost of the nation's oldest farm group." The Grange was founded soon after the Civil War in a period of unfavorable economic conditions for farmers. Frontier farmers had contracted debts during the high-price period of the Civil War and could not repay them when farm prices fell. Midwestern farmers burned their corn because it was cheaper, at 15 cents a bushel, than fuel. Farmer resentment was directed toward the middlemen and the railroads.

Oliver Hudson Kelly founded the Grange (also known as the Patrons of

Husbandry) in 1868. Kelly was a thirty-second degree member of the Masonic Temple, a secret fraternity for men. As a government employee of the newly established U.S. Department of Agriculture, he made a tour of the agricultural conditions of the postwar South. He conceived the idea of a farmers' fraternity while on this tour, as a means of seeking solutions to some farmers' ills. In 1868, Kelly resigned from the USDA and went on the road to sell his idea to American farmers. After encountering a lack of farmer enthusiasm, Kelly established several local Granges in Minnesota. These local organizations marked the beginning of the greatest expansion of any farmer organization in the United States. The high point of Grange membership was reached in 1875, with 850,000 members in 32 states.

Why did the idea of a farmer fraternity suddenly catch on after its abortive first attempt? One sociologist has presented documents to show a decided change occurred in the promised benefits of Grange membership. Early Grange organizers shifted the emphasis from Kelly's notion of fraternal fellowship to legislative and economic benefits. These organizers claimed that the best way to sell a Grange membership was to show a farmer how much money could be saved through economic services and, less directly, through pressure group activities (Taylor, 1953).

A decline in Grange membership came as suddenly as had its growth. The Grange failed for the same reasons that it originally succeeded. The economic advantages had been oversold. Grange enterprises often failed, and when a local Grange store went bankrupt, all the members of the local Grange organizations were liable for whatever debts it had accrued.

Grange membership in the United States is now at about 400,000. Membership has also shifted in the geographical locations of Grange activity, from the Midwest and the South, to New England (plus Ohio, New York, and Pennsylvania) and the Pacific Northwest. This geographical location influences the legislative policies of the Grange, as we shall see.

FIGURE 11-2
Membership   Trend   of   the   Grange.

Most farmer organizations seem to follow a similar path of sudden membership growth, sharp decline, and then a gradual growth. Grange membership followed this general pattern from its beginning in 1868.

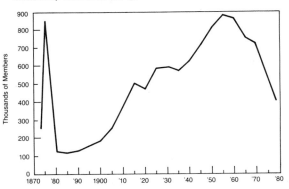

Membership trend of the Grange.

The Farmers Union

The era of the declining Grange movement in the late 1870s was a time of unfavorable economic conditions for farmers, especially cotton farmers in the South. The time was ripe for the founding of a new farmer organization.

This organization was the Farmers Educational and Co-operative Union of America, or more simply, the Farmers Union. Soon a membership of 200,000 farm families was scattered throughout the Southern states. The Union was originally a secret fraternal society with a racial clause to prevent black membership. Both the racial ban and the secret nature of the Union were dropped when the Union shifted membership from the South to the wheat region of the Midwest. Instead of building cooperative cotton gins, the Union began constructing grain elevators. Union membership is today concentrated in six Western states: Oklahoma, Colorado, Montana, the Dakotas, and Minnesota. There are also substantial memberships in Nebraska and Wisconsin. The Union has never been strong in the Far West, or the East, or the Corn Belt states.

In 1969, there were 250,000 dues-paying farm families as members of the Farmers Union, which makes it smaller in membership than the Grange and the Farm Bureau, and perhaps smaller than the NFO.

The economic services provided by the Farmers Union are almost entirely cooperative. These farmer cooperatives contribute in two ways to the Farmers Union: The cooperatives pay an educational fund, usually 5 percent of net earnings to the state Union, and the co-ops pay the Union membership dues of their patrons through a "check-off" system. A farmer who intends to do business with a local Farmers Union cooperative supposedly must first become a member of the Farmers Union. Membership dues in the Union local are deducted from the farmer's co-op annual savings before the savings check is issued; the dues are thus "checked off." The farmer may not even know or care about belonging to the Farmers Union, and thus is not likely to attend meetings of the Union local or to have a say in its legislative policies. So the check-off system may provide more members for a farmer organization, and ensure their continued loyalty over a period of years, but it may ultimately be detrimental because these members are not involved or committed to the organization.

The connection between the Farmers Union and its cooperatives is largely historical and voluntary, rather than legal. Today less than half of the members in Farmers Union cooperatives are actually Farmers Union members. While economic services contribute to a pressure group's high, stable membership, they also may lead to inactive members who are unlikely to support the organization's legislative positions.

The Farm Bureau

The first Farm Bureau was organized in Broome County, New York, in 1911. The Chamber of Commerce in the town of Binghamton, New York, was composed of a number of sections or bureaus, one of which was known as the "Farm Bureau." It was composed of farmers and businessmen interested in improving agriculture. This first Farm Bureau was an educational agency designed to help farmers learn better methods of agriculture. Funds to support this program were supplied in part by the Delaware, Lackawanna, and Western Railroad. The employees of the Farm Bureau became known as "farm agents" because it was the custom of the day to refer to any railroad employee as an agent.

The educational program of the Broome County Farm Bureau initiated the idea of an extension "agent" residing in the county. The county agent movement was spurred by the Smith-Lever Act of 1914, which provided federal funds to pay for such extension work. By 1918, there was a county agent in almost every county in the United States. So the Farm Bureau of Broome County was rapidly copied throughout the United States.

The original purpose of these county Farm Bureaus was strictly educational. A county Farm Bureau consisted of several hundred farmers who annually contributed dues toward the hiring of a county extension agent. In return, they received intensive technical assistance from the agent through farm visits and in group meetings. Farm Bureau leaders soon realized these county units, if organized into state and national bodies, could function as an effective pressure group. The formation of the American Farm Bureau Federation (AFBF) in 1919 signaled a change in the purposes of the Farm Bureau.

When the AFBF moved into pressure politics, a conflict arose due to the divergent purposes of the organization. At the county level, the educational program of the Farm Bureau was partially supported by public tax funds, thanks to the Smith-Lever Act. At the national and state level, the Farm Bureau acted as a legislative pressure group. The county extension agent was in the position of having to serve two masters with two widely different purposes: Adult agricultural education and pressure group activities. This role conflict (Chapter 4) was resolved by a separation of the Farm Bureau and the extension services (which began in 1919 but was not completed in some states until 1954). Thereafter, the extension service has been solely supported by tax funds.

Membership in the Farm Bureau was about 3,297,000 in the mid-1980s, which marks it as the largest farmer organization in the United States. Many members, however, are not farmers; they may be rural nonfarm people, small town merchants, and others who are involved in the agricultural sector (including college of agriculture professors) who join for the insurance and other economic benefits of Bureau membership. Memberships in the Farm Bureau are family rather than individual, which greatly increases the number of people involved. Farm Bureau membership is concentrated in the Midwest and the South. It tends to represent the better-established and more-commercialized farmers.

So the Farm Bureau developed from the local organizations that originally sponsored county extension agents. To this extent, the Bureau is unlike the other major farmer organizations, which were founded in response to unfavorable economic conditions.

The National Farmers Organization

The National Farmers Organization (NFO) sprang up, as did earlier farmer movements, from the seeds of rural discontent among economically disadvantaged farmers. The NFO began in 1955 from a speculative conversation between an Iowa farmer and his feed salesman in Corning, Iowa, about what to do about dropping livestock prices. The two agreed to invite their neighbors to a meeting to protest the plummeting prices. Thus, Wayne Jackson and Jay Loughry founded the NFO, which was to have over 200,000 members within nine months. From countywide meetings in Iowa sale barns, the organization quickly grew to cover the Midwest.

In the first phase of the NFO's growth, membership dues were only one dollar, and most Midwestern farmers were willing to invest that much in any cause that might help their economic plight. The NFO pursued legislative goals in the mid-1950s, but this early era of mushrooming membership growth was followed by a sudden drop when the NFO could not produce rapid legislative aid for depressed farm prices.

Starting in the late 1950s, the NFO switched its tactics to collective bargaining. Emphasis was put on withholding farm products from market until prices rose, and bargaining contracts were signed with members which allowed the NFO to control the sale of their products. Membership dues rose from one dollar to $75. The number of members slowly began to rise again;

FIGURE 11-3   Two NFO members atop a truck signal the dumping of 11,500 gallons of milk as part of a 1967 milk-holding action. Similar mass dumpings occurred in other Midwestern states on the same day.

growth spread in a widening circle from Iowa until it reached New York, Georgia, and Idaho in 1970. This growth was not like the "spontaneous combustion" of the mid-1950s; it was the result of high-pressure membership organizers. In fact, the NFO employs several hundred paid organizers, although many only work part-time.

The NFO's collective bargaining era revitalized and extended its membership. Paid organizers lead well-planned and well-executed membership drives. Collective bargaining is a forceful system that farmers can understand; holding products from market is far more visible than legislative procedures.

BOX 11-2   *INSIDE THE NFO*

Insight into the organization and growth of the National Farmers Organization is provided by a former rural sociology student of one of this book's authors. He interviewed his father, a North Dakota farmer who joined the NFO and worked as an organizer in the 1960s. Mr. Sauer, in partnership with his son, farms about 1,200 acres in southeastern North Dakota, growing primarily soybeans, corn, small grain, and feeder calves. He joined the NFO in 1962 through the urging of his father, who persuaded him to join with some literature about agricultural economics. Mr. Sauer became actively involved in the NFO, starting as a county organizer and moving up quickly to the position of executive assistant to the president of the National Farmers Organization. He became a full-time, salaried employee, traveling to different states to organize farmers. He eventually served on the National Board of Directors.

INTERVIEWER: What attracted you to the NFO?
MR. SAUER: Karl Wilkins' books on how the economy operates, and the importance of agriculture to the total economy: As agriculture goes, so goes the rest of the economy.
INTERVIEWER: Was that analysis an integral part of NFO philosophy?
MR. SAUER: We used this material all across the United States to recruit NFO members.
INTERVIEWER: How was the NFO different from the other organizations that had gone before it, such as the Farmers Union?
MR. SAUER: The new concept was collective bargaining. None of the other organizations were using or espousing it at that time. They seemed to be doing nothing about the farm problem. With the NFO, farmers could get actively involved.
INTERVIEWER: How was the NFO organized?
MR. SAUER: Build county organizations. You recruit members in that county until you had enough members to charter the county, a minimum of 25 members. We went into a new area and got acquainted—visiting farmers—and then we rented a meeting hall. We printed meeting notices, and hung them up around the town. Then we went out to some farmers and told them about the meeting. At the meeting,

we explained the NFO program and encouraged farmers to enroll that night. Any new member you did enroll got a new membership packet. He went out and enrolled new members the next day. When the meeting was over, we announced there would be another meeting—same time, same place—the next day. When we had enough members recruiting new members, we went on to the next county and did the same thing. After a county was chartered, we tried to recruit organizers from the group to keep on multiplying our effort.

INTERVIEWER: How difficult was it to sell the NFO program to people who had never heard of it before? The idea of collective bargaining was alien to many farmers.

MR. SAUER: No it wasn't. I suppose some people immediately associated collective bargaining with labor unions, and certain people who were oriented against labor were probably turned off. But basically the concept wasn't that difficult to sell. Using the direct approach, we'd say, "We're all going to get together and sell our commodities together, and we're going to set a price together, and they won't be sold unless we get our price."

INTERVIEWER: Some NFO tactics were criticized, such as holding actions. What were the objectives of holding actions and were the holding actions successful?

MR. SAUER: The big objective was to secure contracts with processors— to hold the product off the market until the processor would sign the contract. But more than that, the holding action was mainly to get press coverage so that we could call public attention to the farm problem. That's no different than what the farmers do in Europe—go on strike. So yes, they were successful. We secured contracts with packers and processors. The holding actions also advertised to farmers that the NFO was around, and thus we recruited a lot of members. Farmers that didn't join on the first go-around were saying maybe I want to be in on it.

INTERVIEWER;   Were any economic benefits realized from these contracts achieved through the holding action?

MR. SAUER: No! Because they were not to be implemented until there were enough contracts signed with processors of a certain commodity. Usually there were not enough farmers that signed the contracts.

INTERVIEWER: How much of a commodity within a region would have to be under contract before a benefit would be received?

MR. SAUER: They were all the same, generally 60 percent at early recruiting; later it was said 10 to 20 percent of a commodity. But I'm not sure of that—those figures don't seem reasonable.

INTERVIEWER: Was that a selling tool for recruiting new members, saying that as soon as the NFO gets 50 to 60 percent of the farmers in this area signed up, we can get an additional five cents or more per bushel or pound?

MR. SAUER: Yes! The selling point was that as soon as we can get enough of the commodity under control then we'll bargain with other members and we'll get the benefits of higher prices.

Unfortunately, because of poor management of the contracts in the NFO's national office, members marketing through the NFO were not getting paid. To correct this situation in 1972, some NFO leaders tried to oust Oren Lee Staley and change the NFO by-laws. The ensuing battle led to the disenchantment of a number of prominent NFO members, including Mr. Sauer, who left the organization. They later became active in the American Agricultural Movement and in other farm protest movements of the 1980s. Mr. Sauer himself participated in the AAM and its tractorcades.

The goal of the NFO, as recently stated by an NFO official, is to control at least 20 percent of the nation's farm production. At that point it will have enough strength for a national impact on farm prices (Browne, 1983). Through a combination of volume and forward contracting (guaranteeing delivery of a certain amount of produce at a specified time for a specified price), the NFO claims its members are already making a good profit while other farmers are losing money (Leonard, 1986).

Later in this chapter, we shall examine the nature of NFO growth to demonstrate the process of institutionalization through which a social movement becomes an organization.

Commodity Organizations

As U.S. farmers become more specialized, general farm organizations are being replaced by specialized commodity organizations. A *commodity organization* is a specialized farmer organization that promotes a specific farm product or a related group of farm products. Some commodity organizations are as large as the general farmer organizations. The American Dairy Association is a federation of 20 regional and state dairy farmers' associations with a membership of 210,000. The National Cattlemen's Association has 230,000 members, all involved in some aspect of beef production. The Cattlemen's Association mounts a public information campaign to promote beef consumption and promotes favorable legislation for beef farmers. A smaller and more specialized commodity organization is the Napa Valley Grape Growers Association. It has 200 members, and provides marketing assistance for wineries and promotes local and state legislation that will benefit grape growers.

Recent Agricultural Protests

The 1970s were so prosperous for farmers that the U.S. Secretary of Agriculture remarked wryly that some farmers were spending six months of the year in the field and the other six months sunning themselves in Florida or the Caribbean. In the 1980s, a downturn in the economy and a decline in land values occurred. Many farmers were disappointed with the implementation of the new farm bill, the Food and Agricultural Act of 1977. Farmers were prepared once again to challenge the existing economic and political structure, and a new era of agricultural protest began. As an agricultural policy analyst stated:

> Young farmers who had begun operating during the euphoria of the mid-seventies and then had experienced the down side of the roller-coaster were pinched for cash. Drought had hurt farmers in parts of the Midwest and in the Southeast. The Great Plains, the southeast, and the Gulf Coast were trouble centers. (Paarlberg, 1980, p. 50)

The American Agricultural Movement   Popularly called "the farm strike," the American Agricultural Movement (AAM) demanded that the U.S. Congress support prices for farm products at 100 percent of parity and limit all meat and livestock imports to the United States, and threatened to shut down agricultural production until farmers' demands were met. The AAM began in the summer of 1977 through informal discussions over coffee by several farmers in Campo, Colorado (Browne and Dinse, 1985). In September 1977, meetings were held to recruit farmers to the AAM. A second meeting, held in Springfield, Colorado, attracted 700 farmers and ranchers, some traveling hundreds of miles from neighboring states. The farmers' enthusiasm at these early meetings, combined with widespread leaflet distribution and media coverage, soon resulted in similar rallies across the United States.

By January 1978, approximately 1,100 local chapters had been organized and 40 states were represented at the National AAM convention (Browne, 1983). Although the AAM had a national leadership, it was actually a non-organization, having no dues, no membership, and no officers. State spokespersons were designated to provide a formal linkage for coordination of communication and activities between the state and national levels.

As the AAM grew, a strike deadline of December 14, 1977, was established, at which time all farm production and marketing would stop. The "strike" used some rather uncommon tactics, compared to previous farm protests. Drawing on the repertoire of tactics from other recent protest movements—such as the environmental, anti-Viet Nam War, and civil rights movements—farmers stormed and occupied the U.S. Secretary of Agriculture's office, thronged Congressional offices and hearing rooms, created traffic jams in Washington, D.C., and even released a herd of goats and a flock of chickens in the nation's capital. The mass media eagerly brought national attention to these events. The issues raised by the AAM were quickly addressed by the U.S. Congress.

But after this initial overreaction by Congress, legislative gains from the AAM farm strike were minimal. The major impacts were an increase in the target price for wheat and an increase in the loan rate for cotton. Furthermore, when spring 1978 came, the AAM farmers who had been striking returned to their farms. With the nation's other farmers, they planted and reaped a record crop.

The AAM is best remembered for its "tractorcades," especially the Washington, D.C., tractorcade of 1978. To continue the protest, the AAM sponsored tractorcades—hundreds of farm tractors driven together in a convoy. The 1979 tractorcade left North Platte, Nebraska, in mid-January, heading for Washington, D.C. Along the way the " 'cade" was joined by many hundreds of other tractors. When the farmers reached Des Moines, Iowa, the tractorcade was two miles long! Four thousand farmers driving tractors and

FIGURE 11-4 Tractorcades were used by the American Agricultural Movement to focus public attention on the plight of the farmer. In February 1979, four thousand farmers driving tractors and campers rolled into Washington, D.C. They received coverage from all the media, but because of unruly and crude tactics used by the farmers, many of the news stories did not leave favorable impressions with the public.

Source: Photo by Peggy Brisbane

campers, some from as far away as Colorado, eventually rolled into Washington ("Farmers Raising Cain," 1979). These farmers disrupted traffic, scuffled with police, and the national television networks even broadcast footage of a tractor driving through the reflecting pool on the Capitol grounds. Because of unruly, crude tactics, the 1979 tractorcade probably earned the AAM more public indignation than support.

By the time of the second Washington tractorcade in 1979, the AAM was already beginning to decline, although its followers engaged in additional activities, including political involvement in later presidential and Congressional elections. The same informality and spontaneity that helped the AAM's initial rapid growth also led to its decline. Because of its "no members, no dues, and no officers" philosophy, the American Agricultural Movement was never institutionalized into a farmer organization. It did not go through the process by which a relatively informal protest group becomes a recognized formal institution (discussed later in this chapter). Mainline farmer organizations and farm commodity groups did not overtly support the philosophy or tactics of the AAM (Browne, 1983). The original movement eventually split into a political committee headquartered in Washington, D.C., called AAM, Inc., and a less formally organized protest group called AAM-Grassroots (Downs, 1986). At the state level, the followers of the American Agricultural Movement have organized their own groups or joined other organizations. Many of AAM's early activists now work in other farmer organizations.

Radical right organizations.   In July 1984, the Nebraska State Police and the Richardson County sheriff raided an 80-acre hog farm near Rulo, Nebraska. They found truckloads of stolen farm equipment, as well as an arsenal of rifles, 150,000 rounds of ammunition, camouflage gear, and a hillside bunker stocked with food and water and having its own power supply. A further search led to the discovery of two bodies—a five-year-old boy and a 26-year-old man. Residents of the farm, two men and a 15-year-old, were arrested and charged with murder.

The story that emerged was one of incredible horror. Local people referred to the individuals living on the farm as "survivalists, members of a fanatic 'religious cult' whose leader said he was the 'archangel,' and claimed that Yahweh (God) was speaking through him. They were vehemently anti-Semetic, talked about Armageddon, and kept in touch via a hot line to find out what the Jews were up to." The boy and the man were killed in response to Yahway's bidding (Ridgeway, 1985).

Evidence suggests that the farm was a base camp for a white supremacist underground organization called Posse Comitatus. Posse Comitatus, organized in Portland, Oregon, in 1969, literally translated from Latin means "the power of the county." Its followers believe that the county sheriff is the highest elected official, that we do not have a democracy but a Christian Republic, that the Bible is the sole inspiration of the Constitution, and that

Christian common law is the ultimate authority. Political targets of the Posse are the Federal Reserve System, "believed to be controlled by a cabal of Zionist bankers," and the Internal Revenue Service.

The appeal of Posse Camitatus and similar extremist right groups to farmers is that they provide the farmer with an explanation of farm economic problems, and a source to blame: an international conspiracy (Lundgren, 1986). High interest rates and low land values, major factors in farmer problems, are blamed on the Federal Reserve System. Further, it is claimed that the Federal Reserve System is controlled by Jews, who are orchestrating the downfall of rural America.

Exact membership in Posse Comitatus and similar groups is difficult to determine because of the groups' extreme secrecy. A research organization that monitors the Ku Klux Klan and similar groups has estimated that Posse-type extremist groups have from 2,000 to 5,000 hard-core activists, and perhaps as many as 50,000 sympathizers in the Midwest (Nix, 1985).

North American Farm Alliance.   Decline of the American Agricultural Movement in the early 1980s did not end the farm protest or halt the emergence of new farmer organizations. The continuing farm crisis spawned numerous farmer organizations in the United States and in Canada. To present a unified front for farmers' problems, a national meeting was held in April 1983, which included farmer organization leaders from 23 states and two Canadian provinces. The North American Farm Alliance was created as a coalition of over 20 farmer, labor, and community organizations in the United States and Canada. The basic principles of the alliance include price supports for farm commodities, an end to forced farm sales, and support of the family farm. The Alliance is committed to nonviolent action.

Farm Aid.   On September 25, 1985, an impressive roster of country and rock singers gathered at the University of Illinois in Champaign to perform a fund-raiser for 80,000 fans in support of American farmers. The concert was organized by country singer Willie Nelson. Farm Aid emulated the highly successful Live Aid concert of July 1985, which raised money to fight world hunger, especially in Ethiopia. The 14-hour Farm Aid benefit concert raised $9 million for farmers through concert ticket sales and a telethon. The funds raised are used to help U.S. farmers, but the national attention that the Farm Aid concert called to farmers' problems is even more important. In 1986, a second Farm Aid concert was held in Austin, Texas.

LEGISLATIVE ACTIVITIES OF FARMER ORGANIZATIONS

How do farmer organizations decide what issues they want enacted into law? What type of government farm program does each farm pressure group

FIGURE 11-5   Farm Aid, a concert organized by country singer Willie Nelson, raised money in support of American farmers. Nine million dollars were raised through ticket sales and a national telethon. More important than the money that was raised is the national attention the concert called to farmers' problems.

Source: The *Champaign-Urbana News Gazette*

want? How does the location of their membership affect their legislative policies?

Each farmer organization determines its policies through an annual process in which resolutions are framed at the local level and then passed up through county, state, and national levels. Each organization makes a concentrated effort to involve its members in the policy-making process for two major reasons: (1) The purpose of the organization is to represent its farmers' interests; (2) and when the legislative policies are developed by the members, they are more likely to support their leaders in getting these policies enacted into laws.

The Policy-Formation Process

Each of the major farmer organizations follows slightly different methods of policy-making. In the Farm Bureau, the annual "resolutions process" begins in July and ends in December with the formation of a set of legislative positions on various public issues. In July of each year, public hearings are held at which interested persons present resolutions or proposals for legislative action. A state committee prints the tentative resolutions in questionnaire form, and they are mailed to each Farm Bureau member. These resolutions are discussed in local meetings by the members. Positions on these resolutions are sent to the state level. Voting delegates for each county are instructed to support their county's resolutions at the state Farm Bureau convention. Thus state policy is formulated on each issue.

The AFBF annual convention in December is the end of the annual resolutions process. Delegates from state Farm Bureaus attempt to develop a national Farm Bureau policy for the year ahead. A main issue at this convention each year is the desired type of federal farm program. Once the organization's annual policies are determined, the lobbyists and other Farm Bureau leaders seek to get these policies enacted into law. In Iowa, a strong Farm Bureau state, the chief lobbyist once noted that 17 of 19 Bureau resolutions were enacted into law the following year.

The resolutions process of the Farmers Union is conducted according to procedures generally similar to those of the Farm Bureau. The process begins in the union locals, where policy issues are discussed and decided, and culminates in a national convention each year.

In the Grange, questionnaires calling for responses on current policy issues are mailed to each subordinate Grange. State Granges tabulate the completed questionnaires and send the results to the national Grange. The issues are then voted on by delegates at the annual national convention.

The NFO is mainly involved in collective bargaining and direct economic action, rather than pressure group activities. Nevertheless, it holds annual conventions, where attention is paid to public issues, and a legislative position for the year ahead is mapped out.

Membership Location and Legislative Policies

U.S. farmer organizations are "national" in membership representation, but actually are regional in membership concentration. Grange members are concentrated in New England and the Pacific Northwest and are mostly dairy and crop farmers living within easy marketing distance of large East and West Coast cities. Farmers Union members are found throughout the western Midwest and northern Great Plains area, states ideally suited to the raising of hard red winter wheat. Droughts every four or five years add an element of financial risk. Farm Bureau membership centers in the corn-hog Midwest with important strength in the South. NFO membership is centered in the Midwest.

The membership location of each of these farm pressure groups has considerable influence upon their legislative policies. The organizations' policy positions on the federal farm program reflect the agricultural needs of the majority of their members. For example, the Farm Bureau prefers a gradual reduction and eventual elimination of price supports. This preference is an indication of the more economically secure position of Midwestern farm people in comparison with the Farmers Union members, whose main crop (wheat) is subject to more precarious weather and price conditions. The Farmers Union favors a governmental program of high price supports and export subsidies. Many Grange members in New England states, Ohio, Pennsylvania, and New York are dairy farmers who purchase wheat and corn. So they are less favorable to guaranteed prices for grains.

It might seem that all farmers would favor an extensive government program to provide them with financial security. This is not the case, however; farmers realize that in order for the federal government to provide price security, it must also exert a great deal of control over farmers' actions. For example, if the government is to guarantee a set price for a bushel of corn, farmers must also allow the government to tell them how much corn they can raise. Many farmers (especially Farm Bureau and Grange members) prefer a minimum program of farm price supports, so as to remain relatively free of government acreage allotments.

The NFO tends to view the federal farm program as an inadequate solution to economic problems and prefers to seek solutions via such direct action as collective bargaining with agricultural processors. The Farm Bureau, on the other hand, is strongly opposed to this NFO policy of withholding actions, even though its regional membership concentration overlaps closely with the NFO's in the Midwest.

The Grange and the Farm Bureau tend to favor conservative political approaches, while the Farmers Union and the NFO are the most liberal of the major farmer organizations in the United States.

FARMER MOVEMENTS, FARMER ORGANIZATIONS, AND SOCIAL CHANGE

In the history of U.S. rural society, farmer movements have flared like bright, exploding lights, momentarily directing the public's attention to farmers' economic problems as described early in this chapter. How do these movements facilitate social change? Why did the NFO become institutionalized into a lasting farmer organization while the AAM quickly disappeared?

What Is a Farmer Movement?

A *social movement* is a type of collective behavior in which a large number of individuals organize for social change to solve a perceived problem or crisis. A social movement involves collective, rather than individual, problem solving. Farmer movements began when individuals were faced with problems they could not solve alone, such as falling farm prices. These economic difficulties require group action. A single farmer cannot secure needed legislation, create new government relief agencies, or effectively mount a farm strike.

A *farmer movement* is a type of collective behavior in which a large number of farmers organize for social change to solve a perceived crisis in agriculture, usually an economic crisis. So a farmer movement is simply a particular kind of social movement in which the actors are farmers and the crisis is agricultural. The solutions sought by farmer movements, at least originally, involved changing some aspect of society's social structure. The purpose of a social movement is to change some aspect of society's social structure.

Most social movements pass through a series of developmental stages. Social unrest and upheaval lead to the founding of a formal organization with an ideology and a hierarchical structure, which later becomes institutionalized.

Perceived Crisis

Social movements begin when people in groups experience relative deprivation, and often flower when conditions are beginning to improve and further improvement is expected. *Relative deprivation* (or disadvantage) is the degree to which an individual perceives a situation with dissatisfaction owing to comparing the present situation with aspirations. These wants may arise when one's lot is compared with that of others, or with one's situation at some other time or place.

The history of farmer movements provides evidence that it is not objective disadvantage but rather perceived deprivation that strikes the spark of revolt. Once objective conditions begin to improve, but when such improvement does not occur immediately and dramatically, a social movement burns brightest. Consider the following examples of this principle.

The Whiskey Rebellion of 1792 began because farmers in Western Pennsylvania who distilled whiskey felt it was unfair that only this product was taxed, and not other farm products. Their movement became violent shortly after the U.S. Congress's decision to lighten the whiskey tax by allowing its payment in monthly installments.

The Farmers Union began in 1902 among small tenant farmers in Texas soon after prices for their main crop, cotton, were actually beginning to rise.

The NFO started in Southwestern Iowa in 1955, a time of low hog prices (which had fallen from $26 to $10 per hundredweight in the previous 20 months) and severe drought, which cut corn yields to less than half their expected levels. The founder of the NFO, Jay Loughry, had previously tried to launch an organized protest in 1953, when hog prices were $20. After weeks of effort, Loughry had concluded: "You can't organize the farmer." Yet two years later, when they felt the sting of relative deprivation, these same farmers swarmed by the thousands to Loughry's sales barn meetings.

Analysis of statewide samples of Midwestern NFO members in the 1960s showed them to be economically well-off (Morrison and Steeves, 1967). They definitely were not small, marginal farmers making a last-ditch stand for survival. How can this paradox be explained? When compared with nonmembers, the NFO members expressed greater dissatisfaction with their farm incomes. Their dissatisfaction stemmed in part from much higher income aspirations than nonmembers. Even though they were better off financially, the NFO members perceived themselves as relatively deprived in terms of their desires.

Similarly, larger, commercial farmers participated in the strikes and tractorcades of the AAM. The high socioeconomic status of the participants eventually contributed to the lack of public sympathy for their cause.

Institutionalization and Charismatic Leadership

Why do some social movements flare into fiery protest and then fall silent and disintegrate? Why do other movements survive to become established, systematic organizations? The answer is *institutionalization*, the process through which a relatively simple, informal grouping becomes a recognized and formalized institution.

What are the signs of this process? As in the case of the rural church (Chapter 8), institutionalization is evidenced by a growing concern for the long range, by the professionalization of organizational staff, and by policies that are increasingly less shrill in their protest. Importantly, there is also a basic change in leadership style that must accompany institutionalization.

There is a trend from charismatic-type leaders to bureaucratic-type leaders as a social movement becomes institutionalized. *Charisma* is the ability to secure the devoted following of large numbers of people. This quality of appearing "larger than life" seems to be common to all leaders who launch social movements. They must be persuasive proselytizers, able orators, fanatic thinkers, and crystallizers of action. "It needs the iron will, daring, and vision of an exceptional leader to concern and mobilize existing attitudes and impulses into the collective drive of a mass movement. . . . He articulates and justifies the resentment damned up in the souls of the frustrated" (Hoffer, 1951, p. 111).

Once a social movement becomes institutionalized, however, the charismatic leader becomes excess baggage. "The danger of the fanatic to the development of a movement is that he cannot settle down. Once victory has been won and the new order begins to crystallize, the fanatic becomes an element of strain and disruption" (Hoffer, 1951). So yesterday's charismatic hero is replaced by today's bureaucratic administrator.

The NFO was begun by a charismatic individual, Jay Loughry, a traveling feed salesman who had gone bankrupt in farming. Loughry was an emotional speaker who delivered short, choppy sentences in a high-pitched voice. His verbal blasts against middlemen and the U.S. Secretary of Agriculture attracted cheering, foot-stomping crowds. Although he had little education and was an economic failure, Loughry's charisma was apparent in the remarks of hundreds of farmers who waited in line, "just to shake his hand."

As a crowd attraction, Loughry was superb, but he had little administrative ability. In the early weeks of the movement, huge bags of mail were delivered to the NFO offices in Corning, Iowa, containing membership dues, requests for speakers, and so on. They remained unopened. Loughry was also given to an occasional incautious remark during the heat of his oratory, such as his public announcement in 1955 that all farmers would be "unionized," and required to wear a union badge in order to market their livestock.

The resulting farmer reaction led the NFO to offer their founder an early "retirement" at $75 per week if he would promise to do no more public speaking. He refused this offer and was fired by the NFO as an organizer.

At the end of the NFO's first three months of life, Oren Lee Staley was elected its National President. A college graduate, he was a successful purebred livestock farmer and an effective but careful public speaker. He spent several days each week at NFO headquarters, answered letters promptly, and administered the organization in a dedicated but bureaucratic fashion.

Like NFO's Jay Loughry, Milo Reno, leader of the Farmers Holiday Association, was a fiery speaker who could generate enormous enthusiasm through his emotional appeals. Though uniquely qualified to motivate the movement, he did not have the organizational skills to maintain a stable structure or to successfully carry out complex plans of action. Unlike Jay Loughry and the NFO, Reno was not replaced by a bureaucratic leader, and the Farmers Holiday Association soon faded.

Institutionalization and Organizational Goals

There is greater emphasis on future goals and less on solving immediate problems as a social movement becomes institutionalized. As the here-and-now crisis that launched the movement is partially solved or forgotten, the movement must look to future problems if it is to survive.

Each of the four major farmer organizations was begun in order to solve a different problem than it attacks today. The Grange was launched as a secret fraternity to "get" the railroads; now it mainly provides social fellowship for its members. The Farmers Union started out to help the Southern cotton farmer; now it tries to save the Western wheat grower. The Farm Bureau began as financial sponsor of local extension service workers; now it is mainly a pressure group. The NFO began as a protest group aimed at legislative and political targets; when early legislative efforts failed, it turned to collective bargaining.

Although the Farm Bureau is something of an exception, farmer organizations in general pass through three stages of membership growth: (1) a surprising early spurt, (2) a staggering decline, and (3) a slow, gradual growth requiring many years to regain the original membership level. In order to come out of the tailspin of the second stage, a major redefining of the organization's goals is often necessary. If the movement is not sufficiently flexible in its goals, it dies. For instance, five other farmer organizations began in Iowa in 1955 as a result of the same economic conditions that led to the NFO. None exists today. Among the reasons for their demise was the inflexibility of their goals.

SUMMARY

There are four major farmer organizations in the United States: the Grange, the Farmers Union, the Farm Bureau, and the NFO. All of these organizations provide economic and educational services to their members, but their main function (the NFO is a partial exception) is to secure favorable legislation. A *pressure group* is a formal organization composed of people with common interests or occupations who seek to secure desired legislation by improving communication with their legislators.

Economic services may consist of providing farm supplies at low cost to members through farmer cooperatives, or of direct economic efforts, such as the NFO's withholding actions and collective bargaining. While economic services contribute to a pressure group's high, stable membership, they also may lead to inactive members who are unlikely to support the organization's legislative positions.

The membership location of each of the farm pressure groups influences their legislative positions. For example, Farm Bureau strength is in the Midwest and South, and its economically secure members desire a minimum government program to support farm prices. But Farmers Union members in the wheat belt of the western Midwest states are subject to greater price and weather uncertainty, and consistently stand for high, rigid price supports for grain with accompanying government acreage allotments.

With increasing specialization, many farmers are joining commodity organizations rather than the general farmer organizations. A *commodity organization* is a specialized farmer organization that promotes a specific farm product or a related group of products, such as beef or dairy products.

The purpose of a *social movement* is to change some aspect of society's social structure. A *farmer movement* is a social movement in which farmers organize for social change to solve a perceived crisis in agriculture. A social movement is begun by a collectivity of individuals who experience relative deprivation, often when their conditions are beginning to improve and they expect further improvement. *Relative deprivation* (or disadvantage) is the degree to which an individual perceives a situation with dissatisfaction due to comparing the present situation with aspirations. Falling farm prices frequently have provided the spark to launch farmer movements.

As a social movement becomes institutionalized, charismatic-type leaders are replaced by bureaucratic-type leaders. *Charisma* is the ability to secure the devoted following of large numbers of people. We see illustrations of this proposition in the case of the Grange, the Farmers Union, the Farmers Holiday Association, the NFO, and the AAM.

There is greater emphasis on future goals and less on solving immediate problems as a social movement becomes institutionalized. Farmer organizations typically pass through three stages of membership growth: (1) an early spurt, (2) a decline, and (3) a slow growth over many years to the original membership level.

A farmer's organization must redefine its objectives in order to stop the membership tailspin of the second stage.

REFERENCES

ADLER, RAY P. (1932, March 9). *Iowa Union Farmer.*
BROWNE, WILLIAM P. (1983). "Mobilizing and Activating Group Demands: The American Agricultural Movement." *Social Science Quarterly, 64,* 19–34.
BROWNE, WILLIAM P., and JOHN DINSE. (1985). "The Emergence of the American Agricultural Movement, 1977–1979." *Great Plains Quarterly, 5,* 221–235.
DOWNS, PETER. (1986, July). "Seeds of Discontent: Farmers Plow New Political Ground." *The Progressive,* pp. 31–33.
"Farmers Raising Cain." *Time.* (1979, February 19).
HATHAWAY, DALE E., et al. (1966). *Michigan Farmers in the Mid Sixties: A Survey of Their Views of Marketing Problems and Organizations,* Research Report 54. East Lansing, MI: Michigan Agricultural Experiment Station.
HOFFER, ERIC. (1951). *The True Believer.* New York: Harper and Row.
LEONARD, LORI. (1986, February 22). "NFO: Marketing Strength through Numbers." *Iowa Farmer Today.*
LUNDGREN, MARK. (1986). "The Ideological Campaign of the Radical Right." Paper presented at the Annual Meeting of the Rural Sociological Society, Salt Lake City.
MORRISON, DENTON E., and ALLAN D. STEEVES. (1967). "Deprivation, Discontent, and Social Movement Participation: Evidence on a Contemporary Farmer's Movement, the NFO." *Rural Sociology, 32,* 414–434.
NICHOLS, WADE H., and IKE VERN. (1948, April 24). "The Farmer's Best Friend." *Colliers.*
NIX, CRYSTAL. (1985, September 21). "Extremists in Farm Belt Are Assailed." *The New York Times.*
OLSON, MANCUR. (1971). *The Logic of Collective Action.* Cambridge, MA: Harvard University Press.
PAARLBERG, DON. (1980). *Farm and Food Policy Issues of the 1980s.* Lincoln: University of Nebraska Press.
RIDGEWAY, JAMES. (1985, October 22). "Posse Country: Murder and White Supremacy in the Farm Belt." *The Village Voice.*
STOFFERAHN, CURTIS W., and PETER F. KORSCHING. (1986). "Ecological Determinants of Agrarian Protest." *Iowa State Journal of Research, 61,* 123–141.
TAYLOR, CARL C. (1953). *The Farmers Movement 1620–1920.* New York: American.

Chapter 12

Agricultural Industries

It doesn't seem to make much difference what business you are in, a modern company has to be big to be competitive, big enough to employ the most competent personnel, big enough to afford research in all areas, and big enough to bury your mistakes because you're going to make some.

—An agricultural business executive

Today the corporation is the dominant form of North American business enterprise; even before World War II, corporations accounted for 92 percent of the total manufacturing output. There is a trend toward the concentration of U.S. business in fewer hands. This trend occurs in agriculture as well. The present era in the U.S. is one of Big Business and Big Government.

The trend in most agricultural industries is toward fewer and larger businesses. This change means that economic power will become more concentrated. And these companies are not only dominating a larger share of their industry, but they are expanding vertically to control more stages in the producer-to-consumer process. For example, the four largest national food chains, which handle about 16 percent of the total food store business in the

United States, all own and operate bakeries, milk plants, and coffee-roasting factories. Two food chains also own egg-candling plants and butter and cheese factories. One chain owns laundries, bottling plants, meat-dressing facilities, and produce-packaging plants. These companies have vertically integrated from selling food products to extending their control in the direction of processing and producing these products (Chapter 10).

Food manufacturing companies have much higher advertising expenditures than do other industries producing consumer goods. Further, the expenditures are highly concentrated among a few large firms. Although there are over 1,100 companies that used the media for advertising their food products, over 80 percent of the expenditures were made by the 50 largest food advertisers (Connor et al., 1985). Concentration of food manufacturing is also shown by the decline in the number of firms from 26,549 in 1967 to 16,600 in 1982. The top 50 of these 16,600 firms increased their share of production from 1967 to 1982 from 35 percent to 43 percent. The next 450 firms represent 34 percent of total food manufacturing, leaving only 23 percent for the remaining 16,100 firms (McDonald, 1985).

AGRIBUSINESS

One important change in U.S. agriculture is the increasing interdependence of farmers and agriculture-related industries. This basic change in the nature of farming led to the term agribusiness. *Agribusiness* includes the manufacture and distribution of farm supplies, plus the processing, handling, merchandising, and marketing of food and agricultural products, plus farming itself (Davis, 1956). So agribusiness is much broader than farming; it includes 30 percent of the total U.S. labor force, while farming includes only about 3.5 percent. Farmers and food-related industries have become much closer in recent years. Farmers today buy almost all of their supplies in the form of machinery, building materials, tractor fuel, fertilizer, and feeds, all of which come from nonfarm business.

The farmer of a century ago was mainly a producer and not a purchaser. He seldom bought fuel, equipment, seed, or fertilizer off the farm. Modern farm technology has changed all that; today farmers are important consumers in themselves. Fertilizer, farm machinery, and seed companies now furnish the farmer with needed supplies. These companies usually supply these inputs more cheaply and efficiently than the farmer can.

Most urban people do not understand that a one dollar loaf of bread contains only about 12 cents worth of wheat. In fact, the wheat producers could give their entire crop free of charge to the consumer public without having more than a minor effect on the retail price of bread. Overall, the farmer receives only 25 cents out of each food dollar spent in the United

FIGURE 12-1   Agribusiness firms are increasingly larger in size, fewer in number, and more complex in organization. This grain elevator stretches for blocks; its size makes for efficiency and bargaining power. However, along with its size come human relations problems as the farmer-members of this co-operative have difficulty understanding how their co-op is organized, and in feeling that they have any voice in how it is run.

States. Yet few farmers or consumers would want to eliminate any of the processing stages of agricultural products. For example, few people want raw milk as it comes from the cow; they want it pasteurized and homogenized.

Vertical integration by agribusiness firms is occurring in the supply, processing, and marketing sectors of agriculture. Agribusiness involvement in the supply sector is evident from the wave of acquisitions and mergers that has "swept virtually every American seed company of any size into the corporate folds of the world's industrial elite. Burpee is now owned by ITT, Joseph Harris by Celanese, Ferry-Morse by the French conglomerate Limagrain, Henry Field by AMFAC. Northrup King is now owned by the pharmaceutical giant Sandoz, Jacques by Lubrijol, O's Gold by Upjohn, Pfister by W.R. Grace, and Funk by Switzerland's Ciba-Geigy" (Kloppenburg, 1986).

Whereas the United States once had many domestic tractor manufacturers, today we have the "big four," Ford New Holland, John Deere, Case

International, and Deutz-Allis. The others were lost through bankruptcies, acquisitions, and mergers over the past 40 years.

The growth of agribusiness is illustrated by the changes occurring in the meatpacking industry, one of the largest segments of U.S. food manufacturing (Nelson, no date). It employs over 150,000 workers. Nearly all sales of meat animals, which account for over one-fourth of all farm product sales, funnel through the meatpacking industry. The four top firms account for 45 percent of the beef (steers and heifers) slaughter, and 36 percent of the hog slaughter. Packing plants are increasing in size. The number of hog plants slaughtering over 1 million head per year increased from 23 to 35 between 1972 and 1982. These 35 plants accounted for 59 percent of all U.S. hogs slaughtered in 1982.

BOX 12-1 *IBP GOES WHOLE HOG*

Iowa Beef Packers (IBP) founded in Denison, Iowa, in 1960, took the beef industry by such a storm that it quickly became the nation's largest meatpacker. In just two-and-one-half years, IBP made *Fortune* magazine's list of the 500 largest industrial companies. IBP dominates the beef sector. In 1985, the company, which has 15 plants and 17,000 employees, slaughtered 7.6 million head of cattle, accounting for about one-fourth of the U.S. cattle slaughtered and more than one-third of the country's boxed beef (cut and trimmed) production (Erb, 1986). Together with a slaughter of 3.5 million hogs, IBP had sales totaling 6.5 billion dollars (Erb, 1986).

Several years ago IBP gave notice that it planned to revolutionize the pork industry in the 1980s much as it had revolutionized the beef industry in the 1960s. "IBP was probably the single most determining factor in the concentration of the beef industry. Their designs are to do the same thing in pork, starting with the monopolization of the slaughter end of it," said Lewie Anderson, of the United Food and Commercial Workers Union (Erb, 1986: 1).

IBP moved into the pork business as quickly as it moved into beef packing. In 1981 IBP purchased an old slaughterhouse abandoned by Hygrade Food Products Corporation. It spent approximately 20 million dollars to renovate the old slaughterhouse into a modern pork plant with 900 workers who kill and process 12,000 hogs daily (Erb, 1986). Then IBP established itself as a production leader in the pork industry by purchasing Wilson Foods Corporation,. the nation's largest producer of fresh pork.

1985 and 1986 saw more expansion for IBP. In 1985 IBP bought the defunct Rath Packing Company pork plant in Columbus Junction, Iowa and in 1986, it purchased an old pork plant in Council Bluffs, Iowa, from Goehring Meats Incorporated. IBP spent more than 26 million dollars to modernize and expand the two plants. The Columbus Junction, Iowa plant is a modern behemoth that in itself doubled IBP's annual hog slaughter capacity to 7 million from 3.5 million. The plant employs more than 1,000 workers in slaughtering, cutting, boning and cold storage operations (Erb, 1986).

IBP is itself owned by another industrial conglomerate, Occidental Petroleum Corporation. Its expansion in pork production will probably continue with the acquisition of additional plants and even direct marketing to consumers through name-brand products.

FARMER COOPERATIVES

Farmer cooperatives are of increasing importance. The following facts demonstrate the importance of, and changes in, farmer cooperatives:

1. Cooperatives marketed about one-third of the total U.S. farm output in 1982.
2. Farm cooperatives completed almost $70 billion worth of business in 1982, compared to $26 billion in 1969.
3. Total membership in farmer co-ops in 1982 was about 5.1 million; this figure is down from 10 years ago, but is impressive considering the large decline in farm population. Because each farmer may belong to more than one cooperative, there are not necessarily 5.1 million different farmers who belong to co-ops. But most farmers belong to at least one.

The importance of agricultural cooperatives is shown by this hypothetical case of Farmer Joe Cosby. Farmer Cosby purchases lumber for a new dairy shed at his local farm supply cooperative with capital that he borrowed from his National Farm Loan Association. While in town, he also buys livestock feed with money secured at his Production Credit Association. Farmer Cosby checks with the manager of his Dairy Herd Improvement Association on the production records of his herd, and decides how many herd replacements to have bred by his local Artificial Breeding Cooperative. His last stop in town is at the office of his Rural Electrification Association, where he pays his monthly bill. Thus Farmer Cosby belongs to six cooperatives, each of which provides him with different goods and services. If he were asked why he belongs to these co-ops, he might reply, "Because I get better prices on what I buy and a patronage refund from each co-op at the end of the year. Their profits are passed along to me." Farmers belong to cooperatives mainly for the economic advantages they can secure.

Co-ops are more popular among farmers than they are with other occupational categories because cooperatives provide farmers with a norm of economic organization particularly well-suited to the conditions of agriculture. An individual farmer has little power in the marketplace, but when organized in cooperatives farmers can meet power with power. Cooperatives provide farmers with this economic power, while at the same time preserving for them much of their individuality and freedom. Some types of business are too complicated or difficult for farmers to manage cooperatively, or else they involve more risk than farmers are able to assume. Cooperative meatpacking plants, for example, have seldom been successful.

Major efforts to organize farmer cooperatives in the United States began in the late nineteenth century by the Grange, the oldest of today's farmer organizations (Chapter 11). The Grange established marketing, processing, manufacturing, and purchasing cooperatives for its members. The purpose was for farmers to bypass what they perceived as exorbitant profits by the middlemen in buying farm inputs or selling farm products (Cochrane, 1979). The perception of the exorbitant profits of middlemen was part of a general theme against big business of the farmers' Populist movement of that era. The farmers, however, lacked capital, were unable to work together, and most importantly, lacked business experience. With competition from private business and with the panic of 1873, most were out of business by 1880 (Cochrane, 1979).

The biggest growth in farmer cooperatives occurred between 1890 and 1920. Nearly 10,000 farmer cooperatives were organized between 1900 and 1920 (Cochrane, 1979). With the growth in number and size of the farmer cooperatives and the possibility of monopoly control in purchasing farm inputs and selling farm products, questions were raised about their legal status under antitrust laws. The Clayton Antitrust Act of 1914 and the Capper-Volstead Cooperative Marketing Act of 1922 exempted farmer cooperatives from antitrust laws and provided their members some degree of monopoly power in purchasing farm inputs and marketing farm products (Cochrane, 1979).

Cooperatives have traditionally been stronger in Scandinavian and Western European countries than in the United States. For example, Danish cooperatives handle about 91 percent of the milk, 65 percent of the butter exported, and 90 percent of the pig slaughter for export. Areas in the United States settled by Scandinavian immigrants are strongholds of the cooperative movement. Today, Minnesota and Wisconsin (states with large numbers of Scandinavian immigrants) rank first and third in the number of farmer cooperatives. Scandinavian immigrants brought cooperatives with them as a part of their culture, just as they transplanted the Lutheran Church. The grain and dairy areas of the northern Midwest and the Northeast have traditionally been centers of co-op membership in the United States; the traditional cotton-growing areas of the South have fewer farmer cooperatives.

What Are Cooperatives?

A *cooperative* is a voluntary association (Chapter 5) of individuals who join together to secure goods and services at cost. Several farmers become associated so that a part of their individual business operations are conducted jointly, thus making these functions more efficient and less costly than if each farmer acted individually. For example, several farmers may cooperate to market their lambs in a lamb pool; their purpose is to save some marketing and transportation costs, and to secure a higher selling price.

When farmers decide to start a cooperative, they each extend a part of their own farm business. For instance, they not only raise the lambs but also extend their sheep-production enterprise into marketing their product. The participating farmers must agree to give up some of their own independence in the part of their business they conduct cooperatively. For example, the farmers in the lamb pool must decide jointly when to sell their livestock.

FIGURES 12-2
and 12-3   Supplies Handled and Products Marketed by Cooperatives.

Over one-third of all products cooperatives sell to their members are petroleum products, with fertilizer and feed being second and third. The three constitute three-quarters of all sales for cooperatives. The most important commodities marketed by cooperatives are grains, soybeans, and dairy products, making up 66 percent of all farm products marketed by cooperatives.

Source: U.S. Department of Agriculture Economics, Statistics and Cooperatives Service.

Relative Importance of Major Farm Products Marketed by Cooperatives

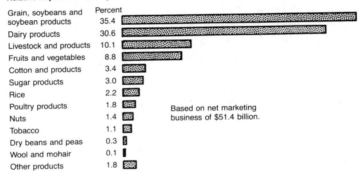

	Percent	
Grain, soybeans and soybean products	35.4	
Dairy products	30.6	
Livestock and products	10.1	
Fruits and vegetables	8.8	
Cotton and products	3.4	
Sugar products	3.0	
Rice	2.2	
Poultry products	1.8	Based on net marketing
Nuts	1.4	business of $51.4 billion.
Tobacco	1.1	
Dry beans and peas	0.3	
Wool and mohair	0.1	
Other products	1.8	

Relative Importance of Major Farm Supplies Handled by Cooperatives

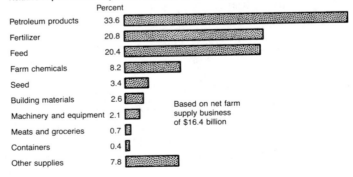

	Percent	
Petroleum products	33.6	
Fertilizer	20.8	
Feed	20.4	
Farm chemicals	8.2	
Seed	3.4	
Building materials	2.6	
Machinery and equipment	2.1	Based on net farm supply business of $16.4 billion
Meats and groceries	0.7	
Containers	0.4	
Other supplies	7.8	

Social Change and Farmer Co-ops

One co-op leader remarked: "Our cooperatives do not change as fast as do farmers themselves." In the face of a rapidly changing agriculture, farmer co-ops are forced to adjust their structure, size, and operation. This adjustment to change has not occurred as quickly as would be ideal for economic efficiency and member satisfaction. But farmers' co-ops are changing.

Co-ops are increasing in size. Both the dollar volume of business and the average number of members have jumped sharply. In 1985, 15 farmer cooperatives were among the list of the 500 largest U.S. industrial corporations as ranked by *Fortune* magazine. These cooperatives included four farm supply, three dairy, three diversified, two fruits and vegetables, one sugar, one rice, and one grain co-op (Davidson and Roger, 1986). Membership per cooperative in the United States increased from 120 in 1915, to 859 in 1981.

Cooperatives are also becoming increasingly complex in their organization. They are more formalized and institutionalized than formerly. When co-ops were initiated, their founders were their enthusiastic supporters. Today the founders' sons or grandsons are co-op members; these hereditary members may be less knowledgeable about their cooperative and less active in their support. Professionally trained managers and large-scale educational programs are required to keep a cooperative operating effec-

TABLE 12-1   Fifteen Cooperatives Rank Among the *Fortune* 500 Largest Corporations in the United States.

COOPERATIVE	'85 SALES IN $1,000	RANKING
Farmland Industries	$4,371,028	87
Agway	4,067,208	95
Land O' Lakes	2,267,148	164
Gold Kist	1,449,740	236
CENEX	1,375,813	250
Mid-America Dairymen	1,344,280	254
CF Industries	920,851	326
NCRA	894,568	339
Ag Processing	643,469	402
Riceland Foods	542,260	442
C & H Sugar	537,134	448
Ocean Spray Cranberries	531,999	452
Michigan Milk Producers	517,113	460
Sun-Diamond Growers	487,233	471
Wisconsin Dairies	464,363	483

tively. The U.S. Department of Agriculture assists farmer cooperatives through its Agricultural Cooperative Service.

The trend is toward co-op merger and consolidation.   The number of farmer cooperatives in the United States decreased from 12,000 in 1930, to 6,211 in 1981. Improved transportation and economic efficiency are basic reasons for co-op merger, as in the case of church and school consolidation. Old loyalties and vested interests sometimes operate as barriers to merger; the members of a co-op board of directors may fear the loss of their positions if they combine with a neighboring cooperative.

Cooperatives began as friendly neighborhood groups; now many have grown to become complex, sprawling bureaucracies.   Because of limited transportation facilities, early cooperatives were of necessity organized on a neighborhood or community basis. But these early cooperators soon realized that much could be gained in economic efficiency by combining into larger units. Community-wide co-ops became county-wide enterprises, which after a few more years became state and regional organizations.

Today, the volume of farmer cooperative business in the United States is growing, while co-op membership is declining slightly.   Over the last ten years, dollar business has increased two-and-one-half times. Co-ops in the future will be larger in size and fewer in number. As a result, co-op members will find themselves in organizations that are growing in geographical area, that have larger, more widespread, and more complicated operations; and that are increasingly dependent on U.S. government agencies.

Vertical integration in cooperatives today is occurring through greater involvement in food processing to assure outlets for farmer-members.   Cooperatives have acquired fluid milk plants, sugar refineries, and fruit and vegetable canning plants. At present, however, cooperatives are relatively unimportant in food manufacturing. In 1977 the largest 100 marketing cooperatives accounted for only about 6 percent of the total value of manufactured shipments and 3.4 percent of the value added in food manufacturing (Connor et al., 1985).

Structure of Farmer Co-ops

Co-op members are not merely customers of their organization, but have the responsibility, in addition, of controlling its policies and practices. They are also the owners. It is important that the members participate in co-op activities, are informed about their co-op's organization, and understand its operations. A recent Iowa survey of farm cooperative members showed that 58 percent of the members of farm marketing or supply cooperatives were very active or moderately active in their co-op, and 67 percent stated that their co-op needed their support to survive (Lasley, 1985).

Previously we defined a cooperative as a voluntary association of individuals who join together to provide goods and services at cost. One often thinks of a grain elevator, a dairy plant, or electrical power lines when one hears the term "cooperative." Actually, however, the elevator, dairy plant, and power lines are just the *joint plant;* they are not the *cooperative.* The cooperative is the association of individuals who own and operate the joint physical plant.

Ideally, the power to make basic policy decisions in a cooperative rests with the members. In practice, many members never take part in these decisions and many never realize that they have the responsibility to do so. Almost every co-op has an annual meeting which all of the members are urged to attend. They are asked to select the board of directors, establish credit policies, and make decisions on such matters as the addition or discontinuation of departments within the co-op, and whether to do business with nonmembers.

As in most other large organizations, the members delegate the authority to make certain decisions to a board of directors. The directors are members who are elected to the board at the annual meeting. They usually meet monthly and fulfill such functions as employing the manager and establishing the co-op's policies.

In a study of six Arkansas cooperatives, a rural sociologist found that board members had more education and much higher social status, participated more in formal organizations, and were younger than the average member (Folkman, 1958). Those who have a larger share of the power in farmer cooperatives are not typical of the average member; there is no evidence, however, that board members do not fairly represent the members.

The co-op manager is hired and fired by the board of directors. The manager carries out the policies made by the board of directors. The manager has the power to hire and fire all other employees of the cooperative and can also make recommendations to the directors. Through college training, experience, and close contact with the business, the manager is in a unique position to render advice to the board of directors on policy matters. Ideally, the manager only provides information and advice. In actual practice, however, the Arkansas study indicated that co-op managers often have a good deal of influence over their boards of directors. Some managers reported that a good manager has his board "in his pocket."

Consolidation and Merger in Cooperatives

As in the case of schools, churches, and other rural organizations, there is an unmistakable trend toward the consolidation of farmer cooperatives. However, there is often considerable opposition to co-op merger, particularly on the part of those members with a vested interest. A cooperative leader remarked: "I have often said that farmers cooperate much better than co-operative managers and directors. The reason is rather easy to find. Farmers usually have everything to gain and nothing to lose, whereas the co-op manager may be eliminated in the case of a merger." Farmers may not necessarily feel they have everything to gain. A recent survey of farmer co-op members showed that only 28 percent felt that large co-ops improve farm prices more than do small co-ops. Forty percent disagreed with the statement, and 32 percent were uncertain (Lasley, 1985).

Like other rural and farm-related businesses, farm cooperatives face financial difficulties. Many co-ops extended credit to farmers in financial difficulty, and in turn became insolvent. Dairy cooperatives are particularly vulnerable under farm legislation that attempts to reduce the amount of milk production by reducing subsidies and buying dairy herds by the federal government (Mengel, 1986). Marketing cooperatives are subject to the vagaries of market accessibility and transportation. Proximity to large loading facilities reduces transportation costs. Many shippers and exporters provide discounts for volume shipments, such as trains of 75 rail cars. Smaller cooperatives do not have the rail facilities nor the storage capacity to load 75 rail cars at one time, and thus they cannot obtain volume discounts. A recent trend is for large farmers to deliver their harvest directly to grain or livestock terminals, rather than marketing it through their local cooperative. This leads to further decline in cooperative business, financial failure of some cooperatives, and consolidation and merger of other cooperatives (Ginder, 1982).

One method of cooperative consolidation, by which co-ops can achieve many of the advantages of a large-scale operation, is forming a regional federation. *Federated cooperatives* consist of two or more member cooperatives organized to market farm products, purchase production supplies, or perform bargaining functions. A federated co-op is a co-op of co-ops. Individual farmers are not members of a federated cooperative, but are members of one of the cooperatives that make up the federation. In 1982 there were 111 federated cooperatives in the United States.

OTHER AGRIBUSINESS SECTORS

The agricultural industry contains several other sectors or components that are a part of agribusiness. Often, we do not think of them as part of agribusiness in the sense that Iowa Beef Packers, John Deere, or Cargill are.

Industrial Farms

In Chapter 10 we discussed the trend toward an increased number of large farms and the concentration of agricultural production. Many of these large farms are family-owned farms or closely held corporations. However, an increasing amount of food is produced on farms owned by larger industrial corporations. Tenneco is one of the largest of U.S. industrial corporations with subsidiaries that produce gas and other oil products, chemicals, tractors and farm implements, and food containers, and that also sell food products through a chain of supermarkets. Tenneco owns Kern County Land Company in California, the state's third-largest landowner (Vogeler, 1981), which produces a wide variety of crops. "Tenneco plows its own land, fertilized and sprayed with chemicals from its own chemical division, using its own tractors fueled with gas and oil from its own oil wells and refineries. The food is processed, packaged and distributed by Tenneco subsidiaries" (Casalino, 1972, p. 33).

Farmer Organizations

Farmer organizations are also part of agribusiness. The major functions of all farmer organizations (Chapter 11) are educational, political, and economic. The Farm Bureau provides its members with insurance and farm supplies through its affiliated cooperatives. The National Farmers Organization assists its members in marketing their farm products through collective bargaining. The specialized commodity groups, particularly those representing major crops such as corn, soybeans, cotton, and tobacco, invest large amounts of human and financial resources to promote their products and to obtain favorable legislation for their members at state and national levels.

Organized Labor

When we think of organized labor in agriculture, we often think of destitute migrant workers, who are members of a minority group, in confrontation with large corporate farmers. Organized labor in the agricultural industry is more than just the organizations of those who work directly in the field such as the United Farm Workers Union (Chapter 15). Other agribusiness workers' unions include the United Food and Commercial Workers, whose members work primarily in grocery stores; the National Brotherhood of Packinghouse and Industrial Workers, representing workers in the meatpacking industry; and the United Auto Workers, whose members make not only cars and trucks but also tractors and farm implements.

The U.S. Department of Agriculture/Land-Grant College System

The U.S. Department of Agriculture and its partners at the state level, the land-grant colleges, were developed primarily to assist farmers and other rural people improve their agricultural production, home economics, and quality of life through resident education, agricultural research, and extension work (Chapter 15). Critics of this system claim it has strayed from its initial objectives and is providing benefits to corporate agriculture and agribusiness (Hightower, 1973; Vogeler, 1981). Benefactors of the U.S. Department of Agriculture commodity support programs and other financial assistance programs are the larger farms, not the traditional family-size farms. Research supported by the U.S. Department of Agriculture and conducted at the land grant agricultural experiment stations has had the effect of promoting commercial agriculture, larger farms, and concentration of resources, at the expense of smaller farms.

Many private corporations provide grants to agricultural experiment stations to initiate research. The agricultural experiment stations then develop long-term research programs around the needs of the sponsoring corporations and make major investments of money, facilities, and scientists to continue the research (Hadwigger, 1982). The Cooperative Extension Service is also criticized for providing assistance to those farmers who least need this help.

PUBLIC REACTION TO AGRIBUSINESS

The public has a strong interest in agriculture and in agribusiness. The total annual budget for the U.S. Department of Agriculture and its programs is over 40 billion dollars, a major allocation of federal tax money. The public also has an interest in maintaining low food prices. To support the interests of the consumer, there are over 60 national or large regional consumer organizations and groups with food and agricultural interests (Hadwigger, 1982).

Public opinion polls consistently indicate that the American public supports maintaining small family farms (Korsching and Stofferahn, 1987; Coughenour, 1986). But what is the public's perception of agribusiness? Although 36 percent of the respondents in a recent national survey agreed with the statement that small farms produce better food than large farms, only 18 percent felt that most farms are too large. Fifty-five percent disagreed, and 27 percent were undecided. So the public apparently does not feel that small family farms are in serious danger.

Only 16 percent stated that the U.S. government should create laws to limit farm size, but 65 percent felt that corporate farms should pay more taxes. Unfortunately, public perceptions do not necessarily conform to reality. The world's largest poultry producer, Tyson Foods, paid virtually no income tax over the last five years. Tyson benefits from a provision of the tax law that allows large tax deferrals for family-owned farms, defined as "any agricultural-related firm owned by three or fewer families who control at least 50 percent of the company's stock" ("Biggest Poultry Producer," 1986). Tyson has annual sales of more than 1 billion dollars.

Urban lawmakers are becoming outraged by the skyrocketing costs of government farm subsidy programs. One member of the House of Representatives, speaking of legislators from rural areas, recently stated, "We get on the floor and they invoke Ma and Pa Kettle with six chickens and a row of lettuce, when in fact we're talking about multi-million dollar corporations getting lots and lots of money" ("Urban Lawmakers Irked," 1986). Agribusiness, especially the production sector, will probably get closer scrutiny by lawmakers and the public in the future.

SUMMARY

As in other industries, the trend in agricultural industries is toward fewer and larger businesses. The increased linkage between the farm and industrial sectors of society is aided by agribusiness and the increased importance of agricultural industries. *Agribusiness* includes the manufacture and distribution of farm supplies, plus the processing, handling, merchandising, and marketing of food and agricultural products, in addition to farming itself.

Of extreme importance to farm people are farmer-owned cooperatives. A *cooperative* is a voluntary association of individuals who join together to secure goods and services at cost. Co-op members are not only customers of their organization; they also are the owners. They elect a board of directors that makes policy decisions for the co-op. Day-to-day operation of the co-op is carried out by a hired manager who is responsible to the board of directors.

Like other agribusiness firms, cooperatives are increasing in size and declining in numbers, primarily through merger and consolidation. Changes in domestic and international markets and in U.S. government farm policy are affecting the survival of farmer cooperatives. One survival strategy is to form a federated cooperative. *Federated cooperatives* consist of two or more member cooperatives organized to market farm products, purchase production supplies, or perform bargaining functions.

Agricultural industry also includes several other sectors or components that we often do not associate with agribusiness. These include farms owned by large, industrial corporations; general farmer organizations and commodity groups; organized labor, including both field and factory worker unions; and the U.S. Department of Agriculture/land-grant college system that conducts agricultural research and disseminates the research results to users.

REFERENCES

"Biggest Poultry Producer Reportedly Deferred Taxes." (1986, September 8). *Des Moines Register.*
CASALINO, LARRY. (1972, July). "This Land Is Their Land." *Ramparts.* pp. 31–36.
COCHRANE, WILLARD W. (1979). *The Development of American Agriculture: A Historical Analysis.* Minneapolis: University of Minnesota Press.
CONNOR, JOHN M., RICHARD T. ROGERS, BRUCE W. MARION, and WILLARD F. MUELLER. (1985). *The Food Manufacturing Industries.* Lexington, MA: D.C. Heath.
COUGHENOUR, C. MILTON. (1986). "Farming in American Life: Report on a National

Survey." Paper presented at the Annual Meeting of the Rural Sociological Society, Salt Lake City, UT.

DAVIDSON, DONALD R. and JEFFREY S. ROGER. (1986). "Sales of 100 Largest Co-ops Drop Nearly $6 Billion in 1985." *Farmer Cooperatives, 53,* 4–9.

DAVIS, JOHN H. (1956). "From Agriculture to Agribusiness." *Harvard Business Review, 34,* 107–115.

ERB, GENE. (1986, June 10). "IBP Causing Tremors in the Pork Industry," *Des Moines Register.* pp. 1,6.

FOLKMAN, WILLIAM S. (1958). "Board Members as Decision Makers in Farmers Cooperatives." *Rural Sociology, 23,* 239–252.

GINDER, ROGER. (1982, October). "Country Elevator Survival: Looking Ahead." *Grain and Feed Review.* pp. 17,18.

HADWIGGER, DON F. (1982). *The Politics of Agricultural Research.* Lincoln, NE: University of Nebraska Press.

HIGHTOWER, JIM. (1973). *Hard Tomatoes, Hard Times.* Cambridge, MA: Schenkman.

KLOPPENBURG, JACK, JR. (1986, January). "First the Seed." *As You Sow . . . Social Issues in Agriculture.*

KORSCHING, PETER F. and CURTIS W. STOFFERAHN. (1987). "Structural Reform, Family Farm Preservation and Free Market: Public Preference of Agricultural Policy." Paper presented at the Annual Meeting of the American Association for the Advancement of Sciences, Chicago, IL.

LASLEY, PAUL. (1985, December). "Membership in Cooperatives." *Iowa Farm and Rural Life Poll: Summary,* pp. 10,11.

McDONALD, JAMES M. (1985). "Food Manufacturing." In *Food Marketing Review, 1985,* Report 59. Washington, DC; Economic Research Service, U.S. Department of Agriculture.

MENGEL, JOHN. (1986). "Spinoffs of 1985 Farm Legislation May Challenge Dairy Co-op Survival." *Farmer Cooperatives, 53,* 12–15.

NELSON, KENNETH E. (No date). *Issues and Developments in the U.S. Meatpacking Industry.* Washington, DC: Economic Research Service, U.S. Department of Agriculture.

"Urban Lawmakers Irked by U.S. Farm Policy." (1986, September 8). *Des Moines Register.*

VOGELER, INGOLF. (1981). *The Myth of the Family Farm: Agribusiness Dominance of U.S. Agriculture.* Boulder, CO: Westview.

Chapter 13

Agriculture and Environmental Quality

Man has lost the capacity to forestall. He will end by destroying the earth.

—Albert Einstein

That ugly Bitch, what's she trying to do, destroy U.S. Agriculture?

The former dean of a U.S.
College of Agriculture,
after reading Rachel
Carson's (1962) *Silent
Spring*

The then dean of a prominent Midwestern agriculture college was visibly upset that Rachel Carson questioned the agricultural use of such "safe" pesticides and herbicides as 2-4-D; 2,4,5-T (Agent Orange); DDT and other chlorinated hydrocarbons. The dean knew that the control of weeds by these powerful chemicals increased the production of corn and soybeans by approximately 40 percent. Nitrogen fertilizers were also an important part of the new chemical farming.

Rachel Carson died in 1964. She did not know that her book would touch off an environmental revolution, changing the way that the world looked at chemical substances in the environment. Despite the 1971 U.S. ban on DDT, the volume of applied pesticides more than doubled between 1965 and 1985 (*New York Times,* 1986).

This chapter traces the changes that have taken place in agriculture and other rural industries due to recent attempts to artificially control and exploit the world's natural ecosystem. Here we look at a 1930s government agency that began with a goal of improving environmental quality.

BOX 13-1   *TVA: A REGIONAL CONSERVATION AGENCY*

Established by the U.S. Congress in 1933, the Tennessee Valley Authority (TVA) was an unprecedented experiment in regional planning covering the 41,000 square mile Tennessee River Basin of Kentucky, Tennessee, North Carolina, Alabama, and other Appalachian states (Selsnik, 1953).

Anchored on the Muscle Shoals, Alabama, hydroelectric plant built for munitions production during World War I, the TVA system today includes 42 dams, a number of coal-fired power plants, eight nuclear power sites, and a major (Land Between The Lakes) recreation area. The most famous name is Oak Ridge, Tennessee, site of early work on the atomic bomb.

TVA began in a depressed rural area with the goals of improving agriculture in Appalachia, developing the fish and wildlife resources, improving flood control, reducing soil erosion, and providing electricity for an ambitious program of rural industrialization and agricultural mechanization. TVA was a semi-autonomous agency of the federal government.

Working with state extension services and the region's colleges of agriculture, TVA introduced soil conservation measures, chemical fertilizer, and other agricultural innovations to improve farm production and bring about vast improvements in Tennessee Valley communities. As a model for hydroelectric power, dam-building, and soil conservation, TVA was widely heralded as a success. In fact, the TVA model was copied around the world.

However, the demand for electricity by agriculture and industry soon outstripped the hydroelectric capacity of the TVA plants. By then, the population in the Tennessee Valley was hooked on cheap electricity. In response to demands by the textile industry (attracted from New England by cheap labor, cheap electricity, and the absence of labor unions), TVA built coal-fired generators to meet the increased demand for its electricity.

Soon the high-quality, deep-mined coal of Eastern Kentucky and Tennessee became too expensive, and so TVA turned to cheaper, low-quality lignite coal from strip mines in Western Kentucky and Tennessee. Surface or strip mining soon transformed the landscape of these two states. The frequent rains mixed with the overburden above the coal seam polluted streams and silted rivers. Eventually, the upper reaches of the reservoirs built for hydroelectric power became giant mud flats. The original TVA goals of soil conservation, clean water, healthy fish and wildlife, and clean air fell prey to demands for cheap electricity.

Under increased pressure to use less coal from strip mines, TVA in the 1960s turned to nuclear power plants. Plans in 1970 called for eight nuclear reactor

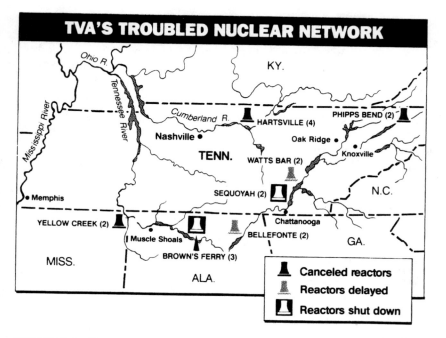

TVA'S TROUBLED NUCLEAR NETWORK

KY.

Ohio R.

Tennessee River

Mississippi River

Cumberland R.

HARTSVILLE (4)

PHIPPS BEND (2)

Nashville •

Oak Ridge •

TENN.

WATTS BAR (2)

Knoxville •

SEQUOYAH (2)

N.C.

• Memphis

YELLOW CREEK (2)

Chattanooga

BELLEFONTE (2)

GA.

Muscle Shoals

BROWN'S FERRY (3)

MISS.

ALA.

Canceled reactors

Reactors delayed

Reactors shut down

FIGURE 13-1   The pressure to provide cheap electricity to an expanding population and industrial base in the Tennessee Valley led TVA away from its original goals of soil conservation, sustainable agriculture, quality water and forest products, coupled with abundant fish and wildlife, and recreational opportunity. Severe environmental damage as well as air pollution has been the result of attempts to continue the supply of cheap electricity by building coal-burning plants and nuclear-powered generators.

Source: Leon Lindsay, *Christian Science Monitor*, July 9, 1986, p. 6. Used by permission.

sites. By 1987, 15 billion had been spent, but not one reactor was actually producing electricity. Existing nuclear power projects were closed, others were delayed, and many were shut down. As one safety engineer put it, "We are talking about [the nuclear] plants out here shot full of every defect known to man, and it does not seem to bother anyone" (Ingwerson, 1986, p. 6).

TVA has now come half circle from an organization with lofty conservation goals, to one of the main contributors to destroying environmental quality in the Tennessee Valley. TVA's last attempt at environmental alteration (in cooperation with U.S. Army Corps of Engineers) was completion of the Tennessee-Tombigbee waterway connecting interior waterways to the Gulf of Mexico. Billions of dollars of taxpayers' money were used to build this project with only dubious economic benefits. Each year it will take millions of federal dollars to maintain the waterway along its new course.

So while the TVA has greatly assisted the development of the region over the past half century, it has also lowered the environmental quality of Appalachia.

HISTORY OF THE ENVIRONMENTAL MOVEMENT

The warning by Rachel Carson that spring might come without the sounds of birds and insects led to the environmental movement in the United States. Pictures of oil-soaked birds after the Santa Barbara oil tanker spill in 1965 helped raise the issue of environmental concern. The activism of the 1960s spawned by the Vietnam War was accelerated in the early 1970s by the public concern for environmental problems. The 1970s were the decade when environmental and energy issues became a permanent part of the public consciousness in America. Here are the key events:

1970 EARTH DAY.

The first celebration of environmental concerns took place on April 22, 1970, and it has been observed each year since. Celebrations feature environmentally sound lifestyles, and an emphasis on cleanup, recycling, and conservation.

1970–1973.

Major environmental legislation that was signed into law included the National Environmental Policy Act (NEPA), Amendments to the Air Quality Act and the Clean Water Act, and other legislation on the use of herbicides and pesticides. The Environmental Protection Agency (EPA) was established in 1970 as a separate government agency to enforce environmental regulations and to monitor the progress in pollution cleanup. The discovery of a housing development built on a former toxic dump site in Love Canal, New York, kept public attention focused on environmental issues.

1973–1974.

The Yom Kippur War in 1973 led to an Arab oil embargo of the United States, an ensuing oil shortage, and sharply increased energy prices. The public was sensitized to the issues of an inadequate domestic energy supply.

1979.

The Iranian revolution created a second energy crisis, and that year the price per barrel jumped from 12 to 34 dollars. Farmers' production costs increased due to the input of oil in fertilizers, chemicals, and petroleum for tractors and vehicles.

1981.

Ronald Reagan took office as President of the United States and appointed James Watt of Colorado, a lawyer for mining interests, as U.S. Secretary of the Interior. Membership in the Sierra Club tripled and other environmental organizations received more donations. Environmentalists received public sympathy as Watt attempted to circumvent the letter and spirit of much environmental legislation.

1984.

The Bhopal chemical disaster in India, where thousands were killed by cyanide gas leaks from a Union Carbide plant. This event brought the destructive potential of chemical manufacturing to the attention of the general public.

1986.

The Chernobyl nuclear power plant disaster occurred near Kiev, Russia. Fallout radiation was recorded in North America. Milk, reindeer, lettuce, and other agricultural products in Europe had to be destroyed due to their radiation content. Worldwide public opinion turned against nuclear power as an energy source.

Public opinion polls conducted on a regular basis since 1965 show that environmental quality issues are a priority item and have remained so through the 1980s. Despite the economic cost, the majority of the U.S. public wants a high-quality environment (Dunlap, 1987, and Mitchell, 1979).

Unlike the labor and equal rights movements, the environmental movement was started by, and draws continued support from middle- and upper-middle-class persons (Harry et al., 1969; Dunlap and Van Liere, 1980). A *social movement* is collective behavior in which a large number of individuals organize for social change to solve a perceived crisis (Johnson, 1986, p. 647).

Conservation organizations that sustain the environmental movement in the United States like the Sierra Club, National Audubon Society, National Wildlife Federation, Friends of the Earth, and the Environmental Defense Fund have well-educated members who provide strong financial backing. They articulate environmental issues to state legislators and the U.S. Congress. The environmental movement in the 1960s emphasized street demonstrations, hike-ins, and public protests. Effective environmental pleas are now made in city council meetings, legislative hearings, and in courtrooms.

Unlike other social movements, the environmental movement found allies in a strange place: Inside the government that they were protesting against. Bureaucrats within the land management agencies (described later in this chapter) hold conservationist and preservationist values because these agencies are charged with preserving and protecting natural resources and parks. Thus major support from environmental pressure groups legitimized their long-held belief system. The U.S. environmental movement has become an effective lobby that can stand off powerful business interests.

IMPACTS OF AGRICULTURAL AND RURAL INDUSTRIES ON ENVIRONMENTAL QUALITY

Rural industries are industrial, extractive, and production activities not associated with the production of food, but commonly found in rural areas. Examples are fishing, mining, forestry, and recreation and parks. These rural industries along with agriculture were not considered an environmental problem until Rachel Carson published *Silent Spring*. Until 1945, fertilizers, pesticides, and herbicides were virtually unknown in U.S. agriculture. The environmental consequences of the chemical transformation of agriculture and rural industries have occurred mainly in recent years. What are these consequences?

1. Loss of soil. The average U.S. Midwestern farm loses about 12 tons of topsoil per acre each year. The amount varies, depending upon the slope, amount of snow and rain, cropping, tillage practices, and crop residues. Post-harvest plowing and use of the mold board plow increases soil loss considerably.

Farmers are generally slow to adopt measures that conserve soil. Only in recent years has *conservation tillage* been widely adopted. This practice is an alternative to fall plowing where a disc or modified plow breaks up the soil but leaves stocks and other crop residue to protect the soil against rain and wind. Increased soil erosion is due in part to row cropping, the elimination of natural and artificial windbreaks, and to dry-land grain farming in highly erodible, drought-prone regions.

2. Declines in water quality and the loss of water resources. The factory that dumps sewage into a stream is more easily recognized than is the contribution of agriculture to water pollution. Herbicides, pesticides, nitrates, and phosphates mix with water runoff, and flow into streams, rivers, and lakes. Chemicals stored in plants and animals get into the food chain. Classic cases were DDT and 2,3,4-T, which killed many unwanted plants but did not then dissipate into the environment. These chemicals instead concentrated in animal and human tissue, leading to mutagenic and carcinogenic conditions, producing cancer cells (Plewa, Dowd, and Wagner, 1984).

The eagle population in the United States declined because of DDT in the fat tissue of the fish that the eagles ate, led in turn to thin-shelled eggs that broke before the eaglet hatched. DDT was banned in the United States in

FIGURE 13-2   The average midwestern farm loses about 12 tons of topsoil per acre each year. About 5 acres of topsoil are regenerated each year through natural processes, leaving an average net loss of seven tons of soil per year per acre. Most farmers are concerned about soil erosion but do not see it as a problem on their own farms.

1971, but the compound is still found in salmon and lake trout that are caught in Lake Michigan.

Contamination of underground water by agricultural chemicals is a serious problem because wells and aquifers account for 50 percent of the U.S. water supply. Acid from strip mining is now seeping into underground water supplies in the Appalachian states, Illinois, and the coal-mining areas of the Northern Great Plains.

The depletion of water supplies by agriculture in the Plains states and the Columbia River Basin of the Pacific Northwest is a serious problem. Pollution of groundwater by agricultural chemicals is even more critical. About 95 percent of all rural residents obtain their drinking water from a groundwater supply. Because of the slow movement of chemicals through the soil, the pollutants now detected in groundwater are the result of chemical fertilizers and pesticides applied many years ago. With the intensification of chemical use in production agriculture, concentration of pollutants in ground water may continue to rise making much water unusable. Another problem is the ground water contamination from large feed lots. The amount of manure and urethra is so concentrated that, unless a sewage treatment facility is installed on site, contaminants seep into underground water supplies.

Groundwater pollution is an important environmental issue since all farmers have a direct stake in drinking clean well water. A study of Midwestern farmers found that protecting water quality was as important as profitability of their farms (Korsching et al., 1983). Most farmers recognized the problem of groundwater pollution and appeared willing to accept governmental intervention. In the case of soil erosion, opinions are not unanimous. Many farmers feel that their neighbors' fields are eroding, not their own (Padgett, 1986).

3. Increased use of chemical fertilizers   The trend is to increase fertilizer use as a substitution for the natural, nitrogen-fixing properties of soil. Fertilizer use in the U.S. Corn Belt doubled from a half ton to over one ton per acre from 1965 to 1985.

Gains in farm production have been accompanied by undesirable environmental consequences. Farmers are now discovering that heavy reliance on fertilizer can lead to sterile land. The trend to organic farming in recent years (described in Chapter 10) is a reaction in part to excessive use of chemical fertilizers (Rodefeld, 1978).

FIGURE 13-3   As the amount of agricultural, industrial, and domestic waste increases, disposal becomes a problem. During the period 1982–1988, only three out of five Illinois communities were successful in siting a new solid waste landfill. Most rural and farm people recognize waste as a problem, but do not want the landfill near their homes.

Runoff water containing chemical fertilizers has led to increased eutrophication in ponds, lakes, and streams. *Eutrophication* is the process whereby excessive plant growth stimulated by the fertilizer in the runoff, produces oxygen that chokes off most marine life, including fish.

4. Increased use of herbicides and pesticides   At the time the first edition of this textbook was published in 1960, pesticides and herbicides were viewed as a miracle cure for farm pests. One of the authors of the present book interviewed an Ohio farmer 30 years ago about 2,4-D weed spray, then an important agricultural innovation recommended to farmers by agricultural scientists. This Ohio farmer had rejected the chemical spray because he claimed that it "killed the earthworms in my fields." He was an organic farmer who was convinced that pesticides, weedicides like 2,4-D, and chemical fertilizers, were substances dangerous to human life. At the time, the present author thought this farmer was a harmless nut, and most agricultural experts would have agreed.

Today, we realize that the Ohio farmer was not all wrong. In fact, 2,4-D spray and DDT are now unavailable to farmers because of their long-term carcinogenic consequences. However, a study of Illinois farmers showed that only one-fifth favored controlling on-the-farm use of chemicals and fertilizers. On the other hand, 70 percent of the farm respondents favored stricter control of food additives (Fliegel et al., 1980). The Environmental Protection Agency (EPA) has banned most chlorinated hydrocarbons like DDT, but these chemicals are still used outside of North America, as related in the box that follows.

FIGURE 13-4   This photo shows a biplane spraying chemicals on a Colorado onion field. As inorganic methods of farming become more expensive and the health effects are more uncertain, many farmers are turning to organic farming.

BOX 13-2   *PESTICIDES IN THE THIRD WORLD*

One illustration of the environmental problems that often come with agricultural development in Third World countries is the overuse of pesticides. The use of chemical sprays came in with the rapid diffusion of high-yielding varieties of rice and wheat in the 1970s. Once almost all farmers in an area were growing the same variety of these "miracle" seeds, which often doubled or tripled yields, it became necessary to adopt insect pesticides. Otherwise, a nation's entire crop might be wiped out by a particular insect. So governments and chemical companies combined forces in the 1970s to push heavy applications of pesticides. Around 1980, entomologists in many Third World countries suddenly became alarmed at the problems being caused by pesticide overuse, and by the fact that many insect pests were becoming immune to the chemicals.

One difficulty was that the pesticides were killing spiders and other natural enemies of crop pests, so that when an insect epidemic occurred, it swept through the fields rapidly and with complete destruction. Songbirds, crickets, and frogs were also killed by the pesticides. Most farmers thought that if applying a little pesticide was a good thing, applying much more was even better. A common practice for Asian rice farmers was to spray their fields every week, whether any insect pests were present or not. Farmers had been taught that "a good bug was a dead bug," and it proved extremely difficult to wean farmers from using heavy applications of the chemicals. About 85 percent of all pesticide use on rice fields in Asia was unnecessary and uneconomical. Yet most Integrated Pest Management programs (see Chapter 10) launched in Third World countries in the 1980s to discourage overuse of pesticides have not been successful. One reason is that such IPM programs were strongly opposed by chemical companies, who continued to promote heavy pesticide applications by farmers through company advertising, by distributing free samples of chemicals, and through a vast network of local dealers.

The human cost of the pesticide problem is also severe. Each year in the Third World, an estimated 10,000 people die and 400,000 suffer from acute pesticide poisoning. These individuals are mainly farmers who are harmed by contact with the pesticides on their crops, but the deaths and injuries include farmers' children (who accidentally drink the poisonous sprays).

In the face of these serious environmental, economic, and health problems, the heads of state of several nations finally decided to take direct action in late 1986. The president of the Philippines declared that Integrated Pest Management was officially recommended to Filippino farmers. The president of Indonesia issued a decree banning the sale or use of 57 pesticide chemicals for rice-growing, allowing only seven chemicals not harmful to friendly insects to continue to be sold. However, government subsidies for pesticides, amounting to about half of the selling price to farmers, have not yet been dropped in most nations.

So getting the unadoption of insect pesticides in the Third World is proving to be very difficult. Meanwhile, the environmental problems of pesticides and herbicides continue.

5. The rise in energy-intensive agriculture   The amount of energy required for agricultural production has increased. Scientists use the kilocalorie to measure the amount of energy inputs required to produce an equivalent amount of food. Energy inputs include the production costs of farm machinery, fertilizers, herbicides and pesticides, as well as petroleum fuels. Modern agriculture depends upon mechanized and chemical inputs, the amount of human inputs and of organic inputs, such as animal wastes, have declined along with the number of farmers.

6. Expanded irrigation   Irrigation has allowed farming on many areas with fertile soil but limited or unreliable rainfall. These irrigation projects originally assumed that energy for water pumps would be cheap and available.

However, environmental problems as well as conflict over water rights soon emerged. In the United States, most irrigation was located in the Central and Western high plains and the arid Southwest. Growing populations and expanded industrialization led to competing demands for water. The Colorado River, powerful and deep as it flows through the Grand Canyon, is a dribble by the time it reaches the Gulf of California. The water has been used for municipal, industrial, and agricultural use. The water for irrigation on the high plains is pumped from the Ogallala aquifer. By the year 2000 these wells will begin to dry up and the area will revert to dry farming and grazing with major changes in the number and size of farms and a decline in the size of rural communities.

Irrigation also causes increased salinity of the soil. Salts in the water do not completely run off. The resulting build up eventually makes the soil unusable for agriculture.

Rural sociologists from the University of Arizona predict that in the Western states water for energy companies and energy development and urban expansion will gradually eliminate irrigated agriculture. Urban and industrial users of water can afford to pay more than farmers, therefore farmers relying upon irrigation will eventually be forced to give up their water rights. So the demand for the fixed resource of water will force many farmers out of agriculture.

7. Deforestation   Some Third World countries have serious problems with desertification, the formation of desert in arid and semiarid regions from overgrazing, deforestation, poor agricultural practices, and climate change. Clearing rain forests for agriculture in tropical areas provides land that is lush and green. When cleared and cultivated, however, the thin soil is acidic and lacks essential trace nutrients for agriculture and plantation timber. After abandonment, these lands are subject to flooding and massive soil erosion. Furthermore, regeneration is a slow process because of competition for available wood (the fuel oil of the poor). If the stripped area is near existing desert areas, it quickly becomes barren and regenerates only through protected planting. About 18 million acres of forest cover is lost each year. About half of the clearing takes place in undisturbed forests; the rest in already logged forests (Lewis, 1986; Chiras, 1985, p. 253).

In the United States, Canada, most of Eastern and Western Europe, and New Zealand, the amount of forest cover is increasing through an aggressive program of reforestation and selective cutting. At the same time, rain forests and other wooded areas in Third World countries are losing forest cover through the use of wood for fuels and the clearing of land for grazing. The result is poor water retention, increased soil erosion, and the destruction of large rain forests vital to the survival of many varieties of plants and animals.

8. Unintended consequence of predator control

What do the rabbit, cain toad, water buffalo, and fox have in common? Each was introduced in Australia to control a natural predator or as a supplemental food source. The cain toad refused to eat the proper insect for which it was introduced and now harasses small children and pets in urban areas. In the absence of natural predators water buffalo quickly multiplied and destroyed large areas of flora. The fox and the cat were brought to Australia for hunting and as pets. The foxes attack sheep and the cats became feral, and are now killing native species like the koala. The rabbit multiplied so fast that grass was no longer available for sheep, cattle, or the kangaroo.

An introduced disease reduced the rabbit population. No solution is yet in sight for the cain toad or the fox. The water buffalo are being killed to avoid transmission of diseases to domestic cattle.

The introduction of nonnative species in a new environment led to unintended consequences for the entire ecosystem. Humans are part of that ecosystem; they make the decisions and evaluate the consequences of their behavior on the environment.

9. Contamination of fish and wildlife

A main concern among U.S. fishers and hunters today is not so much their success, but whether what is killed or caught is safe to eat. A study by the Environmental Protection Agency found that all fish species in the Great Lakes evidenced contamination by chemicals. Big fish eat smaller fish and absorb the chemicals in their bodies. People eat the big fish and absorb the chemicals from the fat tissue of the fish. As the chemicals move up the food chain they pose a health threat to humans if concentrations become high enough.

The use of pesticides like Dioxin by farmers in the Great Lakes region led to contamination of the fish population, threatening the $90 million sport industry in Illinois. The largest trophy fish have absorbed the highest concentration of dangerous chemicals. Commercial Great Lakes fishermen are forbidden to take more than a limited catch, however sport fishers may catch and eat fish at their own risk.

The main point in the present discussion of environmental issues is that *technological and economic changes lead to changes in environmental quality*. Many of the consequences of agricultural change were unanticipated. Benefits of increased food production have led to a loss of environmental quality, the reduction of natural resources, and increased risk to human health.

CONSEQUENCES OF ENVIRONMENTAL PROBLEMS FOR HUMAN COMMUNITIES

The previous section outlined the environmental consequences of agricultural chemicals. How have environmental alterations changed the lives of rural people, communities, and organizations?

Parks for Fauna and Flora, or Parks for People

Except for the northern Rocky Mountains from Yellowstone National Park north to the Canadian border (including the Bob Marshall Wilderness Area and Glacier National Park), the grizzly bear has disappeared from the continental United States. Efforts to preserve its numbers continue in Yellowstone National Park. Bear-human interaction increases with more park visitors, and bears associate easy food with humans. Grizzlies cause injuries to humans each year and several deaths have occurred (Thompson, 1986).

At Fishing Bridge (located near the center of Yellowstone Park), the Park Service proposes to move the campsite many miles to the edge of the park and then bus people each day to the center of the park. Resident grizzlies will have free rein, untempted by the food that campers bring. In Denali (Mt. McKinley) National Park, Alaska, visitors are bused into the park each day to view wildlife. In the evening they return to the campsites and lodges at the edge of the park.

The management question is whether the parks are for people or just a kind of zoo with humans passing through and observing the fauna and the flora? Parks and recreation areas contribute much to the economy of rural communities as outlined in Chapter 6.

Mining

"Coal has always cursed the land—the ebb and flow of the black stream has hurt many miners and disrupted their families. The land has always been worst for it—leaving behind a devastated landscape with smoking slag and polluted streams" (Caudill, 1962, p. 231).

Coal mining is a rural industry that extracts natural resources and brings physical changes to the landscape. Coal mining in the Appalachian region began with underground shaft mining. Large numbers of people were attracted to the region to build railroads and towns and work in the mines.

Unemployment occurred as mechanization replaced hand labor in the coal mines.

In the 1950s strip mining (also called surface or cut mining) became the dominant means of coal extraction in Appalachia. High energy and capital costs were involved but low labor requirements. Unemployment increased. Today the landscape is devastated and rural communities in Appalachia are populated with the unemployed, injured survivors, and the relatives of dead miners.

When resource-extraction industries like mining and lumbering invade a traditional agriculture area, conflicts often result from differences between the old-timers and the new residents (Recer, 1978, pp. 407–409). The new industry brings competition for control of local government offices. Often the new population earns higher incomes, thus increasing living costs for local people (Gold, 1985). In rural communites *in-group* relationships are the key to most social interaction. If you are a member of the *out-group* breaking into community relationships is difficult. Being an outsider and getting in is even more difficult if you are part of the activity that is bringing unwanted change to rural communities (see Chapter 5).

BOX 13-3   *THE TRAGEDY OF THE COMMONS*

As each of us knows, life on earth depends on the land, water, and air. These resources are akin to the English commons, communal land where all grazed their livestock. Garrett Hardin wrote about the commons and their abuse in a classic paper, "The Tragedy of the Commons" (1968, p. 162). In England, each man was free to graze his herd on the commons along with his neighbors. The system became imperiled, though, as users became caught in a blind cycle of self-fulfillment. As grazers sought to maximize their personal gain from the commons, they increased their herds. Because each additional cow meant a gain in income with only a little extra expenditure, the addition seemed like a smart one. Individual farmers realized that such actions might lead to overgrazing and the deterioration of the pasture: they also knew that the negative effects of overgrazing would be shared by other members of the community. Thus, each rational herdsman arrived at the same conclusion: he had more to gain than to lose. Such thinking resulted in a spiraling decay of the commons. Over and over, each grazer increased herd size, sharing the environmental costs with his cohorts. Hardin summarized the situation as follows: "Each man is locked into a system that compels him to increase his herd without limit in a world that is limited." As each pursued what was best for himself, the whole was pushed toward disaster. As Hardin noted, "Freedom in a commons brings ruin to all" (Hardin, p. 162).

The logic that leads people to disregard the impact of their individual behavior on common property has always been with us. However, faced with massive deterioration of our natural resources, the time is here to be concerned about the problem of the "commons." And the tragedies are as common as each of the environmental problems around us. The Midwestern farmer who practices poor soil conservation or the Third World peasant who applies too much pesticide may increase production in the short run. But in the long run streams become polluted and downstream farmers must deal with flooding and heavy runoff (Erickson, 1984). In the meantime, those pesticides may provide serious disruption to the food chain.

Nowhere is the "commons" tragedy more evident than in the conflict over grazing land in the western United States. Much of the pastureland is public—hence part of the commons. Each grazier pressures the Bureau of Land Management to allow more animals. The amount of cattle and sheep able to graze increases up to a point and then the pastures have difficulty regenerating, the soil erodes, and the process of desertification begins. Now many public grazing lands in the West may never recover. All because individual ranchers were improving their economic position at the expense of the "commons."

The "Darling Downs" area of Eastern Australia was traditionally restricted to grazing and dry farming. With the discovery of a huge underground "lake" the large "stations" and "properties" were divided into smaller farms for row-cropping. However, no restrictions or joint cooperation have been developed to keep the withdrawal of water at the replacement level. Within 20 years the lake will be dry and "the tragedy of the commons" will force present farmers out of business.

LAND MANAGEMENT AGENCIES

U.S. Department of Interior

U.S. government land management agencies are public bureaucracies designed to manage and conserve resources on public lands. Most are located within the U.S. Department of Interior (USDI). Like the U.S. Secretary of Agriculture, the Secretary of the Interior is a member of the President's cabinet. In the early 1800s the Secretary of the Interior was charged with overseeing the distribution of western lands to settlers and with supervision of the native Indian population. Today, the main USDI programs are:

1. *Management of Federal Lands:* With few exceptions, most federally owned lands come under the management of the U.S. Department of the Interior. Exceptions are the U.S. Forest Service (administratively located in the U.S. Department of Agriculture) and the U.S. Army Corps of Engineers (located in the U.S. Department of Defense), which manages rivers and harbors and most flood control reservoirs.

2. *Regulation of Private Sector Activity on Government Land:* Most governmental land management agencies are charged with the administration of Federal laws and regulations that apply to private sector business and public activities.

3. *Conservation of Resources:* Most U.S. Department of Interior agencies are charged with conservation, maintaining basic resources for future generations. An example is the preservation of wilderness areas and the maintenance of national parks.

TABLE 13–1   Major Government Land Management Agencies

INITIALS	NAME	CONTROLLED ACREAGE* (IN MILLIONS)	PURPOSE
1. USDI	United States Department of Interior	—	Overall responsibility for federal lands and waters, as well as for regulating resource extraction.
2. NPS	National Park Service	74	Manage the National Park system
3. BLM	Bureau of Land Management	310	Issue grazing and logging permits; regulate mining and mineral extraction on public lands
4. USFWS	U.S. Fish and Wildlife Service	88	Maintain and enhance all fish and wildlife species
5. USFS	U.S. Forest Service	187	Manage and conserve public forest preserves
6. CORPS	U.S. Army Corps of Engineers	31	Manage and maintain all navigable rivers and streams and costal waterways
7. EPA	Environmental Protection Agency	—	Certify all pesticides and herbicides used in agricultural products

*About two-thirds of all the land in the United States and Alaska is in the private sector, counting Indian reservations. Most of the remaining one-third, or about 755 million acres, is administered by government land management agencies, most of which are housed in the departments of the Interior and Agriculture. Military lands account for the remainder.

Source: Jeanne Nienabor Clarke and Daniel McCool, *Staking Out the Terrain: Power Differential Among Natural Resource Management Agencies,* Albany, NY: State University of N.Y. Press, 1985.

4. *Resource Extraction:* This function involves the orderly removal of mineral resources like oil and coal.
5. *Outdoor Recreation:* Almost all federal provision of outdoor recreation facilities and lands is administered through the USDI, much of it built through matching grants funded by the Land and Water Conservation Act of 1964.

National Park Service

Early trappers, hunters, and explorers marveled at the natural beauty of many locations in the mountains of the western United States. The conservation movement in the late 1800s sought to preserve these lands as public parks. The founding of Yellowstone National Park in 1872 and Yosemite

National Park in 1895 led to the establishment in 1916 of the National Park Service. Over the next 40 years, spectacular scenic and unique biological areas came under the management of the National Park Service. The U.S. model of a national park system is now followed in more than 100 countries worldwide.

The National Park Service has traditionally been preservation oriented and staffed by biologists. This agency maintains a very positive image in the eyes of the U.S. public. The Park Ranger dressed in forest green and wearing a wide-brimmed hat represents a symbol of protection.

In the late 1960s the Park Service began to increase the number of U.S. national parks through an active acquisition program. New parks were located in the East, near larger cities. While ecosystem protection was a main goal of the Yellowstone, Yosemite, and Grand Canyon Parks, the new parks emphasized historical preservation and reconstruction, and the provision of outdoor recreation opportunities for urban people.

However, many parks are now threatened by overuse, air pollution, crowding, lack of funds for maintenance, proliferation of businesses within their boundaries, and mineral and energy development both within and around their borders. For example, at times the Grand Canyon is so blanketed with air pollution from the Navajo Power Plant in Page, Arizona, that one cannot see the opposite rim (Rudzitis and Schwartz, 1982). The Department of Energy proposed the siting of a nuclear waste repository facility next to Kings Canyon National Park in Utah. While the facility would be out of sight, the road and railroad leading to it would be visible to persons viewing the scenic canyon.

Visitors to the National Park System increased from 190 million in 1976, to 270 million in 1986 and should reach 350 million by the year 2000. Although the number of parks 'has more than doubled since 1945, the acreage has increased only slightly.

Bureau of Land Management

The activities of the U.S. Bureau of Land Management are little known outside of the ranching and mining areas of the western part of the United States. During the settlement of the United States west of the Mississippi, all land not claimed by settlers, placed in Indian reservations, given to railroads, or made a part of the Park Service or Forest Service system, came under the jurisdiction of the General Land Office. The Grazing Service (which issues grazing permits on public land) and the General Land Office were combined in 1946 to form the Bureau of the Land Management (BLM). The local Bureau manager is usually officed with the county extension agent, and is responsible for issuing grazing permits to local ranchers as well as enforcing regulations to reduce soil erosion.

The Bureau manages more land than all other federal agencies combined. Until the Alaska Lands Bill was signed in 1980, the Bureau administered 96 percent of Alaska. In addition, the Bureau of Land Management is responsible for all offshore areas extending out 200 miles.

BLM traditionally has been responsive to local interests, and in this sense is a participative bureaucracy (see Chapter 5). Almost all decisions on mineral leases (generally mining and prospecting permits) and grazing permits (cattle and sheep) are made at the state and local level. The Bureau's land management practices began to come under public scrutiny when leases were issued for strip mines in Wyoming, Montana, and the Dakotas; when public lands were overgrazed; when pipeline permits were issued without consideration of their impact on wildlife and the fragile permafrost of arctic Alaska; and when coyotes were killed by cyanide poisoning. The environmental movement coincided in the mid-1970s with a revival of exploration for oil and other minerals (particularly coal) on federal lands. Vast oil, coal, and lignite reserves were discovered, both on and offshore in Alaska.

U.S. Fish and Wildlife Service

The Alaska Lands Bill increased the acreage managed by the Fish and Wildlife Service from small holdings along migratory bird routes, to an area

FIGURE 13-5 Stripmining in Wyoming, Montana, and North and South Dakota takes place on public lands administered by the Bureau of Land Management. The Bureau has been the focus of public attention because ranchers (a traditional client) want to keep the land for grazing, while mining companies (a new client) want the coal mined.

the size of the state of Ohio. The USFWS is a line-action agency with responsibility for administration of the Endangered Species Act, issuing commercial fishing permits for coastal areas, controlling the hunting of migratory waterfowl, and management of wildlife refuges, preserves, and reserves.

The Fish and Wildlife Service was established in 1903 as an extension of the general conservation efforts of that period in response to public concern with overhunting and fishing. The native American bison was hunted almost to extinction. The last passenger pigeon was shot in 1927. The major objective of the Fish and Wildlife Service is the improvement of hunting and fishing opportunities, however more attention is now placed on nongame species.

As is the case with many federal land management agencies, the USFWS is caught between two major pressure groups with different views of environmental protection: (1) hunting and fishing groups seek the maintenance and enhancement of game and fish for hunting and fishing, and (2) environmental groups and the general public that see wildlife preservation as a major issue.

Western ranchers complained in the 1970s that their sheep were being killed by an increased population of coyotes. To eliminate the coyotes, the FWS laced sheep with deadly cyanide as bait for coyote. But instead of coyotes eating the sheep decoys, eagles, lynx, marmots, and other animals were killed. The poison killed the wrong victims.

Forest Service

The purpose of the U.S. Forest Service is to manage and conserve public forest resources. Forest rangers are best known by the U.S. public for their role in preventing forest fires. Most fires are set by humans, many of them on purpose. Some purposive fires are of a grudge nature, intended to burn someone out. Other fires are set by low-income rural people as a means of gaining employment; they know they will be hired to help put out the forest fire. Contrary to popular belief, firefighting is really only one of many roles played by forest rangers (Kaufman, 1960).

The Forest Service, established in 1905, is a centralized government agency located within the USDA. The Forest Service is one of the best-organized and most effective of all government agencies. It hires professional (that is, college graduate) foresters, and there is a high esprit de corps among Forest Service employees.

Like other land management agencies, the Forest Service is caught between traditional clients (the forest products industry, loggers, and so forth) and environmental and recreational groups that want to limit timber cutting, maintain natural environments, and improve wildlife habitat.

Major environmental problems include clear-cutting of forests for logs, the building of erodible logging roads through mountainous forest areas, logging too close to streams, and the use of inappropriate pesticides. Each practice contributes to steam sedimentation and pollution, and destroys the aesthetics of the forest environment.

U.S. Army Corps of Engineers

The "Corps" is responsible for the management of all navigable rivers and harbors in the United States (shared with the Bureau of Reclamation in the West). This agency has built most of the large flood-control reservoirs in the United States. Located in the U.S. Department of Defense, the Army Corps of Engineers is the military service with the most contact with civilians. Corps activities are organized on the basis of watersheds.

The Corp of Engineers has a rather poor image among people in rural communities who resent the damming of their streams, the removal of land from agricultural use, and the disruption of their communities (Burdge and Opryszek, 1981). As a Kentucky woman stated: "The Corps is meaner than a barrel full of fishhooks" (Korsching, Donnermeyer, and Burdge, 1980). Such benefits of reservoir construction as reduced downstream flooding and improved recreational opportunites accrue over a wide area, while the environmental and social impacts are borne by the local community.

The Corps is not responsive to local interests and is perceived as a distant bureaucracy that makes decisions with little concern for local people's lives.

Other Government Agencies

The *Bureau of Reclamation* has major responsibility for managing rivers, streams, and lakes, mostly in the Western United States. Most of the large dams and irrigation projects west of the Rockies were built and are managed by the Bureau of Reclamation. The *Bureau of Indian Affairs,* located in the Department of the Interior, is the principal agency relating to the affairs of the American Indian population. The agency manages land for tribal organization. The *Environmental Protection Agency* reports directly to the President and is responsible for the licensing of all herbicides and pesticides. In addition, the agency supervises the training programs for the application of on-farm chemicals. The licensing of farmers to apply pesticides and herbicides is done through the individual state environmental protection organizations.

SOCIAL IMPACT ASSESSMENT

So far in this chapter we have talked about the environmental consequences of agricultural and rural industries. Environmental change has equal consequences for rural families and rural communities.

Elected officials, community leaders, and county extension agents in rural areas who must approve or disapprove future proposals for public and private development need information on the possible social consequences of the proposed action. Rural sociologists have been leaders in providing research on the new methodology of social impact assessment.

Social impact assessment is the systematic appraisal of the impacts on the day-to-day quality of life of persons and communities whose environment is affected by a development or policy change (Burdge, 1985). Examples of social impact setting are school and plant closings, reservoir construction, resource development projects, and the siting of hazardous and solid waste facilities (Finsterbush, 1985).

The social impact assessment process alerts community leaders, planners, and project proponents to the likelihood of future impacts. Social impact assessment developed out of a need to apply the findings of rural sociology and other social sciences to predict the social effects of environmental alteration as required under the National Environmental Policy Act of 1969 (NEPA). These mandates require project proponents to assess the social effects of a development before a decision is made to proceed. Most importantly, social impact assessment evaluates the social effects of a development or new policy while the action is still in the planning stage (Dietz, 1987).

The social assessor first identifies similar projects presently in operation, and based on those experiences, predicts the impacts likely to result from the planned project. For example, water empoundment for hydroelectric power is a common development in many parts of the world. Rural sociologists were asked to evaluate what went wrong in a New Zealand project (Freudenberg, 1986).

BOX 13-4   *DEVELOPMENT FOR WHAT? THE CASE OF HYDRO-POWER DEVELOPMENT IN NEW ZEALAND*

The South Island of New Zealand is blessed with beautiful scenery, swift-flowing streams and rivers, snow-covered mountains, and green fields dotted with sheep and cattle. To provide electricity for the population of 3.2 million, hydroelectric plants were built on the lower parts of the Waitaki and Clutha Rivers, and on the Upper Waitaki. Several dams, canals, and power stations were constructed. A boomtown called Twizel was built in 1960 to accommodate the approximately 8,000 workers and their families.

In 1976, an aluminum smelting plant was proposed at Madsen Point in Otago Bay, near the city of Dunedin, 120 miles downstream from Twizel. Cheap power would come from the new Upper Waitaki complex and from development on the Upper Clutha. The main power source for the Upper Clutha will come from the Clyde High Dam. The dam was started in 1980 and was completed in 1988.

A new boomtown named Clyde, expected to eventually have a population of 10,000 persons, was built near the dam site, and Twizel closed down and its residents moved to Clyde. Meantime, the world price of aluminum collapsed (mainly because additional plants were built in many Third World countries), and the plant at Madsen Point was canceled.

The Clyde High Dam backed up water for 50 miles. The town of Cromwell was relocated and two scenic gorges were flooded, and many people were forced to leave their homes. Although water will run through the gates of the Clyde Dam, its electrical generators will not turn. At present, New Zealand has more electricity than it can use. Three more dams and reservoirs are planned for the Upper Clutha River. The rationale for continuing the projects is that a trained work force needs work.

How could this series of disastrous attacks on the environment have been averted? A social impact assessment completed during the planning stage would have alerted project proponents to the impacts of relocating entire families and communities, to the problems of excess construction workers, and to the recreational patterns of rural New Zealanders.

BOX 13-5   *RURAL LAND USE PLANNING IN ALASKA*

The lack of rural land use planning will lower the benefits and raise the costs of natural resource development. Rural communities can have better roads, schools, improved medical facilities, quality water, and good police and fire protection. However, without control over development, a community cannot articulate its needs to developers and outside funding agencies (Burdge and Opryszek, 1981).

Skagway, Alaska (located on the inland waterway in Southeast Alaska), has been subjected to a rapid influx and outflow of population since the days of the legendary Klondike Gold Rush. First came the stampeders of the 1898 gold rush and the Yukon-White Pass Railroad in 1900. Next was a mini-tourist invasion in the early 1920s. The building of the Alaska Highway in the early 1940s brought an "army" of construction workers. A postwar boom in the Yukon brought increased export trade. The Park Service began a National Park in 1976, and in 1980 a road was built over the mountains connecting Skagway to the Alaska Highway. In 1983 competition from the newly built road forced the railroad to close. In 90 years a small community (population 786 in 1986) has seen wild fluctuations in both its permanent and temporary populations (Burdge, Field, and Wells, 1982).

In 1941 the town's population decided they needed to plan for infrastructure support and zoning laws, and to gain a say in development decisions. As a result, adequate roads have been built and a restored main street now is a stable tourist attraction. Sewage treatment is adequate and a town plan has led to grants from the State of Alaska. So the Skagway story demonstrates that planning can help alleviate the problems of sudden population growth and decline.

The town of Skagway, with the aid of a resident rural sociologist, was able to benefit from the proposed new park. Based on past experiences, the community was able to identify future social impacts. The National Park Service was asked to include those benefits in the proposal to develop the new Klondike Gold Rush International Historical Park.

SOIL CONSERVATION

After 50 years of U.S. conservation programs, why is soil erosion still a problem of such great magnitude? Conservation professionals today realize that human factors are the most important determinant of why farmers do not adopt soil conservation practices (Bultena and Hoiberg, 1983). The means for controlling and indeed reversing soil erosion has been known for many years. But adoption of conservation practices by U.S. farmers lags. Rural sociologists have studied the adoption of soil conservation practices for many decades and have some important conclusions (Lovejoy and Napier, 1986).

1. A major problem is that many soil conservation practices are not profitable to farmers. The Soil Conservation Service has been advocating conservation tillage since 1975. However, the Cooperative Extension Service has been slow to support this practice, and only then by underemphasizing its conservation aspects while overemphasizing its energy-conserving and profitability aspects. Farmers do not perceive that government agencies present a unified program of soil conservation. This lack of harmony may be one reason why farmers are slow to adopt conservation tillage (Nielson, 1986, p. 8).

2. Despite years of educational programs, many farmers remain oblivious to their personal soil loss, or else they discount the importance of this loss. Many farmers perceive that adoption of soil conservation techniques will interfere with their crop production.

3. Users of no-till farming have more education, higher incomes, and larger farms. Adopters also travel more widely to seek information and rely less on their neighbors (Carlson, 1986, p. 11).

4. Finally, some of the most productive land used for farming is also the most erosion prone, particularly bottom lands and former swamps. Many of the individual states are cooperating in a wetland restoration program.

SUMMARY

In a 1962 book, *Silent Spring,* Rachel Carson predicted that continued application of herbicides, pesticides, and chemical fertilizers would have serious environmental consequences. The U.S. environmental movement began in the 1960s due in part to this book and such disasters as the Santa Barbara oil spill. The movement reached full bloom in the 1970s with the passage of such legislation as the National Environmental Policy Act (establishing the Environmental Protection Agency, EPA) and improvements in the Clean Air and Water Acts.

Some of the more serious consequences of agricultural production on environmental quality are: (1) loss of soil, (2) decline in water quality, (3) ground water pollution, (4) increased use of fertilizers, herbicides, and pesticides, (5) energy-intensive agriculture, (6) expanded irrigation, (7) desertification, (8) predator control, and (9) the contamination of fish and wildlife.

The USDI (Department of Interior) provides guidance and coordination for the major land management agencies. The National Park Service (NPS) has management control of national parks, recreational areas, monuments, and historic sites. The Bureau of Land Management (BLM) issues grazing and logging permits for federal lands, and regulates mineral exploration and extraction on public lands and off-shade sites. The Fish and Wildlife Service (USFWS) maintains preserves, sanctuaries, and reserves for fish and wildlife. The Forest Service (USFS), located in the U.S. Department of Agriculture, conserves and manages forest resources. The U.S. Army Corps of Engineers, located in the U.S. Department of Defense, is responsible for the management and maintenance of all navigable streams and rivers, reservoirs, and coastal waterways. The Environmental Protection Agency (EPA) is responsible for regulation of all herbicides and pesticides used in agriculture.

Farmers generally agree that pollution of groundwater is a serious problem and could require government intervention. However, they differ sharply from the rest of the U.S. population on government regulation of chemical fertilizers and pesticides (about 4 out of 5 farmers oppose on-the-farm regulations). Meantime, the problem of soil erosion persists. Profitability generally takes precedent over soil conservation.

Social impact assessment is the systematic appraisal of the impacts on the day-to-day quality of life of persons and communities whose environment is affected by a development or policy change. Rural sociologists have utilized the social impact assessment process to help rural people to plan in advance for natural resource developments in their communities.

REFERENCES

BULTENA, GORDON L., and ERIC O. HOIBERG. (1983). "Factors Affecting Farmers' Adaption of Conservation Tillage." *Journal of Soil and Water Conservation, 38*, No. 2, pp. 281–283.

BURDGE, RABEL J. (1985, August). "Social Impact Assessment and the Planning Process." *Planning and Public Policy, 11*, No. 2., pp. 1–4.

BURDGE, RABEL J., and PAUL OPRYSZEK. (1981, June). *Coping With Change: An Interdisciplinary Assessment of the Lake Shelbyville Reservoir,* UILU-IES 81 0008, IES Report No. 8.

BURDGE, RABEL J., DONALD R. FIELD, and STEPHEN R. WELLS. (1982). "Understanding Social Impacts in the Context of Community History: The Case of Skagway, Alaska." In *Sociological Abstracts,* S14690/RSS/1982/1320.

CANDILL, HARRY R. (1962). *Night Comes to the Cumberlands.* Boston, MA: Doubleday.

CARLSON, JOHN E. In Steve Lovejoy and Ted Napier. *Conservation Soil: Insights from Socio-Economic Research,* NCR-162. Ankeny, IA: Soil Conservation Society of America.

CARSON, RACHEL. (1965). *Silent Spring.* New York: Penguin Books. (First published by Doubleday in 1962.)

CHIRAS, DANIEL D. (1985) *Environmental Science: a Framework for Decision-Making.* Menlo Park, CA: Benjamin/Cummings Publishing Co.

CLARKE, JEANNE NIENABOR, and DANIEL McCOOL. (1985). *Staking Out the Terrain: Power Differential Among Natural Resource Management Agencies.* Albany, NY: State University of N.Y. Press.

DIETZ, THOMAS. (1987). "Theory and Method in Social Assessment." *Sociological Inquiry, 57,* No. 1, pp. 54–69.

DUNLAP, R. E., (1987, July/August). "Polls, Pollution and Politics Revisited: Public Opinion on the Environment in the Reagan Era," *Environment,* Vol. 29, pp. 6–11, 32–37.

DUNLAP, R. E., and K. D. VAN LIERE. (1980). "The Social Bases of Environmental Concern: A Review of Hypotheses, Explanations and Empirical Evidence," PUBLIC OPINION QUARTERLY 44.

ERICKSON, WILLIAM. (1984, March 5). Blomquist and Elinor Ostrom, "Institutional Response and the Resolution of a Commons Dilemma." Workshop in Political Theory and Policy Analysis. Indiana University, Bloomington, IN.

FINSTERBUSCH, KURT. (1985, March). "State of the Art in Social Impact Assessment." *Environment and Behavior, 17*, No. 2, pp. 193–221.

FLIEGEL, F. C., J. C. VAN ES, RABEL J. BURDGE, and HARVEY J. SCHWEITZER. (1980, September). *Farming in an Urban Environment*, AERR 167, Department of Agr. Econ. Agr. Exp. Sta., Urbana, IL.

FREUDENBURG, W. (1986). "Social Impact Assessment." *Annual Review of Sociology, 12*, pp. 451–478.

GOLD, RAYMOND A. (1985). *Ranching, Mining, and the Human Impact of Natural Resource Development*, New Brunswick, NJ: Transaction Books.

HARDIN, GARRETT. (1968, December 13). "The Tragedy of the Commons." *Science.*

HARRY, JOSEPH, *et al.* "Conservation: An Upper-Middle Class Social Movement." *Journal of Leisure Research, 1:3* (summer), pp. 246–254.

INGWERSON, MARSHALL. (1986, July 9). "Depression-Born TVA Falls on Hard Times." *Christian Science Monitor.*

JOHNSON, ALLEN G. (1986). *Human Arrangements: An Introduction to Sociology.* Harcourt, Brace and Jovanovich.

KAUFMAN, HERBERT. (1960). *The Forest Ranger.* Baltimore: Johns Hopkins Press.

KORSCHING, PETER F., J. F. DONNERMEYER, and R. J. BURDGE. (1980). "Perception of Housing and Property Settlement Among Displaced Person." *Human Organization, 39*, pp. 332–338.

KORSCHING, PETER F., *et al.* (1983). "Adaption Characteristics and Adaption Patterns of Minimum Tillage: Implications for Soil Conservation Programs." *Journal of Soil and Water Conservation, 38*, No. 5, pp. 428–431.

LEWIS, ROGER. (1986, October 10). "Damage to Tropical Forests, or Why Were There so Many Kinds of Animals." *Science, 234*, pp. 149–150.

LOVEJOY, STEVE, and TED NAPIER. *Conservation Soil: Insights from Socio-Economic Research*, NCR-162. Ankeny, IA: Soil Conservation Society of America.

MITCHELL, R. C. (1979). "Silent Spring/Silent." *Public Opinion, 2*, 16–20, 55. *New York Times.* (1986, April 21).

NIELSON, JAMES. In Steve Lovejoy and Ted Napier. *Conservation Soil: Insights from Socio-Economic Research*, NCR-162. Ankeny, IA: Soil Conservation Society of America. (1986).

PADGETT, STEVE. (1986). Paper given at the Annual Meeting of the Rural Sociological Society, Salt Lake City, Utah, August 27.

PLEWA, M. J., P. A. DOWD and E. D. WAGNER. (1984). "Calibrations of the Maize yg^2 Assay Using Gamma Radiation and Ethyl Methonesulfonate." *Environ. Mutagenesis, 6*, 781–795.

RECER, PAUL. "Strip Mining Boom Jars Plains States." In Rodefield, Richard D., *et al.* (1978). *Change in Rural America: Causes, Consequences, and Alterations.* St. Louis, MO: C.V. Mosky.

RODEFELD, RICHARD D., *et al.* (1978). *Change in Rural America: Causes, Consequences, and Alterations.* St. Louis, MO: C.V. Mosky.

RUDZITIS, G., and J. SCHWARTZ. (1982). "The Plight of Parklands." *Environment, 24* (8).

SELSNIK, PHILIP. (1953). *TVA and the Grass Roots.*, N.Y., Harper & Row

THOMPSON, JAMES G., (1986, May 10–15). "Visitor Behavior Characteristics and Value Preferences In Yellowstone National Park: A Changing Agenda." Paper presented at the first National Symposium on Social Behavior and Resource Mgt., Corvallis, Oregon.

Chapter 14

Diffusion of Innovations

And he gave it for his opinion . . . that whoever could make two ears of corn, or two blades of grass, to grow upon a spot of ground where only one grew before, would deserve better of mankind, and do more essential service to his country, than the whole race of politicians put together.

—Jonathan Swift

In order to aid in diffusing among the people of the United States useful and practical information relating to agriculture and home economics and to encourage the application of the same, there may be continued or inaugurated in connection with the college or colleges in each state . . . agricultural extension work which shall be carried on in cooperation with the United States Department of Agriculture.

The Smith-Lever Act of 1914, the federal law creating the extension service

The most important immediate cause of social change in the rural United States is technological innovations in agriculture. New ideas largely result from the efforts of agricultural scientists in the USDA, commercial companies, and state agricultural experiment stations. The agricultural extension services then communicate these innovations to their rural audiences. Both the experiment stations and the extension services are part of the land grant system in the United States, which is centered in each state university. The consequences of agricultural technology, while beneficial to many Americans, are far-reaching and sometimes unpredictable. Rural sociologists have been studying the diffusion of agricultural innovations for over 40 years; the results of these studies are summarized in the present chapter.

IMPORTANCE OF DIFFUSION

A technological determinist is one who believes that technology is the main cause of social change in society. The present authors are "soft" technological determinists, in that we believe technology has been one of the main causes of social change in rural society, but not the only cause. Also important are government policies, the actions of farmer organizations, international events, and natural disasters like floods, hurricanes, and earthquakes. Nevertheless, *any full understanding of U.S. rural social change must begin with the diffusion of agricultural innovations.*

The purpose of this chapter is to describe the process through which technological innovations are communicated to farmers. First, let us see how one farmer decided to adopt a microcomputer. Here we describe his behavior at each stage in the innovation-decision process:

1. *Knowledge Stage:* Farmer A is exposed to many magazine and television advertisements for home computers over a period of several years, thus acquiring a general idea of what a home computer is and some of the advantages of owning one. Farmer A also is vaguely aware that several of his neighbors have computers, but he has not discussed this topic with them.

2. *Persuasion Stage:* Farmer A pays a social visit to the home of his friend, Farmer B, who shows him his computer and demonstrates a software program that allows him to select the least-cost rations for his pig-feeding operation. Farmer B is a very satisfied adopter who has become quite knowledgeable about microcomputers. He tells Farmer A about the details of price, brands, and the nature of needed computer peripherals. Much of B's technical expertise was obtained from reading computer magazines. The following day, Farmer A discusses buying a home computer with his wife (she is not enthused, even though Farmer A tells her how Mrs. B files her recipes on a computer).

3. *Decision Stage:* After several weeks of further family discussions, Farmer A decides to adopt. The salesperson at the computer retail store could not answer A's questions to his satisfaction, but gave him several brochures, plus an owner's manual written in rather technical jargon.

4. *Implementation Stage:* Farmer A encounters about a month of extreme frustration as he seeks to put the innovation into use. He has difficulty in connecting

such peripherals as his printer and modem, and in learning how to format floppy disks. The salesperson at the computer store is not helpful, nor are such printed material as the owner's manual. Farmer B owns a different model computer, but provides useful advice. Finally, Farmer A joins a computer club, where he finds more helpful information. Within a few months, A's computer is being used about 15 hours per week, and A has become a satisfied adopter.

5. *Confirmation Stage:* Farmer A seeks further information about his computer through the monthly meetings of his computer club and by subscribing to several computer magazines (where he learns of a new software program that allows him to analyze the ideal crop rotation pattern for his fields). Farmer A tells about eight other individuals per month about his computer, and shows it to an average of five farmers per month.

This illustration is fairly typical of the innovation-decision behavior of a computer adopter in the United States in the 1980s. Note the role that different channels of communication played in this individual's innovation-decision process. Peer communication with Farmer B seemed to be crucial to Farmer A at the persuasion stage, after Farmer A already possessed awareness-knowledge of the innovation that he had obtained from the mass media.

The first important diffusion studies were investigations of the spread of agricultural innovations among U.S. farmers. The early agricultural diffusion studies were mainly conducted by rural sociologists, and over 800 studies have been completed by rural sociologists since. The prototype early diffusion study was the Ryan and Gross (1943) investigation of the spread of hybrid seed corn among Iowa farmers. This inquiry, more than any other diffusion study, influenced the methodology, theoretical framework, and interpretations of later diffusion scholars. Even though the hybrid corn study was conducted before most readers of this book were born, it is still one of the best illustrations of how new ideas spread.

BOX 14-1   *THE DIFFUSION OF HYBRID CORN IN IOWA*

The innovation of hybrid corn was a very important new farm technology when it was released to Iowa farmers in 1928, and it ushered in a whole set of agricultural innovations that have amounted to an "agricultural revolution" in farm productivity. Hybrid seed had been developed by agricultural scientists at Iowa State University and at other state land-grant universities. The diffusion of hybrid seed was heavily promoted by the Iowa agricultural extension service and by salesmen from seed companies. Hybrid corn yielded about 20 percent more per acre than the open-pollinated varieties that it replaced, and it was also more drought resistant and better suited to harvesting with mechanical corn pickers. But the seed lost its hybrid vigor after the first generation, so farmers had to purchase hybrid seed each year. Previously, farmers had saved their own seed, selected from their best-looking corn plants. The adoption of hybrid corn meant that a farmer had to make important changes in his behavior.

Corn was the main farm crop in Iowa in the 1930s; in fact, Iowa's official state song describes it as "the tall corn state." The hybrid seed was adopted rapidly in Iowa. By 1941, about 13 years after its first release, the innovation was adopted by almost 100 percent of Iowa farmers. Still, adoption of the new technology was far from instantaneous.

Administrators in the Iowa Agricultural Experiment Station sponsored the hybrid corn diffusion study in Iowa because they wanted to improve their understanding of this case of successful diffusion in order to learn lessons that might be applied to the diffusion of future farm innovations. These officials may also have been puzzled and frustrated as to why such an obviously advantageous innovation as hybrid corn was not adopted more rapidly. They wondered, for example, why some farmers waited 13 years to adopt, during which period they were surrounded by neighbors who were using the innovation successfully.

In 1941, Bryce Ryan and Neal Gross (1943), two rural sociologists at Iowa State University, personally interviewed 259 farmers living in two small communities. Each of these respondents was asked to recall when and how he had adopted hybrid corn, and to provide certain information about themselves and their farm operation.

All but 2 of the 259 farmers had adopted hybrid corn between 1928 and 1941, a rather rapid rate of adoption. When plotted cumulatively on a year-by-year basis, the adoption rate formed an S-shaped curve over time. After the first five years, by 1933, only 10 percent of the Iowa farmers had adopted. Then, the adoption curve shot up to 40 percent adoption in the next three years (by 1936). Soon the rate of adoption began to level off as fewer and fewer farmers remained to adopt the new idea. The overall shape of the rate of adoption looked like an "S" (as in Figure 14–1).

Ryan and Gross assigned farmers to adopter categories on the basis of when they adopted the new seed. Compared to later adopters, the innovators had larger-sized farms, higher incomes, and more years of formal education. The innovators were more cosmopolite, as measured by the number of trips they had taken to Des Moines (Iowa's largest city, located about 75 miles away).

Although hybrid corn was an innovation with a high degree of relative advantage over the open-pollinated seed that it replaced, the typical farmer moved rather slowly from awareness-knowledge of the innovation to adoption. The innovation-decision period from first knowledge to the adoption decision averaged about nine years for all respondents, a finding that led to a clearer realization that the innovation-decision process involved considerable deliberation by most adopters, even in the case of an innovation with such spectacular results. The average respondent took three or four years after planting his first hybrid seed, usually on a small trial plot, before deciding to plant 100 percent of his corn acreage in hybrid varieties.

Communication channels played different roles at various stages in the innovation-decision process. The typical farmer first heard of hybrid seed from a salesperson, but neighbors were the most frequent channel leading to persuasion. Salespersons were more important channels for earlier adopters, and neighbors were more important for later adopters. The Ryan and Gross (1943) find-

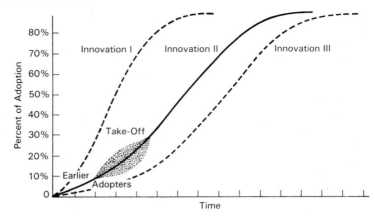

FIGURE 14-1   The *Diffusion* Process.

Innovation I has a more rapid rate of adoption than innovation III. Each of the three diffusion curves are S-shaped, with a take-off in the rate of adoption at about 10 to 25 percent adoption. This take-off occurs when the opinion leaders in a system adopt, thus activating interpersonal diffusion networks.

Source: Rogers (1983). Used by permission.

ings suggested the important role of interpersonal networks in the diffusion process. The farmer-to-farmer exchange of personal experiences with use of the hybrid seed seemed to lie at the heart of diffusion. When enough such positive experiences were accumulated by farmers (especially the innovators and early adopters) and exchanged within the community, the rate of adoption really took off. This threshold seemed to occur in about 1935. After that point, it would have been impossible to halt the further diffusion of hybrid corn. The farm community, including the networks linking the individual farmers within it, was a crucial element in the diffusion process.

Ryan and Gross (1943) concluded that hybrid corn spread in the two Iowa communities as a kind of social snowball. They wrote: "There is no doubt but that the behavior of one individual in an interacting population affects the behavior of his fellows. Thus, the demonstrated success of hybrid seed on a few farms offers a changed situation to those who have not been so experimental. The very fact of acceptance by one or more farmers offers new stimulus to the remaining ones." Thus, the two rural sociologists intuitively sensed what later diffusion scholars were to gather more detailed evidence to prove: *The heart of the diffusion process consists of people exchanging information and borrowing ideas.*

Source: Adapted from Everett M. Rogers, *Diffusion of Innovations,* New York: Free Press, 1983, pp. 32–34, 55. Used by permission.

DIFFUSION OF INNOVATIONS

The Innovation

Diffusion is the process through which (1) an *innovation* (2) is communicated through certain *channels* (3) over *time* (4) among the members of a *society*.

An *innovation* is an idea, practice, or object perceived as new by an individual or other unit of adoption. The characteristics of an innovation, as perceived by the members of a social system, determine its rate of adoption. Five attributes of innovations are: (1) relative advantage, (2) compatibility, (3) complexity, (4) trialability, and (5) observability.

1. *Relative advantage* is the degree to which an innovation is perceived as better than the idea it supersedes. The degree of relative advantage can be measured in economic terms, but often social prestige factors, convenience, and satisfaction are important. It matters little whether the innovation has a great deal of "objective" advantage to a potential adopter. What does matter is whether or not an individual *perceives* the innovation as being advantageous. The greater the perceived relative advantage of an innovation, the quicker its rate of adoption.
2. *Compatibility* is the degree to which an innovation is perceived as consistent with the existing values, past experiences, and needs of the receivers. An idea that is compatible will be adopted more rapidly than one that is incompatible. Adoption of an incompatible innovation often requires creation and adoption of a new value system.
3. *Complexity* is the degree to which an innovation is perceived as difficult to understand and use. Some innovations are readily understood by most members of a social system; others are more complex, and will be adopted more slowly.
4. *Trialability* is the degree to which an innovation may be experimented with on a limited basis. New ideas that can be tried on the installment plan will generally be adopted more quickly than innovations that are not divisible for trial. Ryan and Gross (1943) found that none of their farmer-respondents adopted hybrid seed corn without first trying it on a partial basis. If the new seed could not have been sampled experimentally, its rate of adoption would have been much slower. Essentially, an innovation that is trialable reduces the risk for the individual who is evaluating it.
5. *Observability* is the degree to which the results of an innovation are visible to the receiver and to others. The easier it is for an individual to observe the results of an innovation, the more likely the individual is to adopt it.

Communication Channels

Once an innovation with certain attributes exists, communication between the source and receivers must take place if the innovation is to spread beyond its inventor. *Communication* is the process through which information is exchanged between two or more participants. The essence of the diffusion process is the human interaction through which one person communicates a new idea to one or several others. In its most elementary form, diffusion occurs when there is a new idea, an individual who has knowledge of the innovation, another individual who is not yet aware of the new idea, and a communication channel connecting the two individuals. The nature of the social relationships between the two persons determines the conditions under which the source will or will not tell the receiver about the innovation, and the effect that this telling has on the receiver.

The communication channel that carries a new idea is important in determining an individual's decision to adopt or reject it. The choice of communication channel usually lies with the source and depends on the purpose of the communication act and the audience to whom the message is directed. If the source wishes to inform the receiver about the innovation, mass media channels are the most rapid and efficient way, especially if the audience is large. *Mass media channels* are those methods of transmitting messages that enable a source of one or a few individuals to reach an audience of many. Mass media include radio, television, film, newspapers, and magazines. On the other hand, if the source's objective is to persuade the receiver to form a favorable attitude toward the innovation, an interpersonal channel is more effective. *Interpersonal channels* involve face-to-face communication exchange between two or more individuals. Previously, we noted the role of mass media and interpersonal channels in Farmer A's adoption of a computer.

Time

Time is one of the most important elements in the process of diffusion. The time dimension is involved (1) in the *innovation-decision process* through which an individual passes from first knowledge of an innovation to adoption or rejection, (2) in the *innovativeness* of an individual, the relative earliness/lateness with which an individual adopts an innovation when compared with other members of a social system, (3) and in the innovation's *rate of adoption* in a social system, measured by the number of members of the system who adopt in a given time period.

The *innovation-decision process* is the mental process through which an individual or other decision-making unit passes from first knowledge of an innovation, to forming an attitude toward the innovation, to a decision to adopt or reject, to implementation of the new idea, to confirmation of this decision. Figure 14–2 presents these five stages in the innovation-decision process, thus illustrating the importance of the time dimension.

Adoption is a decision to make full use of a new idea as the best course of action available. The innovation-decision can lead to a negative result; the final decision can be *rejection,* a decision not to adopt an innovation. Another decision may be made at a later point in time to *discontinue* or cease use of an innovation after previously adopting it. Discontinuances sometimes occur because an innovation is replaced with an improved idea.

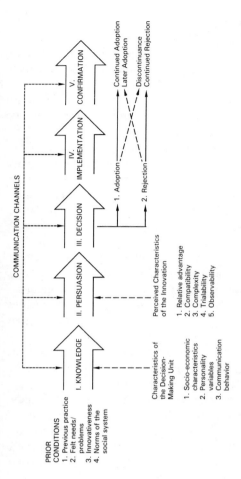

FIGURE 14-2 Stages in the Innovation-Decision Process

Source: Rogers (1983), p. 165. Used by permission.

The last stage in the innovation-decision process is *confirmation,* where the receiver seeks reinforcement for the adoption or rejection decision he/she has made. Occasionally, however, conflicting and contradictory messages about the innovation reach the individual, and this may lead to discontinuance on one hand, or later adoption (after rejection) on the other.

Innovativeness is the degree to which an individual or other decision-making unit is relatively earlier in adopting new ideas than the other members of a system. Rather than describing an individual as "less innovative than the average member of his social system," it is easier to refer to this individual as being in the "late majority" adopter category. This shorthand notation saves words and contributes to clearer understanding. Diffusion research shows that each of the adopter categories has a great deal in common. For example, most individuals in the "late majority" category are below average in social status, making little use of mass media channels, and secure most of their new ideas from peers via interpersonal channels.

Adopter categories are the classifications of members of a social system on the basis of their innovativeness. The five adopter categories are (1) innovators, (2) early adopters, (3) early majority, (4) late majority, and (5) laggards. *Innovators* are the first individuals in a system to adopt new ideas, while *laggards* are the last. Table 14–1 summarizes the characteristics of the five adopter categories.

1. *Innovators:* Venturesomeness is almost an obsession with innovators. This focus leads them out of a local circle of peers into more cosmopolite social relationships. Innovators make little use of local extension workers, preferring to go directly to agricultural scientists for information about new agricultural technologies. Innovators are research-minded and often read research bulletins. Being an innovator has two prerequisites: Control of substantial financial resources, and the ability to understand and apply complex technical knowledge. Innovators are characterized by high levels of formal education, large-sized farms, high incomes, and high social status.

But innovators are seldom asked for information and advice by their neighbors, even though they are technically expert. As one innovator said in a research interview: "Fifty percent of the farmers around here think that I'm crazy, and the other fifty percent are sure that I am." Another innovator remarked: "The way I operate my farm is *not* the way to win popularity contests among one's neighbors." Because they deviate from community norms, innovators are seldom regarded by their peers as opinion leaders.

2. *Early Adopters:* In contrast with innovators, early adopters are well integrated members of the local system. While innovators are cosmopolites, early adopters are localites. Because early adopters are sought by their neighbors for information and advice, they constitute a key audience for change agents, who seek them as local missionaries for speeding the diffusion process. The early adopters are not too far ahead of the average individual in innovativeness, so they serve as appropriate role-models whose behavior is copied by

TABLE 14-1   Characteristics of Adopter Categories

CHARAC-TERISTIC	INNOVA-TORS	EARLY ADOPTERS	EARLY MAJORITY	LATE MAJORITY	LAGGARDS
1. Time of adoption	First 2.5 percent to adopt new ideas	Next 13.5 percent to adopt	Next 34 percent to adopt	Next 34 percent to adopt	Last 16 percent to adopt
2. Attitudes and values	Scientific and venturesome	Progressive	More conservative and traditional	Skeptical of new ideas	Conservative beliefs; fear of debt
3. Education and abilities	High level of education; ability to deal with abstractions	Above average education	Slightly above average education	Slightly below average education	Low level of education; difficulty in dealing with abstractions
4. Group memberships	Leaders in country-wide or state organizations; travel widely	Leaders in local organizations	Many informal contacts within the community	Little travel out of community; little activity in formal organizations	Few memberships in formal organizations other than church; semi-isolates
5. Social status	Highest social status, but their farming practices are not respected locally	High social status; neighbors regard as "good" farmer"	About average social status	About average social status	Lowest social status
6. Farm businesses	Largest, most specialized, and most efficient	Large farms; slightly less specialized and efficient	Slightly larger than average-size farms	Slightly smaller than average-sized farms	Small farms; low incomes; seldom farm owners
7. Main sources of information about agricultural innovations	Scientists; other innovators; research bulletins	Highest contact with local change agents; farm magazines; extension bulletins	Farm magazines; friends and neighbors	Friends and neighbors	Mainly friends and neighbors; radio farm shows

others. Early adopters are the embodiment of successful and discreet use of new ideas. Early adopters know they must continue to earn the esteem of their colleagues if their influential position in the local social structure is to be maintained. The great influence of early adopters in the diffusion process stems from their ability to change the norms of the system toward the innovation.

3. *Early Majority:* This adopter category adopts new ideas just before the average members of the system. The main social value of the early majority seems to be deliberateness. "Be not the last to lay the old aside, nor the first by which the new is tried," might be the motto of the early majority. They follow with deliberate willingness in adopting innovations, but seldom lead. Until the system's norms favor the innovation, the early majority will not adopt. Their education, readership of farm magazines, participation in formal organizations, and contacts with change agents are slightly higher than for the average farmer.

4. *Late Majority:* For this adopter category, adoption is both an economic necessity and a response to increasing pressures from peers. The late majority approach innovations with skepticism and do not adopt new ideas until most others in their system have done so. They are convinced only when the weight of community opinion reflected in the system's norms definitely favors the new idea. The pressure of peers is a necessary motivating factor for innovation adoption by the late majority.

5. *Laggards:* This adopter category is the last to adopt an innovation. Its members possess almost no opinion leadership; many laggards are socially near-isolates. The point of reference for laggards is the past, and they interact primarily with others who also hold traditional values. Laggards tend to be suspicious of innovations, innovators, and change agents. Their older age and tradition-direction slows the innovation-decision process to a crawl. They have small farms, low incomes, and little formal education. While most individuals in a social system are looking down the road of change, laggards have their attention fixed on the rear-view mirror.

Most change agents find it useful to think of their audience in terms of adopter categories. They use different communication channels and different appeals in their messages about innovations when they are dealing with early adopters than when they seek to reach laggards. The measure of innovativeness and the classification of a system's members into adopter categories are based on the relative time at which an innovation is adopted.

The rate of adoption is a third way in which the time dimension is involved in the diffusion of innovations. *Rate of adoption* is the relative speed with which an innovation is adopted by members of a social system. It is usually measured by the length of time required for a certain percentage of the members of a system to adopt an innovation. Figure 14–1 shows that innovation I has a more rapid rate of adoption than does innovation III. *If individuals perceive an innovation as possessing greater relative advantage, compatibility, and so on, the innovation will have a more rapid rate of adoption.*

Society

It is important to remember that diffusion occurs within a society because the social structure of the society affects the innovation's diffusion patterns in several ways, such as by providing boundaries within which innovations diffuse. Here we explain how societal norms affect diffusion, and the roles of opinion leaders and change agents.

Until 1960, most diffusion studies were conducted in the United States. Thereafter, diffusion investigations were carried out in many Third World nations. The diffusion model fit well with the development programs in agriculture, health, nutrition, and family planning then being carried out in Latin America, Africa, and Asia. In these settings, the norms of a peasant community often were a barrier to change. For instance, resistance to new ideas may be found in a system's norms relating to food. In India, sacred cows roam the countryside while millions of people are undernourished. Pork cannot be consumed in Moslem countries. Polished rice is eaten in most nations, even though whole rice is more nutritious. So norms can act as barriers to the introduction of certain new foods. Of course, norms can also give a push to the adoption of innovations. As we noted in our previous discussion of adopter categories, most individuals will not adopt an innovation until the norms of their system are favorable to the new idea. The counter-norm adoption behavior of innovators earns them the disdain of others in their society.

Opinion leadership is the ability to informally influence individuals' attitudes or behavior in a desired way with relative frequency. It is a type of informal leadership rather than a function of the individual's formal position or status in the system. Opinion leadership is earned and maintained by technical competence, social accessibility, and conformity to a system's norms. Due to their close conformity to the system's norms, opinion leaders serve as models for the innovation behavior of their followers. In general, when opinion leaders are compared with their followers, we find that they (1) are more exposed to communication about new ideas, (2) are more socially accessible to their followers, (3) are more cosmopolite, (4) have higher social status, and (5) are more innovative, but not too much so.

Lack of information about an innovation is seldom an important factor retarding an individual from adopting a new idea. Often the problem is finding trustworthy information. Most individuals evaluate technological innovations through the personal experiences of adopters who are much like themselves. If the near-peer (someone almost like the individual) with whom an individual discusses an innovation is a satisfied adopter, this interpersonal network influence is a force for adoption; if the near-peer is a dissatisfied adopter, rejector, or discontinuer, an individual is influenced toward rejection. Following the example of innovation behavior of others seems to be a fundamental process underlying the diffusion of innovations.

Opinion leaders are members of the social system in which they exert their influence. In some instances, individuals with influence in the social system are professionals who represent change agencies external to the society. A *change agent* is a professional who influences innovation-decisions in a direction deemed desirable by a change agency. He or she usually seeks to obtain the adoption of new ideas but may also attempt to slow down diffusion and prevent the adoption of undesirable innovations.

Change agents often use opinion leaders within a given society to prime the pump of the diffusion process. Opinion leaders can be "worn out" by change agents who overuse them. This problem may occur when the opinion leaders are perceived by their peers as becoming too much like the change agents. The opinion leaders' close identification with the change agents makes them lose credibility with their former followers. This wearing out may happen because, through intensive contact with change agents, the opinion leaders become too innovative and are then regarded as deviants from the society's norms (Figure 14–3).

When the S-shaped diffusion curve starts to climb (at 10 to 20 percent adoption), further change agent activity in promoting an innovation has little effect on the rate of adoption. The relationship of change agent effort to

FIGURE 14-3   An Early Extension Agent Conducts a Demonstration on the Farm of an Opinion Leader.

The extension worker is a *change agent,* a professional who influences innovation-decisions in a direction deemed desirable by a change agency. One strategy of change, suggested by rural sociological research on the diffusion of innovations, is for a change agent to conduct a demonstration of an innovation on the farm of an opinion leader. The demonstration, shown in the photo below was conducted in the early days of the agricultural extension services in the United States.

Source: University of Illinois, College of Agriculture, Office of Agricultural Communication. Used by permission.

success is not linear, probably because of the influence potential of individuals who adopt at different times. Innovators, who adopt very early, are seldom active in diffusing the innovation via interpersonal channels to their local peers. Early adopters, who adopt next, possess a high degree of opinion leadership in most societies. These individuals influence their peers to adopt the innovation. This influence causes the diffusion curve to shoot upward in a self-generating fashion. Then the change agent can begin to retire from the scene. Thereafter, the diffusion curve continues to climb, independent of change agents' efforts, under further impetus from opinion leaders.

To be effective, a change agent must gain rapport with his clients to learn of his clients' needs and to introduce new ideas to them. However, because he is so different from his clientele in education, technical competence, and style of life, a change agent often has difficulty in gaining rapport and in achieving effective communication with his clients.

Most human communication occurs between a source and a receiver who are similar, or homophilous. *Homophily* is the degree to which pairs of individuals who interact are similar in beliefs, values, social status, and so on. The opposite of homophily is *heterophily,* the degree to which pairs of individuals who interact are different in such attributes. When a source can interact with any one of a number of receivers, there is a tendency to select a receiver most like oneself.

Communication is most effective when source and receiver are homophilous. When they share common meanings and are alike in personal and social characteristics, the communication of ideas is likely to have greater effects in knowledge gain, attitude formation, and behavior change. Heterophily leads to ineffective communication, an uncomfortable state for the source, so individuals tend to avoid heterophilous situations when they can.

One of the most difficult problems in the diffusion of innovations is that the source is usually quite heterophilous to the receiver, at least in respect to competence with the innovation. The extension worker, for instance, is much more technically competent than his farmer-clients. This heterophily frequently leads to ineffective communication. The two individuals simply do not talk the same language. The very nature of diffusion demands that at least some degree of heterophily be present between source and receiver.

Change agents interact most frequently with clients who are most like themselves, at least in social status and technical competence, even though these clients may need the change agent's help less than lower-status or less-educated clients. So change agents tend to assist those clients who need their help the least.

DIFFUSION STRATEGIES

Here we describe five strategies, each based on the results of research on the diffusion of innovations.

1. Understand Society's Norms

One strategy of change is for the professional to understand the norms of the client society. *Unless a change agent adjusts the program of innovations to the way of life of clients, diffusion activities are unlikely to be successful.* U.S. farmers place a high value on maximizing farm production, and thus usually are resistant to soil conservation innovations, which they perceive as lowering their crop yields per acre (at least in the short-range). Unless a change agent understands this emphasis on production and introduces soil conservation innovations that do not interfere with high yields, the rate of adoption will be very low.

2. Respond to Clients' Needs

A change agent will be more successful if innovations are introduced that match clients' needs. A diffusion program should be constantly reevaluated as it progresses, so as to ensure that it continues to meet clients' needs. Feedback information from clients is needed to determine the effectiveness of a program, and how it should be changed to more closely match needs.

3. Stress Compatibility with Clients' Past Experiences

Change agents should design diffusion programs so that the innovations are compatible with their clients' past experiences with innovations. A change agent often enters a system unaware of previous events and activities. The new change agent should investigate the outcomes of past diffusion campaigns, to determine how they might affect future diffusion efforts. For example, powdered milk was distributed for the first time in a Latin American village the same week that a smallpox epidemic broke out. Later efforts by change agents to secure the adoption of powdered milk were unsuccessful.

4. Use Opinion Leaders

As already stressed, *it is important for change agents to work through opinion leaders in a society.* When the "right" person is the first to adopt a new idea, its diffusion will be speeded. Often, however, the first individuals in a society to seek assistance from a change agent are innovators, who seldom are opinion leaders.

5. Anticipate Consequences

Change agents should try to predict the social consequences for their client system of the innovations that they introduce. Sometimes when an innovation is introduced and adopted in a society, the resulting changes may be largely unanticipated. For instance, certain of the agricultural chemicals recommended to American farmers in the past 30 years were later found to be cancer causing, and now are unavailable.

CONSEQUENCES OF INNOVATION DIFFUSION

Consequences are the changes that occur to an individual or to a society as a result of the adoption or rejection of an innovation. Although of obvious importance, the consequences of innovations have not received much attention by change agents or by diffusion researchers. Consequences have not been studied adequately because (1) change agencies have overemphasized adoption per se, assuming that the consequences will be positive; (2) the usual survey research methods may be inappropriate for investigating consequences; and (3) consequences are often difficult to measure.

Consequences are classified as (1) desirable versus undesirable, (2) direct versus indirect, and (3) anticipated versus unanticipated. *Desirable consequences* are the functional effects of an innovation to an individual or to a society. *Undesirable consequences* are the dysfunctional effects of an innovation to an individual or to a society (Chapter 1).

Direct consequences are the changes to an individual or a society that occur in immediate response to an innovation. *Indirect consequences* are the changes to an individual or a society that occur as a result of the direct consequences of an innovation.

Anticipated consequences are changes due to an innovation that are recognized and intended by the members of a society. *Unanticipated consequences* are changes due to an innovation that are neither intended nor recognized by the members of a society.

The undesirable, indirect, and unanticipated consequences of innovations usually go together, as do the desirable, direct, and anticipated consequences. We see an illustration of this generalization in the introduction of the mechanized tomato harvester.

BOX 14-2   *HARD TOMATOES IN CALIFORNIA*

The nature of an innovation's diffusion and its consequences are often determined in part by R&D that created the innovation. We see an illustration of how diffusion is predetermined by decisions and events that occurred prior to the first diffusion, in the case of the mechanized tomato harvester in California.

California is the number-one agricultural state in America, and tomatoes are one of California's most important farm products. Most U.S. tomato production is concentrated in California. Prior to the introduction of the mechanized harvester in 1962, about 4,000 farmers produced tomatoes in California; nine years later, only 600 of these growers were still in business. One effect of the new machine was to reduce the number of tomato farmers to about one-sixth of what it had been. In 1962, about 50,000 farmworkers, most of them immigrant Mexican men, were employed as tomato pickers in California. They were replaced by 1,152 machines (each costing about 65,000 dollars), plus about 18,000 workers who rode the harvesters to sort out the damaged and immature tomatoes. About 80 percent of these sorters were women; only a few were Mexican-Americans.

There were many other consequences of the mechanized harvesters. Tomato growing moved out of California's San Joaquin County into Yolo and Fresno counties, where the soil and weather conditions were more ideally suited to mechanized farming. And the tomatoes changed, too. To enable machine picking, agricultural scientists bred hard tomatoes that would not bruise so easily. Unfortunately, American consumers prefer soft tomatoes (of course how hard a tomato is does not matter much when the tomatoes are made into paste or catsup). But the housewives who purchased tomatoes gained one important advantage: The mechanized tomatoes were cheaper in price than they would otherwise have been.

So the development of the mechanized tomato picker had many far-reaching consequences. Were these effects anticipated by the R&D workers who developed the mechanized pickers at the University of California at Davis? Not at all, say rural sociological analysts of this case, such as Friedland and Barton (1975, p. 28), who conclude that these agricultural scientists were "social sleepwalkers." The creators of the mechanical harvesters were motivated to save the tomato industry for California when it was threatened by the termination of the Mexican *bracero* program in 1964 (which meant the end of cheap labor). The fact that agricultural scientists showed little concern for how the social consequences of this new technology would adversely affect human lives, led James Hightower (1973) to title his book about this technological change, *Hard Tomatoes, Hard Times.*

Almost all of the research to develop tomato harvester technology was conducted by agricultural professors at the University of California at Davis, using over one million dollars of public funds (Schmitz and Seckler, 1970). The chief researcher was G. C. "Jack" Hanna, a specialist in vegetable crops. He took the lead in breeding a hard-tomato variety that could be machine harvested, despite the vigorous opposition of his colleagues and administrators who believed that his idea of mechanized picking was ridiculous. In fact, at the time, they feared that his bizarre project would damage the reputation of their department and of the University of California. But Hanna was so certain that his approach was correct that in 1947 he went on leave for six weeks to visit New York in his search for hard-tomato varieties. He returned with some seeds of the "Red Top" variety, a tomato that was almost as hard as a green apple when it was ripe. Hanna began to adapt this New York tomato to California conditions.

Finally, Hanna teamed with an agricultural engineer at Davis named Coby Lorenzen in a systems approach to mechanizing tomato harvesting. Lorenzen worked to design a machine that would cut off the tomato plant at soil level, pluck the fruits from the vine, and elevate them past a crew of female tomato-sorters into a gondola truck for transportation to market. In 1971, Hanna developed a tomato variety, VF-145, that was ideal for machine picking. It was firm enough for machine harvesting, the fruits were easily detachable from the vine, and most of the tomatoes ripened at about the same time.

The other key element in the new technology cluster was the harvester, designed by Lorenzen, and produced by Hanna's friend, Ernest Blackwelder, a farm machinery manufacturer who contracted with the University of California. Twenty-five machines were produced the first year. They had many technical problems: Eighteen broke down immediately and, of the seven remaining machines, only one completed the harvest season successfully. But the mechanical harvesters cut labor in half. In 1962, the 25 machines were improved, and harvested 1 percent of the total crop. By 1963, there were 66 machines in use, and they picked about 3 percent of all the tomatoes.

The big boost occurred in 1964, when 224 tomato-picking machines brought in 25 percent of all tomatoes grown. This sudden increase in adoption occurred because the U.S. Congress ended the *bracero* program through which Mexican workers were brought to California. Professors Hanna and Lorenzen had foreseen this possibility, and that is one reason why they had rushed to develop the mechanized harvester. The tomato industry honored Hanna as the individual who "saved the tomato for California." Six years later 1,521 of the machines harvested 99.9 percent of the tomato crop. And 32,000 former hand-pickers were out of work.

In retrospect, one might wonder how differently the diffusion and adoption of this innovation might have been had the R&D workers designed a smaller machine, one that more of the 4,000 tomato farmers (as of 1962) could have adopted. What if the impending threat of a severe labor shortage in 1964 had not forced Hanna, Lorenzen, and Blackwelder to rush their prototype machine into production? What if the University of California at Davis had conducted social and economic research on the impacts of farm mechanization prior to 1962, so that the destructive consequences of the new technology on employment and on tomato consumers might have been anticipated and mitigated?

Answers to such questions suddenly became very important in 1979, when California Rural Legal Assistance, an advocacy group representing farm workers, filed a lawsuit against the University of California. The suit charged this land-grant school with (1) spending public tax dollars to benefit private interests and (2) driving small farmers out of business and displacing thousands of farm workers, while benefiting agribusiness firms. The legal group sought to require the University of California to weigh such social consequences of mechanization research as loss of jobs before such research is begun. Several rural sociologists were asked to testify as expert witnesses. The legal suit illustrates the public concern about the consequences of technological innovations.

So we see that, unfortunately, *it is difficult to predict the social impacts of technology.*

Source: Based on Rogers (1983), pp. 150–153. Used by permission.

BOX 14-3   *THE GAP-WIDENING CONSEQUENCES OF COFFEE INNOVATIONS IN COLOMBIA*

The consequences of the adoption of innovations usually tend to widen the socioeconomic gap (1) between the earlier and later adopting categories in a society and (2) between the audience segments previously high and low in socioeconomic status. Two rural sociologists, A. Eugene Havens and William Flinn (1974), examined the consequences of two new coffee varieties among Colombian farmers over the eight-year period from 1963 to 1970. Of their original sample of 56 coffee growers, 17 adopted the new varieties, which considerably increased their yields.

Chemical fertilizers and herbicides were adopted along with the new coffee varieties in order to achieve the high yields. The 17 adopters raised their net income from 6,700 pesos in 1963 to 21,000 pesos in 1970, an increase of 213 percent. The 39 coffee farmers who did not use the new varieties raised their net income from 4,500 pesos to 12,000 pesos, an increase of only 166 percent. So one effect of the coffee variety innovations was to widen the income gap between the adopters and nonadopters from 2,200 pesos in 1963 to 9,000 pesos in 1970. The improved coffees caused much greater income inequality among the Colombian farmers.

How much of this increased inequality among the Colombian coffee growers was due to the adoption of the new coffee varieties, and how much of it was due to other factors, such as the initially larger farms, higher education, and other characteristics of the adopters? Most of the increased income inequality was due to the introduction of the new coffees. For example, Havens and Flinn (1974) computed the net income per acre of coffee grown, thus removing the effect of the larger-sized farms of the adopters. The adopters and nonadopters both began at about the same level of income per acre in 1963: 290 pesos per acre and 220 pesos per acre, respectively. But by 1970, when the adopters were getting the higher yields from growing the new varieties, their income per acre shot up to 1,640 pesos per acre (an increase of 1,352 pesos), while the nonadopters' income per acre rose to only 632 pesos (an increase of only 413 pesos). So the increased income inequality between the adopters and nonadopters was due mainly to the introduction of the new coffee (Figure 14-4).

What did the adopters do with their higher income? Some bought larger farms, with some of the land coming from the nonadopters. In 1963, the adopters averaged farms of 18.9 acres and the nonadopters 8.0 acres; by 1970, the adopters had increased their farms to 33 acres, while the nonadopters' farms shrank to an average size of 6.4 acres. In addition, 11 of the nonadopters dropped out of farming and either became farm laborers or else migrated to the city. Their farms were purchased by the adopters.

If adoption of the new coffee varieties were to have such important consequences, why didn't the 39 nonadopters also start growing the new varieties? Adopting a new coffee variety is a major decision in Colombia because three years are required for the new trees to come into production; many farmers need credit to tide them over this period before their investment in the new variety begins to pay off. Smaller farmers who did not have much land to put up as collateral, were unable to borrow funds to enable them to adopt the new coffee varieties, so they lost the potential advantage of the higher yields and farm incomes that they could have achieved by adopting the new coffee varieties. In this case the system was to blame; one can hardly blame the individual farmers for not adopting the new coffee varieties.

This vicious circle explains, in large part, how adoption of the coffee variety innovations widened the socioeconomic gaps (1) between the adopters and nonadopters and (2) between those individuals originally high and low in socioeconomic status. The effect of the innovation was like a huge lever, prying wider the gap between the rich and the poor.

Source: This case draws on Rogers (1983), pp. 398–400. Used by permission.

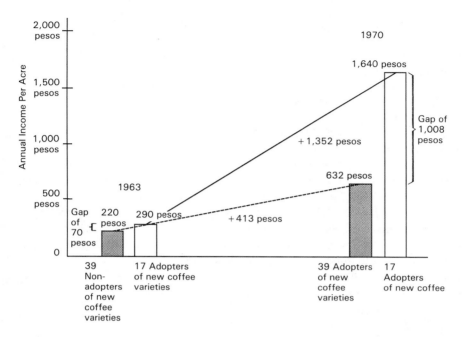

FIGURE 14-4   Gap-Widening Consequences among Colombian Farmers Adopting and Not Adopting Coffee Innovations

Smaller farmers were unlikely to adopt the new coffee varieties because they were not eligible for agricultural credit. The nonadopters' annual income per acre rose 413 pesos from 1963 to 1970, while the adopters' income per acre increased by 1,352 pesos, thus widening the socioeconomic gap.

Source: From Havens and Flinn (1974) and Rogers (1983), pp. 398–399.

Equality and Inequality of Consequences

The equality versus inequality consequences of innovations depend on *how* an innovation is introduced, whether it is high-cost or not, and so forth. An illustration comes from an investigation of the impact of adopting irrigation wells by villagers in Bangladesh and Pakistan (Gotsch, 1972). In each country, an irrigation well cost about the same amount and was able to provide water for 50 to 80 acres of farmland. The introduction of new wheat and rice varieties created a need for irrigation in both nations. But the equality of the consequences of an identical innovation were quite different in Pakistan from those in Bangladesh, mainly because of the different social organization that accompanied the new technology.

In Pakistan, the irrigation wells were purchased mainly by large farmers, so the wells made the rich richer. And the poor farmers became *relatively* poorer.

But in Bangladesh, less than 1 percent of villagers had farms large

enough to justify private ownership of an irrigation well. So village cooperatives purchased the wells, and provided irrigation water to everyone who
belonged to the co-op. Farm incomes were approximately doubled because
farmers could raise a winter crop of rice during the season when rainfall was
scarce. In Bangladesh, the consequences of the innovation were distributed
much more equally than in Pakistan.

Both the study of irrigation wells in Bangladesh and Pakistan and the
investigation of the coffee innovations in Colombia show that social structure
partly determines the equality versus inequality of an innovation's consequences. *When a society's structure is already very inequal, it is likely that an
innovation (especially if it is a relatively high-cost innovation), will lead to even
greater inequality in the form of a wider socioeconomic gap.*

*Social structure variables are not a complete barrier to greater equality in
the consequences of innovations.* Change agents can often modify the social
structure in certain ways, as the Bangladesh-Pakistan study of irrigation wells
suggests. Gap-widening inequality will usually result from technological innovations unless a change agency devotes special efforts to prevent it. In the
Bangladesh illustration, the change agency organized cooperatives so that the
introduction of irrigation wells did not widen the socioeconomic gap.

What other strategies for gap narrowing can be used by change agencies?

1. Messages that are redundant or that are of less interest and/or benefit to the higher socioeconomic audience, but that are appropriate and of interest to the lower
   socioeconomic audience, should be provided. This strategy enables the lower socioeconomic audience to catch up.
2. One should tailor communication messages especially for the lower socioeconomic audience in terms of their particular characteristics, such as education,
   beliefs, communication habits, and the like.
3. Change agents should concentrate their efforts in diffusing innovations, especially to their lower status clients.

THE PRO-INNOVATION BIAS AND INDIVIDUAL BLAME

The *pro-innovation bias* is the assumption underlying most diffusion research
that an innovation should be diffused and adopted by all members of a society, that it should be diffused more rapidly, and that the innovation should be
neither re-invented (that is, modified by the adopter) nor rejected. The pro-
innovation bias leads diffusion researchers to ignore the study of ignorance
about innovations, to underemphasize the rejection or discontinuance of innovations, to overlook re-invention, and to fail to study antidiffusion programs
designed to prevent the diffusion of "bad" innovations (like drugs or cigarettes or aircraft skyjacking, for example). The net result of the pro-
innovation bias in diffusion research is that we have failed to learn about
certain very important aspects of diffusion.

There has also been a source bias in most past diffusion research, that is, a tendency for diffusion research to side with the agencies that promote innovations rather than with the audience of potential adopters. This source bias is perhaps even suggested by the words that we can use to describe this field of research: *Diffusion research* might have been called something like *problem solving, innovation seeking,* or the *evaluation of innovations* had the audience originally been a stronger influence on the design of this research.

As a result of who sponsors diffusion research, along with other pro-source factors, one can detect a certain degree of individual blame, rather than blaming the system, in much diffusion research. *Individual blame* is the tendency to hold an individual responsible for his or her problems, rather than the system of which the individual is a part. In other words, an individual-blame orientation implies that "if the shoe doesn't fit, there's something wrong with your foot." An opposite point of view would blame the system, not the individual; it might imply that the shoe manufacturer or the marketing system could be at fault for a shoe that does not fit.

When coupled with the pro-innovation bias, the individual-blame view-point assumes that an individual is at fault for not adopting an innovation. Perhaps on closer analysis it would become apparent that the system is at fault for not providing an innovation more appropriate to the individual's needs, and so the individual may be quite justified in rejecting the new idea. Or perhaps the innovation is appropriate, but it is simply not available to the potential adopter; an example would be the Indian farmer who does not adopt a new rice variety because the seed is not available in his village store.

An individual-blame orientation is not, in and of itself, always inappropriate. Perhaps individual-level variables *are* the most appropriate explanations of why an innovation is adopted or rejected. But we should keep a more open mind toward system-blame explanations of diffusion behavior than we have in the past.

SUMMARY

Diffusion is the process by which (1) an *innovation,* (2) is *communicated* through certain *channels* (3) over *time* (4) among the members of a *society.* An *innovation* is an idea, practice, or object perceived as new by an individual or other adopting unit. The characteristics of an innovation, as perceived by the members of a social system, determine its rate of adoption. Five attributes of an innovation are (1) relative advantage, (2) compatibility, (3) complexity, (4) trialability, and (5) observability.

Communication channels are the means by which a message gets from a source to a receiver. Mass media channels are more effective in creating knowledge of innovations, while interpersonal channels are more effective in forming and changing attitudes toward a new idea.

Time is involved in diffusion in the innovation-decision process, innovativeness, and an innovation's rate of adoption. The *innovation-decision process* is the mental process through which an individual or other decision-making unit passes from first knowledge of an innovation, to forming an attitude toward the innovation, to a decision to adopt or reject, to implementation of the idea, and to confirmation of this decision. *Adoption* is a decision to make full use of a new idea as the best course of action. *Rejection* is a decision not to adopt an innovation. *Discontinuance* is a decision to cease use of an innovation after previously adopting it.

Innovativeness is the degree to which an individual or other adopting unit is relatively earlier in adopting new ideas than other members of his or her society. There are five *adopter categories,* classifications of the members of a social system on the basis of innovativeness: (1) innovators, (2) early adopters, (3) early majority, (4) later majority, and (5) laggards. *Rate of adoption* is the relative speed with which an innovation is adopted by members of a society.

A *society* is a set of interrelated units that are engaged in joint problem solving to accomplish a common goal. It is important to remember that diffusion occurs within a social system because the society's norms have an important influence on the spread of new ideas.

Opinion leadership is the ability to informally influence other individuals' attitudes or behavior in a desired way with relative frequency. A *change agent* is a professional person who attempts to influence innovation decisions in a direction that his or her organization feels is desirable.

Consequences are the changes that occur to an individual or to a society as a result of the adoption or rejection of an innovation.

REFERENCES

ANDERSON, G. LESTER, ed. (1976). *Land-Grant Universities and Their Continuing Challenge.* East Lansing: Michigan State University Press.

FRIEDLAND, WILLIAM H., and AMY BARTON. (1975). *Destalking the Wily Tomato: A Case Study of Social Consequences in California Agricultural Research.* Santa Cruz: University of California at Santa Cruz, Research Monograph 5.

GOTSCH, CARL H. (1972). "Technical Change and the Distribution of Income in Rural Areas." *American Journal of Agricultural Economics,* 54; 326–341.

HAVENS, A. EUGENE, and WILLIAM L. FLINN. (1974). "Green Revolution Technology and Community Development: The Limits of Action Programs." *Economic Development and Cultural Change,* 23, 469–481.

HIGHTOWER, JAMES. (1973). *Hard Tomatoes, Hard Times: The Failure of America's Land-Grant College Complex.* Cambridge, MA: Schenkman.

PAARLBERG, DON. (1981). "The Land-Grant Colleges and the Structure Issue." *American Journal of Agricultural Economics,* 129–134.

ROGERS, EVERETT M. (1983). *Diffusion of Innovations.* New York: Free Press.

RYAN, BRYCE, and NEAL C. GROSS. (1943). "The Diffusion of Hybrid Seed Corn in Two Iowa Communities." *Rural Sociology,* 8, 15–24.

SCHMITZ, ANDREW, and DAVID SECKLER. (1970). "Mechanized Agriculture and Social Welfare: The Case of the Tomato Harvester." *American Journal of Agricultural Economics,* 52, 569–577.

Chapter 15

Rural Poverty, Rural Development, and Government Agencies

The farmer has not received the attention that the city worker has received and has not been able to express himself as the city worker has done. The problems of farm life have received very little consideration and the result has been bad for those who dwell in the open country, and therefore bad for the whole nation.

—President Theodore
Roosevelt

Although this statement by President Roosevelt was made in 1910 in the introduction to the report of the Country Life Commission, the sentiment expressed is markedly similar to statements made today by advocates of farming and rural life. It recognizes that rural America has not benefited to the same degree as urban areas from the economic prosperity characteristic of life in the United States. During this century, the federal government has tried, with assistance from state and local governments, to solve the social problems of rural areas. Efforts to improve certain physical necessities of rural areas, such as electricity, roads, and water and sewer systems, have been very successful. But other problems, such as unemployment, inadequate housing, poor health care, and persistent poverty have seen little progress despite the amount of time, money, and effort spent.

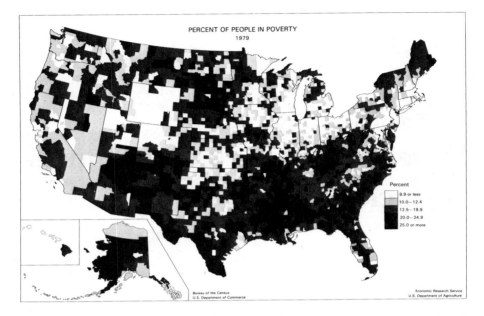

FIGURE 15-1   Poverty is higher in rural than in urban areas. About 18 percent of rural Americans live in poverty compared to 14 percent of urban Americans. Rural poverty is particularly severe in the Appalachian and Ozark mountains and parts of the South, but there are also other pockets of rural poverty.

This chapter is about disadvantaged rural Americans—the people in poverty—about *rural development,* the organized efforts to improve the quality of life in rural areas, and about the U.S. Department of Agriculture agencies that assist rural people. The main categories of the rural poor include migratory laborers, Chicanos, Southern black sharecroppers and subsistence farmers, native Americans living on reservations, and poor whites of the Appalachian and Ozark mountains. There are other poor, disadvantaged rural people living in every county of the United States who are not in any of these categories.

How rural people become poor is a complex process. Causal factors include the agricultural economy, the mechanization and specialization of American agriculture, rapid technological developments, and the failure of rural institutions to adjust to change.

THE NATURE OF RURAL POVERTY

Rural poverty affects over 13 million people in the United States and is so widespread and so acute that it is rightly called a national disgrace. Most of today's urban poor are yesterday's rural poor who moved to the city (Dorner,

1983). Many urban slum dwellers today have rural backgrounds. So there is a relationship between rural and urban poverty in First World countries like the United States.

The rural poor live everywhere, but certain regions of the United States stand out, particularly the Appalachian and Ozark mountains and parts of the South. Chicano workers in the Southwest and American Indians in New Mexico and Arizona are pockets of rural poverty, and concentrations of the poor can also be found in the upper Great Plains, the coastal areas of the Pacific Northwest, parts of northern New England, and the areas of the upper Great Lakes where the timber has been removed (Figure 15-1).

BOX 15-1   *RURAL POVERTY IN APPALACHIA*

One of the areas of persistent poverty in the United States is the Appalachian mountain region stretching from New York in the north to Alabama in the south. A recent study of poverty in a community in upper Appalachia described the life situation of Mary and Bill Crane, who are rural poor in Chestnut Valley.

Mary and Bill Crane live in an old house—it was already old and in poor condition when Bill lived there as a child. Those were hard times; his father was not often home, and eventually he just drifted away. His mother did all she could to keep food on the table and a roof over their heads. Bill remembers eating mostly potatoes, which they grew out back on the hill. Years later, after his mother died, Bill came back to live in the family house, bringing his wife and two small children with him.

Mary, just 35, grew up over on the east side of the hill. Her mother still lives there in the old farmhouse. Mary's parents were originally tenant farmers, but the landowner sold his property to the state during the Depression. Mary's father managed to buy the house and a little plot of land around it. That took place during the last year he was sober and healthy, 30 years ago. Since then, Mama has worked the night shift as a hospital janitor to keep the family going. Mama's "new husband," Shorty, used to work in construction off and on, but now he's on a disability pension.

Life is not easy. There has never been enough money to keep up with each day's needs—let alone to pay off the back bills. It never seems possible to get ahead. So many things have to be put off "until we have enough money"—like fixing up the house. It always seems as if there isn't any place in the house to sit down, as if every bit of space is taken up by furniture, clothing, toys, junk, and kids. After all these years, there is still no running water in the bathroom. Mary wonders if there will ever be a time when they will have enough money to be able to fix up the house the way they'd like.

Recently, Mary has been thinking that it would ease the money problems if she went back to work. But so far, there hasn't even been enough free time for her to go look for a job, let alone actually go to work. It seems to Mary that it is all she can do just to cope with each day's living and family care. There is always something extra coming up that has to be taken care of. The house is almost always a mess; she is usually days behind in the laundry. Lord knows, she's sure no one could say she's a lazy person. Once she thought about taking on a night job at the hospital where one of her friends worked, or working a night shift in a factory, but Bill told her in no uncertain terms that she wasn't going to be taking any night jobs. As for daytime jobs, that would mean arranging for someone to watch the children after school. And what would she do about all the times a child stayed home from school? So for this year at least, Mary has decided to give up the idea of getting a job. Maybe next year.

What could a government rural development program do to help Mary Crane and her family escape poverty?

Source: From Janet M. Fitchen, *Poverty in Rural America: A Case Study* (Boulder, CO: Westview, 1982).

Characteristics of Rural Poverty

Many rural poor are members of minority and ethnic groups such as Southern blacks, Chicanos, and American Indians, but these categories represent only a fraction of the poor in the United States, most of whom are white.

There are about 34 million poor people in the United States. Included are 13 million rural poor who represent 18 percent of the total rural population. About 21 million or 14 percent of the urban population are classified as living in poverty. So rural people in the United States are more likely to be poor then are urban people.

Income is the major criterion used to determine who is poor. For 1984, the U.S. government poverty guideline was annual income of less than 11,000 dollars for a family of four. However, for many rural persons 11,000 dollars would be a substantial family income.

Being poor in America means being poorly educated. About 60 percent of all rural adults complete a high school education. But in the 100 U.S. counties with the highest incidence of poverty (see Figure 15-1), only 41 percent of the adults have completed a high school education (Morrissey, 1985). Children coming from families with low levels of education receive little education. Chapter 9 showed that children from lower-class families, which place a low value on education, are likely to drop out of school at the earliest possible age. So low education and poverty operate in a continuing and vicious circle.

The rural poor are likely to be unemployed or underemployed. In the 100 U.S. counties with the highest incidence of poverty, only 31 percent of all persons 16 years old or older were employed, compared to 40 percent for all rural persons of that age. In these poverty counties, a higher proportion of incomes comes from *transfer payments,* that is, government assistance programs such as social security, aid to families with dependent children, and from food stamps. About 20 percent of the income in the 100 high poverty counties comes from these government payments, versus only 15 percent for all rural counties in the United States.

Employment opportunities in many rural areas have both changed and diminished. Many low-skill labor-intensive industries that initially moved from urban to rural areas of the United States in search of cheap labor, have moved again in search of even cheaper labor, this time out of the United States. So industry is scarce in rural areas, particularly in the more isolated places where the poor are concentrated. Although some industrial growth continues in rural areas, it tends to be in high-technology and other industries that require high-level skills or education. Poor persons are especially handicapped for these jobs because they lack the basic skills necessary for employment.

Major changes have occurred in farming as an occupation. It no longer can be learned by a simple father-son apprenticeship. Farming is a highly competitive business which requires the latest skills and managerial know-how, plus substantial capital.

The rural poor are in poor health. They do not have proper diets, they may not have been raised on an adequate nutritional base, and professional medical care is not readily available. The birth rates of the poor are high, as poor families tend to be large. So family earnings must be spread among many dependents, both young and old.

People in poverty are likely to live in communities with high out-migration. Except for retirement communities in the Sun Belt, the migration turnaround of the 1970s has largely ceased (Beale and Fuguitt, 1986). Even during the peak of the 1970s' "rural renaissance," many rural areas did not benefit.

The high migration from rural areas leaves behind many acute problems. The out-migrants tend to be the young, the better-educated, and those with the most marketable occupational skills. Those individuals left behind in rural areas are the least prepared to solve the problems of dying rural communities. One rural sociologist described colorfully this selective out-migration when he said that rural communities were like "pools of fished-out suckers and bullheads."

DISADVANTAGED RURAL AMERICANS: RURAL MINORITY GROUPS

Minority groups are groups that have certain distinct and recognizable social or physical characteristics different from those of the general population. Minority groups are generally perceived as inferior by the majority population. What makes up the "majority"? In the United States, the majority is made up of the 85 percent of the population that has been sufficiently assimilated into the society so that it is not readily identifiable as a separate grouping, and is classified as "white." Rural minority groups are those minority groups that live in rural areas. Black Americans are the largest minority group in the United States; others are Chicanos and American Indians. We shall discuss each of these rural minority groups, as well as migrant farm workers.

Migrant Farm Workers

A migrant worker is a farm laborer who follows the harvest, moving during the year to jobs in scattered locations. Migration follows a seasonal course, often through several states, with the migrant usually returning home when the farm work season is over.

Migrant workers constitute about 5 percent of hired agricultural labor. John Steinbeck's *The Grapes of Wrath* drew nationwide attention to the plight of migratory laborers who left their bank-foreclosed farms in Oklahoma because of crop pests, drought, and mechanized cotton farming to become migrant laborers in California.

Because migratory families are continually on the move, family members often are not eligible for benefits that accrue to permanent residents. Children often work in the fields and are seldom able to attend school. Because the migratory families change residence so often, workers are seldom protected by such legislation as the Fair Labor Standards Act, minimum wage laws, and social security, and they are not eligible for unemployment insurance. The undesirable aspects of migratory labor are seasonality of work, relatively low wages, necessity of moving frequently and for long distances, social disorganization and exploitation inherent in the migratory pattern, and the inaccessibility of minimal public facilities for education, health, recreation, and welfare.

One study of migratory workers by a rural sociologist in Wisconsin disclosed that few are wanderer or hobo types (Slesinger, 1985). Typically, the migratory workers were temporary settlers or work-seekers traveling with family or friends. Low educational levels were found among these agricultural migrants. Thirty percent had completed fewer than five years of school and more than 70 percent had completed eight years or less.

Migrant agricultural workers are probably among the most underprivileged of the rural poor. Unfortunately, their particular social problems will probably become worse. Machines are rapidly taking over many phases of agricultural production and harvesting. Mechanized equipment is now available for picking apples, peaches, and tomatoes, and for digging carrots and other below-ground crops. In a few years, large-scale farming will be freed from most hand labor, and will depend upon a few skilled operators and technicians, rather than migratory workers.

Attempts have been made to organize migrant agricultural workers. The most determined efforts have been in California under the leadership of Cesar Chavez and the United Farm Workers Organizing Committee.

FIGURE 15-2 **Migratory Laborers Are an Important Rural Social Problem in the United States.**

This young boy works as part of a gang of migratory laborers. They make up about one-fourth of the farm labor force, are exploited by the owners of large farms who employ them, and are often Chicanos, or members of other minority groups. Because they change residence so often, migratory workers or their families are seldom eligible for welfare, educational help, or other community services.

In 1968 a drive was launched to limit consumer purchase of California table grapes, which were harvested despite the strike of organized grape-pickers. Buttons, bumper stickers, and leaflets were widely distributed throughout the United States. The campaign met with some success in Eastern states, where the price of grapes dropped and many supermarket chains would not stock them. The excess grapes were shipped to the South and Midwest, where consumers were less sympathetic about the plight of migratory workers. In most areas, however, organized campaigns succeeded in stopping the sale in all but the largest supermarket chains. The grape boycott called attention to the plight of the migrant laborer, and eventually produced a union contract between the growers and the migrants. But the long-range effect was probably to speed the process of mechanization and reduce the number of jobs for migrant workers.

Chicanos

Several terms such as "Spanish-Americans," "Latin Americans," "Mexican-Americans," and "Hispanics" have been used for descendants of Spanish-speaking people who migrated to the United States from Central or South America. They are concentrated largely in Texas, California, Arizona, New Mexico, and Colorado. Several million Spanish-speaking persons live in the United States, constituting about 11 percent of the population of the five main states.

The fastest-growing ethnic minority group in the United States is Chicanos. Over one-third of all Chicano rural households have incomes below the poverty level, twice as many as rural households in general and three times as many as urban households (Durant and Knowlton, 1978). The low incomes of Chicanos, the low levels of schooling, the large families, and for many, their inability to speak, read, or write English have been barriers to improving their social situation.

"Wetbacks" are Mexican citizens who illegally enter the United States by crossing the U.S.-Mexican border (often the Rio Grande River) to seek employment. They are usually young adult males from the interior of Mexico. Many are illiterate and few are fluent in English. If they are apprehended by U.S. immigration authorities, they are returned to Mexico. Then, under cover of darkness, they may slip back across the border. Although the undertaking is hazardous, and the "coyotes" they pay to smuggle them across the border have little concern for their welfare, the improved work opportunities are perceived as being worth the risk.

Because of the attention the national media gave to the work of organizing migrant farm laborers in California by Cesar Chavez, many people have a stereotype of Chicanos as migrant farm workers. Actually, only about 7 percent of Chicanos in general are farm workers (Carlson, Lassey, and Lassey, 1981).

Blacks

Blacks are the most important U.S. minority group in terms of numbers. About 12 percent of the U.S. population in 1980 were black. At one time black Americans were concentrated in the South, and especially in the deep South. Due to migration, blacks are now one of the most urban minority groups. As recently as 1950, about 34 percent of black workers were in farming either as farm operators, renters, or laborers. In fact, agriculture was the single most important occupation for blacks.

Out-migration of the black farm population from the South has taken place on a massive scale since the 1920s. Much of the former Southern black population now lives in the "black ghettos" of northern cities. Occupational and educational opportunities for blacks in the North and West were the attraction, as well as less visible segregation. Push factors include segregation and antiblack activity in the rural South.

Today, less than 1 percent of the black population is engaged in agriculture, and only a small fraction of blacks outside of the South are in farming. Overall, the number of U.S. black farmers has been declining rapidly. In 1978, the number of all farms in the United States was 38 percent of the number in 1920. But the number of black farms was only 6 percent of the number in 1920. Black farmers in the South in 1974 represented only 13 percent of their numbers (Schulman et al., 1985). The mechanization of cotton farming displaced many black sharecroppers to Northern urban areas. Young blacks have little desire to enter farming as a career, and often sell inherited land. The composite picture of the Southern black farmer is one of low income, limited education, advancing age, and inferior social status.

Unlike farming in general, in which the decline is the result of consolidation of land and larger farms, the size of the farms of black farmers is not growing, but in fact, shrinking. In Florida, black-owned farmland has decreased from 10 percent in 1930 to less than 1 percent of the total farmland in 1982, while average farm size has increased only 13 acres from 47 to 60 over the same period of time (Gladwin and Zabawa, 1985).

Government agencies dealing with Southern black farmers could do much to upgrade their level of living. Many of these agency employees are white, middle-class individuals who share the prejudices of the general population. Among the causes of black land loss are clouded land titles and inadequate wills (Schulman et al., 1985). Extension services could develop educational programs to make black landowners aware of the need for wills. The Farmers Home Administration also could play a more positive role in providing black farmers with needed credit for farm purchases. Loans to black farmers under the Farm Ownership Loan Program declined from 3.1 percent in 1980 to 1.4 percent in 1982, and operating loans to blacks declined from 7.9 percent in 1980 to 4.5 percent in 1982 (Martin, 1985).

American Indians

The 1980 U.S. census indicated there are about 1.4 million American Indians and Alaskan natives. About 24 percent live on reservations, mostly in Oklahoma, Arizona, and New Mexico. They are the most rural of the large ethnic minorities, with over half living in rural areas. American Indians who have left the reservation generally acquire more education and achieve higher status and better paying jobs than those who remain behind. But assimilation into the larger society and culture for those who leave the reservation remains a problem for them, and they often are subject to the same prejudices and discrimination as are members of other ethnic groups.

The federal government has tried for years to increase involvement of American Indians in commercial agriculture (Kuvlesky et al., 1982). Yet the percentage of American Indians employed in farming decreased from 68 percent in 1940 to 6 percent in 1980. Most successful commercial farms or ranches

FIGURE 15-3   Agriculture was once the single most important occupation for blacks in the South, but the number of black farmers is declining rapidly. Of those who remain, the composite picture is one of low income, limited education, poor housing, and inferior social status. Government programs have been of little help to black farmers in improving their social and economic position.

Source: Southern Rural Development Center.

are operated by tribal governments or producer cooperatives. Like black farmers, few American Indians have sufficient land, capital, or available markets to succeed in commercial agriculture. Land is either hopelessly fragmented into small plots because of multiple ownership or has been absorbed by white farm operators (Kuvlesky et al., 1982).

RURAL DEVELOPMENT

Rural development is organized efforts to improve the well-being of rural people. It is based on the judgment that people in rural areas should have the same opportunities for a desirable quality of life as urban residents. Rural development includes improvements in employment, income, health, education, housing, nutrition; in services, such as police and fire protection and solid waste disposal; and in physical facilities, such as water and electric systems, roads, bridges, parks, and playgrounds.

Rural development encourages the use and enhancement of local resources and leadership, but at the same time recognizes that much that happens in the local community is due to national and international events (Council for Agricultural Science and Technology, 1974). Improvements in rural areas will occur only to the degree that rural people recognize their interdependence with the larger system. Rural people must determine how their communities can best benefit from these linkages.

History of Rural Development

Major efforts to improve the well-being of rural people began in 1908 with the appointment of the Country Life Commission by President Theodore ("Teddy") Roosevelt. Chairman of the Commission was Liberty Hyde Baily, the son of a Michigan farmer and dean of the College of Agriculture at Cornell University. The Commission was appointed to investigate the nature of rural life and to make recommendations as to what the federal government could do to improve it. The Commission's recommendations included establishing a parcel post system and a postal savings program, an agricultural extension service, increased construction of rural roads and highways, and a land bank credit system. Many of the Commission's recommendations were enacted by the U.S. Congress during the two presidencies following Roosevelt's. The original impetus for the scientific field of rural sociology also grew out of the Country Life Commission's recommendation for surveys and analyses of rural social problems like poverty.

The federal government renewed its rural development activities in the New Deal program of President Franklin D. Roosevelt, enacted to cope with the Depression of the 1930s. Through the Agriculture Adjustment Acts of 1933 and 1938, several rural development programs were established to assist farmers. The Resettlement Administration sought to rehabilitate poor communities, resettle the rural poor, and to establish experimental community farming (an idea criticized because it seemed too communistic). The Resettlement Administration evolved into the current Farmers Home Administration.

One of the most successful new agencies was the Rural Electrification Administration. The REA brought electricity to rural areas in the United States through cooperatives, which continue to this day.

Contemporary efforts aimed at finding a solution to the persistent problems of rural poverty began in 1954 with publication of President Dwight Eisenhower's study report, *Development of Agriculture's Human Resources* (Rasmussen, 1985). Rural development programs in the U.S. Department of Agriculture were established that emphasized the important role of states and counties. Under the leadership of the county extension offices, other federal agencies and community leaders were organized into Rural Development Committees at the local level. The concept of a rural development partnership was established involving federal government agencies, local and state government agencies, and private sector entrepreneurship and capital. This shared effort at improving rural well-being continues to this day.

The next major effort came under President Lyndon Johnson's "Great Society," with the Rural Poverty Commission's 1967 report, *The People Left Behind.* One result of the report was increased involvement of the extension service in rural development.

The Rural Development Act of 1972 provided state extension services and experiment stations with federal funds to establish pilot projects to increase income and employment opportunities, involve local, state, and federal agencies and the private sector in these efforts, and target rural development programs to areas with the greatest need. Under this act, states continue to receive funds for rural development work from the U.S. Department of Agriculture.

The Rural Development Act established four regional centers for rural development: the Northeast center, at Pennsylvania State University; the Southern center, at Mississippi State University; the North Central center, at Iowa State University; and the Western center, at Oregon State University.* Each center works primarily with the faculty at the land-grant universities in its region to bring together relevant expertise to examine rural problems and possible solutions. Financial support is provided to develop programs to solve the social problems.

Since the early years of the 1972 act, the federal government has gradually withdrawn its financial support for rural development activities, so that state and local initiatives are dominant. U.S. Department of Agriculture agencies cooperate with state and local government agencies, with some private nonprofit organizations, and with business and industry. Other federal agencies, like the U.S. Department of Housing and Urban Development (in housing and industrial development) and the Department of Labor (in job retraining programs), also cooperate in rural development.

How successful is the federal government's rural development program? Many of the drawbacks of rural life have been corrected through surfaced roads, electricity, water and sewer systems, improved housing, and recreational facilities. Rural development has had a major role in these improvements. Compared to urban areas, however, economic opportunities still lag behind in rural areas. We are no closer to solving the problems of unemployment, persistent poverty, and inadequate housing than we were when President Theodore Roosevelt appointed the Country Life Commission. The federal government has not adequately funded its rural development programs. Rural policy analyst Wayne Rasmussen (1985 p. 9) concluded that "rural development programs so far have left their goals unmet. A full scale rural development program is still needed."

Rural Sociologists in Rural Development

Rural sociologists have had a major role in shaping rural development in the United States. Rural development encourages the enhancement of local

---

*The director of the North Central center is, in fact, one of the authors of this book.

resources and leadership within the broader context of national and international events. Rural sociologists specialize in studying how leadership functions in the community, and how the community organizes itself to carry out activities that benefit the community (Chapter 6). Rural sociologists also study social and economic trends of the larger society, and the impacts of these on local areas. So rural sociologists are uniquely qualified to plan, conduct, and evaluate rural development programs.

As an illustration, for many years dying rural communities saw their salvation in rural industrialization. Local leaders spent much time attempting to persuade industries to locate in their community and invested large sums of money in developing industrial parks for potential industries. Many industrial parks were financed through grants from the federal government. The belief held by local leaders and government agencies was that local industrial development would create jobs, reduce poverty, stimulate the local economy, and improve the tax base of local government. It was the research of rural sociologists that showed that successful "smokestack chasing" does not necessarily provide all those benefits, and indeed, may have additional costs for the community (Chapter 6) (Summers, 1986).

New industries often do not create jobs for local unemployed, underemployed, and low income people because (1) many new jobs are filled by

FIGURE 15-4 Rural industrialization was once considered the panacea for declining rural communities. Communities developed industrial parks with financial help from the federal government. The Boone Industrial Park appears to be successful, but the only growth many industrial parks saw was weeds. Other communities that were successful in attracting industry quickly discovered that industrial development brought costs as well as benefits.

Source: Iowa State University Photo Service.

commuters from outside the community, (2) some jobs are filled by workers who transfer from another plant operated by the firm, (3) some jobs are filled by people who migrate in because they are seeking a job, and (4) some jobs are filled by persons not previously in the labor force (Summers, 1986). Only a small fraction of the new jobs actually provide employment for those for whom they were intended. A problem with industrialization is that people living on a fixed income, such as social security, may actually suffer if the new industry raises wages sufficiently to create local inflation. Other problems are greater demands on government services, such as schools and police protection, and a larger transient population.

The results of this research have provided community leaders and rural development workers with a better perspective on the benefits and costs of rural industrialization. Industrialization should only be part of a more comprehensive strategy to improve the quality of life in rural communities.

GOVERNMENT AGRICULTURAL AGENCIES

Governmental agricultural agencies have become increasingly important to rural people in the United States. These agencies include the Cooperative Extension Service, the Soil Conservation Service, the Farmers Home Administration, the Rural Electrification Administration, and the Agricultural Stabilization and Conservation Service.

These agencies are a necessary part of modern U.S. agriculture. They were inaugurated in the great depresssion of the 1930s to help farmers solve their social problems. One fundamental problem is the surplus of certain agricultural products. Agricultural technology enables American farmers to boost total food output at a faster pace than population growth. It is much more difficult for farmers to adjust their production downward, due to the complexity of farming. The result is low prices for farm products and correspondingly low incomes for farmers. In the words of former President Harry Truman, "Prosperous farmers make for a prosperous nation, and when farmers are in trouble, the nation is in trouble." This belief in the importance of farmers' well-being to the well-being of the nation, one tenet of the ideology called *agricultural fundamentalism* (Chapter 8), is encouraged by farmer organizations, which have been very successful over the years in convincing political leaders and the U.S. public that government agricultural programs are a necessity.

Why Does the U.S. Government Aid the Farmer?

U.S. government agencies seek to improve the contribution of the agricultural economy to the nation's growth, and to help solve the social problems of rural people and their declining communities. Very few farmers had ever received a government check before the Depression of the 1930s. It was during this depression period that the number of government agencies multiplied rapidly.

U.S. farmers probably receive more help from the government than any other occupational category. There are five main reasons why the government aids farmers:

1. The nature of the farm economy is unique. The two million farmers and producers would never be able to make or maintain a voluntary agreement to limit agricultural production. In other parts of the U.S. economy, the small number of producers can mutually cooperate to limit their production to meet existing demand. For instance, the six major U.S. and foreign automobile manufacturers can easily prevent a car glut. To ensure that farmers have an adequate income, the government helps them control surpluses and provides price supports when the market price for farm products is too low.

2. The federal government gives farmers preferential treatment at the request of the U.S. public. Citizens have shown rather consistently at election time that they want their government to help solve farm problems. Many people in the United States believe that a surplus of agricultural products and a decline in farm prices is the first indication of coming depression for the total economy. They think that government agricultural programs are insurance against a general depression. Such thinking is based on agricultural fundamentalism.

3. Another important role of government agencies is to administer conservation programs to preserve natural resources. Chapter 13 pointed out that the public is concerned with the erosion of soil on millions of acres of farmland and with the quality of drinking water. Legislators realize the public anxiety about natural resources, and know that farm legislation labeled as conservation is easily passed.

4. With international competition from other countries in selling manufactured goods such as automobiles and electronic products, the United States has become a debtor nation. The 'sale and export of U.S.-produced agricultural products to other countries is one means of protecting the trade imbalance.

5. The activities of farm pressure groups secure special government aid for farmers. As we saw in Chapter 11, these organizations obtain the passage of legislation favorable to farmers.

MAJOR GOVERNMENTAL AGRICULTURAL AGENCIES

The major government agencies that administer agricultural programs, and their special functions, are:

INITIALS	NAME	PURPOSE
1. USDA	United States Department of Agriculture	Coordinate and direct the activities of most government agricultural agencies
2. AES	Agricultural Experiment Stations	Perform agricultural research

3.	CES	Cooperative Extension Service	Communicate farm and home innovations to clients and conduct other educational programs
4.	SCS	Soil Conservation Service	Provide technical assistance and secure the adoption of soil and water conservation practices
5.	ASCS	Agricultural Stabilization and Conservation Service	Restrict food surpluses, maintain farm prices, and pay farmers to adopt soil conservation practices
6.	FmHA	Farmers Home Administration	Provide loans and farm management assistance to low-income farmers
7.	FCA	Farm Credit Administration	Provide loans through local cooperatives (NFLAs and PCAs) for the purchase of farm supplies, equipment, land, and buildings
8.	REA	Rural Electrification Administration	Make loans to local cooperatives (RECs) who provide electric power or telephone service to rural people

The traditional purpose of agricultural agencies is to improve the lives of farmers, their families, and their community. The paid employees of these agencies are change agents, who attempt to secure their clients' adoption of change. For example, a change agent for the Soil Conservation Service encourages the adoption of conservation tillage by farmers. The soil conservationist is changing these farmers' behavior in relationship to their land. The farmers thus increase the profitability of their farms, preserve their land for future generations, and protect streams and lakes from sedimentation.

Another type of change is the adoption of production-increasing innovations, the goal of agencies like the Cooperative Extension Service. Agencies such as the ASCS attempt to convince farmers to restrict farm production in order to decrease food surpluses. Credit agencies such as the FmHA provide loans to rural families to encourage them to adopt new technologies, to improve production, and to improve their farmstead and home. The theory is that improved farm production and a higher quality of life helps farmers stay on the land rather than migrate to cities and thus add to urban social problems.

U.S. DEPARTMENT OF AGRICULTURE

The USDA provides the overall guidance, and part of the funds, for most government agricultural agencies. The USDA is a bureaucracy and has the characteristics of a bureaucratic organization (Chapter 5). The top officer of the USDA is the U.S. Secretary of Agriculture, a member of the President's Cabinet. USDA employees are selected on technical qualifications, often a civil service examination, and promoted on the basis of seniority and ability.

USDA programs have been classified into five categories on the basis of their function:

1. *Stabilize farm prices and income* through agencies like the Agricultural Stabilization and Conservation Service.
2. *Conserve resources.* The Soil Conservation Service and certain aspects of the ASCS are included in this function.
3. *Credit and agricultural loans* through such agencies as the Rural Electrification Administration and Farmers Home Administration.
4. *Conduct research and provide education.* Land-grant colleges and universities carry out these programs with funds provided by grants-in-aid from the federal government. Administration of these grants is a responsibility of the federal Extension Service and the Cooperative State Research Service. In addition, the USDA performs considerable research work itself.
5. *Miscellaneous functions,* such as the school lunch program, food stamps, crop and animal disease control, pest control, crop and livestock estimates, food inspection and certification, and market development are also responsibilities of the USDA.

In addition to the government agricultural agencies administered by the USDA, several agencies serve rural people through rural development activities organized in other federal departments. The U.S. Department of Education administers grants-in-aid for vocational agriculture and homemaking. The Small Business Administration in the U.S. Department of Commerce provides low interest loans for business development. And the U.S. Department of Housing and Urban Development provides grants-in-aid for rural communities to improve their public facilities and services. The Department of Interior includes agencies that manage vast tracts of public land (Chapter 13).

Land-Grant Colleges

Several government agencies operate through land-grant colleges and universities. This teamwork between the USDA and land-grant colleges results in the operation of two very important agricultural agencies: state Cooperative Extension Services and the state Agricultural Experiment Stations.

Land-grant colleges were begun by the Morrill Act, passed in 1862, and were brought together with the USDA, which had previously existed as a part of the U.S. Patent Office. Several attempts to pass a land-grant college bill had been made previous to 1862, but these laws were consistently defeated by legislators who viewed the federal grant of land to the states as a threat to the states' power. In 1862, during the Civil War when the Southern states' rights enthusiasts were absent from Congress, the legislation was passed quietly. This law provided that in each state, federal land was to be set aside, with the income from this property used to support a college or university for teaching "agriculture and the mechanical arts." The 1890 land-grant colleges were founded in most Southern states because blacks were excluded from the 1862 schools. Today, the 72 land-grant universities enroll about 16 percent of all U.S. college students. The land-grant law gave a tremendous increase in prestige to agricultural occupations.

The early professors of scientific agriculture in the land-grant colleges soon realized that they had little real knowledge about agricultural topics. This realization caused a demand for research on agricultural problems in agronomy, animal breeding and nutrition, horticulture, and other fields. The Hatch Act of 1887 provided federal funds to state Agricultural Experiment Stations. These research centers were developed in most states as an adjunct to the land-grant college of agriculture. The Cooperative State Research Service in the USDA annually reviews the research projects in each state to ensure that they meet federal stipulations. About one dollar out of three spent at the experiment stations comes from the federal government.

FIGURE 15-5 The land-grant college concept was established by the Morrill Act of 1862. The original purpose of the Act was to provide states with funds to support a college or university for teaching agricultural and mechanical arts. Subsequent legislation provided additional funding of Agricultural Experiment Stations and the Cooperative Extension Service as part of the land-grant institutions. The picture shows the main campus of the University of Illinois, a land-grant university at Urbana-Champaign, Illinois.

Source: University of Illinois, College of Agriculture, Office of Agricultural Communications.

Soon after 1900 the state extension services were established as another addition to the land-grant colleges and universities. By 1914, the Smith-Lever Act provided federal grant-in-aid funds to each state for extension purposes. The extension workers in each state are staff members of that state's land-grant institution.

Agricultural experiment stations   Why do farmers need a government agency to perform their research while other private business firms must perform their own? The answer lies in the special nature of farming. Millions of farm operators could not independently afford or justify the expenditure for agricultural research. If any agricultural research is to be completed for application to farm problems, the government must do it. Most farmers agree that agricultural research should be carried out by the state experiment stations. The ordinary farmer feels that he cannot do a good job of farming and experimenting at the same time.

New seed varieties, fertilizers, farm machines and equipment, livestock feeds, weed sprays, insecticides, and other new farm ideas are constantly being developed and recommended to farmers. These innovations have tremendously increased the productivity and efficiency of farming in recent years. Today, one farm worker provides farm products for about 78 persons, as compared with 45 in 1970 and only 15 in 1950 (Rasmussen, 1982).

Agricultural technology is developed by state and federal agencies supported by public tax funds. This research benefits the farmer directly, and it benefits the consumer indirectly. The increased efficiency in raising farm products lowers food prices for the consumer. The economic returns to society from most agricultural research provides justification of its cost. A recent study showed that public investment in experiment station research since the 1930s has had an annual rate of return of 30 to 50 percent, well above the 10 to 15 percent return that private firms consider adequate (Eddleman, 1985).

The U.S. Department of Agriculture spends about 10 percent of its total budget on research and development. Research sponsored by the U.S. Department of Agriculture is supplemented by commercial companies who sponsor agricultural research. Most new farm and home ideas involve the purchase of a new product. Commercial concerns dealing in farm products conduct research to develop agricultural innovations. Farm people generally believe that most agricultural research is performed by scientists at the state experiment stations, rather than by commercial researchers. Farm people not only believe that publicly sponsored agricultural research is more important, but they place more credibility in experiment station scientists than in commercial researchers.

Cooperative extension service   One of the most important government agencies is the Cooperative Extension Service. It is called the Cooperative Extension Service because it is cooperatively financed by the federal

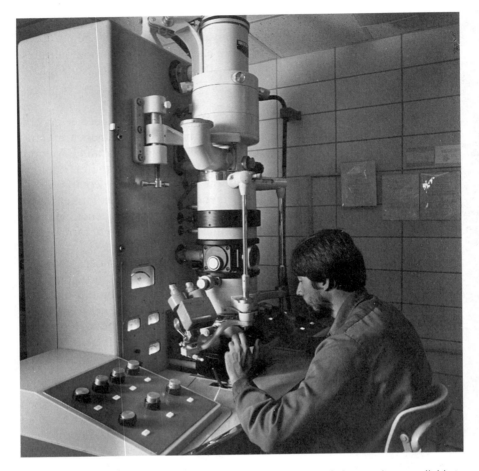

FIGURE 15-6   Agricultural Experiment Stations ensure that U.S. farmers have available to them the latest farming technology. Agricultural scientists are working in such emerging fields as biotechnology and robotics. This electron microscope enables scientists to see the DNA structure of cells.

Source: Iowa State University Photo Service.

government, by each state government, and by each county government. Farmers perceive the county extension agent as their most important link with agricultural scientists. County extension workers, more than any other change agent, set off the agricultural revolution of the past 60 years.

The work of the Cooperative Extension Service is categorized into four or five program areas. Agriculture is the major program area. Many extension employees feel their agency should work only with farm clients, although there is nothing in the agency's charter to imply this limitation. Certainly the major share of extension funding goes to support agricultural programs. Na-

FIGURE 15-7   County Extension Agent Gives On-The-Farm Technical Advice To a Corn Grower About a New Pest That is Threatening His Crop.

The county agent is the grass roots element in the land-grant college complex. Historically, the county agent idea began in 1904 in the campaign to control the cotton boll weevil in Texas, and then took final shape in 1911 in New York State. Extension work was facilitated by the Smith-Lever Act of 1914, which provides federal funds to land-grant colleges to carry out agricultural extension work. The land-grant system in the United States is a tremendous success in a technological sense and an awesome failure in a human sense.

Source: University of Illinois, College of Agriculture, Office of Agricultural Communication. Used by permission.

tionally, 36 percent of Cooperative Extension Service staff work in agriculture (Warner and Christianson, 1984).

Two other well-established program areas are home economics and 4-H/youth work. The basic change strategy of 4-H/youth work is to introduce innovations to parents through their children, and to help youth become competent adults.

Less well established is extension work in rural development, which is officially termed "community resource development" (CRD) by the Cooperative Extension Service. Some states have extension agents responsible for CRD in every county; other states have few, if any, agents with CRD as a major responsibility. Nationally, only 6 percent of Cooperative Extension Service staff work in CRD (Warner and Christianson, 1984). Even with so few workers in CRD, the Cooperative Extension Service can claim credit for many successful rural development programs. The Rural Development Act of 1972 helped make CRD a legitimate activity as well as providing funds for CRD to each state. The regional rural development centers work with the states' Cooperative Extension Services to facilitate sharing of rural development ideas, knowledge from research, educational materials, and information on successful programs, thus expanding individual states' efforts and impacts. Unfortunately, when public support for extension service activities declines, usually during economic downturns, Cooperative Extension Service administrators shift their emphasis to such traditional programs as agriculture. Yet these are the times when rural development programs are needed most by disadvantaged rural people.

A fifth program area recently identified by the Cooperative Extension Service is natural resources. Continuing problems of soil erosion and emerging problems of contamination and depletion of water (especially groundwater) are the focus of natural resource activities by the Cooperative Extension Service. Ninety-five percent of all rural people are dependent upon groundwater for their water supply. Extension promotes forest and rangeland management on private land in cooperation with the Forest Service (Chapter 13).

Extension agents increasingly work with urban and rural nonfarm people. As the number of farmers continues to decline, the Cooperative Extension Service is losing its traditional clientele. Urban legislators find it increasingly difficult to maintain support for the Cooperative Extension Service. To survive, the Cooperation Extension Service is becoming more innovative in delivering its programs to clients.

Soil Conservation Service

Conservation efforts are designed to minimize future decreases in production. The soil conservation program began in the U.S. Department of Interior, but in the 1930s it was transferred to the USDA. The major aim of the SCS in its early days was to provide work for unemployed men at conservation tasks. As the Depression ended, and the need for a work relief program decreased, the SCS became more of a technical assistance program.

At a farmer's request, the SCS will provide technical advice about soil conservation problems. Technical help is given only on request: A farmer applies to the county SCS office, the local SCS farmer-board approves the application, and the SCS employees lay out a farm plan for soil conservation. The farmer is under no obligation to adopt the soil conservation practices that are recommended, and many do not.

The SCS places considerable emphasis on the group approach to soil conservation, as water runs off of one farm onto neighboring farms. Local farmers who are opinion leaders play a key role in the SCS's group approach.

A rural sociological study in Stephanson County, Illinois, was influential in convincing the SCS to work through opinion leaders. Here is how one local leader was described:

> Arthur Laible was the first man in the county to sign up with the conservation program. His farm was badly run down, his soil was eroded, and both he and his neighbors knew it. He put a complete conservation plan on his farm, and within a few years had made such a remarkable change in the place that people for miles around were impressed. A small nucleus of neighbors had meanwhile followed Laible's lead in adopting conservation practices, and these, in turn, were demonstrations for others.
>
> Of 16 farmers interviewed in the mile-and-a-half radius, 14 mentioned the Laible farm as the place, or one of the places, where they had first seen contour practices in operation. Many said they were influenced to make their initial trial by what they had learned in firsthand observation on the Laible farm, or on one of the other farms which had adopted conservation under the stimulation of the Laible operation. In contrast, in a neighboring community, only a handful of farmers using contouring had gotten the idea through close observation of practices carried out on someone else's farm. There was no one there like Arthur Laible to exert opinion leadership for the SCS.

The Soil Conservation Service's need to maintain popular political support interferes with its overall efficiency in controlling erosion. "The agency never seemed to have felt free to attack severe erosion problems only in the regions or locations where they existed; a program with something for every area, and, if possible, for every farmer was politically, if not technically, necessary" (Held and Clawsen, 1965, p. 98). Some critics of the SCS point out that it plays to farmers' values on production, which outweigh their values on conservation. The SCS has sought to change this image by "targeting" its financial and staff resources on areas identified as having especially serious erosion.

Agricultural Stabilization and Conservation Service

Dear Senator: My friend Albert received a $5,000 check from the government this year for not raising hogs, so I am going into the no-hog-raising business next year. I want to know what is the best kind of hogs not to raise, and the best kind of farm not to raise hogs on? I would prefer not to raise razorbacks, but will gladly not raise Berkshires or Durocs. My friend has been raising hogs for 20 years and the best he ever made in a year was $500, until this year when he got $5,000 for not raising hogs. If he can get $5,000 for not raising 50 hogs, then can I get $10,000 for not raising 100 hogs? P.S. Can I raise 10 or 20 hogs on the side while I am in the no-hog-raising business? Enough just to get a few sides of bacon?

The government agricultural agency that employs the largest number of workers and spends the most money is the Agricultural Stabilization and Conservation Service (ASCS). As its name indicates, the purposes of the

ASCS are to restrict food surpluses, to maintain farm prices, and to financially assist farmers in adopting soil conservation practices. The first two objectives are accomplished by the restriction of crop acreages and by government purchase of surplus production. These surpluses of corn, wheat, dairy, and other farm products are stored, resold on the open market, marketed to foreign countries, used in school lunch programs, destroyed or disposed of by other methods. The farmer's letter to his senator humorously illustrates some dilemmas in the ASCS program.

A recent innovation in paying farmers not to plant certain crops was the PIK (payment-in-kind) program. Rather than receiving cash for not planting certain crops, farmers received certificates for a specified amount of government-owned surplus grain. The object was to reduce the surplus of specific commodities, while minimizing the direct outlay of cash by the federal government.

The third purpose of the ASCS is to financially assist farmers to adopt contour plowing and conservation tillage, and to establish terraces, farm ponds, and grassed waterways. To secure ASCS subsidies for these practices, a farmer must develop a farm conservation plan with the SCS.

The ASCS was established in the 1930s as the Agricultural Adjustment Administration (AAA). Its efforts to limit farm production and hence raise farm prices have met with limited success. Why?

1. It is impossible to control crop production by limiting the acreage planted in a crop. For example, if a farmer's corn acreage allotment is decreased from 80 to 60 acres, the farmer can apply more fertilizer or plant more seed on the remaining acres, and produce almost as much on the 60 acres as on the 80 acres. Farmers recognize this fact. In a survey of Iowa farmers about the PIK program, 85 percent believed it would give farmers short-term benefits but only 9 percent believed it would give them long-term help through higher prices (Lasley, 1984).

2. The programs are not comprehensive. A farmer can raise wheat or cotton on vacated corn land even though these crops are raised under acreage allotments in other states. As one farmer remarked, "All that Washington has done is chase the acres around."

3. Almost every farmer would have to participate in crop acreage allotments for these allotments to affect total crop production. However, the level of participation in the ASCS program is only about one-third of all farmers, in spite of the fact that a guaranteed price is paid for participation.

4. There are inconsistencies in the goals of agricultural agencies. Some perform agricultural research to produce new technology which increases farm production, while other agencies attempt to control agricultural production and maintain farm prices.

Rural Electrification Administration

The farm windmill has creaked to a halt in most of the rural United States. It has lost its function due to the work of the Rural Electrification Administration (REA). Electric pumps have now replaced wind power. The purpose of the REA is to provide electrical power and telephone service for rural families. In the 1930s most farm homes in the United States lacked electricity. Less than 20 percent of the farms in the United States had electricity when the REA was founded, even though electrification was then commonplace in the nation's towns and cities. Today over 99 percent of U.S. farms are electrified, with about 54 percent of the nation's electrified farms served by REA-financed cooperatives.

The REA is a loan-type agency. The loans are made to local cooperatives that provide electrical power and/or telephone service to their members. The loans are eventually repaid, so the only real loss to the federal government is the expense of administering the program.

The distinction between the REA (a government agency) and the local electrification cooperatives is not understood by the typical co-op member. The member thinks the electricity is provided by the government, rather than the cooperative. As an Iowa farmer told one of this book's authors in a research interview, "I don't belong to no communistic co-op!" This remark was made while the farmer was standing in the very shade of his REA barnyard pole.

Local rural electric cooperatives are organized in state organizations and in a national association called the National Rural Electric Co-operative Association (NRECA). The NRECA is a powerful friend of the REA in achieving favorable legislation.

The clientele of the REA has changed since its early days. Today, five

FIGURE 15-8
As recently as 50 years ago, few farms had electricity: That meant no running water, no electric lights, hand-washing of clothes, and hand-milking of cows. Today, few farmers or other rural residents are without electricity, due largely to the work of the Rural Electrification Administration.

Source: U.S. Department of Agriculture Rural Electrification Administration.

out of six new member-customers are industrial, commercial, or rural non-farm consumers.

Agricultural Credit Agencies

Inadequate credit has long been one of the U.S. farmer's major problems. The Farm Credit Administration is the USDA agency designed to oversee a vast program of agricultural credit:

1. *The Federal Intermediate Credit Bank* supervises local production credit associations (PCAs), through which the local PCAs obtain loan funds for their member-borrowers. PCAs are local farmer cooperatives that make production loans for fertilizer, seed, feed, and machinery. These loans are usually repaid at the end of the crop year.
2. *The Federal Land Bank* provides capital for local National Farm Loan Associations. NFLAs are local cooperatives that loan funds to farmers for the purchase of farmland and buildings. These loans offer longer-term credit than those provided by PCAs.
3. *The Bank for Cooperatives* provides loans to all types of farmer cooperatives, particularly those that sell farm supplies or market farm products.

Agricultural credit is largely distributed by the Farm Credit Administration through farmer cooperatives, thus giving the borrower-member some control of the organization from which the capital is secured (farmer cooperatives are discussed in Chapter 11).

Another important source of low interest credit for both farm and nonfarm rural residents is the Farmers Home Administration. The FmHA provides loans for purchasing farmland, constructing buildings, and buying homes (for both farm and nonfarm rural residents), as well as for the development and expansion of rural business and industry. The FmHA provides loans to farmers who cannot get credit elsewhere, so the FmHA is the "last resort" for farmers on the verge of bankruptcy.

Changing Attitudes Towards Agencies

U.S. farmers' attitudes toward government agencies are changing from resistance to passive acceptance to dependence. A rural sociologist was conducting a research interview with a farmer on his back porch. During the interview, the farmer indicated his dislike for all agricultural agencies: "There's too many people a'tryin' to tell me how to farm my place here." At the conclusion of the interview the sociologist thanked the farmer and started to leave. As he walked off, he heard the farmer yell in through the screen door to his wife, "Emma, have you been down to the mailbox yet? I don't know what we'll do if that government check don't come today."

Farmers have a generally favorable attitude toward most government agricultural agencies, but they definitely prefer programs that provide assistance while leaving the initiative for action to the farmer. For example, farmers oppose "cross compliance" that requires farmers to participate in the federal crop insurance program or to implement soil conservation plans to qualify for other government assistance.

When agricultural credit agencies began, many farmers were embarrassed to be in need of a loan. They wished to keep their dependence on credit agencies hidden from their neighbors. Some local PCA headquarters had a private office for discussing loans; many clients left by the back door. Today, the majority of PCAs have a desk or counter in their lobby where farmers come openly to negotiate loans.

The long-range trend is for farmers' attitudes toward government agricultural agencies to become more positive as they become more dependent on these agencies, and as they obtain more understanding of them. As farming becomes more complex and specialized, however, government agencies do not always have the most current information. Many farmers thus turn to manufacturers or dealers and to management consulting services for assistance in making decisions about purchasing, production, and marketing.

Changes in Government Agencies

The United States continues to experience urban growth. U.S. farmland is being withdrawn from crop production at an average rate of 3 million acres per year. The proportion of all U.S. residents living on farms has fallen to 2.2 percent. Technological expansion and population growth causes cities to expand into the countryside, covering former farmlands with suburbs, housing developments, and factories. The technological revolution in agriculture makes it possible for farmers to produce more crops on fewer acres. These social changes have consequences for government agricultural programs.

Government agencies originally established to serve farm people must adjust to the specialized needs of a smaller farm audience and to an increased nonfarm audience. The U.S. Department of Agriculture has become more consumer-minded in recent years and less inclined to serve only the farmer.

This shift in the client audience has been accompanied by changes in the programs provided by agricultural agencies. The extension services have changed the content of their 4-H programs to serve suburban members. They now include such topics as lawn care, golden hamsters, and automotive mechanics. The Home Economics Expanded Food and Nutrition Education Program (EFNEP) aims at a primary clientele of inner-city low-income people. Recent extension services programs reflect a change from "things" to "people."

The REA, having fulfilled its original purpose of providing electricity to the U.S. farmer, now makes its services available to the expanding nonfarm population. REA co-ops sell about half of their electrical power to nonfarm buyers. The FmHA has expanded its role to provide housing for any rural resident who qualifies and to assist rural business and industry.

Greater cooperation among agencies is occurring. The SCS, ASCS, CES, and FmHA cooperate with the local soil conservation district commissioners in soil conservation programs. The SCS provides technical assistance in developing and implementing farm conservation plans, the ASCS provides funds for the practices, the extension service conducts educational programs, and the FmHA provides low interest loans to farmers for installing the conservation practices.

A rural sociological study in Iowa showed that such cooperation among these agencies faced many problems (Hoban, Korsching, and Huffman, 1986). Battles over areas of responsibility were common. Officials complained they did not receive proper credit for their accomplishments when they worked with other agencies. The specific responsibilities of these agencies for soil conservation were blurred to many farmers and even to the agencies.

Government agricultural agencies are also important in Third World countries, but these agencies are less powerful than in the United States. Most Third World countries have an extension service and an experiment station modeled after their counterparts in the United States. Their task is to increase

FIGURE 15-9   To adjust to an increased nonfarm audience, agricultural agencies are changing the programs they provide. The Cooperation Extension Services' Expanded Food and Nutrition Education Program aims at a primary clientele of inner-city low-income people using paraprofessionals or volunteers as educators. The EFNEP program is far removed from the traditional homemakers clubs that worked with farm women.

Source: University of Illinois. College of Agriculture, Office of Agricultural Communications.

food production rather than to control surpluses. Often lacking in Third World countries is a link between extension and research agencies, such as the land-grant colleges of agriculture seek to provide in the United States. Agricultural researchers are not aware of the problems that farmers face and extension agents cannot obtain research-based information to help farmers with their problems. In First World countries like the United States, agricultural agencies are more concerned with conservation and with regulating the quality of agricultural products than with increasing total farm production.

Agency Clientele and Socioeconomic Status

Change agents theoretically make their services equally available to all clients and make special efforts to reach those clients with the greatest need. However, the results of numerous studies indicate that agricultural agencies are utilized most by those who have the least need for assistance from the standpoint of socioeconomic status.

Why are clients with the most critical problems least likely to use the services of government agricultural agencies? As pointed out in Chapter 14, the change agent has difficulty communicating and empathizing with lower-class clients because of the barrier of social and economic differences.

This barrier between agents and clients can be broken by employing aides who come from low-income backgrounds. For example, the extension service in Detroit hired housewives from low-income urban families to explain the agency's home economics program to other low-income housewives. This strategy of the EFNEP program may only be successful for a limited period of time. The aides often begin to identify with the professional change agents, rather than their clients. Even the nominal salaries they earn as aides place them in a different economic position than their clients. When the aides begin to act and empathize more with the change agent than with their clients, they are no longer useful in bridging the socioeconomic gap with their clients.

SUMMARY

Rural America has not benefited to the same degree as urban areas from the economic prosperity characteristic of the United States. About 13 million rural people live in poverty. Although the rural poor may be found everywhere, there are areas in which poverty has been particularly persistent. These include the Appalachian and Ozark mountains, parts of the South and Southwest, and parts of the upper Great Plains and upper Great Lakes.

Income is the major criterion used to determine who is poor. A family of four with an income of less than $11,000 is in the poverty category, according to U.S. government criteria. Being poor means being poorly educated, being unemployed or underemployed, having high birth rates, and having poor diets and health.

Rural *minority groups,* groups that have certain distinct and recognizable social or physical characteristics different from those of the general population, are a major proportion of the rural disadvantaged. They include (1) *migrant workers* who follow the harvest by moving during the year to jobs in scattered locations, (2) *Chicanos* who are descendents of Spanish-speaking people who migrated to the United States from Central or South America, (3) *black farmers* who are concentrated mainly in the South, and (4) *American Indians* in New Mexico and Arizona.

Rural development is the organized effort to improve the well-being of rural people. Such efforts began with the appointment of the Country Life Commission by President Theodore Roosevelt in 1908. Rural development programs supported by the U.S. government have had limited success. Problems of poverty, unemployment, and inadequate housing persist.

The scientific field of rural sociology grew out of the Country Life Commission's recommendation for surveys and analyses of rural social problems. Rural sociologists have played a major role in shaping rural development programs.

Government agricultural agencies have become increasingly important to rural people in the United States. The agencies are a necessary part of modern U.S. agriculture, but they have assumed an increasing role in assisting the nonfarm rural population. These agencies and their responsibilities are listed below.

1. The *United States Department of Agriculture* coordinates and directs the activities of most government agricultural agencies.
2. *Agricultural Experiment Stations,* located in the land-grant colleges and universities, perform agricultural research.
3. The *Cooperative Extension Service,* operating from the land-grant colleges and universities, communicates farm and home innovations to clients and conducts other educational programs.
4. The *Soil Conservation Service* provides farmers with technical assistance to secure the adoption of soil and water conservation practices.
5. The *Agricultural Stabilization and Conservation Service* helps to reduce food surpluses, maintains farm prices, and pays farmers to adopt soil conservation practices.
6. The *Farmers Home Administration* provides loans to farmers and other rural residents and provides farm management assistance to financially troubled farmers.
7. The *Farm Credit Administration* provides loans through local cooperatives for the purchase of farm supplies, equipment, buildings, and land.
8. The *Rural Electrification Administration* makes loans to local cooperatives that provide electrical power or telephone service to rural people.

U.S. farmers' attitudes toward government agencies are changing from resistance to passive acceptance to dependence. The agencies are also changing to serve the changing needs of a smaller farm audience and an increased nonfarm audience. One change is more work with low-income clients.

REFERENCES

BEALE, CALVIN L., and GLENN V. FUGUITT. (1986). "Metropolitan and Nonmetropolitan Population Growth in the United States Since 1980." In Joint Economic Committee, ed. *New Dimensions in Rural Policy: Building Upon Our Heritage.* Washington, DC: U.S. Government Printing Office.

CARLSON, JOHN E., MARIE L. LASSEY, and WILLIAM R. LASSEY. (1981). *Rural Society and Environment in America.* New York: McGraw-Hill.

Council for Agricultural Science and Technology. (1974). *Rural Development.* Ames: Iowa State University.

DORNER, PETER. (1983). "Technology and U.S. Agriculture." In Gene F. Summers, ed. *Technology and Social Change in Rural Areas.* Boulder, CO: Westview.

DOWNING, THEODORE E. (1985). "The Crisis in American Indian and Non-Indian Farming." *Agriculture and Human Values, 2,* 18–24.

DURANT, THOMAS J., JR., and CLARK S. KNOWLTON. (1978). "Rural Ethnic Minorities: Adaptive Response to Inequality." In Thomas R. Ford, ed. *Rural U.S.A.: Persistence and Change.* Ames: Iowa State University.

EDDLEMAN, B. R. (1985). "National and Regional Analysis, Evaluation Planning and Financing of Agricultural Research, IR-6." In the Experiment Station Committee on Organization and Policy, eds. Research Perspectives, College Station, Texas Agricultural Experiment Station.

GLADWIN, CHRISTINA H., and ROBERT ZABAWA. (1985). "Survival Strategies of Small, Part-Time, Black, Florida Farmers: A Response to Structural Change." *Agriculture and Human Values, 2,* 49–56.

HELD, R. BURNELL, and MARION CLAWSON. (1965). *Soil Conservation Perspectives.* Baltimore, MD: Johns Hopkins Press.

HOBAN, THOMAS J., PETER F. KORSCHING, and TERRY HUFFMAN. (1986). *The Selling of Soil Conservation: A Test of the Voluntary Approach, Vol. 2: Organization Survey.* Sociology Report No. 158, Ames: Iowa State University.

KUVLESKY, WILLIAM P., CLARK S. KNOWLTON, THOMAS J. DURANT, JR., and WILLIAM C. PAYNE, JR. (1982). "Minorities." In Don A. Dillman and Daryl J. Hobbs, eds. *Rural Society in the U.S.* Boulder, CO: Westview.

LASLEY, PAUL. (1984, December). "Evaluation of the PIK Program." *Iowa Farm and Rural Life Poll: Summary,* pp. 3–5.

MARTIN, PHILIP L. (1985). "Labor in California Agriculture." *Agriculture and Human Values, 2,* 60–67.

MORRISSEY, ELIZABETH S. (1985). *Characteristics of Poverty in Nonmetro-Counties.* Rural Development Research Report No. 52. Washington, DC: Economic Research Service, U.S. Department of Agriculture.

RASMUSSEN, WAYNE D. (1985). "90 Years of Rural Development Programs." *Rural Development Perspectives, 2,* 2–9.

RASMUSSEN, WAYNE D. (1982). "The Mechanization of Agriculture." *Scientific American, 247,* 77–89.

SCHULMAN, MICHAEL D., PATRICIA GARRETT, REGINA LUGINBUHL, and JODY GREENE. (1985). "Problems of Landownership and Inheritance among Black Smallholders." *Agriculture and Human Values, 2,* 40–44.

SLESINGER, DORIS P. (1985). "Migrant Farmworkers in Wisconsin." *Rural Development Perspectives, 2,* pp. 35–38.

SUMMERS, GENE F. (1986), "Rural Industrialization." In Joint Economic Committee, ed. *New Dimensions in Rural Policy: Building Upon Our Heritage.* Washington, DC: U.S. Government Printing Office.

WARNER, PAUL D. and JAMES A. CHRISTIANSON. (1984). *The Cooperative Extension Service: A National Assessment.* Boulder, CO: Westview.

Chapter 16

Development and the Third World

Why is it important to understand the problems of development in the Third World nations of Latin America, Africa, and Asia? One reason is because over 3 billion of the world population of 5 billion live in the Third World. From now until the year 2000, nine hundred and fifty of every 1,000 babies born will live in the Third World. Only 50 will live in First World countries like the United States.

WHAT IS THE THIRD WORLD?

As defined in Chapter 1, First World countries include the rich, industrialized nations of North America, Western Europe, and Japan. Second World nations include the socialist nations of the Soviet Union and Eastern Europe. The term *Third World* was coined by French intellectuals as an analogy with the historical term *the third estate,* a residual category for individuals who did not belong to the privileged estates of the nobility or the clergy (Mody, 1985, p. 135). *Third World countries* are all those not privileged to become industrialized and wealthy during the past several centuries. All countries in Latin America, Africa, and Asia are usually considered Third World, except for Japan and South Africa (Figure 16-1). The First and Second World include

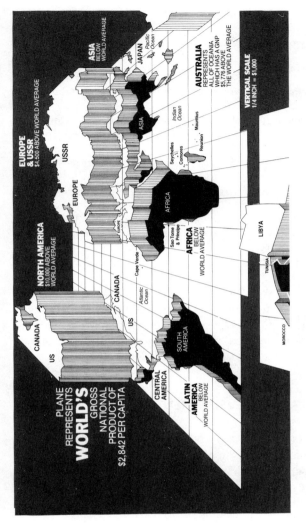

FIGURE 16-1 The Level of Development Indexed By Per Capita Income By Continent.

The continents of Latin America, Africa, and Asia are the Third World, ranking below the world's average in per capita income. African nations are furthest below average in per capita income and face the severest developmental problems. The average citizen of the First and Second Worlds can expect to finish high school, rarely be hungry, and live for more than 70 years. Half of the Third World citizens are illiterate, 20 percent are hungry and malnourished, 25 percent die before age five, and the average survivor can expect to live to only 50.

Source: Horn in *The Christian Science Monitor* ©1985 TCSPS. Used by permission.

355

only 25 percent of the world's population, but have 80 percent of the world's income.

Individuals living in the Third World countries of Latin America, Africa, and Asia:

1. Have a lower life expectancy than North Americans (it is presently about half, but rising).
2. Suffer—due to a lack of adequate health care—from malaria, dysentery, tuberculosis, and many other diseases that have largely been eliminated in industrialized nations.
3. Have a daily food intake about one-third less—measured in calories—than that of the industrial countries.
4. Have limited educational opportunities, with only about half attending school for more than four years.
5. Possess an average income that is a fraction of that in the United States; the lowest income class in North America is better off economically than the average individual in most Third World countries.
6. Have a birth rate much higher than that of people in industrial countries.

These problems of Third World countries are highly interrelated. For example, overpopulation leads to malnutrition, and illiteracy affects both. Development in Third World nations is like a series of locked boxes, with the key to each box inside of another box. The development problems of low income, malnutrition, disease, and illiteracy are highly interrelated.

THE DOMINANT PARADIGM OF DEVELOPMENT

In the 1960s, social scientists thought they understood the nature of development and the role of communication in the development of Third World countries. Here, we (1) describe the old concept of development and contrast it with emerging alternatives, and (2) summarize what we have learned from development programs in the Third World countries of Latin America, Africa, and Asia.

What is a *paradigm?* We use *paradigm* as essentially synonymous with *model,* that is, a way of looking at some social problem or scientific puzzle. It is a scientific approach to some phenomenon that provides model problems and solutions to a community of scholars. In the case of the development paradigm, the intellectual model provided a neat, simplified way of understanding what was holding back the socioeconomic advance of Third World countries. At least until the early 1970s.

Through the late 1960s, a dominant paradigm ruled intellectual definitions and discussions of development and guided national development programs. This concept of development grew out of certain historical events, such as the Industrial Revolution in Europe and the United States; the colonial experience in Latin America, Africa, and Asia; the quantitative empiricism of North American social science; and capitalistic economic/political philosophy. Implicit in the ruling paradigm of development were numerous assumptions which were generally thought to be valid, or at least were not widely questioned, until about the 1970s. The level of national development at any given point in time was defined as the gross national product (GNP) or, when divided by the total population in a nation, per capita income.

Now we look at the major academic and historical influences on the old conception of development.

1.   *The Industrial Revolution* was usually accompanied by foreign colonization and domestic urbanization during the latter 1800s. The rapid economic growth during this period in Europe and the United States implied that such growth was development, or at least was the driving engine of development. Industrialization, based on applications of the steam engine, was seen as the main route to development. So Third World countries (they were called underdeveloped in the 1950s and 1960s) were advised by development planners to industrialize. Build steel mills and hydroelectric dams. Construct manufacturing industries. Assign a low priority to agricultural development.

The old paradigm stressed economic growth through industrialization as the key to development. At the heart of industrialization were technology and capital, which substituted for labor. However, this simple approach to development could not be applied successfully to very different sociocultural settings, such as Third World countries, where labor was generally in very ample supply. What had happened in Western nations regarding development was not an accurate predictor of the developmental process in non-Western nations.

2.   *Capital-intensive technology.* First World countries possess expensive technology, while Third World countries have less of it. Appropriate social and cultural change was expected to accompany the material technology that was introduced. When needed social structures did not always materialize in Third World countries, the fault was accorded to "traditional" beliefs and social values. Social science research was aimed at identifying the individual variables on which rapid change was needed, and the modernization of traditional individuals became a priority task of various government agencies.

The capital that was required to purchase the high-capital technology was often obtained by international loans and through the activities of multinational firms (usually owned and controlled by First World countries). The newly independent nations began to realize that economic independence did not necessarily accompany political freedom. The end of colonialism in the Third World did not mark the end of financial dependence on the First World. Often it increased such dependency. Capital-intensive technology, including military armaments, was one reason.

3.   *Economic growth.* It was assumed by development officials that individual behavior was economic, responsive rationally to cash incentives, and that the profit motive would stimulate the widespread behavior changes

required for development. Economists were in the driver's seat of most development programs in Third World countries. They defined the problem of underdevelopment largely in economic terms, as a problem of raising per capita income. Certainly achieving higher incomes was an important part of development, but it was not all of development. Also important was how the added income was spent, whether for alcohol or for children's education.

4. *Quantification.* One reason for reliance on per capita income as the main index of development was its deceitful simplicity of measurement. If some dimension of development could not be measured and quantified in numbers, then it probably did not exist. Or so it seemed in the 1960s.

Further, the quantification of development invoked a very short-range perspective of 10 or 20 years at most. It was easy to forget that India, China, Persia, and Egypt were old, old centers of civilization, and that their rich cultures had in fact provided the basis for contemporary Western cultures. Such old cultures were now poor (in a cash sense), and even if their family life displayed a warmer intimacy and their artistic triumphs were greater, that was not development. It could not be measured in dollars and cents.

The drive for the quantification of development, an outgrowth and extension of North American social science empiricism, helped define what development was and what it was not. Material well-being could be measured. Values such as dignity, justice, and freedom did not fit a dollars-and-cents yardstick. Development began to have a somewhat dehumanized meaning. Political stability and unity were thought to be necessary for continued economic growth, and authoritarian leadership increasingly emerged, often in the form of military dictatorships. And in the push for government stability, individual freedoms often were trampled.

CRITICISMS OF THE DOMINANT PARADIGM

In short, the old paradigm implied that poverty was equivalent to underdevelopment. The obvious way for Third World countries to develop was for them to become more like the industrialized countries of the First World.

It was less obvious that First World countries largely controlled the rules of the game of development. Balances of payment and monetary exchange rates were largely determined in New York, London, and Tokyo. International technical assistance programs sponsored by the rich nations often made the recipients even more dependent on the donors.

Theoretical writings about development in the 1960s generally were rather ethnocentric in a cultural sense. The leading theorists were Westerners. What if Adam Smith had been Chinese or a Sikh?

Western models of development assumed that the main causes of underdevelopment lay within a Third World country rather than external to it. Specific causes were thought to be (1) of an individual-blame nature (for example, peasants were said to be traditional, fatalistic, and generally unresponsive to technological innovation) and (2) of a social-structural nature within the nation (for example, a tangled government bureaucracy, a top-heavy land tenure system, and so on). The importance of external constraints on a nation's development were less likely to be recognized. These constraints include international terms of trade, the economic imperialism of international corporations, and the vulnerability and dependence of the recipients of technical assistance programs. The dominant paradigm put the blame for underdevelopment on Third World, rather than on industrial First World countries.

ALTERNATIVE PATHWAYS TO DEVELOPMENT

In the early 1970s, the dominant paradigm began to be widely questioned.

1. The world oil crisis, beginning in 1973, demonstrated that certain Third World countries could make their own rules of the international game. The escape from national poverty of the OPEC nations was a lesson to other countries in Latin America, Asia, and Africa. No longer were these nations willing to accept the formerly held assumption that the causes of underdevelopment were internal.

2. The opening of international relations with the People's Republic of China in the early 1970s allowed the rest of the world to learn details of China's pathway of development. Here was one of the poorest and largest countries in the world that in two decades had created a miracle of modernization: a public health and family planning system that was envied by the richest nations plus well-fed and well-clothed citizens, increasing equality, an enviable status for women. The Chinese experience suggested that there must be alternatives to the dominant paradigm.

3. Perhaps most convincing of all was the discouraging realization that development was not going very well in the Third World countries that had closely followed the dominant paradigm. However one might measure development in most of the nations of Latin America, Africa, and Asia in the past several decades, not much development had occurred. Instead, most "development" efforts had brought further stagnation, a concentration of income and power, high unemployment, overurbanization, and food shortages in these nations. If past development programs represented any kind of test of the intellectual paradigm on which they were based, the model had been found rather seriously wanting.

From these events in the early 1970s grew the conclusion that there are several pathways to development. Their exact combination of components might be somewhat different in every nation. What are the main elements in the newer conceptions of development?

1. Equality. This new emphasis in development programs led to the realization that villagers, urban poor, and women should be the priority audience for development programs. The general strategy was to target development programs at the subaudiences that were lagging in socioeconomic status.

2. *Participation in self-development.* Development came to be less a mere function of what national governments did *to* villagers, although it was recognized that perhaps some government assistance was necessary even in local self-development. An example of local participation is the "group planning of births" at the village level in the People's Republic of China, where the villagers decide how many babies they should have each year, and who should have them. A participation approach to development usually meant establishing some kind of organized group at the local level, which makes certain decisions for development programs.

3. *Integration of traditional with modern systems.* The integration of Chinese medicine with Western scientific medicine in contemporary China is an example of this integrated approach to development. Acupuncture and antibiotics mix quite well in the people's minds. Until the 1970s, aiming at development implied that traditional institutions would have to be entirely replaced by their modern counterparts. Belatedly, it was recognized that these traditional forms could contribute directly to development. National family planning programs in many Third World countries trained traditional birth attendants to promote contraception to village couples. After all, the birth attendants (midwives) were numerous, perceived as highly credible, and entrusted with the delivery of about 80 percent of the babies born in the Third World.

WHAT IS DEVELOPMENT?

The various criticisms of the dominant paradigm of development questioned whether development was equivalent to materialistic, economic growth. Newer definitions of development implied such other valued ends as social advancement, equality, and freedom. These valued qualities should be determined by the people themselves through a widely participatory process. Thus, each nation might pursue a somewhat different pathway to development, depending on exactly what style of development was desired. In this sense, development is simply a powerful social change toward the kind of social and economic system that a country decides it wants.

Today we define *development* as a widely participatory process of social change in a society, intended to bring about both social and material advancement (including greater equality, freedom, and other valued qualities) for the majority of the people through their gaining greater control over their environment. Thus the concept of development was expanded and made much more flexible and at the same time more humanitarian in its implications.

EQUALITY IN DEVELOPMENT

Not much attention was paid to equality in development until the 1970s. When the issue of equality began to be investigated, development programs were usually found to widen social-economic gaps between the higher and lower status segments of a system. The information-rich and the information-poor often tended to grow apart as one consequence of development programs.

Research on the diffusion of innovations was begun in the United States by rural sociologists (Chapter 14). In the early 1960s, diffusion studies were conducted for the first time in the Third World countries of Latin America, Africa, and Asia. The diffusion paradigm, imported from the United States, was followed rather closely. Many of the Third World diffusion studies were conducted by researchers from the United States and Europe, or else by Latin American, African, or Asian scholars who had learned the diffusion approach during their graduate studies in the United States. A strong stamp of "Made in America" characterized this early diffusion research in the Third World. At first, during the 1960s, it seemed that most diffusion research methods and theoretical generalizations were cross-culturally valid. The diffusion process in Third World countries seemed to be generally similar to its counterpart in the richer, industrialized nations of Europe and North America. Even though a peasant village in the Third World was characterized by much more limited financial resources, lower levels of formal education, and a paucity of mass media, innovations seemed to diffuse in approximately the same way as in Iowa or in Ohio. Similarities in the diffusion process were more striking than were the differences. For example, the rate of adoption of an innovation followed the familiar S-shaped curve over time. As in the United States, innovators were characterized by higher status, greater cosmopoliteness, and more tolerance for uncertainty than were other farmers in villages in Colombia and in Bangladesh. Initially, social science research seemed culturally appropriate, even though it originally grew to strength in the United States and was then applied to very different social-cultural conditions in the Third World.

One of the general criticisms of diffusion research deals with the issue of equality (Chapter 14). *A much greater concern with equality in the benefits of development occurred during the late 1970s and 1980s.* Development programs now give a higher priority to villagers, urban poor, and women as the main targets for development activities. These audiences represent the majority of a nation's population in most Third World countries. Development policies have become less elite-oriented and more concerned with equalizing the socio-economic benefits of development programs. When concerns about equality in development programs had been raised prior to the 1970s, they were often answered in terms of the trickle-down theory—that is, a certain sector of society would lead in adopting new ideas and that these benefits would then be passed on to the lagging sectors. Today the trickle-down theory is largely rejected; it is just too slow. Most development theorists now consider the trickle-down theory to be an excuse for inequality.

In Latin America, Africa, and Asia the social structure of a nation or of a local community is often very different from that in Euro-America. Power, economic wealth, and information are usually highly concentrated in a few hands in the Third World. Scholars in the 1970s began to question whether the usual development program could contribute much to real development unless greater emphasis was placed upon the equity issue. The social problem of underdevelopment was thus being redefined, along lines that seriously questioned whether communication alone could play a very important role in changing the social structure of society. Shingi and Mody (1976) in India and Röling and others (1976) in Kenya designed and evaluated development approaches that narrowed, rather than widened, socioeconomic gaps. Essentially, these newer approaches sought to overcome the inequity bias of the usual diffusion programs. They introduced appropriate innovations to lower socioeconomic audiences via a special kind of development program. These studies in India and in Kenya suggested that if development strategies were used effectively in narrowing the socioeconomic benefits gap, then the social structure might no longer be a major barrier to innovation diffusion among the most disadvantaged segment of a national population. Thus it might be possible to bring about a more equitable development through appropriate planned change strategies.

In the United States and other First World countries, there often is a general faith in free market forces. Certain individuals and companies succeed in a competition in which others fail. Without restraint, a free market acts as an amplifier of inequalities by increasing differences in wealth, information, and social status. Many Third World governments do not feel that market forces will enable them to catch up socioeconomically with the rich, industrialized nations. The leaders of Latin America, Africa, and Asia know that they are late in entering the development game. These leaders seek alternatives to free market forces, especially as a means to achieving greater equality as a result of development programs.

If the more equitable distribution of socioeconomic benefits were an important goal of development programs, the following strategies might be followed:

1. Identify the opinion leaders among the disadvantaged segment of the total audience, and concentrate development efforts on them, so as to indirectly reach the information-poor.
2. Use change agent aides selected from among the disadvantaged audience to work for development agencies in contacting their peers.
3. Establish special development agencies to work only with disadvantaged audiences.
4. Disseminate development communication messages that are redundant to the "ups," but which meet the needs of the "downs."

Women in the Third World

Perhaps the most extreme form of inequality in the Third World is based on gender (Chapter 4). Women are the poorest, the least-educated, and toil the hardest. They produce 70 percent of the food in Africa and Asia, and 40 percent in Latin America. So most farm work in Third World countries is done by women. Women put in two-thirds of total work-hours worldwide, but receive only 10 percent of the income, and own less than 1 percent of the property. Seldom are Third World women consulted in decisions that involve them.

Until the 1980s, women were not considered in designing development programs. But once development experts became more sensitive to issues of equality, women in Third World settings became a key concern in development programs. To the surprise of many development experts, women accomplished impressive goals when they were involved in development programs (Figure 16-2). That lesson is strikingly illustrated by the case of mothers' clubs in Korea.

FIGURE 16-2   West African Women Conduct Most of the Small-Scale Trading and Much of the Farm Work in Their Society.

Until the 1970s, the role of women in the Third World was almost completely ignored. Then, as part of the new paradigm of development, much greater emphasis was placed on equality consequences of development programs. Women in the Third World are the poorest, least well-educated, and toil the hardest. Today women are a priority audience for development programs. In West Africa women do most of the petty trading, and in some cases even own and operate large trucks (called "mammy-wagons" in Nigeria). The experience to date in the Third World indicates that women can achieve considerable economic progress when given the opportunity.

Source: University of Illinois, College of Agriculture, Office of Agricultural Communication. Used by permission.

BOX 16-1   *THE MIRACLE OF ORYU LI*

When one of the authors of the present book first saw the Korean village of Oryu Li in 1973, he was not very impressed. The 100 or so homes were cramped in a narrow valley between a pair of railroad tracks and the steep foothills of a mountain range. The village homes looked small and poor. The roofing was only straw thatch. There were no TV aerials, not even a school. In fact, before the women of Oryu Li began their self-development activities in 1971, Oryu Li was one of the poorest villages in one of the poorest counties in one of the poorest provinces in the Republic of Korea. Here in a nutshell were exemplified the major problems of rural Korea: overpopulation, low education, poverty, lack of cooperative trust, underdevelopment. Certainly the village had little to distinguish it from the hundreds of thousands of other hamlets in Asian countries, caught in their dusty circle of poverty.

How Oryu Li escaped this vicious cycle is a fascinating story. If you like success stories, you'll like the "miracle" of Oryu Li. In 10 years, it became one of the richer villages in Korea. Oryu Li represents what is possible for other peasant villages to achieve, regardless of their economic resources, through strong leadership, local organization for self-development, and adequate government support.

On arriving at Oryu Li back in 1973, we met the leader of the mothers' club in Oryu Li, Mrs. Moon Ja Chung, and some of the club members. The mothers' club leader was modest and respectful, but one sensed a quiet strength. Her mothers' club had accomplished such development progress that the provincial governor had been moved to tears during his recent visit to Oryu Li. Mrs. Chung had a high school education (somewhat unusual for a village woman in Korea), but her most important quality was enthusiasm, vision, and a shrewd grasp of strategies of change. Mrs. Chung's home served as a sort of headquarters for the mothers' club. On her wall was the ubiquitous performance chart with the number of family planning adopters per month (IUDs in red on the graph, oral contraceptives in blue, and condoms in black). In one corner of the main room was a small cabinet in which supplies of pills and condoms were stored.

We asked: "How many members does this mothers' club have?"

Mrs. Chung: "We are now 53."

"How many have adopted family planning?"

Mrs. Chung: "Every member is an adopter. No baby has been born in this village for more than one year now."

The national rate of adoption of family planning was then about 36 percent in Korea; Oryu Li had achieved 100 percent adoption by its mothers' club members.

"How many *won* does your mothers' club fund now have?"

Mrs. Chung answered with evident pride, "We have almost 600,000 *won* [about $1,500 U.S.]. We also own 2,000 chestnut trees that are growing up there on the mountainside." The club leader gestured to the steep slopes above the village. "And we own a cooperative grocery store down there." She pointed to a small building near the church tower. "It was once the village wineshop."

The typical mothers' club in Korea is a small discussion and action group, composed of several dozen members. These small groups are an ideal means of changing individuals' attitudes and behavior. Originally designed by the Korean government's family planning program, the women's clubs soon were also involved in a variety of other development activities. In Oryu Li, the club members pooled their savings to buy cloth from which they sewed uniforms to sell to nearby school children for their school's annual sports competition. The profit from this project of 6,000 *won* U.S. $15) was used to start the club's treasury. The mothers' club members were thus convinced that they could create ways to earn money for their fund. The club members hoped to break the hold of the village moneylenders, who often charged 6 percent interest *per month*. In order to provide an alternative credit source, however, the club would have to amass a considerable fund, and they would have to operate a village store (because the moneylenders managed credit at the time of villagers' purchases of food).

Mrs. Chung rallied the womenfolk against the local wineshop, where many of their husbands drank and gambled. The Oryu Li wine house was a symbolic object of much female concern. Wives felt their husbands were throwing away their earnings, which could be better spent for food, clothes, and other essentials. Mrs. Chung challenged her club members to greater heights of sacrifice by appealing to their hatred for the moneylenders and the wineshop. She urged each club member to begin saving 100 *won* (U.S. 25 cents) per month.

The first successes of the mothers' club in Oryu Li were small-scale projects that did not directly threaten traditional norms regarding the role of women. But when the temperance drive was launched in Oryu Li, the mothers' club sought to change not just their own members' behavior, but that of their husbands. The wineshop, a rather low-class tavern in a tiny building, served rice wine and a vodkalike rice liquor. The wineshop was a place of male comradeship and relaxation after a hard day's work. "Chopstick girls" were employed in the wineshop. Perhaps these waitresses increased the potential for male pleasure (and their wives' displeasure). The expense of drinking, and the gambling which usually accompanied it, was a main source of village disharmony and family conflict. Drunken fights among village men were common occurrences.

The first step in the mothers' club's temperance drive was to fix a 100 *won* fine on each club member whose husband was seen drinking. Next, the club offered to buy the wineshop, whose owner was now more willing to sell, due to a sharp decline in sales. The mothers' club then converted the former winehouse into a cooperative grocery store operated by the mothers' club. Needless to say, the co-op did not sell alcoholic spirits. It stocked items like soap, salt, and socks made by the club members. The wineshop was dead, and gambling and drinking declined (athough a few husbands occasionally slipped off to the wineshop in a nearby village for a quick cup). Some of the club members' husbands indicated being vexed at the loss of their social center. But most male attitudes were typified by the comment of one husband who indicated both pride and considerable wonderment, in what the village's "little women" had accomplished.

The end of the wineshop was a turning point in the process of Oryu Li's self-development. The women gained a strong sense of solidarity and collective efficacy, a feeling that they could control their own future rather than simply wait to have their fate defined for them (usually by males).

Perhaps the experience of Oryu Li implies that development is easy. It is not. The real miracle of the "miracle" of Oryu Li lies in the similar success stories in hundreds of other Korean villages. Women in many other villages organized through their mothers' clubs to remove their local winehouse. In other villages, the mothers' club accumulated a mutual fund, so as to challenge the local money-lenders. The previously untapped women's power in Korea, unlocked by organizing mothers' clubs, became an important force for development. The can-do spirit exemplified by mothers' clubs in Korea was incorporated into a national community development program, the New Village Movement, which continues to the present.

Source: This reading is adapted from Rogers and Kincaid (1981), pp. 1–27. Used by permission.

RURAL-URBAN MIGRATION AND URBAN SLUMS

One undesirable and often unanticipated result of improved agricultural technology is a massive rural-to-urban migration of peasants. The most important contemporary social problem in most Third World countries is overurbanization, the too-rapid growth of a city's population. One highly visible symbol of this social problem is urban slums. Every capital city in the Third World has a ring of substandard houses surrounding it in a tightening belt of human misery. These slums are one of the negative consequences of rural development program in villages. Every sack of chemical fertilizer applied by a peasant farmer to make land more productive, and every new tractor put into use, reduces the labor requirements in rural villages. *Mechanization and improved technology bring higher farm production and improved levels of living for peasant farmers, but they also bring a massive movement to the cities of technologically unemployed ex-peasants.* The supercities of the Third World like Mexico City, São Paulo, Calcutta, and Lagos provide a grim picture of what happens when public services cannot keep pace with exploding population growth.

Former villagers enter the city environment with little preparation, woefully unprepared to cope with their new milieu. They cannot read, a skill that was not necessary in their former setting. But street signs, price tags, labels, and instructions are an essential part of city life. Nor does the new immigrant possess occupational skills that are useful in the city. The ex-peasant is often unemployable, and he and his family are forced to live in a slum.

The lure of higher wages and better living conditions, as depicted in the mass media of television and radio, draws rural people to the Third World supercities. The migration pattern is similar to what happened early in the Industrial Revolution in Europe. But there is a key difference: the rate of change. Manchester, England, considered one of the first industrial cities in the world, doubled its population in the 50 years between 1851 and 1901. In comparison, Mexico City's population was 3 million in 1950, and will be 26 million in the year 2000, an increase of 750 percent in 50 years! Mexico City will then be the world's largest metropolitan center, followed closely by São Paulo, Brazil, with 24 million inhabitants. Such supercities will be virtually unlivable. Large portions of the urban population will consist of vast shanty-towns of cardboard dwellings.

Most urban slums consist of thrown-together shacks located illicitly on vacant land near a city's boundaries. Because the inhabitants are often squat-ters, city authorities do not feel responsible for providing them with water or sewers. Urban governments simply do not recognize that the slum squatters exist. In Chile, the slums are called *callampas,* a Spanish word meaning mush-rooms. And the slums grow up as rapidly as their namesake. In Mexico, squatters are called *parachutistas.* One of the authors of the present book, while conducting a survey of slum dwellers in a Latin American city, was drawing a map of the slum in order to select a sample. He found that his map was in error because three new cardboard shanties had been constructed during the night.

Life in the urban slums of Latin America, Africa, and Asia is indescrib-ably miserable. The lack of water, electricity, and sanitary facilities results in high infant death rates. High levels of political and economic frustration lead the slum dwellers to welcome violent methods of social change.

What can be done about the problem of overurbanization in the Third World? One approach, tried in India and in several other nations, is for the national government to provide job opportunities in rural areas. An example is to locate agribusiness companies like food processing plants, meat packing sheds, and cold storage plants in market towns in the countryside, so that excess farm labor can work in these companies, without having to migrate cityward. Some nations (Mexico is an example) have tried to change the content of the mass media, so that the reality of urban life (such as slums, unemployment, and traffic) is shown, as well as the attractive image of city lifestyles depicted in advertisements and entertainment programs.

THE FOOD-PEOPLE PROBLEM IN THE THIRD WORLD

When most Americans think of Latin America, Africa, and Asia, the image of famine comes to mind, like that which occurred in Ethiopia. In the 1980–1986 drought, eight million Ethiopians were affected and an estimated one million died. There are indeed starving children in certain Third World countries, and there would be many more, were it not for food aid from American farmers.

Food Aid

The most pressing problem of Third World countries is too many people and not enough food. Thomas Malthus's famous principle is that population increases geometrically while the food supply increases arithmetically, leading to famine, disease, and social disorganization. Malthusian problems operate with special poignancy in the Third World. Enriched by the nineteenth-century Industrial Revolution that Malthus could not foresee, Europe and the United States have escaped his pessimistic predictions. But experts worry that a Mathusian scenario could occur in certain Third World nations. One preventive strategy is food aid.

Not only do American farmers, who represent less than 3 percent of the U.S. population, produce the food and fiber for their own country's consumption, but they produce more than 85 percent of the world's food surplus, which is consumed abroad (Lemons, 1986). Much of this food is sent overseas to alleviate problems of malnutrition and starvation in the Third World. The U.S. public strongly supports giving food aid. Partly for this reason, the federal government pursues agricultural policies contributing to high farm yields in America. U.S. farmers value high production, and are proud to contribute to combating world hunger. So here is a case of a fortunate congruence between U.S. farmers' values and the moral imperative to combat world starvation. About 40 percent of all food imported by Third World countries in the past 30 years comes from the United States (Lemons, 1986).

Further, U.S. food exports earn about $40 billion annually, thus contributing toward a more balanced U.S. foreign exchange. In fact, U.S. farm exports have offset about two-thirds of the nation's expenditures for imported oil since 1973 (Lemons, 1986).

BOX 16-2   *THE ETHIOPIAN DROUGHT*

The food-people problems of Third World countries impress the U.S. public from time to time when natural disasters such as droughts occur. One of the worst such disasters in recent years was the Ethiopian drought of the 1980s. An estimated one million people and several million cattle died. Perhaps one of the gravest aspects of this tragedy was that most of these losses had already occurred by 1984, when the news media finally "discovered" the drought, which had actually been underway since 1980.

The Ethiopian drought was just one part of a more general disaster in 20 African nations lying in an arid belt from Mali to Kenya, in which at least 30 million people did not have enough food on which to live. Ten million Africans abandoned their homes and farms to search for food and water. Many drifted to government relief camps like Korem in Ethiopia. This camp became famous in October 1984, when a film taken by a BBC TV crew showing children dying of starvation, was shown on national television news in the United States. Immediately, cash contributions began pouring in to the TV network. Public pressure forced the U.S. government to launch a massive food aid program to Ethiopia, which the United States had previously failed to do because Ethiopia was ruled by a Marxist government. English and American rock musicians recorded songs like "We Are the World" and held benefit concerts like Live-Aid in 1986, raising millions for drought relief in Ethiopia. Soon, two huge grain ships each week were landing sacks of food in Ethiopian ports.

But the human suffering in Ethiopia continued. Why? For one thing, much of the food aid did not get through to the starving people in Korem and the other relief camps. The Ethiopian government simply did not have enough trucks to move the food inland to the camps. So it piled up at dockside. Further, the donated food could not be unloaded until the American relief agencies paid an exhorbitant fee of $30 per ton to the Ethiopian government. These funds were then used to purchase arms for use in suppressing the people in the two breakaway provinces in northern Ethiopia where the drought was most severe. So the food aid donations were indirectly providing military hardware to the Ethiopian government to further suppress the drought-striken victims. In fact, some observers claimed that the Ethiopian government did not really want to aid the famine victims, whom it regarded as political enemies.

More fundamental questions could be raised about whether food aid was a viable long-range solution to Ethiopia's drought. A basic reason for the drought lay in the gradual desertification of vast areas of Africa (Chapter 13). The Sahara Desert was moving south across the continent at the rate of 20 or 30 miles per year. Why? A gradual deforestation of vast areas in Africa, due to an exploding population's need for firewood, upset the environmental balance so as to cause decreased rainfall. A solution to African desertification lay in massive reforestation campaigns across Africa, with relief agencies providing tools, seeds, and know-how. And effective national planning programs to control overpopulation were necessary to stop further deforestation in the future.

So we see that the Ethiopian drought of the 1980s was caused by much more than just a lack of rain. The drought also has important political aspects, and stems from overpopulation and deforestation, leading to desertification. The real solution must consist of much more than just shipping food. The Ethiopian drought is a development problem.

The Population Explosion

Unless the rate of population growth is slowed, catastrophe lies ahead for the human race. Let us consider India as an illustration of the problem. It took that ancient land thousands of years to raise its population to today's 800 million, but at the present rate of growth it will require only 30 more years to double that figure. Why the sudden increase?

For centuries it has been traditional to have large families in India; having many children provided a kind of old age security for the parents. Until about 1920, India's birth rate was high—49.2 per 1,000 population—but so was the death rate—48.6 per thousand. As a result, the population grew very slowly. Then improved public health due to insecticides, antibiotics, and better sanitation cut the death rate dramatically. The social norms on family size changed much more slowly. In fact, today, despite a much lower death rate, India's birth rate has declined only slightly. So the gap between births and deaths widened, and India's population grew at a very rapid rate. Obviously, the solution for India (and many other Third World countries) is to mount a national family planning program to convince the public to have smaller-size families and to provide the contraceptive methods to prevent unwanted births.

Family Planning Programs

Most development experts agree that efforts, no matter how massive, on only the agricultural side of the food-people imbalance will not be enough. So family planning programs by the governments of Third World countries are a necessity. About 50 Third World countries now have family planning programs, but only a few of these national programs have yet affected population growth rates very much. It is an extremely difficult and complex task to introduce contraceptives to millions of peasant and urban poor families. Providing family planning methods is not enough to affect birth rates in many Third World countries. Educational campaigns are also necessary to change attitudes toward ideal family size. When parents want smaller families, then they will use contraceptives. But changing ideal-size family norms is no easy task, and so population growth rates in the Third World change slowly (Figure 16-3).

Why do family planning programs fail? First, contraception is an extremely sensitive issue in most cultures, especially traditional ones, because it involves sex, which is usually considered a taboo topic. In fact, it is even considered inappropriate to ask a couple in most Third World countries whether or not they are using a contraceptive method. Thus the taboo nature of family planning restricts the rate of diffusion of contraceptive techniques. The word for condom in many Third World languages is particularly taboo because the use of condoms is often associated with prostitution. For example, in India condoms were commonly called "French leathers" until the early 1970s, when the government family planning program began promoting condoms as a contraceptive method for young parents. In order to reposition the public image of French leathers, they were renamed *Nirodh*, a Sanskritic word meaning protection. A huge advertising campaign was launched in India for *Nirodhs*, and they were available at almost every drugstore and tea stall at a cheap price (subsidized by the Indian government). Similar campaigns for condoms were launched for *Kinga* in Kenya, *Preethi* in Sri Lanka, and for similar products in Jamaica, Bangladesh, and Mexico. The general result of these condom campaigns has been promising, suggesting that the taboo na-

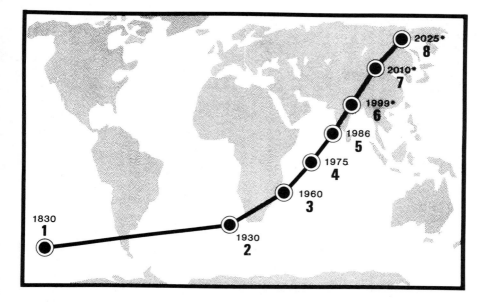

FIGURE 16-3   The Rapid Increase in World Population is Crowding the Globe.

World population reached 5 billion in mid-1986. Global population is presently growing by one million people every four or five days; this rate of increase amounts to about 85 million a year. According to United Nations' projections, world population will reach 6 billion by 1999, 7 billion by 2010, and then the rate of growth will slow somewhat to 8 billion in 2025. Clearly, world population cannot continue to increase at these rates. National family planning programs seek to help parents avoid unwanted births.

ture of contraception can be overcome through an intensive communication effort.

A further problem facing family planning programs in Third World countries is that many couples do not want to have fewer children. Until real economic advance occurs as a result of rural development activities, and until alternatives to children for old-age security are provided (like social security programs), most parents are not motivated to have small families. Patriotic appeals by the national leaders of Third World countries to their people (like India's "Have two or three children, that's enough, stop") have little effect. When rapid agricultural development has occurred, as in India's Punjab during the 1970s and 1980s when "miricale" varieties of wheat and rice were introduced, the rate of population growth dropped sharply.

So again we see an illustration that *all aspects of development problems are highly interrelated.* An advance in one development sector usually leads to improvement in another development dimension. Certainly the food and population problem consists of complex interrelationships that touch almost every aspect of a culture.

BOX 16-3 *BOTTLE BABIES*

Nowhere is the cultural interrelatedness of Third World development problems better illustrated than in the tragic case of bottle babies. A major cause of infant death in Third World countries is the bottle baby syndrome, often characteristic of babies that are fed powdered milk. Because most drinking water is contaminated in the Third World, and facilities for boiling it are usually not available, many bottle-fed babies contract diarrhea, leading to severe dehydration and malnutrition. Their sunken eyes, prominent ribs, swollen bellies, and thin little arms and legs are signs of approaching death. They are not protected by the natural immunities against various diseases provided by a mother's milk. Further, the cost of purchasing powdered milk is a major problem for poor parents in Third World countries, requiring up to one-third of their total income.

Given all of the disadvantages of bottle-feeding, why is it so prevalent today in the Third World? One reason is the profits being made by milk food companies, like Nestle's, the largest seller of powdered milk products. Total annual sales of baby formula in the Third World are more than $300 million. Bottle-feeding is one of the most heavily advertised products in the Third World today, and many of the ads are targeted especially at poor parents, who have the most children. The ads utilize status appeals, showing upper-middle class parents bottle-feeding healthy-looking, happy babies. The ad campaigns seem to be successful in promoting bottle-feeding; for example, in Chile bottle-feeding increased from 5 percent in 1955 to 80 percent in 1980. It is estimated that no more than 10 percent of mothers need to bottle-feed their babies because of a lack of natural milk. Nevertheless, the practice of breast-feeding is decreasing rapidly in most Third World countries.

Once consciousness about the bottle-feeding problem was created in the 1970s, various efforts were launched to correct it. A boycott of all Nestle's products including candy bars, tea, and soups, was established in 1977 on many U.S. university campuses. Other attempts to force the powdered milk companies to change their advertising and marketing practices in Third World countries were initiated by religious organizations and private foundations. They purchased stock in the powdered milk companies, and then brought stockholders' pressures to bear in order to force a change in advertising practices targeted at poor parents in the Third World. The World Health Organization (WHO) also became involved in the bottle babies problem, establishing a set of ethical standards for the companies to follow in marketing powdered milk products. National ministries of health launched campaigns in several Third World countries to promote a return to breast-feeding. Several nations simply banned all advertising for infant formula, or prohibited the sale of the product entirely.

The case of bottle babies illustrates the conflict between the profit-making orientation of the multinational companies versus the health concerns of parents, Third World governments, and international agencies. Also involved are the ethical issues of advertising an unhealthy product in Third World nations. We see the interrelatedness of development problems: nutritional, advertising, health, and economic factors are complexly intertwined.

A documentary film entitled "Bottle Babies" was widely shown by church groups in the United States to raise awareness of the problem. The film ends with a shot of a child's grave near Lusaka, Zambia. The small grave is decorated with a powdered milk can and a baby bottle. The narrator says, "Mothers put empty Nestle's Lactogen cans and feeding bottles on their dead babies' graves, for they believe to the end that powdered milk and feeding bottles were the most valuable possessions their babies once had."

FROM RISING EXPECTATIONS TO RISING FRUSTRATIONS

Why do development programs in Third World countries so frequently fail? To fully understand the nature of today's programs of directed social change in Third World countries, a brief historical background is necessary.

The Revolution of Rising Expectations

The 1950s and 1960s was an era of increasing expectations. Most Third World countries had gained their independence from former colonial rulers and began to concentrate on development. This period was characterized as "an era of rising expectations." The general public mood was optimistic. National governments told their people that higher incomes, improved nutrition, and a better education for their children were just around the corner.

Development planners in the new nations saw their most important task as creating industry. Third World countries were mainly producers of agricultural products, while the richer countries were mainly industrial. The logic seemed self-evident: Pursue a policy of industrial development. Build hydroelectric dams and huge steel mills. But meanwhile, food production was allowed to lag. Industrial development meant urbanization, and national governments focused on improving city life, while tending to forget about rural development problems. Then food shortages began to occur.

The industrial development phase of the 1950s later gave way to an emphasis on agricultural and rural development in villages. Modernizing the peasant millions became a major goal of most Third World governments. Fertilizer, "miracle" varieties of rice and wheat, and other agricultural innovations were introduced. Villagers began migrating to urban centers, attracted by the rosy image of city life created by the mass media. By 1970, a tidal wave of Third World humanity was moving urbanward.

Rising Frustrations

It soon became apparent that aspirations were more easily aroused in the Third World than satisfied. Satisfaction is a ratio of "gets" to "wants," of achievements to aspirations. As actualities fell far short of aspirations—the denominator in the gets/wants ratio increased faster than the numerator—the 1970s were typified by widespread frustration. Third World political leaders came to realize that their speeches were often promissory notes on which they could not deliver. Government instability became prevalent in Latin America, Africa, and Asia. Military dictatorships increasingly took over Third World countries floundering in development problems. Extreme discontent and revolution set back the rate of development in several nations.

Why did aspirations outrun actualities in many Third World countries? One reason was the mass media, which preached a gospel of increasing expectations. Unfortunately, the media were not equally effective in showing their audiences how to achieve development goals. For example, it is more difficult to teach villagers how to read by way of radio instruction than it is to make city life appear desirable. When mass media audiences were encouraged to want more but not fully informed on how to get more (food production, higher incomes, better education for their children), the net result was frustration.

A second reason for rising frustration is that in many Third World countries, power often lay in the hands of an oligarchy that dominated economic and political life. For example, 26 rich families run Colombia, and 16 dominate Pakistan. They own the mass media and the main industrial enterprises, like the beer companies and banks. Their sons serve as presidents and prime ministers. This power elite often gave lip service to development goals but was generally reluctant to endorse programs that really upset the status quo. Tax reform laws and other restructuring innovations that threatened to alter the social structure of Third World countries were usually sandbagged by the power elite.

So the rigid social structure of countries in Latin America, Africa, and Asia, coupled with a flood of promodernization mass media messages, led to a revolution of rising frustrations. The general disappointment to date with development programs is pervasive in the Third World. We do not need just more of the same.

The question for the next decade is whether our theories, knowledge, and resources can be properly harnessed for the hard pull toward desired development goals.

SUMMARY

The Third World consists of most nations in Latin America, Africa, and Asia. Although there are very important differences among these countries, they all share a common problem of development. Until the early 1970s, most experts agreed on a dominant paradigm or model of development, which (1) was defined as essentially synonymous with the Industrial Revolution that had occurred in Europe and North America, (2) involved the introduction of capital-intensive technology, (3) was measured in terms of economic growth, and (4) was quantified as the rate of change in per capita income. This notion of development was seriously questioned in the 1970s, and alternative pathways to development were recognized. Specifically, the newer models of development (1) placed more emphasis upon equality, (2) focused on local participation in self-development, and (3) recognized the integration of traditional with modern systems.

Today, we define *development* as a widely participatory process of social change in a society, intended to bring about both social and material advancement (including greater equality, freedom, and other valued conditions) for the majority of the people through their gaining greater control over their environments. This newer definition means that much greater concern is now being shown to equality of the benefits of development than had occurred in the past. Specifically, the recent focus on equality means that development programs are now targeted especially to reach villagers, urban poor, and women.

A special problem in most Third World countries is the massive rural-urban migration to urban slums. Mechanization and improved technology bring higher farm production and improved levels of living for peasant farmers, but they also bring a massive movement to the cities of technologically unemployed ex-peasants. Adequate solutions to the problem of such super-cities as Mexico City, São Paulo, Lagos, and Calcutta have not yet been found.

Another important problem in many Third World countries is the population explosion caused by decreasing death rates which are not accompanied by a drop in the birth rate. National family planning programs in many Third World countries seek to cope with rapid population growth rates, but unfortunately such family planning programs have not yet been very successful in most countries. As a short-term expedient, food aid programs are mounted to cope with drought, famines, and other disasters. U.S. farmers have a direct stake in food aid programs to Third World countries, because 85 percent of the world's food surplus is made in America.

All aspects of development problems in the Third World are highly interrelated. Food shortages, overpopulation, malnutrition, illiteracy, and so forth are interdependent elements of a total problem. The revolution of rising expectations in the 1950s and 1960s has given way to a revolution of rising frustrations in the 1970s and 1980s as felt needs have increased rapidly in the Third World, but the actualities of filling these needs have progressed at a much slower rate.

REFERENCES

LEMONS, JOHN (1986). "Structural Trends in Agriculture and Preservation of Family Farms." *Environmental Management, 10*(1),75–88.

MODY, BELLA. (1985). "First World Communication Technologies in Third World Contexts." In Everett M. Rogers and Francis Balle, eds. *The Media Revolution in America and Western Europe.* Norwood, NJ: Ablex.

ROGERS, EVERETT M., and D. LAWRENCE KINCAID. (1981). *Communication Networks: Toward a New Paradigm for Research.* New York: Free Press.

RÖLING, NIELS, JOSEPH ASCROFT, and FRED WA CHEGE. (1976). "The Diffusion of Innovations and the Issue of Equity in Rural Development." *Communication Research, 3,*155–170.

SHINGI, PRAKASH M., and BELLA MODY. (1976). "The Communication Effects Gap: A Field Experiment on Television and Agricultural Ignorance in India." *Communication Research, 3,*171–193.

Glossary of Concepts

Accommodation: the process by which two organizations retain their own identities in pursuing similar goals.

Achieved Status: status earned by the individual's own effort.

Achievement Motivation: the social value that emphasizes a desire for excellence in order for an individual to attain a sense of personal accomplishment.

Adopter Categories: classification of the members of a social system on the basis of their innovativeness.

Adoption: the decision to make full use of a new idea as the best course of action.

Agribusiness: the manufacture and distribution of farm supplies, plus the processing, handling, merchandising, and marketing of food and agricultural products, plus farming itself.

Agricultural Adjustment: the process by which social and economic changes are made in order to accompany the technological changes taking place in agriculture.

Agricultural Magic: farming beliefs that lack any scientific explanation.

Agricultural Transition: the change that is occurring in the nature of farming and all other parts of the agricultural industry in response to new technology and the changing world economy.

Anticipatory Socialization: beginning to act like a member of a particular reference group to which one does not yet belong.

Ascribed Status: status that is inherited or determined by birth.

Aspirations: desired future states of being.

Attitude: a relatively enduring organization of an individual's belief about an object, that predisposes the individual's future actions.

Biotechnology: any technology that attempts to improve plants or animals by changing the genetic structure, or the use of living organisms to make or modify products.

Bureaucracy: a secondary, formal type of organization designed, ideally, to coordinate the work of many individuals in the pursuit of large-scale administrative tasks.

Castes: categories of persons arranged in stratified levels according to the social status they possess, with very little mobility of individuals among the stratified levels.

Category: a number of persons who are thought of together but who are not in communication with each other.

Centralized Bureaucracies: bureaucracies in which decision making is not widely shared.

Change Agent: a professional who influences individuals' innovation decisions in a direction deemed desirable by a change agency.

Charisma: the ability to secure the devoted following of large numbers of people.

Church: an organization of believers having a common religious faith.

Cliques: informal groups in which the basis of membership is common interests or friendship.

Communication: the process by which messages are transferred from a source to a receiver.

Community: a locality group that contains the major social institutions.

Community Decision Making: the process by which a community chooses a plan or idea that affects the community and puts this idea into action.

Compatibility: the degree to which an innovation is perceived as consistent with the existing values, past experiences, and needs of the receivers.

Competition: the relationship between two or more individuals or organizations pursuing a similar goal that only one can achieve.

Complexity: the degree to which an innovation is perceived as relatively difficult to understand and use.

Conflict Avoidance: the minimization of role conflict by avoiding life situations that might produce it.

Consequences: changes that occur within a social structure as a result of the adoption or rejection of an innovation.

Conservation Tillage: reduced plowing and cultivating of cropland between and during the growing seasons, so that crop residues are left on top of the soil.

Consolidation: the merger or union of two or more units in order to create one stronger unit.

Contact Change: change produced when sources external to a social system introduce a new idea.

Continued Socialization: the process in which an individual takes on new adult roles and modifies roles.

Continuum: a device that shows the degree to which some characteristic or variable is present.

Contract Farming: an agreement between a farmer and a businessman to partially coordinate the supplying, production, processing, and marketing of a farm product under one management.

Cooperation: agreed-upon action by two or more units that is directed to similar goals.

Cooperatives: voluntary associations of individuals who join together to secure goods and services at cost.

Cosmopoliteness: the degree to which an individual's orientation is external to his/her community.

Cultural Relativism: evaluating the worth of a cultural item in terms of its contribution to the total culture of which it is a part.

Cultural Universals: common elements found in all cultures.

Cultural Variability: the differences among cultures.

Culture: material and nonmaterial aspects of a way of life, shared and transmitted among the members of a society.

Culture Shock: the frustration and disorientation that occurs when an individual experiences a strange culture.

Deferred Gratification: the postponement of short-range rewards by an individual in order to secure long-range goals and satisfactions.

Development: social change in which new ideas are introduced into a social system in order to produce higher per capita incomes and levels of living through modern production methods and improved social organization.

Diffusion: the process by which new ideas are communicated to the members of a society over time.

Directed Contact Change: planned change, caused by outsiders who, on their own or as representatives of change agencies, intentionally seek to introduce new ideas in order to achieve goals they have defined.

Discontinuance: a decision to cease use of an innovation after previously adopting it.

Dual Structure of Agriculture: growing number of small and large farms and a disappearing middle.

Education: the process by which a culture is formally transmitted to learners.

Empathy: the ability of an individual to project himself/herself into the role of another person.

Equalitarian: a type of family in which all members have nearly equal authority in decisions.

Ethnocentrism: the tendency to perceive and value other cultures in terms unconsciously based on one's own, and hence to regard one's own culture as superior.

Eutrophication: the process whereby excessive plant growth stimulated by fertilizer in groundwater runoff produces oxygen that chokes off most marine life, including fish.

Extended Family: a large number of relatives who usually share a common residence.

Familism: the subordination of individual goals to those of the family.

Family Farm: a farm managed and run by a family with a minimum of outside hired labor.

Farm Commercialization: the production of agricultural products for marketing off the farm.

Farmer Movements: collective behavior in which a large number of farmers organize for social change and to solve a perceived crisis in agriculture.

Fatalism: the degree to which an individual perceives a lack of ability to control his/her future.

Federated Cooperatives: two or more member cooperatives organized to market farm products, purchase production supplies, or perform bargaining functions.

Folkways: norms that are only weakly punished if they are violated.

Formal Group: a group that usually has a name, elected officers, written constitution, and a regular meeting place and time.

Government Agricultural Agencies: public bureaucracies designed to provide services to rural people.

Government Land Management Agencies: public bureaucracies designed to manage and conserve resources on public lands.

Grant-In-Aid Government Agencies: public bureaucracies in which a grant of money is made by the federal government to the state or local level without a direct line of authority.

Groups: people in communication and together geographically with common interests or goals.

Heterophily: the degree to which pairs of individuals who interact are different in such attributes as beliefs, values, education, and social status.

Homophily: the degree to which pairs of individuals who interact are similar in such attributes as beliefs, values, education, and social status.

Ideal Types: conceptualizations based on observations of reality and designed to make comparisons.

Immanent Change: change produced when members of a community, with little or no external influence, invent a new idea and then spread it within their community or society.

Incest Taboo: prohibition of marriage or sexual intercourse between certain relatives.

Informal Groups: small primary groups that are based on friendship and mutual interest.

Innovation: an idea, practice, or object perceived as new by an individual.

Innovation-Decision Period: the length of time required to pass through the innovation-decision process.

Innovation-Decision Process: the mental process through which an individual passes from first knowledge of an innovation, to a decision to adopt or reject, to confirmation of this decision.

Innovativeness: the degree to which an individual is relatively earlier in adopting new ideas than other members of the community.

Institution: the aspects of a culture that satisfy some fundamental function of a society.

Institutionalization: the process through which a relatively simple, informal grouping becomes a formalized institution.

Intensification: increasing the amount of food or fiber produced on a given parcel of land by increasing the density of plants or animals on that land or by increasing the number of production cycles for that land in a given period of time.

Interaction: the process of exchanging messages with other persons.

Interpersonal Communication Channels: those means of communication that involve a face-to-face exchange between two or more individuals.

Invention: the process by which new ideas are created or developed.

Learning: a relatively permanent change in an individual's behavior brought about as the result of experience.

Legitimizers: key power-holders in a community who give their approval or sanction to proposed solutions to community problems.

Line-Action Government Agencies: public bureaucracies that have a direct line of authority extending down from the federal level through state and county levels to the farmer.

Loan-Type Government Agencies: public bureaucracies in which a temporary grant of federal money at a relatively low interest rate is made to state or local organizations.

Locality Groups: informal groups in which the basis of membership is that the members live near each other.

Mass Media Communication Channels: all those means of transmitting messages that involve a mass medium, such as newspapers, magazines, film, radio, or television, which enable a source of one or a few individuals to reach an audience of many.

Matriarchal: the mother makes most of the decisions in the family.

Matricentric: the mother exercises most of the control and authority in the family.

Matrilineal: the line of descent is traced through the mother, and kinship ties through the father are ignored.

Matrilocal: the newlyweds move in with the bride's parents after the wedding ceremony.

Migration: the geographical movement of persons.

Minority Groups: categories of persons that have certain distinct, recognizable social or physical characteristics different from those of the general population.

Modernization: the process by which individuals change from a traditional way of life to a more complex, technologically-advanced, and rapidly-changing way of life.

Monogamy: one man marries one woman.

Mores: norms that are strongly punished if they are violated.

Motivation: a driving force behind the individual which directs him/her toward goals to satisfy certain needs.

Neighborhood: a locality group which is not as self-sufficient as a community because it contains fewer of the social institutions.

Neolocal: newlyweds set up a separate residence after they are married.

Norms: the established behavior patterns for the members of a given social system.

Nuclear Family: the husband, wife, and their children until they leave home.

Observability: the degree to which the results of an innovation are visible to others.

Opinion Leadership: the degree to which an individual is able to informally influence other individuals' attitudes or overt behavior in a desired way with relative frequency.

Organic Farmers: farmers who avoid the use of chemical fertilizers and pesticides, as well as synthetically compounded growth regulators and feed additives.

Participative Bureaucracies: those bureaucracies in which major decisions are widely shared by members or employees.

Part-Time Farmers: farmers who spend at least 100 days per year in off-farm employment.

Patriarchal: the father makes most of the decisions in the family.

Patrilineal: the line of descent is traced through the father, and kinship ties through the mother are ignored.

Patrilocal: the newlyweds move in with the groom's parents.

Peasants: farmers oriented largely (but not necessarily entirely) to subsistence production.

Perception: the way in which external stimuli are subjectively interpreted or experienced by an individual.

Personality: the sum total of the attitudes, ideas, values, and habits of an individual.

Polyandry: one woman has several husbands at the same time.

Polygamy: when a man or woman has plural marriage partners.

Polygyny: one man has two or more wives at the same time.

Position: the rights and obligations of a particular role.

Power: the degree to which an individual can influence or control the actions of others.

Pressure Groups: formal organizations composed of people with common interests or occupations who seek to secure desired legislation by improving communication with their legislators.

Primary Groups: groups that are small in size, informal in nature, and characterized by intimate face-to-face relationships among the members.

Rate of Adoption: the relative speed with which an innovation is adopted by members of a community.

Reference Groups: organizations, groups of people, and individuals to whom we look for cues for our behavior.

Rejection: a decision not to adopt an innovation.

Relative Advantage: the degree to which an innovation is perceived as better than the idea it supersedes.

Relative Deprivation (or **disadvantage**): the degree to which an individual perceives a situation with dissatisfaction because the individual compares his/her present situation with his/her aspirations.

Religion: a belief in a supernatural power which distinguishes between right and wrong and which provides answers to some of life's ultimate problems.

Resocialization: the rapid learning of a set of roles which are different from those previously held.

Robotics: the development and use of self-controlled machines through a combination of engineering automation and computerized artificial intelligence.

Role: a pattern of behavior associated with a distinctive social position.

Role Conflict: the clash felt when a person occupies two antagonistic role positions at the same time.

Role Strain: a less serious case of role conflict, when roles are not compatible, but must necessarily occur together.

Rural Development: the organized efforts to improve the well-being of rural people.

Rural Industries: industrial, extractive, and productive companies not associated with the production of food that are found in rural areas.

Rural Nonfarm Persons: those individuals who live in villages or in the open country but not on farms.

Rural Persons: those individuals who live in the country or in towns of less than 2,500 population, and who may be either farm or rural nonfarm residents.

Rural Schools: schools located in the country or in small towns or those schools which rural children attend in larger communities.

Rural Sociology: the scientific study of rural people in group relationships.

Rural Survival: any practice or belief that was well-adapted to former conditions but is retained under changed conditions to which it is no longer well-adapted.

Rural-Urban Fringe: the area that lies immediately outside of the city limits (containing mixed rural and urban land uses), not including suburbs.

School: the social organization in which formal education takes place.

Secondary Groups: groups that are large in size and formal in nature and that are characterized by impersonal relationships among the members.

Sects: uninstitutionalized churches.

Selective Exposure: the tendency to attend to communication messages that are consistent with one's existing attitudes and beliefs.

Selective Perception: the tendency to interpret communication messages in terms of one's existing attitudes and beliefs.

Self-Concept: an individual's perception of his/her own personality that is formed through interaction with others.

Social Change: the process by which alteration occurs in the structure and function of a society.

Social Classes: abstract categories of persons arranged in hierarchical levels according to the social status they possess.

Social Impact Assessment: the systematic appraisal of the impacts on the day-to-day quality of life of persons and communities whose environment is affected by a development or policy change.

Socialization: the process by which an individual's personality is shaped.

Social Mobility: the movement of individuals up or down the social class structure.

Social Movement: collective behavior in which a large number of individuals organize for social change to solve a perceived crisis.

Social Problem: a disturbance in human relationships that seriously threatens society or the important aspirations of people within it.

Social Sciences: the study of various social aspects of human life utilizing scientific methods.

Social Status: the position of an individual or a group relative to others in a society.

Social Stratification: when social status differences in a community or society are prominent.

Society: a collectivity of people who share a common culture.

Sociology: the scientific study of people in group relationships.

Sociometry: a method of mapping informal group relationships in graph or chart form.

Status: the position of an individual or group relative to others in a society.

Status Inconsistencies: when an individual possesses a series of high (low) status factors combined with one or more low (high) status factors.

Status Symbols: objects that convey an indication of the possessor's social status.

Stereotype: an exaggerated and preconceived image of a category of people.

Subculture: a part of the broader culture that shares many elements of it, yet can be characterized by particulars that set it apart from other parts of the culture.

Suburb: a residential community generally located outside the city limits, but dependent on the central city.

Trialability: the degree to which an innovation may be experimented with on a limited basis.

Underemployment: an individual working at a job below his/her skill level.

Urban persons: individuals who live in towns or cities of more than 2,500 population.

Values: abstract and often unconscious assumptions by an individual of what is right and important.

Vertical Integration: the coordination of two or more steps in the chain of supplying materials, producing, processing, and distributing a product under the control of the management.

Voluntary Associations: formal groups that usually have a name or title; selected and titled officers; a written purpose, constitution, bylaws, or charter; and a regular common meeting time and place.

Index